INTERNATIONAL ORGANIZATIONS AND THE FIGHT FOR ACCOUNTABILITY

International Organizations and the Fight for Accountability

The Remedies and Reparations Gap

CARLA FERSTMAN

OXFORD
UNIVERSITY PRESS

OXFORD
UNIVERSITY PRESS

Great Clarendon Street, Oxford, OX2 6DP,
United Kingdom

Oxford University Press is a department of the University of Oxford.
It furthers the University's objective of excellence in research, scholarship,
and education by publishing worldwide. Oxford is a registered trade mark of
Oxford University Press in the UK and in certain other countries

First Edition published in 2017

Published in the United States of America by Oxford University Press
198 Madison Avenue, New York, NY 10016, United States of America

British Library Cataloguing in Publication Data
Data available

Library of Congress Control Number: 2017945343

ISBN 978–0–19–880844–2

Acknowledgements

I am extremely grateful to Guy S Goodwin-Gill, Emeritus Fellow at All Souls College, University of Oxford, for supervising my doctoral thesis, which forms the basis for this book. I am also grateful to my examiners professors Dapo Akande and Guglielmo Verdirame and to professors Dapo Akande, Vaughan Lowe, Mark Janis, and Jure Vidmar for assessing my work at earlier stages and to Nancy Eisenhauer at Mansfield College for her encouragement. I am also very grateful to Sir Emyr Jones Parry and the Board of Trustees at the Redress Trust for their constant encouragement and flexibility, which has enabled me to progress this research and writing. Thank you as well to the Jennings Randolph Senior Fellowship programme of the United States Institute of Peace for hosting me for nine months and in particular to Lilli Cole. I am also grateful to the Regulatory Institutions Network (RegNet) at the Australian National University and Professor Hilary Charlesworth in particular, who sponsored me as a visiting professional as well as the Human Rights Programme of Hunter College Public Policy Institute, Roosevelt House, City University of New York for providing me with the opportunity to present my research at a faculty seminar.

I am very thankful to the range of individuals who provided me with input, feedback, and encouragement in the course of this project. These are far too many to name; however, a few must be mentioned. Thank you to Dr Lutz Oette, Dr Bruce 'Ossie' Oswald, Dr Alice Edwards, Dr Arezou Azad, Dr Rianne Letschert, Dr Barbara Harrell Bond, Dr Marina Sharpe, Baroness Frances D'Souza, Professor Theo van Boven, and Christoph Sperfeldt.

Contents

List of Abbreviations

ACHPR	African Charter on Human and Peoples' Rights
ACtHPR	African Court on Human and Peoples' Rights
ACHR	American Convention on Human Rights
ACJHR Protocol	Protocol on the Statute of the African Court of Justice and Human Rights
ARS	Articles on the Responsibility of States
AU	African Union
CAR	Central African Republic
CDTs	conduct and discipline teams
CEDAW	Convention on the Elimination of All Forms of Discrimination against Women
CERD	Convention on the Elimination of All Forms of Racial Discrimination
CPIUN	Convention on the Privileges and Immunities of the United Nations
CPPED	Convention for the Protection of All Persons from Enforced Disappearance
CPRMW	Convention on the Protection of the Rights of All Migrant Workers and Members of Their Families
CRC–OPSC	Optional Protocol to the Convention on the Rights of the Child on the Sale of Children, Child Prostitution and Child Pornography
DARIO	Draft Articles on the Responsibility of International Organizations
EACJ	East African Court of Justice
ECtHR	European Court of Human Rights
EULEX Kosovo	European Union Rule of Law Mission in Kosovo
Frontex	The European Border and Coast Guard Agency
GC1	Convention (I) for the Amelioration of the Condition of the Wounded and Sick in Armed Forces in the Field
GC2	Convention (II) for the Amelioration of the Condition of Wounded, Sick and Shipwrecked Members of Armed Forces at Sea
GC3	Convention (III) relative to the Treatment of Prisoners of War
GC4	Convention (IV) relative to the Protection of Civilian Persons in Time of War
HRAP	Human Rights Advisory Panel
HRRP	Human Rights Review Panel
ICCPR	International Covenant on Civil and Political Rights
ICJ	International Court of Justice
ICRC	International Committee of the Red Cross
IGO	Inspector General's Office
ILA	International Law Association
ILC	International Law Commission
IOM	International Organization for Migration
KFOR	the Kosovo Force
MINURSO	United Nations Mission for the Referendum in Western Sahara
NATO	North Atlantic Treaty Organization

OAS	Organization of American States
OIOS	Office of Internal Oversight Services
OLA	Office of Legal Affairs
PCIJ	Permanent Court of International Justice
RIO	regional integration organizations
SADC	Southern African Development Community
SEA	sexual exploitation and abuse
UDHR	Universal Declaration of Human Rights
UN	United Nations
UNAT	United Nations Appeals Tribunal
UNCAT	Convention against Torture and Other Cruel, Inhuman or Degrading Treatment or Punishment
UNICEF	United Nations International Children's Emergency Fund
UNMIK	United Nations Interim Administration Mission in Kosovo
UNMIS	United Nations Mission in Sudan
WTO	World Trade Organization

I
Introduction

I.1 The Problem to Be Addressed

This book explores the challenges to obtain remedies and reparation for harm suffered in the context of violations of human rights and international humanitarian law carried out by or attributed to international organizations. Increasingly, international organizations take on State- or quasi-State-like functions in which they exercise control over individuals and societies, particularly in contexts of conflict and transition. However, disciplinary, oversight, and judicial structures that exist in State administrations to promote accountability and forestall abuses have only partially been put into place for international organizations. At the same time, individuals affected by their conduct have had no, or only cursory recourse to domestic, regional, and international courts and they have not been able to rely on their States of nationality to pursue claims on their behalf.

Historically, international organizations operated in limited spheres. They were much more likely to afford assistance or coordinate the engagements of other actors than to engage directly and exert effective control in different locales. Over time, this has changed. As the roles and responsibilities of international organizations have broadened, there are more situations in which they interact with, and in which their actions directly impact on, individuals. These all increase the risks that their conduct may infringe human rights and international humanitarian law. International organizations' engagement in peace operations has progressively widened, with mandates now regularly including the protection of civilian populations and in several new operations containing peace enforcement responsibilities with active combat duties. Other areas which may give rise to human rights infringements include: sanctions; humanitarian assistance and development; when international organizations adopt State functions, such as the administration of territory or more limited contexts such as detention, refugee status determination, or repatriation programmes. Additionally, the circulation of international arrest warrants and the resort to international criminal courts and tribunals opens up the prospect that such actions violate the rights of suspects and possibly victims and witnesses.

The rationales for immunities and other limits on international organization judicial accountability were conceived to ensure the organizations' independence from State influences and their capacity to engage in often difficult circumstances. Many, if not all of these rationales remain relevant today. Nonetheless, there is a

International Organizations and the Fight for Accountability. Carla Ferstman. © Carla Ferstman. Published by Oxford University Press 2017.

need to evaluate whether and, if so, how these principles—which have been framed in absolute terms—should be adapted to better take account of the variety of scenarios in which international organizations are now engaged.

Normatively, there has been insufficient consideration of individuals' ability to obtain reparation from international organizations. The International Law Commission (ILC) Draft Articles on the Responsibility of International Organizations (DARIO)[1] make clear that international organizations are responsible for internationally wrongful acts attributable to them and are obliged to afford reparation for injuries caused. Yet, the DARIO only cover the invocation of responsibility by States or international organizations; responsibility towards individuals harmed by a breach is not considered in the text. The failure to spell out clear rules on this issue mirrors to a large extent the gaps in international law.

When considering whether international organizations are obliged to afford reparation and to whom it is owed and what it entails, one is confronted with how the law of responsibility intersects with the specialized regimes of human rights and international humanitarian law and, particularly, their application to individuals as rights holders, claimants, and beneficiaries. The absence of clear standards for international organizations makes it necessary to extrapolate standards from these other regimes, as well as to imply standards from the functions of international organizations. Both these approaches necessarily require a shift from analysing the law *de lege lata* to *de lege ferenda*.

The normative gaps have led international organizations to operate solely on the basis of internal rules which they have created in their self-interest. While some international organizations have paid lip-service to human rights and international humanitarian law protections by officially declaring their commitment to these principles, the internal structures of accountability that they have developed have not reflected the external and significantly wider human rights and international humanitarian law standards applicable to other actors such as States. In particular, there has been a failure to treat individuals potentially affected by the conduct of international organizations as anything more than humanitarian charges; individuals' access to forums in which they can claim their rights is decidedly limited.

While there may be good reasons for standards applicable to States to diverge from those applicable to international organizations, the lack of standing for injured individuals to challenge international organizations' understandings of the law, affords these organizations a virtual monopoly over the framing of the law and its procedures, which can and has resulted in impunity. The incentives to afford injured individuals greater procedural safeguards and to extend to them adequate and effective reparation are low; there is no reciprocity because the power relationships between potential claimants and international organizations are highly

[1] ILC, Draft Articles on the Responsibility of International Organizations, 'Report of the International Law Commission on the Work of its 63rd Session' (26 April–3 June and 4 July–12 August 2011) UN Doc A/66/10 (DARIO).

asymmetric. Injured individuals have limited sway on the procedures of international organizations and limited influence on their governments to pursue claims on their behalf. As such, there are few consequences when international organizations fail to meet the wider standards which exist under human rights and international humanitarian law.

These gaps have meant that, for the most part, injured individuals lack access to remedies and are unable to obtain reparation for the harm suffered. Many of these individuals come from protracted conflict zones and/or experience other forms of disadvantage and daily hardships including extreme forms of poverty, violence, vulnerability, or marginalization. Indeed, it is often those characteristics of vulnerability which cause international organizations to engage in particular countries or regions in the first place. But it is also those characteristics that underscore why reparation is so needed. At the same time their situation of powerlessness can make it more difficult for injured individuals to assert and realize any rights they may have. As such the absence of adequate and effective reparation for the harms suffered as a result of the abuses of international organizations constitutes a significant and often immediate hardship on the victims.

Much the same as in national contexts, the failure to acknowledge and account for the wrongful conduct can also reduce victims' and societies' faith in the rule of law and entrench vulnerabilities. From the perspective of the international organization, the lack of accountability can produce a situation in which these organizations operate in a legal vacuum which can contribute to recurrence. It also produces the contradictory and unhelpful conundrum whereby the values the organizations seek to instil in others are ones that they do not espouse for themselves. This can have the result of de-legitimizing the international organizations and thereby impeding them from achieving the overall goals of their mandates.

I.2 The Approach Taken

The primary aim of this book is to deepen understanding about the intersections between the law of international organizations, the law of international responsibility, immunities, human rights, and international humanitarian law. I seek to determine where there are gaps in the various legal frameworks, explore why these gaps exist and posit ways in which they might be filled.

The main questions posed in this book are as follows. Do international organizations have obligations under human rights and international humanitarian law and, if so, what do these entail? Is there a right to reparation for harm suffered in the context of violations of human rights and international humanitarian law perpetrated by or attributable to international organizations and, if so, what is its content? Is the ability to obtain adequate and effective reparation from the wrongdoer an essential component of the right to reparation? Are there concomitant obligations on international organizations to ensure access to procedures whereby injured individuals may obtain reparation? I argue that it is possible to derive international organizations' obligations from an analysis of their functions and mandates and by extrapolating from the obligations of other actors, particularly States. This is necessarily a *de lege ferenda* analysis, given the paucity of clear sources of law and the relatively limited practice concerning international organizations specifically.

Do existing mechanisms for adjudication (both those internal to the organization and external avenues of justice such as recourse to domestic, regional, and international courts) have the capacity to afford injured individuals adequate and effective reparation? If not, what steps can be taken to improve such mechanisms? I seek to assess the availability and capacity of existing redress mechanisms to afford reparation to injured individuals, and the extent to which reparation afforded matches up with the obligations I postulate are relevant to international organizations. One objective is therefore to determine the practical impact of available redress mechanisms on injured individuals.

Underpinning this analysis is my view that (i) laws and procedures are meant to be practical and effective and should be capable of addressing wrongs; (ii) the law is not a static edifice; it should be capable of progressive evolution to meet its underlying objectives. The study thus contributes to the ongoing debate about the accountability of international organizations and the practical implications of the DARIO framework and seeks to identify areas in which further clarity or exploration is warranted.

The counter-arguments stem mainly from the philosophical placement of the study. Is this simply a utopian exercise or is it a critical mapping of where the law should be, if law matched purpose? Some would argue that law does not and should not be made to approximate particular purposes, ideals, or values; this is not law's function. Law is simply a reflection of States' (and presumably other actors') willingness to be bound. In this book I have sought to take an approach which Cassese refers to as 'avoid[ing] the extremes of both blind acquiescence to present conditions and the illusion of being able to revolutionize the fundamentals'.[2] This approach necessarily introduces contingency into a discipline which many understand as fundamentally objective. It is also a fine balancing act and there will be necessarily debate as to whether the balance has been tipped too far in favour of revolution, or not far enough. Furthermore, there is a natural tension within the study relating to the distinctions made between where the law is and where it should be.

Thus, counter-arguments may also stem from where I have situated the law within this continuum. These arguments too, tend to stem from different perspectives of the placement and role of law. Within this study, I have understood and sought to use law not only as a descriptor, but also as a process of argumentation. Thus, an important aspect of the book is determining the nature of the arguments that must be made in order to support particular propositions of where the law is, as well as where it should be.

[2] Antonio Cassese, 'Introduction' in Antonio Cassese (ed), *Realizing Utopia: The Future of International Law* (OUP 2012) xvii.

I.3 Methodology

The main methodological approach has been to identify the law through laws and treaties, procedural frameworks, jurisprudence, and declaratory texts and statements and to assess these against international organizations' constituent agreements and related institutional practices. The inevitable gaps have been dealt with by extrapolating and seeking to apply as appropriate, laws from other domains, particularly the law of State responsibility.

Given the emphasis of this book on access to remedies and reparation, there is a heavy procedural component to the study. In this respect, there is a significant amount of space devoted to the analysis of accountability structures, both those internal to international organizations and others operating at the domestic and regional or international level. Where possible, I have sought to consider how these structures currently address remedies and reparation for human rights and international humanitarian law violations attributable to international organizations, as well as how they could do so better.

The reference to 'international organizations' throughout this study entails the notion of a collectivity of States with a constitution and an international legal personality distinct from the Member States that establish them. In essence, the focus is on intergovernmental organizations that have a recognized independence from their Member States that have the capacity to engage on the international plane. This would include organizations like the United Nations and regional organizations like the European Union, African Union and Organization of American States. In certain contexts and for some purposes it might also include the North Atlantic Treaty Organization or the Organization for Security and Co-operation in Europe, but these latter organizations tend to operate with less autonomy and thus are less relevant to this inquiry.

A good portion of the available practice concerns the United Nations. However, the study is not limited to considering UN responsibility, and seeks to draw parallels with the conduct of other international organizations which may also bear responsibility for human rights and international humanitarian law violations. To an extent, the UN's oft-cited failings to put in place adequate and effective redress mechanisms has received most notoriety, and have been considered most by scholars and policy-makers. But there are other organizations which are playing increasingly important roles on the international plane in areas which directly impact vulnerable populations. The European Border and Coast Guard Agency's role in preventing refugees and other migrants from reaching Europe and effectuating returns and the African Union's growing role in peacekeeping operations are but two clear examples. Another is the role of the International Criminal Court, which can exercise enormous powers over defendants and victim populations.

As appropriate, I have sought to note the differences between different types of international organizations which may impact on the ability to attribute conduct to them and on their resulting obligations. I have also sought to analyse the approaches taken by regional courts, which while having limited subject matter and personal jurisdiction stemming from their narrow mandates, provide useful comparators for structures which could be established at the universal level.

There is a natural breadth to what the book covers. This is because the problem areas become most evident in relation to how the various elements canvassed in the study intersect. The choices of what to cover and what to leave out have been made with a view to being able to best analyse those intersections.

In consequence, the relevant but extraneous area of State responsibility has been omitted from my inquiry. Naturally, it can be difficult to situate international organizations' responsibility outside of and without considering the responsibility of States who may act in conjunction with them, or whose conduct may result in multiple or shared attribution of responsibility. Nevertheless, I have operated from the perspective that the existence of State responsibility and the possibility to secure reparation for internationally wrongful acts stemming from that responsibility does not negate the need to address the responsibility of international organizations and the consequences of that responsibility. An international organization may have distinct obligations flowing from its particular mandate and taking into account its capacity to act or refrain from acting. Thus, a breach of an international organization's obligation is a separate and distinct matter requiring resolution, regardless of whether the breaches of other actors such as States have been resolved independently. However, the law of State responsibility has been canvassed as appropriate in order to extrapolate possible features for the responsibility of international organizations, to the extent that the latter framework is deficient.

I.4 The Structure of the Arguments

The book is divided into two main parts. Part I focuses on the responsibility of international organizations for human rights and international humanitarian law violations. Here, I consider whether international organizations may incur responsibility for breaches of human rights and international humanitarian law and analyse the contexts in which such responsibility may arise as well as when breaches may be attributed to the organization. I also consider the legal consequences of such breaches. Part II focuses on the implementation of the regime of responsibility, and canvasses the principal venues where claims against international organizations may be adjudicated. Part II also canvasses the prospects for criminal and civil accountability of international organizations' employees, contractors, and troop contingents.

Part I contains three chapters. Chapter II assesses whether international organizations have obligations to respect human rights and international humanitarian law. Aside from limited exceptions, international organizations are not party to human rights or international humanitarian law treaties and therefore the determination of obligations to comply with the norms in such treaties depends, in large part, on a finding that the norms are binding by virtue of the organizations' direct and voluntary incorporation of them, by implication through the organizations' functions or by their recognition as customary international law binding on the organization irrespective of consent. This analysis is complicated by the relatively limited practice involving international organizations specifically.

Chapter III analyses the circumstances in which international organizations may breach their human rights or international humanitarian law obligations. It first considers principles of liability including the required degree of intentionality for acts and omissions, exceptions to liability as well as the relationship between positive duties to act and the capacity to do so. It also analyses the impact of *ultra vires* acts on the imputation of liability. It then considers the bases for determining whether the conduct can be attributed to the international organization. The contexts and limitations in which international organizations operate are considered and these are analysed in regard to how they impact on findings of effective control.

Chapter IV surveys the obligation to afford reparation under general international law and its potential application to international organizations. Given the absence of clear and objective standards applicable to international organizations, the bulk of the chapter constitutes a *de lege ferenda* analysis. The limitations regarding State-owed obligations also impact on what can be said about international organizations' obligations. This is because of the near total absence of relevant practice on reparation concerning international organizations specifically. Therefore one must use the practice and *opinio juris* emanating from State violations to draw parallels to possible standards for international organizations; unclear State obligations influence what can be said about the obligations of international organizations.

I consider whether and the basis upon which any right which exists against States might also exist against international organizations. I review the content of the right, both from the DARIO perspective which approaches reparation along the same lines as the Articles on the Responsibility of States and through the human rights lens, which takes a broader approach both to the characterization of forms of reparation and the recognition of procedural elements such as the obligation to afford effective access to a fair hearing. I argue that reparation should be guided by what is adequate and appropriate to redress the nature of the breach, and less so by the nature or status of the wrongdoer.

Part II contains four chapters. Chapter V reviews the practice of international organizations in establishing internal adjudicative mechanisms and assesses the extent to which these meet the international law standards on reparation, particularly as is required for human rights and international humanitarian law violations. I also outline the arguments and rationales that have been used by international organizations to limit the scope and functioning of such mechanisms and analyse their cogency.

Chapter VI considers the limited instances in which claims against international organizations may be receivable before domestic courts. In this chapter, I outline the limited ways in which domestic courts have overcome the various jurisdictional and procedural barriers to entertain claims against international organizations and in contrast, the avoidance techniques some courts have used to entrench those same barriers. I review preliminary considerations of jurisdiction as well as the application of immunities to international organizations. I consider the sources of organizational immunities and assess the approaches taken by national courts when deciding on them, including with respect to their nature and content and how these have been considered alongside other rights, such as the right to reparation and the right of access to court.

In Chapter VII, I consider the few instances in which claims against international organizations may be receivable before regional and international courts and associated adjudicative bodies, and the related challenge for individuals to access such forums. I analyse the ways in which certain international courts have managed to assert jurisdiction, and the limitations of such approaches.

Chapter VIII considers the challenges to pursue criminal and civil accountability of international organization employees, contractors, and troop contingents. It reviews the possibilities and limitations of accountability structures in both the sending and host States and considers the associated due diligence obligations of international organizations to ensure progress with criminal investigations and prosecutions and civil reparations claims.

Finally, Chapter IX posits some solutions and paths forward to the myriad lacunae that have been identified throughout the text. Also, it collates the findings and conclusions.

I.5 Particular Issues and Tensions

Several tensions repeat throughout. Overall there is the tension between the *de lex lata* and *de lex ferenda*. The starting point is the weak and inadequate legal framework, thus the bulk of the research focuses on why it is weak, why this is problematic, and what are the necessary steps in argumentation to posit stronger assertions. In many respects, I take on the weak case; there is a heavy history, which goes against all that is posited. But even so, when one arrives at the conclusion, as I do, that international organizations have certain human rights and international humanitarian law obligations, that these may be breached, and that in consequence there are obligations to afford reparation, this does not necessarily imply that one can transpose the entire framework from the law on State responsibility without a process of translation. There is a need to determine what may be relevant or applicable to the international organization, taking into account the particularities of that organization, its functions, and its capacities and limitations.

A second constant theme is the influence of classical international law as a system that regulates relations between States as a constraint on the recognition of the placement of other actors and in particular the rights of individuals. This tension is particularly evident in the area of reparation, where traditionally, individuals' rights were subsumed by their States of nationality who could choose to address internationally wrongful acts affecting their citizens through the law on injury to aliens and diplomatic protection. While certain inroads have been made in the area of State human rights protections, the ability for individuals to lodge claims in respect of international humanitarian law breaches arguably remains circumscribed. It is also evident in respect of individuals' limited *locus standi* before international courts and certain regional ones.

This second theme also influences the development of the law of international organizations. When the DARIO was being developed, the Articles on the Responsibility of States (ARS)[3] formed the basis for the text, with modifications introduced as required.[4] Whilst this sped up the drafting, the method has also been criticized for 'not taking sufficient account of the differences between States and international organizations, and of the diversity among different international organizations'.[5] This tension is evident throughout the text.

A third issue relates to the terminology used in relation to international organizations' secondary obligations following the commission of an internationally wrongful act. I have tended to use the terms 'responsibility' and 'liability' as opposed to 'accountability'. This is because the latter term has a wide meaning, referring to the various aspects relevant to holding public officials and institutions to account including good governance, transparency, and the like. While these aspects have a general relevance, my focus is much more narrowly construed on the legal consequences of a breach of an international obligation. An international organization that is legally responsible and/or liable has the concomitant obligation to afford reparation. It is this relationship between the responsibility/liability of the international organization and the obligation to afford reparation that is central to my inquiry.

I.6 What is Concluded

While there may be no general international organization obligation to respect all human rights and international humanitarian law norms, there are indeed obligations which apply to such organizations in particular contexts. These must be assessed and determined on a case by case basis, and are aligned with international organizations' purposes and capacities to act and react. At the least, these include the obligation to respect international humanitarian law when carrying out enforcement actions and the obligation to respect human rights when international organizations exercise effective control over civilian populations. International organizations also must comply with peremptory norms of international law (which include elements of human rights and international humanitarian law) that apply to all subjects under international law.

[3] ILC, Articles on the Responsibility of States for Internationally Wrongful Acts, 'Report of the International Law Commission on the Work of its 53rd Session' (23 April–1 June and 2 July–10 August 2001) UN Doc A/CN.4/SER.A/2001/Add.1 (ARS).

[4] However, the DARIO Official Commentary makes clear that there is no general presumption that the same principles in the ARS apply to it. See DARIO (n 1) Official Commentary, General commentary para 4.

[5] Christiane Ahlborn, 'The Use of Analogies in Drafting the Articles on the Responsibility of International Organizations—An Appraisal of the "Copy-paste Approach"' (2012) 9 Intl Org LR 1.

When these obligations are breached, there is an obligation to afford reparation. The DARIO is clear that the reparation owed must correspond to the harm. While the DARIO text does not deal with reparation owed to individuals, there is no clear justification to diverge from this standard when considering reparation owed to individuals as opposed to States or other international organizations. For example, the UN has argued that its abridged procedures and curtailed awards amount to an institutional *lex specialis*, yet it is not evident that this is the case. If anything, I argue that the UN's arguments underpin the Organization's general reluctance to engage seriously in these matters, made worse by the monopoly it holds on the framing of the law given the absence of independent judicial scrutiny.

The rationales given by some organizations to refrain from seeking to negotiate special protocols or other means to accede to relevant treaties appear to stem more from their reluctance to be bound than by any formal difficulties associated with the accession process. The example of the European Union which has ratified certain human rights treaties is a useful basis upon which to explore whether other international organizations could follow suit. At the same time the difficulties to secure reparation for injured individuals even when a treaty framework or comparable legal framework is present underscores the overriding challenges for any accountability project.

Having determined that the existing mechanisms do not have the capacity to afford adequate or effective remedies and reparation, the question becomes how to move towards a model that achieves greater compliance. Indeed, should it be accepted that international organizations must afford remedies and reparation for breaches of human rights and international humanitarian law that correspond to the standards that exist in those specialized fields then there is a corresponding obligation for them to establish the framework for that to be achieved. This might include, for instance, strengthening internal adjudicative frameworks, or making more transparent the process for waiving immunity.

PART I

THE RESPONSIBILITY OF INTERNATIONAL ORGANIZATIONS FOR HUMAN RIGHTS AND INTERNATIONAL HUMANITARIAN LAW VIOLATIONS

II

International Organizations' Obligations under Human Rights and International Humanitarian Law

II.1 Introduction

Do international organizations have obligations under human rights and international humanitarian law? Obligations to respect, protect, and fulfil human rights and international humanitarian law can be imputed to international organizations if they are necessary to fulfil the organizations' purposes. They can also derive from treaties and custom. In this respect, it is relevant to consider the extent to which States and international organizations themselves have recognized international organizations to be bound by human rights and international humanitarian law in general or in particular contexts. This is made complicated by the limited practice of both States and international organizations, and the vagary of statements by international organizations of their intention to be bound.

II.2 The Ability of International Organizations to Bear International Obligations and Liability for Breaches of International Law

The ability for international organizations to exist under international law, to bear international obligations, and responsibility for breaches is a function of international legal personality (*persona jure gentium*).[1]

Traditionally, only States were understood to possess such personality,[2] which was recognized as 'the hallmark of sovereign powers'.[3] Neither the Covenant of

[1] *Reparation for Injuries Suffered in the Service of the United Nations* (Advisory Opinion) [1949] ICJ Rep 174, 179 (*Reparation for Injuries*).

[2] Hersch Lauterpacht, *International Law: Being the Collected Papers of Hersch Lauterpacht*, vol II (Elihu Lauterpacht (ed), CUP 1975) 489; David J Bederman, 'The Souls of International Organizations: Legal Personality and the Lighthouse at Cape Spartel' (1996) 36 Va J Int'l L 275, 334.

[3] Philippe Sands and Pierre Klein, *Bowett's Law of International Institutions* (6th edn, Sweet & Maxwell 2009) 473.

the League of Nations,[4] nor the UN Charter expressly conferred international legal personality on the respective organizations, although Article 104 of the UN Charter set out that the UN 'shall enjoy in the territory of each of its members such legal capacity as may be necessary for the exercise of its functions and the fulfilment of its purposes'.[5] Progressively, it has been recognized that non-State entities can possess such personality in limited circumstances or degree,[6] to the extent that specific rights and obligations are expressly set out in constituent agreements or can be implied from same. The position arguably remains in flux, although the starting point remains the State: non-State entities may acquire personality, although this is contingent on States' will.[7]

Aside from the constituent agreement, scholars appear to agree that the main criteria to determine international legal personality are:

1) The nature of the organization; whether the entity is a 'permanent association of States'.[8]
2) The decision-making structure: The entity should have a *volonté distincte*, in terms of legal powers and purposes, from its member States.[9]
3) The objectives must be lawful, and the functions and powers must be exercisable on the international plane, not solely within the national systems of one or more States,[10] that is, whether the organization has the capacity to enter into relations with States and other organizations and to conclude treaties with them.[11]

On the basis of those criteria, intergovernmental organizations like the UN would possess international legal personality. Whether the same can be said of other organizations with more limited fields of application and/or operating only in certain regions has been the subject of debate.

[4] Covenant of the League of Nations (adopted 29 April 1919, entered into force 10 January 1920) [1919] UKTS 4 (Cmd 153) art 7.

[5] Charter of the United Nations and Statute of the International Court of Justice (adopted 26 June 1945, entered into force 24 October 1945) 1 UNTS XVI art 104 (UN Charter). Henry G Schermers and Niels M Blokker, *International Institutional Law: Unity Within Diversity* (5th edn, Martinus Nijhoff 2011) 988.

[6] See Bederman (n 2) 335.

[7] *Legality of the Use by a State of Nuclear Weapons in Armed Conflict* (Advisory Opinion) [1996] ICJ Rep 66 [25]. Yet, some question whether the State-centric approach to personality sufficiently accounts for modern understandings of international society, which recognize a plethora of actors, including but not limited to the State. See James E Hickey Jr, 'The Source of International Legal Personality in the 21st Century' (1997) 2 Hofstra L & Pol'y Symp 1, 14–17; Christoph Schreuer, 'The Waning of the Sovereign State: Towards a New Paradigm for International Law' (1993) 4 EJIL 447, 453.

[8] Ian Brownlie, *Principles of Public International Law* (7th edn, OUP 2008) 678.

[9] ibid; see also Nigel D White, *The Law of International Organisations* (Melland Schill Studies in International Law, 2nd edn, Manchester University Press 2005) 1. As Higgins explains: 'An international association lacking legal personality and possessing no *volonté distincte* remains the creature of the States members who are thus liable for its acts'. Rosalyn Higgins, 'The Legal Consequences for Member States of the Non-fulfilment by International Organizations of their Obligations toward Third Parties' (1995) 66(1) YB Inst Int'l L 252, 254.

[10] See Brownlie (n 8).

[11] Malcolm Shaw, *International Law* (5th edn, CUP 2003) 181, 241.

Reparation for Injuries, and the International Court of Justice (ICJ)'s subsequent jurisprudence,[12] put to rest the view which understood personality to exist only if explicitly conferred in the constituent agreement.[13] In *Reparation for Injuries*, the ICJ was asked to assess whether the UN had the capacity to bring an international claim against a State to obtain reparation for the damage caused to the UN and the victim injured in the course of UN employment. The ICJ considered whether the UN possessed international legal personality as one route to determine if it was competent to present an international claim. It determined that the UN possessed 'a large measure of international personality', which was implied from the functions the organization exercises and the rights it enjoys: 'it could not carry out the intentions of its founders if it was devoid of international personality ... its Members, by entrusting certain functions to it, with the attendant duties and responsibilities, have clothed it with the competence required to enable those functions to be effectively discharged'.[14]

A functional analysis is consistent with the requirement of Article 31 of the Vienna Convention on the Law of Treaties[15] to give effect to interpretations that promote treaties' objects and purposes. The relevance of treaty interpretation to the analysis of constituent agreements was affirmed in the *WHO Nuclear Weapons Advisory Opinion*.[16] The ICJ recognized, however, that constituent instruments 'can raise specific problems of interpretation owing, inter alia, to their character which is conventional and at the same time institutional'.[17]

Both the ICJ and Permanent Court of International Justice (PCIJ) have considered the nature and scope of organizations' purposes and functions, as part of their analyses of organizations' competencies to request Advisory Opinions on legal questions arising within the scope of their activities,[18] as well as in the substantive consideration of the questions put to them. The opinions differ in the relative emphasis placed on the consent of States as the basis for personality and the outline of its powers, but there are no finite or fixed separations. Some decisions only recognize as legitimate those implied powers that are functionally necessary for carrying out express powers set out in the constituent agreement.[19] The *WHO Nuclear Weapons* Opinion refers to these as 'subsidiary powers'.[20] Most of the opinions in this category broadly construe functional necessity so long as the link to the constituent treaty is well evidenced.[21] Early PCIJ opinions interpreting organizations'

[12] *Legality of the Use by a State of Nuclear Weapons in Armed Conflict* (n 7) [25]: '[T]he necessities of international life may point to the need for organizations, in order to achieve their objectives, to possess subsidiary powers which are not expressly provided for in the basic instruments which govern their activities. It is generally accepted that international organizations can exercise such powers, known as "implied" powers'.

[13] See Schermers and Blokker (n 5) 988–89.

[14] See *Reparation for Injuries* (n 1) 179.

[15] Vienna Convention on the Law of Treaties (adopted 23 May 1969, entered into force 27 January 1980) 1155 UNTS 331 (VCLT).

[16] *Legality of the Use by a State of Nuclear Weapons in Armed Conflict* (n 7) [19].

[17] ibid.

[18] UN Charter (n 5) art 96(2).

[19] See *Reparation for Injuries* (n 1) (Hackworth dissent) 198.

[20] *Legality of the Use by a State of Nuclear Weapons in Armed Conflict* (n 7) [25].

[21] Dapo Akande, 'The Competence of International Organizations and the Advisory Jurisdiction of the International Court of Justice' (1998) 9 EJIL 437, 446.

competences take this approach.[22] Somewhat similarly, another line of cases recognize as legitimate, implied powers necessitated by the discharge of the organization's functions—if it is only possible for the organization to act with the power under consideration. Bekker, for instance, has indicated that an international organization is 'entitled to (no more than) what is strictly necessary for the exercise of its functions in the fulfilment of its purposes'.[23] In *Reparation for Injuries*, the ICJ applied a wide approach to acts understood as 'necessary' wherein it reasoned that the acceptance of these powers is necessary 'to ensure efficient and independent performance of these missions and to afford effective support to its agents, the organization must provide them with adequate protection'.[24]

Other jurisprudence has broadened what may be implied to include indirect powers 'relating to' the purposes and functions specified in the constituent agreement.[25] In *Certain Expenses*,[26] where the ICJ established that the UN had capacity to establish a peacekeeping force, it did not analyse whether the establishment of the UN Emergency Force was necessary, instead it was sufficient that the powers to do so related to the general purposes of the UN.[27] Similarly, in the 1971 *Advisory Opinion on Namibia*, where the ICJ considered Security Council resolutions not expressly covered by the wording of Chapter VI or VII of the UN Charter, it determined that the Council had, in addition to its specific powers, certain general powers under Article 24(1).[28]

II.3 Consequences of International Legal Personality

It is possible to derive human rights and international humanitarian law obligations from the conferral of international legal personality. This may be done by maintaining that some obligations are an inherent consequence of the personality bestowed on the international organization. However, a more persuasive position is that these obligations exist by virtue of them being necessary or otherwise required to fulfil the organizations' purposes.

II.3.1 Inherent consequences

Writers debate whether personality is merely declaratory or automatically engenders specific rights and obligations, irrespective of the functions of the organization.

[22] *Competence of the ILO to Regulate Incidentally the Personal Work of the Employer* (Advisory Opinion) PCIJ Rep Series B No 73, 24.

[23] Peter H E Bekker, *The Legal Position of Intergovernmental Organizations: A Functional Necessity Analysis of their Legal Status and Immunities* (Martinus Nijhoff 1994) 5.

[24] See *Reparation for Injuries* (n 1) 183.

[25] See Hickey Jr (n 7) 6.

[26] *Certain Expenses of the United Nations (Article 17, paragraph 2, of the Charter)* (Advisory Opinion) [1962] ICJ Rep 151.

[27] ibid [168].

[28] *Legal Consequences for States of the Continued Presence of South Africa in Namibia (South West Africa) notwithstanding Security Council Resolution 276 (1970)* (Advisory Opinion) [1971] ICJ Rep 16 [52].

The ambiguity may stem from the language in *Reparation for Injuries*. The ICJ held that international legal personality means that the organization is a subject of international law and capable of possessing international rights and duties, and that it has capacity to maintain its rights by bringing international claims.[29] Schermers and Blokker emphasize that 'to be an international person means only to be *capable* of bearing rights and duties', no actual rights or duties are automatically conferred.[30] Brownlie, similarly, has noted that 'the existence of international legal personality implies no automatic consequences',[31] that it is all derived from function. Some have gone so far as to refer to a 'functional personality of international organizations'.[32] *Reparation for Injuries* supports this conclusion when the ICJ holds that unlike a State, 'the rights and duties of an entity ... must depend upon its purposes and functions as specified or implied in its constituent documents and developed in practice'.[33]

The ICJ's later jurisprudence provides further support. In *Legality of the Use by a State of Nuclear Weapons*, it held that international organizations: 'do not, unlike States, possess a general competence. International organizations are governed by the "principle of speciality", that is to say, they are invested by the States which create them with powers, the limits of which are a function of the common interests whose promotion those States entrust to them'.[34]

Yet, it has been argued that to void international legal personality of actual content would make it 'merely a descriptive notion, lacking practical usefulness'.[35] Rama-Montaldo asserts that there are certainly rights which derive directly from the conferral of personality[36] and these should not be confused with those which arise from the precise functions and characteristics of the organization.[37] However, there is indeed confusion, because one of the 'objective' considerations understood to determine the existence of personality is the organization's objectives and the functions and powers accorded to it to attain them. This requires a functional analysis, so this limits the dichotomy in the analyses. Indeed, Rama-Montaldo's argument is circular when pared down to its essentials: one only arrives at a functional analysis

[29] See *Reparation for Injuries* (n 1) 178. See also Manuel Rama-Montaldo, 'International Legal Personality and Implied Powers of International Organizations' (1970) 44 BYIL 111, 124, 129–30, 139–40.

[30] See Schermers and Blokker (n 5) 993.

[31] See Brownlie (n 8) 527. See also Bekker, *The Legal Position of Intergovernmental Organisations* (n 23) 5.

[32] See Schermers and Blokker (n 5) 993; August Reinisch, *International Organizations before National Courts* (CUP 2000) 71.

[33] See *Reparation for Injuries* (n 1) 180.

[34] *Legality of the Use by a State of Nuclear Weapons in Armed Conflict* (n 7) [25].

[35] See Rama-Montaldo (n 29) 113, referring to Eduardo Jiménez de Aréchaga, *Curso de Derecho International Público*, vol I (Centro Estudiantes de Derecho 1959) 276.

[36] Seyersted shares this view, arguing that international organizations have inherent powers, dependent on the international legal order. Constituent agreements may restrict such powers, yet they do not provide an exhaustive and constraining list of powers within which an organization must operate. See Finn Seyersted, *Common Law of International Organizations* (Martinus Nijhoff 2008) 53.

[37] See Rama-Montaldo (n 29).

after satisfying the objective criteria for personality, the third of which requires a functional analysis.

Those that recognize inherent consequences have stuck to general principles,[38] given wide variations in organizations' size, scope, and mandates. Rama-Montaldo lists among the automatic consequences: the ability to operate on an international plane corresponding to 'rights to bring a claim, to negotiate, to conclude a special agreement, protest, request for an inquiry, etc'.[39] Proponents of automatic consequences of personality would also recognize amongst the inherent content the ability of those against whom the international organization has breached a duty, to bring claim against it. The entity is thus internationally responsible for the failure to observe obligations that are attributable to it.[40] This is a consequence of independent will and the power to produce by their acts, legal effects separable from the effects of acts of members.

The two approaches are not inconsistent; they illustrate two different points on the same continuum. Those who recognize no inherent characteristics proceed directly to a functional analysis to determine the international organization's sphere of rights and obligations whereas those who do, consider the inherent content as a preliminary frame, proceeding next to a functional analysis to determine whether a particular right or obligation is properly within the organization's scope of activity. The detailed analysis is thus concentrated on the organization's functions, irrespective of the starting point.

The ICJ has held that, as subjects of international law, international organizations are bound by obligations arising under such law:[41] they are 'bound by any obligations incumbent upon them under general rules of international law, under their constitutions or under international agreements to which they are parties'.[42] Thus, arguably like any other subject of international law, international organizations are bound by custom and/or general principles of law as recognized by civilized nations, which would include fundamental aspects of human rights and international humanitarian law. Verdirame takes this position, having regard to the 'approach adopted in the 1950s and 1960s towards newly independent states'. He asserts that: 'it would, after all, be extremely disruptive for the international system to tolerate the presence of actors that are endowed with legal personality, and thus with the legal capacity to operate upon the international plane, but are exempt from a body of universally or almost universally accepted rules'.[43]

Under this view, one would arguably need to accept the proposition that there is no automatic distinction between the consequences of personality for international

[38] ibid 117–20, referring to what he terms the 'material approach'. See also Seyersted (n 36) 67–69.

[39] See Rama-Montaldo (n 29) 139.

[40] ILC, Draft articles on the responsibility of international organizations, 'Report of the International Law Commission on the Work of its 63rd Session' (26 April–3 June and 4 July–12 August 2011) UN Doc A/66/10 (DARIO) para 87 art 3.

[41] *Interpretation of the Agreement of 25 March 1951 between the WHO and Egypt* (Advisory Opinion) [1980] ICJ Rep 73; *Legality of the Use by a State of Nuclear Weapons in Armed Conflict* (n 7) [16].

[42] ibid.

[43] Guglielmo Verdirame, *The UN and Human Rights: Who Guards the Guardians?* (CUP 2011) 71.

organizations and for States,[44] and then proceed to argue that such obligations are the consequence of the inalienable rights possessed by all persons and as a result are binding on all those having the capacity to ensure those rights. Clapham, for instance, has argued that: '[t]he obligations arise because the international legal order considers these rights and obligations as generally applicable and binding on every entity that has the capacity to bear them'.[45] Clapham focuses on the nature of the rights and obligations as opposed to the degree to which particular entities have expressed consent to be bound.

At least those obligations that have attained peremptory status[46] are binding on international organizations by virtue of the fact that any act of an international organization in conflict with a peremptory norm would necessarily be without effect. Orakhelashvili argues that the obligation to comply with peremptory norms would constitute 'an inherent limitation on any organization's powers'.[47] Similarly, it has been argued that international organizations have a due diligence obligation by virtue of being a subject of international law, not to undermine the obligations of other subjects under international law. Darrow and Arbour contend that international organizations are obligated to ensure that their own 'policies, actions, or possible neglect do not undermine the human rights obligations of other subjects of international law'.[48]

Articles 25 and 40(1) of DARIO refer to peremptory norms of general international law, and in its consideration of 'countermeasures'. Article 52(1) clarifies that: 'Countermeasures shall not affect: (a) The obligation to refrain from the threat or use of force as embodied in the Charter of the United Nations; (b) Obligations for the protection of fundamental human rights; (c) Obligations of a humanitarian character prohibiting reprisals; (d) Other obligations under peremptory norms of general international law'. This would suggest recognition by DARIO that international organizations are always obligated to respect these norms. The content of the norms is not explained in the text, although the Official Commentary notes that: '[p]eremptory norms that are clearly accepted and recognized include the prohibitions of aggression, genocide, slavery, racial discrimination, crimes against humanity and torture, and the right to self-determination'.[49] Furthermore, Article 26 of the DARIO specifies that: '[n]othing ... precludes the wrongfulness of any act of an international organization which is not in conformity with an obligation arising under a peremptory norm of general international law'.[50] The Commentary proceeds, albeit with little analysis, to state that peremptory norms bind international organizations just as they bind States.[51]

[44] See Rama-Montaldo (n 29) 119–21, who criticizes Seyersted's approach on this point.

[45] Andrew Clapham, *Human Rights Obligations of Non-State Actors* (OUP 2006) 87.

[46] See VCLT (n 15) art 53.

[47] Alexander Orakhelashvili, 'The Impact of Peremptory Norms on the Interpretation and Application of United Nations Security Council Resolutions' (2005) 16 EJIL 59, 60.

[48] Mac Darrow and Louise Arbour, 'The Pillar of Glass: Human Rights in the Development Operations of the United Nations' (2009) 103 AJIL 446, 474.

[49] See DARIO (n 40) Official Commentary to art 26 para 2.

[50] ibid art 26.

[51] ibid Official Commentary to art 26 para 3.

The ILC commentary on the *jus cogens* provision of Article 53 of the Vienna Convention on the Law of Treaties between States and International Organizations and between International Organizations 1986 comes to the same conclusion that peremptory norms necessarily bind international organizations, yet this is reasoned not as the necessary result of the conferral of international legal personality but because the organization is bound by virtue of the incorporation of Member States' obligations: 'it can hardly be maintained that States can avoid compliance with peremptory norms by creating organizations'.[52] In this way, international organizations will be bound by the progressive recognition of peremptory norms.[53] But, on the basis of this third argument, it is not only peremptory norms that would bind international organizations—any obligation which binds the founding members of that organization would potentially transfer to that organization.

Given the centrality of the will of States in the creation of an international organization, international organizations arguably can take on the obligations of the States that created them.[54] Reinisch has referred to this as 'something like a "functional" treaty succession by international organizations to the position of their Member States',[55] premised on the notion that States should not be able to avoid their international obligations by creating an international organization to carry out work that States themselves would not be permitted to undertake.[56] When States transfer powers to an international organization, these powers must necessarily be exercised in accordance with States' own obligations, a sort of 'equivalent protection',[57] or else States may be held responsible for any ensuing violations which would otherwise be attributable to the organization.[58] While an international organization is independent from the will of the Member States that founded it, this arguably would not relieve the organization from the obligations of the founding States. This has been affirmed for the EU; when Member States transferred powers to the EU, the CJEU accepted that the EU may de facto succeed Member States' obligations.[59] A transfer of competencies should not have the capacity of creating a gap in human rights protection for rights-bearers. The UN Human Rights Committee has noted, for example that: 'once the people are accorded the protection of the rights under the Covenant, such protection devolves with territory and continues to belong to them, notwithstanding change in government of the State

[52] ILC, 'Report of the International Law Commission on the Work of its 34th Session' (3 May–23 July 1982) UN Doc A/37/10, Official Commentary art 53.

[53] See Orakhelashvili (n 47) 60.

[54] Schermers and Blokker (n 5) 996.

[55] August Reinisch, 'Securing the Accountability of International Organizations' (2001) 7 Global Governance 131, 137.

[56] ibid 137, 143; *Waite and Kennedy v Germany* (GC) App no 26083/94 (ECtHR, 18 February 1999) [67].

[57] *M & Co v Germany* (Decision on Admissibility) App no 13258/87 (ECommHR, 9 February 1990); *Matthews v United Kingdom* App no 24833/94 (ECtHR, 18 February 1999).

[58] Darrow and Arbour (n 48) 464.

[59] Joined Cases 21–24/72 *International Fruit Company* [1972] ECR 1219, para 18: 'It therefore appears that, in so far as under the EEC treaty the Community has assumed the powers previously exercised by member states in the area governed by the general agreement, the provisions of that agreement have the effect of binding the community'. See also Case T 315/01 *Yassin Abdullah Kadi v Council and Commission* [2005] ECR II–03649 para 203.

party, including dismemberment in more than one State or State succession or any subsequent action of the State party designed to divest them of the rights guaranteed by the Covenant'.[60]

At the least, State obligations help to construe the intention of the founders when establishing an international organization—their intention could not have been to establish an organization which had as one of its aims, the violation of law binding on States.

II.3.2 Consequences that are implied because they are necessary to fulfil international organizations' purposes

Under a second reasoning, human rights and international humanitarian law obligations are derived through the constituent agreement and implied by virtue of the obligations being essential or appropriate for the fulfilment of the organization's purposes. Most of the ICJ cases have dealt with a potential expansion of powers not specifically conferred on the organization, and not, as here, whether the organization's actions are necessarily constrained by certain obligations that may be expressly conferred in the Charter or implied as a necessary or essential requirement for the fulfilment of its purposes.[61]

The argument can be made most forcefully in respect of peremptory norms of international law which apply to all subjects under international law and to applicable customary international law and general principles. Beyond this, obligations will be determined on the basis of the constituent agreement, any treaties or agreements to be bound to particular rules, the nature and functions of the organization, and the concomitant capacities to act and react. For example, all international organizations regardless of mandate will be called upon to respect the labour rights of their employees. Given their role, the International Monetary Fund and the World Bank may well have obligations which prevent them from adopting policies or actions that have a regressive impact on individuals' access to health, water, or education; whereas an African Union or UN peacekeeping or police mission which detains civilians will be required to uphold the prohibition on arbitrary detention and refrain from torture. A regional Border Agency which carries out sea patrols in Europe will be obliged to respect inter alia the principle of non-*refoulement*.

The case for affirmative obligations can be made most forcibly for the EU which has acceded to several human rights treaties and its foundational documents recognize the centrality of human rights for EU institutions. Its Charter on Fundamental Rights applies not only to Member States, but also to 'the institutions, bodies, offices and agencies of the Union'.[62] Accordingly, respect for human rights is a

[60] UN Human Rights Committee, 'General Comment 26', Issues Relating to the Continuity of Obligations to the International Covenant on Civil and Political Rights (8 December 1997) CCPR/C/21/Rev.1/Add.8/Rev.1 para 4.

[61] *Interpretation of the Agreement of 25 March 1951 between the WHO and Egypt* (n 41) 89.

[62] Charter of Fundamental Rights of the European Union (proclaimed 7 December 2000, entered into force 1 December 2009) 2010/C 83/02 art 51(1).

condition for the legality of EU action. The planned accession of the EU to the European Court of Human Rights, which Member States have agreed through the Treaty of Lisbon,[63] is another indicator of the EU's understanding of the human rights obligations of EU institutions.

There is no comparable practice in other regional systems,[64] or at the international level. Most constituent agreements emphasize the role of the organization in promoting State adherence to human rights and other obligations. According to the African Union (AU) Constitutive Act: '[t]he Union shall function in accordance with the following principles ... 'respect for democratic principles, human rights, the rule of law and good governance'.[65] The obligations set out in the African Charter on Human and Peoples' Rights do not expressly apply to African institutions.[66] Similarly, the UN Charter makes numerous references to human rights and international law but refrains from explicitly obliging the UN itself to uphold these principles. However, it specifies that the fulfilment of the purposes of the UN must be carried out in conformity with 'the principles of justice and international law'.[67]

For the African Union and the UN, and other organizations with similarly framed constituent agreements, there will be debate about whether the references in those agreements are capable of being translated into hard and binding obligations on the organizations; there are arguments about why they *should*, but it is harder to ground an argument about why they *must*.[68] Human rights and the respect for international law operate as a key lens through which these organizations' work can be understood. Thus, compliance becomes necessary to fulfil the organizations' functions, which arguably requires them to subscribe to the norms that they seek to promote. The ICJ came to a similar view in its 1954 Advisory Opinion, in which it held that to leave one of the UN's own civil servants without access to a remedy would 'hardly be consistent with the expressed aim of the Charter to promote freedom and justice for individuals and with the constant preoccupation of the United Nations Organization to promote this aim'.[69]

A predominant UN purpose is the maintenance of international peace and security.[70] Whilst there are no references in the Charter to the respect of international humanitarian law *per se*, either by States or by the UN, actions must be undertaken 'in conformity with the principles of justice and international law', and Article 24(2), in relation to Security Council actions, affirms that: '[i]n discharging these

[63] ibid; Treaty of Lisbon, Consolidated versions of the Treaty on European Union (TEU) and the Treaty on the Functioning of the European Union (TFEU) (adopted 13 December 2007, entered into force 1 December 2009) [2008] OJ C115/01 art 59(2).

[64] See Chapter VII.

[65] Constitutive Act of the African Union (adopted 11 July 2000, entered into force 26 May 2001) art 4(m).

[66] African Charter on Human and Peoples' Rights (adopted 27 June 1981, entered into force 21 October 1986) (1982) 21 ILM 58 (ACHPR) art 45.

[67] UN Charter (n 5) preamble arts 1(1), 2(3).

[68] Frédéric Mégret and Florian Hoffmann, 'The UN as a Human Rights Violator? Some Reflections on the United Nations Changing Human Rights Responsibilities' (2003) 25 HRQ 314, 334.

[69] *Effects of Awards of Compensation Made by the United Nations Administrative Tribunal* (Advisory Opinion) [1954] ICJ Rep 47, 57.

[70] UN Charter (n 5) arts 1(1), 1(3), 1(6), 11(1), 11(2), 11(3), 13, 14, 34, 26, and 33(2).

duties the Security Council shall act in accordance with the Purposes and Principles of the United Nations'. While it is recognized that the Security Council is empowered to derogate temporarily from rules of both treaty and customary international law as long as it is acting under Chapter VII of the UN Charter to maintain or restore international peace and security, authors have recognized that the Security Council is not empowered to act in a way that would defeat the other purposes and principles of the UN.[71]

II.4 Treaties

II.4.1 Treaties and related texts which establish or recognize the human rights and international humanitarian law obligations of international organizations

There is no treaty framework establishing the human rights or international humanitarian law obligations of international organizations. The Articles on the Responsibility of States (ARS) adopted by the ILC in 2001 do not address 'the responsibility under international law of an international organization, or of any State for the conduct of an international organization'.[72] The DARIO provide no further guidance.[73] Article 4(b) provides that an internationally wrongful act of an international organization is an act which constitutes a breach of an international obligation of that organization, yet the text does not consider which acts would constitute such a breach. The Official Commentary notes simply that an international obligation 'may be established by a customary rule of international law, by a treaty or by a general principle applicable within the international legal order', and is 'likely to arise from the rules of the organization, which are defined . . . as meaning "in particular, the constituent instruments, decisions, resolutions, and other acts of the organization adopted in accordance with those instruments, and established practice of the organization"'.[74] A breach may stem 'either from a treaty binding the international organization or from any other source of international law applicable to the organization'.[75]

[71] Chittharanjan Felix Amerasinghe, *Principles of the Institutional Law of International Organizations* (Cambridge Studies in International and Comparative Law, 2nd edn, CUP 2005) 186. This was also the position taken by the UN Committee on Economic and Social Rights in its General Comment 8 on the relationship between economic sanctions and respect for economic, social, and cultural rights; UN Commission on Human Rights, 'Compilation of General Comments and General Recommendations Adopted by Human Rights Treaty Bodies' (2004) UN Doc HRI/GEN/1/Rev.7 para 1, although the Committee arrives at this position largely on the basis of an extrapolation of Member States' conventional and customary international law obligations, not by virtue of any direct analysis of the institutional obligations of the UN by virtue of the Charter.

[72] ILC, Articles on the Responsibility of States for Internationally Wrongful Acts, 'Report of the International Law Commission on the Work of its 53rd Session' (23 April–1 June and 2 July–10 August 2001) UN Doc A/CN.4/SER.A/2001/Add.1 art 57.

[73] See DARIO (n 40).

[74] ibid Official Commentary arts 10, 31.

[75] ibid art 54.

II.4.2 Accession to treaties

International organizations may enter into treaties[76] and thereby become bound by their terms,[77] to the extent that it 'is necessary for the exercise of their functions and fulfilment of their purposes'.[78] They *may* enter into treaties, but there is no requirement to do so, even if treaty ratification would result in better fulfilment of their purposes.[79] Indeed, international organizations have rarely ratified human rights or international humanitarian law treaties. The reasons for this are practical; ratification would normally require complicated adjustments to treaty frameworks designed mainly with States in mind. The reasons are also connected to international organizations' self-interest; their vulnerability in light of the varied and complex circumstances of their operations; their wish to preserve the greatest possible flexibility and freedom of action, and/or avoid possible liability in case of breach.

Quenivet explains that treaties seldom provide for organizational membership.[80] She lists three human rights treaties which allow for regional organization membership: the European Convention for the Protection of Human Rights and Fundamental Freedoms (ECHR),[81] Convention on the Rights of Persons with Disabilities (CRPD),[82] and Convention on Action against Trafficking in Human Beings (CATHB).[83] To this list, one might add several Council of Europe Conventions: the Convention on Preventing and Combating Violence against Women and Domestic Violence;[84] the Convention for the Protection of Human Rights and Dignity of the Human Being with regard to the Application of Biology and Medicine,[85] and the Convention on the Protection of Children against Sexual Exploitation and Sexual Abuse,[86] all of which allow the European Union to join. Of these, the EU has ratified only the CRPD.[87] No human rights treaty provides explicitly for UN membership.[88] Similarly, while most international humanitarian

[76] See *Reparation for Injuries* (n 1) 178–79.

[77] Vienna Convention on the Law of Treaties between States and International Organizations or between International Organizations (adopted on 21 March 1986, not yet in force) UN Doc A/CONF.129/15, 25 ILM 543 (VCLT 1986) art 11(2). According to art 6, the capacity of an international organization to conclude treaties is governed by the rules of that organization.

[78] ibid preamble.

[79] Note, however, the exceptional obligation in the Treaty of Lisbon. Consolidated versions of the Treaty on European Union and the Treaty on the Functioning of the European Union (TFEU), 2008/C 115/01 (adopted 13 December 2007, entered into force 1 December 2009) art 59(2), as amended by Protocol No 14 to the Convention which entered into force on 1 June 2010.

[80] Nicole Quenivet, 'Binding the United Nations to Human Rights Norms by Way of the Laws of Treaties' (2010) 42 Geo Wash Int'l L Rev 587, 590–92.

[81] Adopted 4 November 1950, entered into force 3 September 1953 (ECHR).

[82] CRPD (adopted on 13 December 2006, entered into force on 3 May 2008) 2515 UNTS 3.

[83] CATHB (adopted on 16 May 2005, entered into force on 1 February 2008) CETS no 197.

[84] Adopted on 11 May 2011, entered into force on 1 August 2014, CETS no 210.

[85] Convention on Human Rights and Biomedicine (adopted 4 April 1997, entered into force 1 December 1999) CETS no 164.

[86] Adopted 25 October 2007, entered into force 1 July 2010, CETS no 201.

[87] The EU signed the CRPD on 30 March 2007 and ratified the Convention on 23 December 2010.

[88] See Quenivet (n 80) 591–92.

law treaties do not exclude explicitly entities other than States,[89] the treaty wording and official commentaries suggest that ratification is open to States only.[90]

The argument has been made that international organizations cannot be bound by certain treaties by virtue of their inability to comply in totality with their terms.[91] However, strategies have been employed successfully to enable international organizations to accede to human rights conventions. These include revising treaty terms and/or allowing them to make reservations at the time of accession to avoid taking on obligations that exceed their competences, provided that the reservations are not incompatible with the object and purpose of the treaty.[92] The challenges are not insignificant, as is attested by the difficulties associated with the EU's pending accession to the ECHR,[93] although they are not insurmountable.

It has been suggested that the UN should accede to certain human rights and international humanitarian law treaties.[94] The Institut de droit international recommended that the UN 'state in an appropriate form that it considers itself bound by the 1949 Geneva Convention in all operations to which its Forces might be parties'.[95] The UN Secretary-General eventually did specify a commitment for the UN to be bound by international humanitarian law principles in a limited way,[96] and international humanitarian law obligations have been incorporated into status of mission and status of force agreements in AU and UN missions with enforcement mandates.[97] Other suggestions have been made to encourage the Parties to relevant treaties to agree a Protocol to enable the UN and other organizations as

[89] Marten Zwanenburg, *Accountability of Peace Support Operations* (Martinus Nijhoff 2005) 136–38. See also Christopher Greenwood, 'International Humanitarian Law and United Nations Military Operations' (1998) 1 YIHL 3, 16, n 42 (referring to the response of the Swiss Government to the deposit of purported instruments of accession by Palestine: 'due to the uncertainty within the international community as to the existence or non-existence of a State of Palestine it was not in a position to decide whether this communication constituted an instrument of accession').

[90] See eg Convention for the Amelioration of the Condition of the Wounded and Sick in Armed Forces in the Field (adopted 12 August 1949, entered into force 21 October 1950) 75 UNTS 31, which refers to the possibility for all 'Powers' to accede to the Convention, and the ICRC Commentary thereto, which clarifies that: '[t]he invitation is addressed to all *States*, whether they are or are not parties to one of the earlier Conventions' (emphasis added). ICRC, 'Commentary to art 60: Accession', 1949 Conventions and Additional Protocols, and their Commentaries www.icrc.org/applic/ihl/ihl.nsf/vwTreaties1949.xsp (last accessed 20 December 2016).

[91] According to Schermers and Blokker (n 5) 1001, the UN Office of Legal Affairs has indicated that the UN cannot adhere to the 1949 Geneva Conventions given its inability to discharge all the obligations contained therein. See also Greenwood (n 89) 15.

[92] *Reservations to the Convention on the Prevention and Punishment of the Crime of Genocide* (Advisory Opinion) [1951] ICJ Rep 15. This was the argument made by the ICRC in relation to the UN's compliance with international humanitarian law. See ICRC, 'Statement at the 47th Session of the GA' (13 November 1992).

[93] See Chapter VII. [94] See Quenivet (n 80) 612–13.

[95] IDI, 'Conditions of Application of Rules, Other than Humanitarian Rules, of Armed Conflict to Hostilities in which United Nations Forces May be Engaged' (Wiesbaden, 13 August 1975) Rec II.

[96] UN Secretariat, 'Observance by United Nations Forces of International Humanitarian Law' (6 August 1999) UN Doc ST/SGB/1999/13 Chapter I para 3.

[97] AU, Status of Mission Agreement between the Transitional Federal Government of the Somali Republic and the AU on the AU Mission in Somalia (6 March 2007) para 9; UN, Status of Forces Agreement between the UN and the Government of the Republic of South Sudan concerning the United Nations Mission in South Sudan (8 August 2011) para 6.

appropriate to join,[98] or for the General Assembly to adopt a resolution that the relevant Conventions apply to UN activities,[99] or a specific regulation or Convention determining the scope of application of such treaties to UN action.[100] As there are no reservation or derogation clauses in The Hague or Geneva Conventions or Additional Protocols, this possibility would need to be introduced by a specific amendment or separate protocol.[101] A further means for this to occur could be through unilateral declaration by an international organization that it accepts that a particular treaty is binding upon it.[102]

II.4.3 Treaty obligations that may bind international organizations regardless of accession

While it is a general principle that treaties bind only those that consent to their terms,[103] there are instances in which entities that are not parties may nonetheless be considered to be bound. For example, the minimum protections and obligations in Article 3 common to the Geneva Conventions 1949 are applicable to all 'Parties to the conflict', not all of whom will necessarily be parties to the Conventions; indeed, they need not be States.[104] The typical non-State entity contemplated by Common Article 3 is an armed opposition group, although this is not explicitly stated and it is plausible that it could also apply to an international organization with troops in the country. While it may be difficult to conceive international organizations' troops as a 'party' to a conflict when they act at the behest of the international community and undertake missions that are primarily humanitarian,[105] if any force is

[98] Derek Bowett, *United Nations Forces: A Legal Study of United Nations Practice* (Stevens & Sons 1964) 510. See also Richard Baxter, 'Constitutional Forms and Some Legal Problems of International Military Command' (1952) 29 Brit YB Int'l L 325, 354–59.

[99] See Bowett (n 98) 511. See also Convention on the Safety of United Nations and Associated Personnel (adopted 9 December 1994, entered into force 15 January 1999) 2051 UNTS 363 arts 2(2), 20.

[100] Gerald Irving Draper, 'The Legal Limitations upon the Employment of Weapons by the United Nations Force in the Congo' (1963) 12 ICLQ 387, 412. See also Nigel D White, 'Towards a Strategy for Human Rights Protection in Post-conflict Situations' in Nigel D White and Dirk Klaasen (eds), *The UN, Human Rights and Post-conflict Situations* (Manchester University Press 2005) 461, 465.

[101] Finn Seyersted, *United Nations Forces in the Law of Peace and War* (AW Sijthoff 1966) 290–92 (arguing that an explicit derogation provision in a treaty binding UN Member States would be required to permit the United Nations to 'deviate from those parts of the laws of war which apply to all types of armed conflict', and concluding that, with a few possible exceptions, 'the United Nations must be bound by the substantive aspects of the traditional laws of war in the humanitarian field').

[102] *Nuclear Tests (New Zealand v France)* [1974] ICJ Rep 253 [43].

[103] VCLT 1986 (n 77) art 26.

[104] *Military and Paramilitary Activities in and against Nicaragua (Nicaragua v USA)* (Merits) [1986] ICJ Rep 14 [219], in which the ICJ indicates that Common Article 3 is applicable to the Contras rebel group.

[105] Yet, the UN has recognized in its Bulletin that its troops may act in enforcement operations as combatants (s. 1 of the Bulletin, (n 96)). The Bulletin suggests that when UN forces use force in armed conflict situations, international humanitarian law will apply. The distinction between UN forces role in enforcement action and peacekeeping is also recognized in the *Convention on the Safety of UN and Associated Personnel* (n 99), which treats only the latter as falling within the purview of the Convention. See Christiane Bourloyannis-Vrailas, 'The Convention on the Safety of UN and Associated Personnel' (1995) 44 ICLQ 560, 567.

drawn into hostilities, then regardless of the reason for their presence, international humanitarian law may be said to apply,[106] although there is debate about whether the fact of an international organization's involvement necessarily gives the conflict an international character.[107]

Certainly, when peacekeepers are authorized to use force as part of offensive actions—as is the case of the Force Intervention Brigade of the UN Stabilization Mission in the Democratic Republic of the Congo (MONUSCO) or the African Union Mission in Somalia (AMISOM), they would be considered combatants under international humanitarian law.[108] Article 1(1) of Protocol II[109] also applies to entities other than contracting parties, although these are more narrowly described as 'dissident armed forces or other organized armed groups which, under responsible command, exercise such control over a part of its territory as to enable them to carry out sustained and concerted military operations and to implement this Protocol'. It is more difficult to conceive of an international organization as a dissident force, although it can be an organized armed group, and may well have control over parts of a territory on an explicit or *de facto* basis.

The direct applicability of human rights treaties to international organizations is less clear. Article 5(1) of the International Covenant on Civil and Political Rights (ICCPR)[110] refers to entities other than States Parties, but it is negatively construed—nothing 'may be interpreted as implying for any State, group or person any right to engage in any activity or perform any act aimed at the destruction of any of the rights and freedoms recognized herein or at their limitation to a greater extent than is provided for in the present Covenant', and even if an obligation could be implied there is no method within the Covenant or other international law instrument to enforce it against an entity other than a State. Similarly, the 2009 Convention for the Protection and Assistance of Internally Displaced Persons in Africa cites as its objectives in Article 2 to '[p]rovide for the respective obligations, responsibilities and roles of armed groups, non-State actors and other relevant actors, including civil society organizations … ', whereas Article 7 lists obligations that may be imposed on those actors, although it lists the obligations of individual members of armed groups and not those of the group itself.

106 See Greenwood (n 89) 14, 23.

107 ibid 25–26.

108 UNSC Res 2098/2013 (28 March 2013), authorizing the Force Intervention Brigade to neutralize, inter alia, armed groups and 'reduce the threat posed by armed groups to state authority and civilian security in eastern DRC'; UNSC, Res 2297/2016 (7 July 2016) paras 4, 6(a), 7(a) authorizing AMISOM 'to take all necessary measures' … to 'continue to conduct offensive operations against Al Shabaab and other armed opposition groups', and … 'conduct joint operations with the Somali security forces, within its capabilities'. See also in relation to Mali, UNSC Res 2100/2013 (25 April 2013) 7. See Magdalena Pacholska, '(Il)legality of Killing Peacekeepers: The Crime of Attacking Peacekeepers in the Jurisprudence of International Criminal Tribunals' (2015) 13(1) J Int'l Criminal Justice 43, 68–69.

109 Protocol Additional to the Geneva Conventions of 12 August 1949, and relating to the Protection of Victims of Non-International Armed Conflicts (adopted 8 June 1977, entered into force 7 December 1978) 1125 UNTS 609 (Protocol II).

110 Adopted 16 December 1966, entered into force 23 March 1976.

II.5 Customary International Law

II.5.1 Are customary international law obligations binding on states directly transferrable to international organizations?

Scholars and others have considered the extent to which particular elements of human rights and international humanitarian law constitute customary international law. For instance, it has been argued that the wide adoption and continuous affirmation of the fundamental human rights listed in the Universal Declaration of Human Rights (UDHR) have transformed many of the principles contained therein into customary international law.[111] The same arguments have been made in relation to many principles in the Geneva Conventions and Additional Protocols.[112] But, a preliminary question is whether customary international law which evidences State practice binds international organizations without any special practice or *opinio juris* emanating from the organizations themselves.[113] Many customary norms have little relevance to international organizations, and international organizations are incapable of fulfilling all the obligations. However, this should not impede the application of those elements that the organizations have the capacity to comply with.

II.5.2 Practice and *opinio juris* providing specific evidence of international organization obligations

Proving a customary norm requires evidence of an identifiable State practice, however it has been recognized that the practice of other international subjects including international organizations is also relevant.[114] This is particularly the case when inquiring into custom binding on international organizations.

(1) State practice and opinio juris

There is some, although not extensive, direct evidence of State practice recognizing that international organizations possess human rights or international humanitarian law obligations.[115] Some of this practice relates to judicial decisions of national and regional courts which have attributed responsibility for violations to

[111] Hurst Hannum, 'The Status of the Universal Declaration of Human Rights in National and International Law' (1995–1996) 25 Ga J Int'l & Comp L 287, 322–25.

[112] Theodor Meron, 'The Geneva Conventions as Customary Law' (1987) 81 AJIL 348; Jean-Marie Henckaerts and Louise Doswald-Beck, *Customary International Humanitarian Law*, vol 1 (Rules) (CUP 2005).

[113] See II.3.1 'Inherent consequences'.

[114] Maurice H Mendelson, 'Formation of Customary International Law' (1988) 272 Recueil des Cours: Collected Courses of the Hague Academy of International Law 165, 188.

[115] See DARIO (n 40) Official Commentary.

international organizations,[116] although in the majority of these cases, judges have refrained from determining the liability of organizations because of limited jurisdiction and the recognition of organizations' privileges and immunities. While this practice is unlikely on its own to provide evidence of a customary rule, there is additionally, no practice of States explicitly denying that international organizations have these obligations. Indeed, no State disputed the DARIO's general framework which outlines that international organizations may be responsible for the breach of international obligations attributable to them, nor the multiple references to international organizations' responsibility for the violation of peremptory norms.[117] States' silence is normally understood as tacit acceptance or acquiescence to a rule, or that they view the rule as self-evident.

As indicated in earlier sections, States have rarely sought to include international organizations in human rights and international humanitarian law treaties, although this is not necessarily evidence of their view of the lack of obligation; it could simply relate to the view that treaties specifying State obligations are not understood by States to be the best forum to outline international organization obligations.

With respect to international humanitarian law, the parties to the Convention on the Safety of UN and Associated Personnel recognized that the Convention does not apply to enforcement actions under Chapter VII, 'in which UN personnel are engaged as combatants to which the law of international armed conflicts applies'.[118] States have also regularly entered into agreements with international organizations concerning the rights and obligations of the organization and of the host State, although these agreements rarely mention, or indeed set out a structure for the liability of international organizations for violations of human rights or international humanitarian law.

In the numerous status of forces agreements States have agreed with international organizations, and indeed in the UN's own Model Status of Forces Agreement,[119] there is no reference to the institutional liability of the UN for breaches of human

[116] See eg *Behrami and Behrami v France; Saramati v France, Germany and Norway* (GC) App nos 71412/01, 78166/01 (ECtHR, 2 May 2007). Attribution is considered in further detail in Chapter III.

[117] ILC, Responsibility of international organizations: Comments and observations received from Governments 'Report of the International Law Commission on the Work of its 56th Session' (3 May–4 June and 5 July–6 August 2004) UN Doc A/CN.4/547; ILC, Responsibility of international organizations: Comments and observations received from Governments and International Organizations, Report of the International Law Commission on the Work of its 57th Session' (2 May–3 June and 11 July–5 August 2005) UN Doc A/CN.4/556; ILC, Responsibility of international organizations: Comments and observations received from Governments, 'Report of the International Law Commission on the Work of its 63rd Session' (26 April–3 June and 4 July–12 August 2011) UN Doc A/CN.4/636, A/CN.4/636/Add.1. Note, however, the Czech Republic comment that the Articles' and Commentary's consideration of whether an international organization can violate *jus cogens* and whether in such case the responsibility is incurred by the organization and/or its Member States failed to provide examples of serious breaches of obligations under peremptory norms of general international law committed by international organizations (A/CN.4/636/Add.1, 16).

[118] Convention on the Safety of United Nations and Associated Personnel (n 99) art 2(2).

[119] UNGA, 'Model Status-of-forces Agreement for Peace-Keeping Operations' (9 October 1990) UN Doc A/45/594 (UN Model SOFA).

rights or international humanitarian law, although these breaches are not explicitly omitted. These agreements recognize the potential liability of employees and contractors, and consistent with the Convention on the Privileges and Immunities of the United Nations (CPIUN), require the UN to establish mechanisms for the settlement of disputes of a private law character or involving officials who benefit from immunities.[120] This is consistent with the opinion of the ICJ, which has recognized that the UN may be required to compensate States for any damages incurred as a result of acts performed by the UN or by its agents acting in their official capacity.[121]

In addition, the Copenhagen Process Principles and Guidelines[122] have sought to identify the baseline of laws applicable to the taking, handling, and transfer of civilian detainees in international military operations, particularly non-international armed conflicts, peace-keeping operations, and law enforcement operations. The principles and guidelines that were eventually adopted by an array of States apply to 'detaining authorities',[123] which in the international military operation context can include international organizations. The Principles and Guidelines are non-binding, nor do they create new commitments or restate customary international law.[124] Nonetheless, they do constitute evidence of practice recognizing that international organizations engaged in detention can possess legal obligations pertaining to detention, which at least as a matter of principle, can straddle human rights and international humanitarian law.

With respect to human rights law, State practice and *opinio juris* is more limited and less capable of generalization. The clearest practice is at the regional level, with the proclamation and later entry into force of the Charter of Fundamental Rights of the European Union and the planned accession of the EU to the ECHR.[125] There is no comparable practice in other regional systems.[126] Universal human rights texts have emphasized the responsibility of States, almost exclusively. But there does not

[120] Convention on the Privileges and Immunities of the UN (adopted 13 February 1946, entered into force 17 September 1946) 1 UNTS 15 (CPIUN) art VIII s 29; UN Model SOFA (n 119) para 51.

[121] *Difference Relating to Immunity from Legal Process of a Special Rapporteur of the Commission on Human Rights* (Advisory Opinion) [1999] ICJ Rep 62 [88]–[89] (*Cumaraswamy Case*).

[122] Danish Ministry of Foreign Affairs, 'The Copenhagen Process on the Handling of Detainees in International Military Operations: Principles and Guideline, and Chairman's Commentary' (Copenhagen, 19 October 2012) http://um.dk/en/~/media/UM/English-site/Documents/Politics-and-diplomacy/Copenhangen%20Process%20Principles%20and%20Guidelines.pdf (last accessed 18 March 2015).

[123] ibid principles 5, 9, and 11. Explicit reference to international organization obligations is set out in principles 15 and 16, and is clarified further in the Commentary, para 4.3 of which provides that: '[D]etention in some international military operations may also be justified as a matter of law pursuant to authorizations by the UN, or on the basis of international law by other competent international organizations such as the NATO, AU or the EU, or arrangements between a host State and State contributing military forces or international organizations. In such operations both international humanitarian law and human rights law may be relevant, depending upon factual circumstances and any specific parameters provided in the particular authorisations'.

[124] ibid Commentary to principle 16. See also Bruce Oswald and Thomas Winkler, 'The Copenhagen Process: Principles and Guidelines on the Handling of Detainees in International Military Operations' (2014) 83 Nordic J Int'l L 128, 149, 164.

[125] Charter of Fundamental Rights of the European Union (n 62); Treaty of Lisbon (n 63) art 59(2).

[126] See Chapter VII.

appear to be State practice or any significant *opinio juris* which speaks to the lack of international organization human rights obligations. Also, there is some developing, albeit limited practice which underscores States' understanding that the actions of international organizations must comply with human rights standards. A number of General Assembly resolutions have underscored the importance for international organizations to comply with human rights standards. The General Assembly has recognized

> [t]he need to continue ensuring that fair and clear procedures under the United Nations terrorism-related sanctions regime are strengthened in order to enhance their efficiency and transparency, and welcomes and encourages the ongoing efforts of the Security Council in support of these objectives, including by supporting the enhanced role of the office of the ombudsperson and continuing to review all the names of individuals and entities in the regime, while emphasizing the importance of these sanctions in countering terrorism.[127]

Also, the General Assembly, in its Declaration of the High-level Meeting on the Rule of Law at the National and International Levels, indicated that: 'the rule of law applies to all states equally, and to international organisations, including the United Nations and its principal organs, and that respect for and promotion of the rule of law and justice should guide all of their activities'.[128] Further, the Declaration on the Right and Responsibility of Individuals, Groups and Organs of Society to Promote and Protect Universally Recognized Human Rights and Fundamental Freedoms,[129] uses broad language to frame prohibitions[130] and refers to the duties of 'everyone'[131] and the responsibilities of 'individuals, groups, institutions and non-governmental organizations',[132] which arguably extends to international organizations.

(2) *International organization practice and* opinio juris

International organizations have recognized, or at times consented to, obligations for their staff to comply with certain aspects of human rights and international humanitarian law. Such obligations feature in staff regulations,[133] and field manuals. For instance, human rights officers employed by the Office of the High Commissioner for Human Rights are 'mandated by the United Nations to monitor and encourage compliance with international human rights norms, [and thus]

[127] UNGA, 'Protection of human rights and fundamental freedoms while countering terrorism' (28 January 2014) UNGA Res 68/178, UN Doc A/RES/68/178 paras 10, 11.

[128] UNGA, 'Declaration of the High-level Meeting of the General Assembly on the Rule of Law at the National and International Levels' (19 September 2012) UN Doc A/67/L.1 para 2.

[129] UNGA, 'Declaration on the Right and Responsibility of Individuals, Groups and Organs of Society to Promote and Protect Universally Recognized Human Rights and Fundamental Freedoms' (8 March 1999) GA res 53/144, UN Doc A/RES/53/144.

[130] ibid; article 10 refers to 'no one', which arguably extends to non-State entities.

[131] ibid art 18(1).

[132] ibid art 18(2), (3).

[133] UN Secretariat, 'Staff Regulations of the United Nations and provisional Staff Rules' (21 October 2009) UN Doc ST/SGB/2009/7 reg 1.2.

officers should in their own conduct exemplify those norms'.[134] There is less evidence that the organizations themselves understand themselves to be bound by human rights and international law.

Below, several (non-exhaustive) areas of human rights and humanitarian law protections which may engage organizations' responsibility are canvassed. To the extent that organizations have set up accountability structures or processes to deal with these and other matters, these are described in Chapter V.

(i) Economic, social, and cultural rights

International organizations recognize that employees should be able to access an internal dispute mechanism to address labour rights. Ombudsperson offices, grievance committees, and administrative tribunals have been established to mediate, offer recommendations, and/or adjudicate such claims.[135] This may stem from the recognition of a fundamental obligation to afford employees access to justice,[136] or a more contractual understanding that the organization's immunity from suit requires it to provide an alternative dispute settlement mechanism;[137] a failure to do so opening up the possibility that a domestic court may ignore applicable immunities.[138] Administrative tribunals have considered a variety of labour rights, including the right to privacy,[139] equal treatment and non-discrimination in the work place, protection from institutional harassment, and whistle-blower protection.[140] For the most part, however, these bodies have focused on whether there has been fair compliance with the rules of the organization pertaining to staff as well as any applicable general principles of international administrative law.[141] While it has been accepted that these tribunals must apply general principles of law which might include fundamental human rights law,[142] there have been fewer acceptances of the applicability of more specific human rights norms which go beyond the internal rules of the organization.[143] However, the practice is mixed. Some tribunal decisions have concentrated on organizations' failure to accede to particular treaties to deny their relevance to those organizations.[144] For instance the Arbitral Tribunal of the Commonwealth Secretariat determined that: 'the Respondent ... is not a

[134] OHCHR, 'Training Manual on Human Rights Monitoring' (Professional Training Series no 7, 2001) para 7.

[135] See Chapter V.4(1).

[136] *Effects of Awards* (n 69) 57.

[137] CPIUN art 29 (n 120).

[138] *Waite and Kennedy v Germany* (n 56); *X v Pacific Community*, French *Cour de Cassation* (soc) 13 May 2014, 12-23805.

[139] Case F–46/09 *V v European Parliament* ECLI:EU:F:2011:101 (EU Civil Service Tribunal, First Chamber, 5 July 2011).

[140] *LN v ILO* No 3250 (ILOAT, 5 February 2014); *PR v WIPO* No 3090 (ILOAT, 8 February 2012); *AE v FAO* No 3593 (ILOAT, 3 February 2016).

[141] *de Merode v World Bank (No 1)* (World Bank Administrative Tribunal, 5 June 1981) para 28.

[142] *In re Franks (No 2) and Vollering (No 2) v EPO* No 1333 (ILOAT, 31 January 1994).

[143] *Al Abani v Secretary-General of the United Nations* No 2016-UNAT-663 (UNAT, 24 August 2016); *A-O v UNESCO* No 2193 (ILOAT, 3 February 2003); *In re Deville and Others, In re Gasser v WHO* No 2097 (ILOAT, 30 January 2002).

[144] *In re Pibouleau* No 351 (ILOAT 13 November 1978) para 8; *Miss EEH v European Patent Org* No 2236 (ILOAT 16 July 2003) para 11.

party to and is not bound by the ICCPR. It is, of course, bound by its own internal instruments and institutional rules which, in any event, substantially embrace rules and principles that are not dissimilar to universally applicable human rights principles'.[145]

The UNAT has been more inclined to refer in its decision-making to general principles of human rights, and has held that the UDHR takes precedence over the Organization's internal rules. In *Chen*, UNAT noted that:

'[d]enial of pay is a violation of the principle of "equal pay for equal work" which is a right granted under Article 23(2) of the Universal Declaration of Human Rights, ... We are puzzled that the Administration seems to contend that these documents do not apply, at least where funding is concerned. To follow the Administration's logic, classification of posts is subject solely to management's discretion, even to the extent that internationally acknowledged human rights may be violated. To state the issue thus is to supply the answer'.[146] Owing to the particular context of the European Union, claims pertaining to employees of EU institutions have benefited from the application of European human rights standards.[147]

Trade and investment and structural adjustment policies may have profound impacts on individuals' enjoyment of economic and social rights, including the right to adequate food, education, health, clean water, work and social security. Financial institutions and organizations have the potential to advance protections in these areas but often their actions have had the opposite impact. Austerity measures taken in response to the global economic crisis have been criticized for negatively impacting the enjoyment of economic and social rights,[148] with the UN Independent Expert on the effects of foreign debt having underscored that: '... the obligation to protect, respect and fulfil human rights is also applicable to multilateral institutions, including international financial institutions ... '.[149] International financial institutions have for the most part paid little attention to the human rights implications of their activities, and the persons most affected have no direct channels to voice concerns or influence policies. While all EU institutions must comply with the Charter on Fundamental Rights of the European Union,[150] the European Stability Mechanism that was established to bail out struggling countries in the Eurozone is outside the purview of the Charter and EU law more generally because of the way in which it was established.[151] The CJEU determined that the involvement of the Commission and the European Central Bank in the work of the ESM

[145] *MH v Commonwealth Secretariat* CSAT/15 (CSAT June 2010) para 54.

[146] *Chen v Secretary-General of the United Nations* No 2011-UNAT-107 (UNAT, 11 March 2011) paras 18–19.

[147] Case F–46/09 *V v European Parliament* (n 139).

[148] UN OHCHR, 'Report on Austerity Measures and Economic and Social Rights' (7 May 2013) UN Doc E/2013/82, 7.

[149] UN HRC, 'Report of the Independent Expert on the Effects of Foreign Debt and Other Related International Financial Obligations of States on the Full Enjoyment of All Human Rights, Particularly Economic, Social and Cultural Rights on His Mission to Greece' (29 February 2016) UN Doc A/HRC/31/60/Add.2 para 19.

[150] Charter of Fundamental Rights of the European Union (n 62) art 51(1).

[151] Case C–370/12 *Pringle v Ireland* [2012] ECR I–756.

does not change this.[152] The ESM treaty contains no reference to human rights concerns.[153] The IMF, which has implemented debt restructuring programmes on a global scale, has no accountability structures in place for affected persons, although its Independent Evaluation Office has the authority to review IMF actions. Its findings on the IMF's actions concerning the crises in Greece, Ireland, and Portugal,[154] however, did not identify or consider whether there are any clear or implied human rights obligations in regards to IMF decision-making.

Development banks have introduced safeguarding policies and impact assessments to assure themselves that plans and policies do not negatively impact on beneficiaries' rights, or that those impacts are appropriately mitigated. Some of these have directly incorporated human rights into those policies like the European Investment Bank[155] and the Inter-American Development Bank[156] as have several UN agencies involved in development.[157] Others like the Asian Development Bank[158] and the World Bank[159] have taken a more limited approach to integrating

[152] Joined Cases C–8/15 P to C–10/15 *Ledra Advertising v Commission and ECB* ECLI:EU:C:2016:701 (Grand Chamber, 20 September 2016); *Mallis and Malli v Commission and ECB* ECLI:EU:C:2016:702 (Grand Chamber, 20 September 2016).

[153] Treaty Establishing the European Stability Mechanism (ESM) D/12/3 (adopted 1 February 2012, entered into force 27 September 2012).

[154] Independent Evaluation Office of the IMF, 'The IMF and the Crises in Greece, Ireland, and Portugal: Evaluation Report' (2016).

[155] European Investment Bank, 'The EIB Statement of Environmental and Social Principles and Standards' (2009).

[156] The Inter-American Development Bank has an independent consultation and investigation Mechanism (MICI), which investigates allegations by complainants of harms in bank-financed projects caused by the failure to comply with its own policies. Among the policies are ones concerning access to information, environment, involuntary resettlement, gender equality, and indigenous peoples. See www.iadb.org/en/mici/operational-policies,20447.html?open_accordion=1 (last accessed 22 December 2016).

[157] UNDP, 'Social and Environmental Screening Procedure' (March 2016): 'The SES and SESP do not only apply a "do no harm" approach but also a quality enhancement approach to strengthen social and environmental sustainability of UNDP programming. In addition to risk screening, the SESP provides a tool to help UNDP fully consider and document how the SES Overarching Policy and Principles, namely a human rights-based approach to development programming, gender equality and women's empowerment, and environmental sustainability, are integrated into Project design'. [para 28] See also UNEP, 'UNEP and Indigenous Peoples: A Partnership in Caring for the Environment' Policy Guidance (November 2012).

[158] Asian Development Bank, 'Social Protection Policy' (January 2001).

[159] The World Bank Inspection Panel (discussed in Chapter V) has been lauded by some for its ability to investigate complaints of harm caused by its projects when its own safeguards have not been followed; however, its general approach to human rights has been criticized. See UNGA, 'Report of the Special Rapporteur on Extreme Poverty and Human Rights' (4 August 2015) UN Doc A/70/274. The new Environmental and Social Framework has received further criticisms. See World Bank, 'Environmental and Social Framework: Setting Environmental and Social Standards for Investment Project Financing' (4 August 2016). The policy framework has been dismissed by some civil society groups who engaged in the consultation process and by 28 UN special procedures mandate holders. See 'Letter from 28 special procedures mandate holders to the President of the World Bank' (12 December 2014). Commenting on an earlier draft, they note that 'As the Bank seeks to revise and adapt its Safeguards approach to the challenges of the twenty-first century, we believe that it is imperative that the standards should be premised on a recognition of the central importance of respecting and promoting human rights. But there is no such provision in the current draft. Instead, by contemporary standards, the document seems to go out of its way to avoid any meaningful references to human rights and international human rights law.' www.ohchr.org/Documents/Issues/EPoverty/WorldBank.pdf (last accessed 21 December 2016). One civil society representative indicated: 'In addition to the

human rights specifically, although both have inspection and compliance panels to deal with breaches of internal policy (including on indigenous peoples, which contain important human rights elements) and to remediate harm. Particularly critical is the UN Special Rapporteur on Extreme Forms of Poverty, who has decried the World Bank's approach to human rights as: 'incoherent, counterproductive and unsustainable. For most purposes, the World Bank is a human rights-free zone. In its operational policies, in particular, it treats human rights more like an infectious disease than universal values and obligations'.[160]

In the area of international trade, agreements negotiated by States under the umbrella of the World Trade Organization (WTO) can have deleterious impacts on enjoyment of social, economic, and cultural rights. Yet, WTO structures allow for only indirect engagement by affected persons or groups in the development and monitoring of trade policies. The WTO's dispute settlement process is only open to the organization's Member States. Non-governmental organizations have sought to intervene in the settlement process in order to bring a wider perspective to the cases, and while this is theoretically possible,[161] intervention applications have usually been denied. The International Law Association has emphasized the importance for trade organizations like the WTO to allow 'individual parties, both natural and corporate, an advisory locus standi in those dispute settlement procedures where their own rights and interests are affected'.[162]

Trade restrictions or embargoes and related economic sanctions have often been adopted by international organizations in response to a variety of circumstances however the harmful impact of these measures on the enjoyment of economic and social rights has not always been considered when such measures were being adopted,[163] although the practice has progressively improved. The UN Committee on Economic, Social and Cultural Rights has underscored that: 'it is essential to distinguish between the basic objective of applying political and economic pressure upon the governing elite of a country to persuade them to conform to international law, and the collateral infliction of suffering upon the most vulnerable groups

glaring absence of binding human rights obligations—the need for which was highlighted repeatedly by civil society groups throughout the public consultation—one of the most concerning policy changes is the dangerous amount of discretion the Framework gives to borrower countries. Under the new safeguards, the World Bank has delegated much of its due diligence duties to borrowers, giving them the responsibility of carrying out Environmental and Social Impact Assessments for projects despite possible (and probable) issues with capacity, conflicts of interest, and even corruption and bad faith'. See Upasana Khatri, 'World Bank's New Environmental and Social Framework is a Huge Step Backward for Human Rights' (17 August 2016) www.earthrights.org (last accessed 21 December 2016). See also Natalie Bugalski, 'The Demise of Accountability at the World Bank?' (2016) 31 Am U Int'l LR 1.

160 UNGA, 'Report of the Special Rapporteur on Extreme Poverty and Human Rights' (n 159) 2.

161 WTO Doc WT/DS58/AB/R, *Shrimp/Turtle Case*, Report of the Appellate Body (12 October 1998) paras 108–109.

162 ILA, 'Resolution No 2/2000 on International Trade Law' The 69th Conference of the International Law Association, held in London, United Kingdom (25–29 July 2000) Annex 3: Declaration on the Rule of Law in International Trade para 3(c).

163 Center for Economic and Social Rights, UN Sanctioned Suffering: A Human Rights Assessment of United Nations Sanctions on Iraq (May 1996) 42.

within the targeted country'.[164] The UN General Assembly has recognized the existence of 'special economic problems arising from the application of sanctions in accordance with the Charter',[165] and mechanisms have progressively been put in place to closely monitor the impact of sanctions on vulnerable populations. For instance, the UN Security Council's sanctions committees monitor mandatory sanctions imposed by the Council, and some procedural safeguards have been progressively introduced.[166]

(ii) Refugee law and migration

Regional and international organizations continue to play major roles in responding to the mass flows of refugees and migrants in recent years. Most of the failings in response result from the actions and inactions of States. However, there are certain areas in which regional and international organizations' human rights responsibilities are engaged. Of the two organizations referred to below, the EU has made numerous unambiguous statements about its commitment to the respect of human rights and refugee law, although its positive actions in fulfilling those commitments are more opaque. The International Organization for Migration has been much less clear in its statements, focusing instead on its operational activities in support of States. This however does not provide much insulation from its responsibilities.

The EU's responsibility is likely to be engaged by the actions of the European Border and Coast Guard Agency and its predecessor the European Agency for the Management of Operational Cooperation at the External Borders of the Member States of the European Union (Frontex). The expanded Agency is mandated to carry out an array of activities including rapid border interventions, assisting Member States with return operations and cooperating with third countries including by organizing training activities in cooperation with Member States and third countries on their territory. Frontex has also supported EU Member States such as Greece in the detention of migrants, notwithstanding the inadequate conditions of detention and heightened risks of ill-treatment.[167] The Regulation establishing the expanded Agency underscores the obligation for the Agency to carry out all activities in full compliance with applicable human rights standards, and a series of measures are contemplated to give this effect, such as training, putting in place a fundamental rights officer with adequate resources and staff.[168] Furthermore, an administrative complaints mechanism is to be established to receive, assess, and follow up on complaints regarding fundamental rights.[169]

[164] UN Committee on Economic, Social and Cultural Rights, General Comment 8 'The Relationship between Economic Sanctions and Respect for Economic, Social and Cultural Rights' (12 December 1997) UN Doc E/C.12/1997/8 para 4.

[165] UNGA, '2005 World Summit Outcome' (15 September 2005) A/60/L.1 para 108.

[166] See Chapter V.

[167] Human Rights Watch, 'The EU's Dirty Hands: Frontex Involvement in Ill Treatment of Migrant Detainees in Greece' (2011).

[168] Regulation No 2016/1624 on the European Border and Coast Guard (adopted 14 September 2016, entered into force 6 October 2016) [2016] OJ L 251/1.

[169] See Chapter V for an analysis of the operation of this complaints mechanism.

The EU has partnered with neighbouring transit countries to stem the flow of refugees to Europe. Many of the partnership agreements contain undertakings that the latter states will respect the rights of persons transferred to them and will not send them to countries where they face a real risk of persecution (*refoulement*). However, the States predominantly do not have satisfactory systems of refugee status determination in place, some are not party to the Refugee Convention and sub-standard conditions of detention and the poor treatment of detained asylum seekers and other migrants, including the lack of protection against attacks by fellow detainees and members of the local populations have been well-documented. A case in point is the negotiation of agreements with Turkey aimed at returning all persons irregularly entering the Greek islands after 20 March 2016, in which it deemed Turkey a 'safe third country'.[170] The EU has funded Turkey to strengthen border controls and build immigration detention facilities.[171] The policy and underlying agreements have been criticized, also on account of a series of reports on poor detention conditions and ill-treatment of refugees.[172]

Another example is the 'Khartoum process', an agreement between the EU and the Horn of Africa migration route States including Djibouti, Egypt, Eritrea, Ethiopia, Kenya, Somalia, South Sudan, Sudan, and Tunisia, agreed on the guise of thwarting trafficking and smuggling rings but clearly also aimed at curbing migration to Europe.[173] In addition, the EU has embarked on a diplomatic offensive to establish partnerships with a range of countries under the European Agenda on Migration, listing as priority countries: Afghanistan, Algeria, Bangladesh, Ethiopia, Eritrea, Ghana, Ivory Coast, Mali, Morocco, Niger, Nigeria, Pakistan, Senegal, Somalia, Sudan, and Tunisia. Additional countries identified as short-term priorities are Egypt, Iran, Jordan, Lebanon, Libya, and Morocco.[174] The majority of these are major refugee producing countries where torture is routinely practised.

The International Organization for Migration, which has recently joined the UN system of organizations, is mandated to facilitate the orderly and humane management of international migration.[175] Among its many functions, it assists with the

[170] EU–Turkey statement (18 March 2016) Press release 144/16.

[171] Esra S Kaytaz, 'At the border of "Fortress Europe": Immigration Detention in Turkey' in Amy Nethery and Stephanie J Silverman (eds), *Immigration Detention: The Migration of a Policy and Its Human Impact* (Routledge 2015) 59–68, 60, which refers to the Twinning Project (2009–2011), 'Support to Turkey's Capacity in Combating Illegal Migration and Establishment of Removal Centres for Illegal Migrants', which 'provided for the construction of removal centres in the cities of Ankara and Erzurum with financial support from the European Commission'.

[172] Report by the Special Rapporteur on the Human Rights of Migrants, François Crépeau, Addendum: Mission to Turkey (25–29 June 2012) UN Doc A/HRC/23/46/Add.2 (17 April 2013) paras 40–58; Committee against Torture: Concluding Observations: Turkey, UN Doc CAT/C/TUR/CO/3 (20 January 2011) para 15; Human Rights Watch, 'Buffeted in the Borderland: The Treatment of Asylum Seekers and Migrants in Ukraine' (6 December 2010).

[173] Declaration of the Ministerial Conference of the Khartoum Process (EU–Horn of Africa Migration Route Initiative) (Rome, 28 November 2014).

[174] See European Commission, 'Communication on Establishing a New Partnership Framework with Third Countries under the European Agenda on Migration' COM(2016) 385 final (7 June 2016).

[175] IOM Constitution (adopted 19 October 1953, entered into force 30 November 1954) as amended.

voluntary return of migrants which the UN Special Rapporteur on Migrants has indicated has been 'criticized for not being genuinely voluntary, particularly when offered to migrants kept in detention centres'.[176] Returns which are not genuinely voluntary may breach the prohibition on *refoulement* if the person faces a real risk of persecution or torture on return. The International Organization for Migration (IOM) has also been involved in the construction and operation of detention centres for migrants. Detention can be unlawful in itself and made worse in contexts of inhumane conditions and when torture and other cruel, inhuman, or degrading treatment is resorted to by prison staff. If an international organization supports involuntary returns and manages detention centres where unlawful practices are known to occur, it may be responsible for the degree of its causal contribution to the wrongful act.[177] International organizations can be responsible even if they are not the principal actors. The Special Rapporteur on Migrants has encouraged the IOM to better incorporate human rights into its mandate, and in order to comply with human rights, it should 'cease any activities in relation to the construction and operation of detention centres, and ... ensure that all its assisted voluntary return programmes are genuinely voluntary and carried out in strict compliance with human rights standards'.[178]

(iii) Human rights and international humanitarian law in the context of peace operations and related political missions

With respect to the distinct context of the administration of territory, several missions have taken a more proactive approach to human rights compliance. For instance, UNMIK was mandated to 'protect ... and promot[e] human rights',[179] and it clarified in internal regulations that it would itself respect human rights law obligations.[180] A special advisory panel was established with powers to assess human rights compliance and recommend remedies.[181] The EU followed a similar approach with the establishment of a Human Rights Review Panel for the European Union Rule

[176] UNGA, 'Report of the Special Rapporteur on the Human Rights of Migrants' (7 August 2013) UN Doc A/68/283 para 59. On criticisms see Julien Brachet, ' Beyond War and Peace: The IOM and International Migration Control in Libya' (December 2015) International Migration Institute, Working Papers No 124 ('Partnerships with local governments were highly valued, and questions of direct coercive power systematically left to them (however bad their human rights record might be)') 7; UNHCR, 'UNHCR monitoring visit to Manus Island, Papua New Guinea 23 to 25 October 2013' (26 November 2013) paras 113–19; Clotilde Caillault, 'The Implementation of Coherent Migration Management through IOM Programs in Morocco' in Martin Geiger and Antoine Pécoud (eds), *The New Politics of International Mobility: Migration Management and its Discontents* (IMIS-Beiträge 2012) 133.

[177] See DARIO (n 40) Official Commentary Chapter IV para 1.

[178] UNGA, Report of the Special Rapporteur on the human rights of migrants (7 August 2013) A/68/283 paras 112, 113.

[179] UNSC Res 1244/1999 (10 June 1999) art 11(j).

[180] UNMIK, 'Regulation 1999/24 on the Law Applicable in Kosovo' (12 December 1999) arts 1.3–1.5; UNMIK, 'Regulation 2001/28 on the Rights of Persons Arrested by Law Enforcement Authorities' (11 October 2001); and similarly, UNTAET, 'Regulation 1999/1 on the Authority of the Transitional Administration in East Timor' (27 November 1999) s 2.

[181] See UNMIK, 'Regulation 2006/12 on the Establishment of the Human Rights Advisory Panel (23 March 2006).

of Law Mission in Kosovo (EULEX Kosovo) for complaints from any person claiming to be the victim of human rights violations by EULEX Kosovo in the conduct of its executive mandate.[182] The United Nations Interim Administration Mission in Kosovo (UNMIK) also signed agreements with the Council of Europe to comply with the Framework Convention for the Protection of National Minorities[183] and the European Convention for the Prevention of Torture,[184] and responded to reporting requests of the UN Human Rights Committee.[185]

There have been progressive undertakings by international organizations engaged in peacekeeping to comply with applicable human rights and international humanitarian law. One of the premises on which the Panel on UN Peace Operations based its report was the importance of '[a]dhering to and promoting international human rights instruments and standards and international humanitarian law in all aspects of its peace and security activities'.[186] Similar statements have been made by the UN Secretary-General in the report 'In Larger Freedom' that: 'United Nations peacekeepers and peacebuilders have a solemn responsibility to respect the law themselves, and especially to respect the rights of the people whom it is their mission to help'.[187]

Most agreements regarding the status of peacekeeping missions recognize, without prejudice to their international status, that the forces should conduct their operations in full respect for the principles and rules of international humanitarian law, and that the host governments would extend reciprocal protection.[188] The rules governing most peacekeeping operations, include the UN Model Agreement, make reference to a need for forces to observe 'the general principles and spirit' of international conventions applicable to the conduct of military personnel, yet they typically refrain from entertaining any duty of compliance with the detailed provisions of the Conventions.[189] The 1999 Bulletin issued by the UN Secretary-General

182 EULEX Human Rights Review Panel Rules of Procedure para 5 (January 2013) www.hrrp.eu/ROP.php (last accessed 22 December 2016).

183 Agreement between UNMIK and the Council of Europe on Technical Arrangements related to the Framework Convention for the Protection of National Minorities (adopted and entered into force 30 June 2004) COE Doc CM/Del/Dec (2004) 890/2.lb/appendix2E.

184 Agreement between UNMIK and the Council of Europe on Technical Arrangements Related to the European Convention for the Prevention of Torture and Inhuman or Degrading Treatment or Punishment (adopted and entered into force 23 August 2004) COE Doc CM/Del/Dec(2004)890/2.lb/appendix3E (2004).

185 UN Human Rights Committee, 'Report Submitted by UNMIK on the Human Rights Situation in Kosovo since June 1999' (2006) UN Doc CCPR/C/UNK//1 paras 123–24.

186 UNGA, 'Report of the Panel on United Nations Peace Operations' (21 August 2000) UN Doc A/55/305–S/2000/809 para 6(e).

187 UNGA, 'In Larger Freedom: Towards Development, Security and Human Rights for All' (21 March 2005) UN Doc A/59/2005 para 113.

188 See eg United Nations Mission in Sudan (UNMIS), 'Agreement between the Government of Sudan and the UN concerning the Status of the UN Mission in Sudan' (28 December 2005) para 6 http://unmis.unmissions.org/Portals/UNMIS/Documents/General/sofa.pdf (last accessed 31 July 2015). An identical provision appears in certain African Union agreements, eg the Status of Mission Agreement between the Transitional Federal Government of the Somali Republic and the African Union on the African Union Mission in Somalia (AMISOM) (6 March 2007) para 9.

189 UNGA, 'Model Agreement between the United Nations and Member States Contributing Personnel and Equipment to United Nations Peacekeeping Operations' (23 May 1991) UN Doc A/46/185, Annex para 28.

'Observance by United Nations Forces of International Humanitarian Law'[190] provides further certainty, detailing a non-exhaustive list of rules of international humanitarian law binding on UN peacekeeping forces which apply to UN forces in combatant situations of armed conflict (enforcement operations) and in peacekeeping missions in self-defence situations.[191] Full respect for international humanitarian law has been incorporated into the status of mission agreements of those AU and UN missions with enforcement mandates.[192]

An intention to comply with international humanitarian law is evidenced by the Convention on the Safety of UN and Associated Personnel, which specifies that UN enforcement operations are bound by international humanitarian law. This is confirmed by various statements of the Secretary-General, which have affirmed expressly, inter alia, that: '[t]he applicability of international humanitarian law to United Nations forces when they are engaged as combatants in situations of armed conflict entails the international responsibility of the Organization and its liability in compensation for violations of international humanitarian law committed by members of United Nations forces'.[193] A review of UN Office of the Legal Advisor memoranda confirms the *opinio juris* of this obligation. For instance, when the United Nations Organization Mission in the Democratic Republic of the Congo (MONUC) troops in the Democratic Republic of the Congo (DRC) were considering joint operations with governmental forces, the UN legal adviser set out a number of detailed conditions to such joint operations, on the basis of the UN's obligations to 'uphold, promote and encourage respect for human rights, international humanitarian law and refugee law'.[194]

The UN's due diligence policy, adopted in 2013, further clarifies the UN's *opinio juris*, that the Organization recognizes that all United Nations entities must take measures 'in order to ensure that any support that they may provide to non-United Nations forces is consistent with the purposes and principles as set out in the Charter of the United Nations and with its responsibility to respect, promote and encourage respect for international humanitarian, human rights and refugee law'.[195] The policy underscores that:

[190] UN Secretariat, 'Observance by United Nations Forces of International Humanitarian Law' (n 96).

[191] ibid s 1.

[192] See eg AU, 'Status of Mission Agreement between the Transitional Federal Government of the Somali Republic and the AU on the AU Mission in Somalia' (6 March 2007) para 9; UN, 'Status of Forces Agreement between the UN and the Government of the Republic of South Sudan concerning the United Nations Mission in South Sudan' (8 August 2011) para 6.

[193] UNGA, 'Financing of the United Nations Protection Force, the United Nations Confidence Restoration Operation in Croatia, the United Nations Preventive Deployment Force and the United Nations Peace Forces headquarters' (20 September 1996) UN Doc A/51/389 para 16.

[194] UN Office of Legal Affairs, 'Note to Mr. Le Roy', MONUC—Operation Kimia 2 (1 April 2009) paras 10, 13, and 14 www.innercitypress.com/OLA2MONUC040109.pdf (last accessed 31 July 2015).

[195] UNGA, 'Human Rights Due Diligence Policy on United Nations Support to Non-United Nations Security Forces' (5 March 2013) UN Doc A/67/775 S/2013/110 para 1.

United Nations support cannot be provided where there are substantial grounds for believing there is a real risk of the receiving entities committing grave violations of international humanitarian, human rights or refugee law and where the relevant authorities fail to take the necessary corrective or mitigating measures. For the same reasons, if the United Nations receives reliable information that provides substantial grounds to believe that a recipient of United Nations support is committing grave violations of international humanitarian, human rights or refugee law, the United Nations entity providing such support must intercede with the relevant authorities with a view to bringing those violations to an end. If, despite such intercession, the situation persists, the United Nations must suspend support to the offending elements. Notwithstanding the present policy, existing obligations of human rights, humanitarian and refugee law continue to apply to all United Nations activities.[196]

This policy has been integrated into joint AU-UN missions such as AMISOM,[197] and it has been recommended that any AU peace support mission which receives UN assessed contributions should comply fully with the human rights due diligence policy and conduct and discipline frameworks.[198] The High-level Independent Panel on Peace Operations has further recommended that:

'[w]here a United Nations peacekeeping operation is deployed in parallel with a non-United Nations force undertaking military counter-terrorism operations or other offensive operations, a clear division of labour and distinction of roles must guide their respective operations. The United Nations must in those situations maintain a strict adherence to its impartial commitment to the respect for human rights. When such non-United Nations forces depart, the United Nations should not be called upon to assume residual tasks beyond its capability'.[199]

Police and peacekeeping policies equally incorporate an array of human rights obligations[200] including guidelines on detention,[201] protection of civilian populations,[202] and protection against sexual exploitation and abuse.[203] Serving officials

[196] ibid. [197] UNSC Res 2297/2016 (7 July 2016) paras 14, 15.

[198] UNGA/UNSC, 'Report of the High-level Independent Panel on Peace Operations on Uniting our Strengths for Peace: Politics, Partnership and People' (17 June 2015) UN Doc A/70/95-S/2015/446 para 249(b).

[199] ibid para 123.

[200] UN OHCHR/DPKO/DPA/DFS, 'Policy on Human Rights in UN Peace Operations and Political Missions' (1 September 2011) 2011.20; UN DPKO/DFS, 'United Nations Police in Peacekeeping Operations and Special Political Missions' (1 February 2014) 2014.01.

[201] DPKO/DFS, 'Standard Operating Procedures on Detention in United Nations Peace Operations' (25 January 2010) 2010.06. To the extent that a particular mandate authorizes detention, and if in the context of that mandate UN police have to detain a suspect, detainees 'shall be released or handed over to national law enforcement officials of the host State or other relevant authorities as soon as possible', normally within a delay of 48 hours. See Katarina Grenfell, 'Detention in United Nations Peace Operations' in Gregory Rose and Bruce Oswald (eds), *Detention of Non-State Actors Engaged in Hostilities: The Future Law* (Brill 2016) 345–64. The operational challenges to comply with such policy particularly in missions with expansive mandates and the consequential liability risks for the UN is canvassed in Scott Sheeran and Stephanie Case, 'The Intervention Brigade: Legal Issues for the UN in the Democratic Republic of the Congo' International Peace Institute (November 2014).

[202] DPKO/DFS, 'Operational Concept on the Protection of Civilians in United Nations Peacekeeping' (9 April 2010).

[203] DPKO/DFS, 'Standard Operating Procedures on Government Provided Corrections Personnel on Assignment with United Nations Peacekeeping Operations and Special Political Missions' (15 April 2014) 2014.07 paras 67–75. On comparable AU policies, see eg AU, 'Easy-to-Read Guide on AMISOM Policy on Prevention and Response to Sexual Exploitation and Abuse' (September 2013).

are obligated to report human rights abuses they witness[204] and risk repatriation on disciplinary grounds in cases which include violation of international humanitarian and international human rights laws, which disqualifies them from further service with the United Nations.[205] The AU has endorsed this approach, and has recommended to 'develop a joint database that will help them [AU and UN] both to ensure that they do not deploy individuals that have been involved in misconduct in previous missions'.[206] These policies have been integrated into missions progressively through training and the involvement of internal oversight bodies, however as described in later chapters,[207] there are serious questions whether the accountability structures that have been put in place have been sufficiently robust and have been fully adhered to.

In addition, as part of standard operating procedures put in place by the UN for the receipt of corrections personnel seconded by their governments, the States contributing personnel must affirm inter alia that the candidates have never been convicted of, or are not currently under investigation or being prosecuted for any violations of international human rights law or international humanitarian law.[208]

II.6 Conclusions

International legal personality enables international organizations to assert rights, negotiate, and be held responsible for acts considered to be internationally wrongful. This personality may directly engender specific rights and obligations, although an analysis of the organization's functions is required to give them effect, a main consideration being whether the rights and obligations may be implied from what is set out in the constituent treaty. International organizations have obligations to comply with peremptory norms and accepted general principles of international law (which include elements of human rights and international law) that apply to all subjects under international law. There are also additional obligations which apply to international organizations in particular contexts and these must be assessed and determined on a case by case basis, and are aligned with organizations' purposes and their capacities to act and react in any given situation.

[204] DPKO/DFS, 'Standard Operating Procedures on Government Provided Corrections Personnel on Assignment with United Nations Peacekeeping Operations and Special Political Missions' (n 203) para 65.

[205] ibid para 61.

[206] AU, 'Common African Position on the UN Review of Peace Operations' (29 April 2015) PSC/PR/2(DII) para 12(ii).

[207] See Chapters V and VIII.

[208] DPKO/DFS, 'Standard Operating Procedures on Government Provided Corrections Personnel on Assignment with United Nations Peacekeeping Operations and Special Political Missions' (n 203) para 8.

III

Human Rights and International Humanitarian Law Breaches Attributable to International Organizations

III.1 Introduction

This chapter considers the circumstances in which international organizations may breach the human rights and international humanitarian law obligations that they are bound to respect and incur liability in the case of breach. It also considers when the conduct is an act of the organization for the purposes of assigning responsibility.

International organizations' ability to operate successfully in fulfilment of their mandates is contingent on the relationships they maintain with States, other international organizations, corporations, entities and individuals that assist them in various ways. In cases of breach, there is therefore a need to determine to whom among the different actors the conduct is attributable. Member States of an international organization may also incur liability as a result of the acts of the organization,[1] and States and others that collaborate with international organizations may incur responsibility for breaches in connection with conduct resulting from such collaboration.[2] These issues are tangential to the liability of international organizations, which exists irrespective of the liability of other actors.

As the roles and responsibilities of international organizations have expanded, there are more situations in which they interact with, and in which their actions directly impact on, individuals. These include: peacekeeping;[3]

[1] See generally Jean d'Aspremont, 'Abuse of the Legal Personality of International Organizations and the Responsibility of Member States' (2007) 4 Int'l Org LR 91; Ralph Wilde, 'Enhancing Accountability at the International Level: the Tension between International Organization and Member State Responsibility and the Underlying Issues at Stake' (2005–2006) 12 ILSA J Int'l & Comp L 395; Andrew Stumer, 'Liability of Member States for Acts of International Organizations: Reconsidering the Policy Objections' (2007) 48(2) Harv Int'l LJ 553; Cedric Ryngaert and Holly Buchanan, 'Member State Responsibility for the Acts of International Organizations' (2011) 7 Utrecht LR 131.

[2] See generally Gordon Christenson, 'Attributing Acts of Omission to the State' (1990–1991) 12 Mich J Int'l L 312; Stefan Talmon, 'A Plurality of Responsible Actors: International Responsibility for Acts of the Coalition Provisional Authority in Iraq' in Phil Shiner and Andrew Williams (eds), *The Iraq War and International Law* (Hart Publishing 2008) 185–230.

[3] See generally Kjetil Mujezinović Larsen, 'Attribution of Conduct in Peace Operations: The "Ultimate Authority and Control" Test' (2008) 19(3) EJIL 509; Tom Dannenbaum, 'Translating the Standard of Effective Control into a System of Effective Accountability: How Liability Should be Apportioned for Violations of Human Rights by Member State Troop Contingents Serving as United

sanctions;[4] humanitarian assistance and development;[5] debt restructuring;[6] when international organizations adopt State functions such as the administration of territory[7] or more limited contexts such as detention[8] or refugee status determination.[9] Additionally, the circulation of international arrest warrants[10] and the resort to international criminal courts and tribunals[11] opens up the prospect that such actions violate the rights of suspects, and possibly also victims and witnesses.

Attribution requires an analysis of the international organization's role vis-à-vis the internationally wrongful act. The organization will normally be operating in some relationship with other parties and therefore the conduct is not usually within its absolute control. Thus, the test which has been adopted by the Draft Articles on the Responsibility of International Organizations (DARIO) and by many courts assesses who had 'effective control'. This involves an analysis of the legal assignation of control and the factual operating context. The context in which abuses occur can be made complicated by an unstable operating environment. This can raise issues of what might be an 'operational necessity' and how this characterization impacts on

Nations Peacekeepers' (2010) 51 Harv Int'l LJ 113; Frédéric Mégret, 'The Vicarious Responsibility of the United Nations for "Unintended Consequences" of Peacekeeping Operations' in Chiyuki Aoi, Cedric de Cooning, and Ramesh Thakur (eds), *The 'Unintended' Consequences of Peace Operations* (UN University Press 2007) 250–67.

4 UN Commission on Human Rights, 'The Adverse Consequences of Economic Sanctions on the Enjoyment of Human Rights' (21 June 2000) UN Doc E/CN.4/Sub.2/2000/33; August Reinisch, 'Developing Human Rights and Humanitarian Law Accountability of the Security Council for the Imposition of Economic Sanctions' (2001) 95(4) AJIL 851; Gráinne de Búrca, 'The European Court of Justice and the International Legal Order After *Kadi*' (2010) 51(1) Harv Int'l LJ 1.

5 UNGA, 'Report of the Office of Internal Oversight Services on the Investigation into Sexual Exploitation of Refugees by Aid Workers in West Africa' (11 October 2002) UN Doc A/57/465; Mac Darrow and Louise Arbour, 'The Pillar of Glass: Human Rights in the Development Operations of the United Nations' (2009) 103 AJIL 446, 474.

6 Case C–370/12 *Pringle v Ireland* [2012] ECR I–756; *Federation of Employed Pensioners of Greece (IKA–ETAM) v Greece* 76/2012 (European Committee of Social Rights, 7 December 2012).

7 Ralph Wilde, *International Territorial Administration: How Trusteeship and the Civilizing Mission Never Went Away* (OUP 2008); Carsten Stahn, *The Law and Practice of International Territorial Administration. Versailles to Iraq and Beyond* (CUP 2008).

8 See generally Scott Sheeran and Stephanie Case, 'The Intervention Brigade: Legal Issues for the UN in the Democratic Republic of the Congo' International Peace Institute (November 2014); Talmon (n 2); Simon Chesterman, 'UNaccountable—The United Nations, Emergency Powers, and the Rule of Law' (2009) 42 Vand J Transnat'l L 1509.

9 Maja Smrkolj, 'International Institutions and Individualized Decision-Making: An Example of UNHCR's Refugee Status Determination' in Armin von Bogdandy and others (eds), *The Exercise of Public Authority by International Institutions: Advancing International Institutional Law* (Springer 2010) 165–94.

10 Mario Savino, 'Global Administrative Law Meets "Soft" Powers: The Uncomfortable Case of Interpol Red Notices' (2010) 43 NYU J Int'l L Pol 263; James Sheptycki, 'Accountability of Transnational Policing Institutions: The Strange Case of Interpol' (2004) 19 Can J L & Soc 107.

11 Guido Acquaviva, 'Human Rights Violations before International Tribunals: Reflections on Responsibility of International Organizations' (2007) 20(3) Leiden J Int'l L 613; Jean d'Aspremont and Catherine Brölmann, 'Challenging International Criminal Tribunals Before Domestic Courts' in August Reinisch (ed), *Challenging Acts of International Organizations before National Courts* (OUP 2010) 111.

attribution and liability. Equally relevant is whether the conduct was undertaken in the proper exercise of the international organization's mandate.

III.2 Attribution of Conduct to an International Organization

The law on attribution developed in the context of State responsibility, which considers whether a State is responsible for the acts of its organs or non-State entities exercising governmental authority. It was understood as important to avoid attributing to the State conduct which was purely private or personal. The rule which developed recognized as acts of State the conduct of any organs of government, or of others who acted under the direction, instigation, or control of those organs.[12]

The Articles on the Responsibility of States for Internationally Wrongful Acts (ARS) provide that: '[t]he conduct of any State organ shall be considered an act of that State under international law, whether the organ exercises legislative, executive, judicial or any other functions, whatever position it holds in the organization of the State, and whatever its character as an organ of the central Government or of a territorial unit of the State'.[13] The comparable provision in DARIO indicates that conduct of an 'organ or agent of an international organization ... whatever position the organ or agent holds in respect of the organization'[14] may constitute an act of the organization. By including 'agents' in this list, the scope for international organization responsibility is widened, going beyond the principal and subsidiary bodies of the organization, beyond recruited staff, to contractors with different levels of relationships with the organization, including secondees.[15] Thus, the focus is on the link such persons or entities have with the organization, and less about their official status.[16]

The DARIO clarify that attributable conduct includes both acts and omissions.[17] Active breaches of human rights or international humanitarian law are relatively discernible, given that prohibited conduct is tangible and reasonably well spelt out in treaties and other applicable law. Conduct that is prohibitive to international organizations specifically is less obvious. Also, omissions are more difficult to attribute. Omissions arise when the organization must take positive action and fails to do so, or where the actions undertaken are inconsistent with or fail to meet the level of the positive obligation.[18] As is later raised in relation to the relevance of international organizations' capacity to prevent when determining effective

[12] James Crawford, *The International Law Commission's Articles on State Responsibility: Introduction, Text and Commentaries* (CUP 2002) 91.

[13] ILC, Articles on the Responsibility of States for Internationally Wrongful Acts, 'Report of the International Law Commission on the Work of its 53rd Session' (23 April–1 June and 2 July–10 August 2001) UN Doc A/CN.4/SER.A/2001/Add.1 (ARS) art 4(1).

[14] ILC, Draft Articles on the Responsibility of International Organizations, 'Report of the International Law Commission on the Work of its 63rd Session' (26 April–3 June and 4 July–12 August 2011) UN Doc A/66/10 (DARIO) art 6.

[15] ibid Official Commentary art 6 para 6.

[16] Marten Zwanenburg, *Accountability of Peace Support Operations* (Martinus Nijhoff 2005) 71–72.

[17] See DARIO (n 14) arts 4, 9.

[18] ibid Official Commentary art 9 para 2.

control, international organizations may be constrained from taking affirmative action, even if in the same factual context, they are able to refrain from acting.

III.2.1 Conduct carried out by the international organization or one of its organs or agents

(1) Ultra vires *conduct may be attributable to the international organization*

According to DARIO, conduct carried out by the international organization or one of its organs or agents constitutes an act of the organization, so long as the organ or agent acts in an official capacity and within its overall functions, even if the conduct is *ultra vires*, eg exceeds the authority or mandate of the organization or was carried out in contravention of instructions.[19] The 'rules of the organization' will help determine what functions are properly within an international organization's scope.[20]

Article 8 of DARIO developed from the corresponding ARS rule, which itself developed in recognition that: 'many, if not most, injuries to aliens are caused by unauthorized acts of officials, and since States may limit the powers of their officials as they may deem appropriate, it is essential for protection of aliens that some measure of responsibility for *ultra vires* acts be admitted'.[21] The principle is reflected in human rights law, wherein 'a State is responsible for the acts of its agents undertaken in their official capacity and for their omissions, even when those agents act outside the sphere of their authority or violate internal law'.[22] In international humanitarian law, the principle is given expression in Article 3 of the Fourth Hague Convention of 1907 and Article 91 of Protocol Additional to the Geneva Conventions of 1949, although both of which indicate that a party to the conflict is responsible for *all* acts by persons forming part of its armed forces.[23] The reference to 'all' makes clear that attribution of conduct to the State includes *ultra vires* conduct, and any other acts regardless of whether they were carried out within the scope of apparent authority.

Unlike the DARIO provision, under the ARS there is no requirement that *ultra vires* acts fit within the overall functions of the State for conduct to be attributed to that State. The only requirement is that the acts are committed within the scope of

[19] ibid art 8.

[20] ibid art 6(2). See generally Christiane Ahlborn, 'The Rules of International Organizations and the Law of International Responsibility', Amsterdam Center for International Law Research Paper, 2011-03, SHARES Series (26 April 2011).

[21] Theodor Meron, 'International Responsibility of States for Unauthorized Acts of their Officials' (1957) 33 Brit YB Int'l L 85, 88–89.

[22] *Velásquez Rodriguez* case (Compensatory Damages) Ser C no 4 (IACtHR, 21 July 1989) para 170.

[23] Hague Convention No IV Respecting the Laws and Customs of War on Land and its annex: Regulations concerning the Laws and Customs of War on Land (adopted 18 October 1907, entered into force 26 January 1910) 36 Stat 2227, TS No 539 art 3; Protocol Additional to the Geneva Conventions of 12 August 1949, and relating to the Protection of Victims of International Armed Conflicts (adopted 8 June 1977, entered into force 7 December 1978) 1125 UNTS 3 (Protocol I).

the actor's apparent authority. These are different but related tests. As is described in the next sub-section, the requirement to act in an official capacity or within the scope of apparent authority is directed at ensuring the exclusion from attribution of purely private acts.

In contrast, the reference to functions suggests a constitutional principle connected to the powers conferred on the organization in its constituent agreement. However, *ultra vires* acts by their nature will necessarily or at least potentially exceed that mandate. Thus, the DARIO provision seems to negate the possibility of attribution to an international organization for all but the most negligible of *ultra vires* acts. The DARIO commentaries are imprecise on the rationale for the reference to functions, simply citing an outdated UN Office of Legal Affairs (OLA) memorandum (in 2011 OLA replaced the memorandum noting that 'the 1986 opinion ... does not reflect the consistent practice of the Organization'[24]), which sets out the UN's own, restricted view as to what types of acts might be attributed to it.[25]

The initial draft of the current Article 8, put forward in the Rapporteur's second report to the International Law Commission (ILC), uses 'functions' in a different way.[26] Instead of limiting the circumstances in which *ultra vires* acts may constitute acts of the organization, they must be carried out 'within its overall functions' (the current text), the initial draft used 'functions' to explain to whom the exception applied; to '[t]he conduct of an organ, an official or another person entrusted with part of the organization's functions'. In his second report, the Rapporteur notes that: '[u]ltra vires conduct of an international organization could be either conduct beyond the powers conferred on the organization or conduct exceeding the powers of a specific organ'.[27]

He refers to the decision of the International Court of Justice (ICJ) in the *Legality of the Use by a State of Nuclear Weapons in Armed Conflict*,[28] which underscores the principle of speciality whereby international organizations have no general competence; their competence is circumscribed by their mandate. He notes that this 'does not imply that conduct which exceeds an international organization's function could never be attributed to that organization'.[29] However, he also refers to

[24] ILC, 'Comments and Observations Received from International Organizations' (17 February 2011) A/CN.4/637/Add.1, 15.

[25] DARIO (n 14) Official Commentary art 8 para 9, particularly n 141 and accompanying text.

[26] ILC, Responsibility of International Organizations, Titles and Texts of the Draft Articles 4, 5, 6, and 7 Adopted by the Drafting Committee, 'Report of the International Law Commission on the Work of its 56th Session' (3 May–4 June and 5 July–6 August 2004) UN Doc A/CN.4/L.648. Draft art 6 provided: 'The conduct of an organ, an official or another person entrusted with part of the organization's functions shall be considered an act of the organization under international law if the organ, official or person acts in that capacity, even though the conduct exceeds authority or contravenes instructions'.

[27] ILC, Second Report on Responsibility of International Organizations by Mr Giorgio Gaja, Special Rapporteur, 'Report of the International Law Commission on the Work of its 56th Session' (3 May–4 June and 5 July–6 August 2004) UN Doc A/CN.4/541 para 51.

[28] *Legality of the Use by a State of Nuclear Weapons in Armed Conflict* (Advisory Opinion) [1996] ICJ Rep 66 [25].

[29] Second Report on Responsibility of International Organizations (n 27) para 51.

the same outdated OLA memorandum. Notwithstanding, he does not derive a functional limitation from the memorandum, and merely notes that: '[a]s with State organs, for responsibility to arise there needs to be some connection between the entity's or person's official duties and the conduct in question'.[30]

Professor Gaja's understanding that the principle of speciality has little impact upon the capacity for international organizations to be responsible for *ultra vires* acts is consistent with Hirsch, who argues that international organizations 'will be responsible for unlawful conduct imputed to them, irrespective of whether the acts were committed within their competence or not'.[31] To say otherwise would give credence to the view that an international organization could not be liable for violating peremptory norms, because to do so is outside the organizations' functions. Reinisch, referring to the treatment of this issue by domestic courts, has similarly underscored that: '[b]y eliminating *ultra vires* acts from the scope of acts attributable to an international organization, a functional concept would thus protect—literally "immunize"—an international organization in its dealings instead of limiting its immunity to certain functional fields'.[32]

Several organizations have argued differently. The International Criminal Police Organization-Interpol (ICPO-Interpol) has maintained that the principle of speciality necessarily means that acts outside the mandate of the organization cannot ever be considered as acts of the organization and thus cannot attract responsibility,[33] and similarly, a joint submission by several international organizations recommended the Rapporteur to take greater account of the principle of speciality in the framing of *ultra vires* acts capable of engendering responsibility.[34]

Differently, the International Labor Organization recognized that an international organization may be held responsible for *ultra vires* conduct of its organs or officials, 'when such conduct exceeds the powers of a specific organ or official under the rules of the organization or, *a fortiori*, when the conduct goes beyond the

[30] ibid para 55.

[31] Moshe Hirsch, *The Responsibility of International Organizations Towards Third Parties: Some Basic Principles* (Martinus Nijhoff 1995) 14–16. See also Noemi Gal-Or and Cedric Ryngaert, 'From Theory to Practice: Exploring the Relevance of the Draft Articles on the Responsibility of International Organizations (DARIO)—The Responsibility of the WTO and the UN' (2012) 13(5) German L J 511, 517, who note that acts of WTO organs that are *ultra vires* the WTO treaty 'may potentially have unlawful consequences and engage the organization's responsibility'.

[32] See August Reinisch, *International Organizations before National Courts* (CUP 2000) 342.

[33] It concluded that 'international organizations cannot be held responsible for actions outside their area of competence, without any qualification'. See ILC, Responsibility of International Organizations: Comments and Observations Received from Governments and International Organizations, 'Report of the International Law Commission on the Work of its 57th Session' (2 May–3 June and 11 July–5 August 2005) UN Doc A/CN.4/556 (comments on Draft Article 6).

[34] ILC, Comments and Observations Received from International Organizations (n 33), Joint submission on Draft Article 7, 24: 'The rules applicable to ultra vires acts of an organ of a State in draft article 7 ... cannot be transposed automatically to those of an agent or an organ of an international organization which can only be held responsible within the framework of the principle of speciality. At least, a better balance should be struck, on the one hand, between attribution of ultra vires acts and the protection of third parties who rely on the good faith of agents or organs acting beyond their mandate, and, on the other hand, on the principle of speciality and the fact that an agent or organ acting ultra vires operate beyond the mandate and functions entrusted to an international organization by its members'.

powers conferred on the organization by its constituent instrument'.[35] However, in the latter scenario, it argued that third parties appear to require less protection. Presumably, although this is not made clear by the submission, States may need less protection as they would be familiar with the limits of an international organization's mandate and would be able to take steps to avoid contracting with it if and when it acts outside its mandate. However, the same would not apply to third parties, particularly individuals and groups that may be vulnerable to human rights and international humanitarian law violations.[36]

Aside from the possible appeal to international organizations of this narrow position, the functional approach arguably also draws from the ICJ's Advisory Opinion in *Certain Expenses of the United Nations*.[37] That case concerned whether expenditure relating to UN operations in the Congo and the Middle East, which had been authorized by the General Assembly, should properly be considered expenses of the UN. The Court determined that acts which are within the UN's functions, but are irregular or non-compliant with the UN's internal structure are *ultra vires* but would nonetheless constitute acts of the UN and thereby bind the UN.[38] The opinion is limited, given the narrowness of the facts. As explained by Seyersted, the Opinion 'gives the impression that the Court might be disposed to deny the external validity only of *procedural* provisions in the constitution, not of those defining the purposes of the Organization. However, the Court was not called upon to pronounce itself upon the latter question, since the expenses obviously had been incurred within the scope of the purposes specified in the Charter'.[39]

Also at issue is the character of the acts subject to attribution. According to Meron, 'States may be responsible for wilfully and maliciously motivated *ultra vires* acts of their officials acting within the scope of their general authority'.[40] While the wilfulness or maliciousness of conduct was generally not understood as

[35] ILC, Responsibility of International Organizations: Comments and Observations Received from International Organizations, Addendum, 'Report of the International Law Commission on the Work of its 58th Session' (1 May–9 June and 3 July–11 August 2006) UN Doc A/CN.4/568/Add.1, submission on Draft art 6.

[36] The International Monetary Fund proposed a formulation which responded to such concerns. It indicated that: 'While we agree with the principle that an international organization may be bound, as to innocent third parties, by an ultra vires act of an organ or official, we believe article 6 should take account of one key exception, drawn from municipal law, which excuses the attribution of an agent's ultra vires conduct to the principal in cases where the injured party was (i) on actual or constructive notice about the ultra vires nature of the conduct and (ii) participated in such conduct. We believe this principle should be considered to be an exception to the provisions of draft article 6'. See ILC, 'Comments and Observations Received from Governments and International Organizations' UN Doc A/CN.4/556 (n 33). This type of exception is also proposed by Hirsch (n 31) 14–16.

[37] *Certain Expenses of the United Nations (Article 17, paragraph 2, of the Charter)* (Advisory Opinion) [1962] ICJ Rep 151, 168.

[38] ibid.

[39] Finn Seyersted, 'Objective International Personality of Intergovernmental Organizations: Do Their Capacities Really Depend Upon the Conventions Establishing Them?' (1964) 34 Nordisk Tidsskrift Int'l Ret 3, 34.

[40] See Meron 'International Responsibility of States for Unauthorized Acts of Their Officials' (n 21) 95–96.

a requirement for State responsibility and went more to the extent of damages,[41] there is no suggestion in the law on State responsibility of an exception to responsibility if conduct was understood to be wilful or malicious. Nevertheless, this principle appears in DARIO Article 39, which specifies that: '[i]n the determination of reparation, account shall be taken of the contribution to the injury by wilful or negligent action or omission of the injured State or international organization or of any person or entity in relation to whom reparation is sought'.[42]

There is no obvious reason why such a principle is different for international organizations; whether particular acts are wilful or malicious should not determine whether the acts may constitute acts of the organization. However, the UN Secretary-General has asserted the organization's responsibility for the *ultra vires* acts of peacekeepers, *except* when peacekeepers exhibit 'gross negligence or wilful misconduct', in which case responsibility falls on the State.[43] This language is also set out in the model contribution agreement relating to military contingents placed at the disposal of the UN, wherein the UN is regarded as liable towards third parties, but has a right of recovery from the contributing State under circumstances such as 'loss, damage, death or injury [arising] from gross negligence or wilful misconduct of the personnel provided by the Government'.[44]

Along the UN's own reasoning, if the mission is UN mandated, as opposed to simply endorsed or authorized by the UN, then it would constitute a subsidiary body of the UN and any actions that occur in the course of the conduct of the mission would constitute acts of the organization. On the other hand, the statement in the Memorandum and model SOFA might simply be a rule about distributing responsibility (as opposed to attributing conduct). This is the explanation provided in the DARIO commentaries.[45] The UN has confirmed that this is the correct interpretation in its comments on Article 7 DARIO, underscoring that: 'Mindful of the realities of peacekeeping operations but keen to maintain the integrity of the UN operation vis-à-vis third parties, the United Nations has struck a balance, whereby it remains responsible vis-à-vis third parties, but reserves the right in cases of gross negligence or wilful misconduct to revert to the lending State'.[46]

[41] ILC, Report by Mr Roberto Ago, Chairman of the Sub-Committee on State Responsibility, 'Report of the International Law Commission on the Work of its 15th Session' (6 May–2 July 1963) UN Doc A/CN.4/152.

[42] See DARIO (n 14) art 39.

[43] UN Secretary-General, *Administrative and Budgetary Aspects of the Financing of the United Nations Peacekeeping Operations: Financing of the United Nations Peacekeeping Operations*, UN Doc A/50/995 (9 July 1996) para 9.

[44] UNGA, 'Model Memorandum of Understanding between the United Nations and [Participating State] Contributing Resources to [the United Nations Peacekeeping Operation]' (27 August 1997) UN Doc A/51/967, Annex; UNGA, 'Contribution Agreement between the United Nations and [Participating State] Contributing Resources to [the United Nations Peace-Keeping Operation]' (9 July 1996) UN Doc A/50/955, Annex art 9.

[45] DARIO (n 14) Official Commentary art 7 para 3.

[46] ILC, 'Comments and Observations Received from International Organizations' (n 24) 14.

(2) The requirement that acts are 'official'

Ultra vires conduct will only be attributed to the international organization if it was carried out in an official capacity.[47] This distinction between official and private acts is derived from the law on State responsibility,[48] and it recognizes the independent will of individuals apart and separate from the State. Nonetheless, criticisms can and have been made, mainly on the basis that the distinction between public and private acts is ambiguous,[49] always shifting,[50] and prone to leave gaps of protection for those who suffer harm.[51]

The UN's position on what acts may constitute 'official acts' appears to be in flux. In 1986, the Office of Legal Affairs took a broad reading of the 'off duty' (and thereby non-official) acts of peacekeepers, noting that: 'a soldier may be considered "off duty" not only when he is "on leave" but also when he is not acting in an official or operational capacity while either inside or outside the area of operations'.[52] Its characterization of *ultra vires* conduct that is 'on-duty' has been correspondingly narrow, and has focused on circumstances such as when peacekeepers open fire and kill civilians without any corresponding order to do so.[53] Under such readings, the private conduct exception might exempt attribution to the organization of conduct of persons working for international organizations who perpetrate sexual assaults and exploitation,[54] human trafficking, bribery, smuggling, or theft, as such acts would not fall under the OLA's reading of what would constitute 'official acts'.[55]

Professor Gaja appears to have relied on the 1986 Memorandum in the preparation of DARIO Article 8, as described earlier.[56] However, in 2011, when the DARIO was being finalized, the OLA issued new comments in which it noted that: 'the 1986 opinion ... does not reflect the consistent practice of the Organization'.[57] It

[47] See DARIO (n 14) art 6(1); Official Commentary art 6 para 7. See also International Law Association, 'Accountability of International Organisations' (Final Report, Berlin Conference, 2004) http://www.ila-hq.org/en/committees/index.cfm/cid/9 (last accessed 11 December 2016), which take a similar approach.

[48] Rosalyn Higgins, *Problems and Process: International Law and How We Use It* (OUP 1994) 153. See also ARS (n 13) Official Commentary art 7 paras 1, 2.

[49] See Meron 'International Responsibility of States for Unauthorized Acts of Their Officials' (n 21) 105.

[50] Christine Chinkin, 'A Critique of the Public/Private Dimension' (1999) 10 EJIL 387, 389.

[51] See Meron 'International Responsibility of States for Unauthorized Acts of Their Officials' (n 21) 105.

[52] UN Office of Legal Affairs, Memorandum to the Director, Office for Field Operational and External Support Activities, 'Liability of the United Nations for Claims Involving Off-duty Acts of Members of Peace-keeping Forces—Determination of "Off-duty" versus "On-duty" Status' (23 July 1986) [1986] 24 UN Juridical Yearbook 300.

[53] The UN has accepted responsibility for the *ultra vires* acts of peacekeepers in the UN Mission in Congo and the UN Emergency Force. See Zwanenburg, *Accountability of Peace Support Operations* (n 16) 106.

[54] Claire Morris, 'Peacekeeping and the Sexual Exploitation of Women and Girls in Post-Conflict Societies: A Serious Enigma to Establishing the Rule of Law' (2010) 14 J Int'l Peacekeeping 184, 192.

[55] Christopher Leck, 'International Responsibility in United Nations Peacekeeping Operations: Command and Control Arrangements and the Attribution of Conduct' (2009) 10 Melb J Int'l L 346, 351.

[56] See earlier section III.2.1.

[57] ILC, 'Comments and Observations Received from International Organizations' (n 24) 15.

referred to its 1974 advice to the Field Operations Service with regard to the activities of the UN Emergency Force Claims Review Board, noting that off-duty actions of force members could engage the UN's responsibility in circumstances when the acts related to the functions of the force member (ie the use of a government issued weapon).[58] On this basis, it encouraged the Rapporteur to modify Article 7 'so as to provide that attribution in any such case could exist only where an organ or agents "acts in an official capacity and within the overall functions of the organization" '.[59]

This is a slight broadening in the OLA's understanding of what may constitute conduct undertaken in an official capacity[60] but, as has been noted, the circumstances that would qualify as official acts remain unclear and, as already raised, the reference to 'the overall functions of the organization' seems ill-placed. Even if a particular act is not carried out pursuant to official functions, often the position of power vis-à-vis the local community engendered by the individual's role in the international organization, particularly although not exclusively in a peacekeeping context, and in certain instances, access to weapons, funds, equipment or other means put at the individual's disposal, might have made the commission of the unlawful act possible.[61]

The 2011 OLA comments already specify that the use of a government issued weapon in the commission of acts, which might otherwise be outside of the official functions of the actor, may suffice to engage the responsibility of the organization.[62] However, this is but one straightforward example of an abuse of power that should engage the organization's responsibility. The overall dynamic of power should arguably favour the broadest possible interpretation, regardless of whether guns or weapons are employed. This is consistent with codes of conduct issued by international organizations, all of which make clear that proper comportment is not limited to particular contexts when an agent or employee is said to be 'on duty'.[63] As Hampson noted in relation to the administration of territory by international organizations, there are circumstances when the distinction makes no sense at all.[64]

58 ibid. 59 ibid.

60 See Comments of Mr Niehaus, ILC member, who criticized the position set out in the 1986 Memorandum as removing from the scope of the Organization's responsibility acts committed off duty, but appearing to be official (ILC, Summary Record of the 2802nd Meeting of the ILC on the Responsibility of International Organizations (Agenda item 2) (21 May 2004) 'Report of the International Law Commission on the Work of its 56th Session' (3 May–4 June and 5 July–6 August 2004) UN Doc A/CN.4/SR.2802, 83 para 14). See also Meron 'International Responsibility of States for Unauthorized Acts of Their Officials' (n 21) 107–12, who cites a series of cases in support of the proposition that when officials' positions are used as the means to carry out the act, these become acts under the colour of their authority.

61 See the *Caire* case *(France v Mexico)* [1929] 5 RIAA 516, 531, set out in ARS (n 13) Official Commentary to art 7 para 5.

62 ILC, 'Comments and Observations Received from International Organizations' (n 24) 15.

63 See in particular UN Secretariat, 'Special Measures for Protection from Sexual Exploitation and Sexual Abuse' (9 October 2003) UN Doc ST/SGB/2003/13, whose provisions apply at all times; UN Secretariat, 'Staff Regulations' (7 February 2003) UN Doc ST/SGB/2003/5 reg 1.2(f); UN DPKO, Directives for Disciplinary Matters Involving Civilian Police Officers and Military Observers (2003) UN Doc DPKO/CPD/DDCPO/2003/001 and DPKO/MD/03/00994 s 4.

64 UNCHR, 'Working Paper on the Accountability of International Personnel Taking Part in Peace Support Operations Submitted by Françoise Hampson' (7 July 2005) UN Doc E/CN.4/Sub.2/2005/42 para 85.

In contrast to both the ARS and DARIO, Article 3 of the Fourth Hague Convention of 1907 contains no requirement for acts to be 'official'. The treaty provides that a belligerent party will be liable to pay compensation for '*all* acts committed by persons forming part of its armed forces',[65] and thereby not exempting from attribution to the State acts committed by individuals in their private capacity. A similar provision is found in Article 91 of Protocol I.[66] Thus, at least in times of international armed conflict, States appear to be responsible for all acts of their military personnel, both private and official.[67] Noting the difference between these international humanitarian law provisions and the approach taken in the ARS, early ILC commentaries referred to the humanitarian law provisions as a *lex specialis*—an exception to the general rule applicable to persons acting in their private capacity.[68] Kalshoven has argued that the international humanitarian law *lex specialis* affords no private capacity exception,

> [b]ecause members of an armed force at war stand a greater chance than do other State organs of becoming entangled in ambiguous situations where it may be unclear whether they were acting in their capacity as an organ of the State ... putting the acts of an armed force to the test whether they were committed "in that capacity" may set an uncertain and certainly undesirable limit on the responsibility of the State. In other words, the wider scope of Article 3 is definitely to be preferred.[69]

He affirms that: '[t]he State should bear responsibility, not merely for (unlawful) acts of war properly so called, but equally for those acts of wantonness or savagery committed by members of its armed forces outside the sphere of duty but in violation of the law of armed conflict. This applies to acts against civilians and enemy combatants alike'.[70] The final ARS commentaries provide no reference to this, however.

Article 63 of DARIO provides that DARIO provisions do not apply where and to the extent that the conditions and the content of international responsibility 'are governed by special rules of international law'. However, as indicated, the

[65] Hague Convention No IV (n 23) art 3 (emphasis added). [66] See Protocol I (n 23).

[67] Note, however, the lack of uniformity in State practice. In relation to US practice exempting the state from responsibility for the private acts of its armed forces see Jean-Marie Henckaerts and Louise Doswald-Beck, *Customary International Humanitarian Law*, vol 1 (Rules) (CUP 2005) Rule 149, 533–34.

[68] Rapporteur Ago notes that the existence of the rule 'naturally does not prevent States from sometimes assuming responsibility for such actions by treaty, as is the case for instance, of the Convention IV respecting the laws and customs of war on land (The Hague, 1907), article 3 of which attributes to the State responsibility for "all acts committed by persons forming part of its armed forces" in violation of the Regulations annexed to the Convention, whether they acted as organs or as individuals. But in the absence of treaty provisions of this nature, States cannot be held responsible for such conduct'. See ILC, 'Report of the International Law Commission on the Work of its 27th session' (5 May–25 July 1975) UN Doc A/CN.4/SER.A/1975/Add.l, 69 (para 26 on Draft art 10). See also Marco Sassoli, 'State Responsibility for Violations of International Humanitarian Law' (2002) 846 Int'l R Red Cross 401, 405–406.

[69] Frits Kalshoven, 'State Responsibility for Warlike Acts of the Armed Forces: From Article 3 of Hague Convention IV of 1907 to Article 91 of Additional Protocol I of 1977 and Beyond' (1991) 40 Int'l & Comp LQ 827, 837–38.

[70] ibid 853.

applicability of Article 3 of the Hague Convention and Article 91 of Protocol I to international organizations is unclear, aside from the particular circumstances of enforcement actions[71] and, as such, it is unlikely that the *lex specialis* referred to has the same applicability for the attribution to the organization of *all* conduct committed by persons forming part of armed forces serving in UN missions. This issue is not taken up in DARIO. As was indicated, DARIO borrows extensively from the ARS, and neither the final ARS text nor its final commentaries makes reference to the international humanitarian law *lex specialis*. Also, as is evidenced in the official statements of the UN, its view is that it is only responsible for acts that occur in an official capacity.[72]

Zwanenburg's view is that the international humanitarian law *lex specialis* should not be applicable to peace support operations because the *lex specialis* is based on the structure of the armed forces, including the chain of command and the disciplinary power of the commander, which afford significant powers to prevent violations that are not reproduced in peace support operations because of the different command structures.[73] However, his approach seems to conflate the question of whether a particular act should be considered as 'official' with the separate question of which body has effective control, relevant to the separate circumstance of when an organ or agent is placed at the disposal of an international organization.

III.2.2 When an organ or agent is placed at the disposal of an international organization

When an organ or agent is seconded to an international organization but still acts as an agent or organ of the body that seconded it, Article 7 of DARIO specifies that attribution of conduct is to be determined by who exercised 'effective control' over the organ or agent that carried out the act.

The criterion of 'effective control' for determining attribution is similar, although distinct[74] from the jurisdictional principle of 'effective control', which determines whether a State had the requisite amount of control over a territory and the persons within it for its obligations to be engaged.[75] Some courts have tied the extent of a State's jurisdiction to the level of their control over the particular situation giving rise to the international wrongful act. In *Al-Skeini*, it was recognized that European Convention rights can be 'divided and tailored' to secure the rights that are relevant

[71] See Chapter II.

[72] ILC, 'Comments and Observations Received from International Organizations' A/CN.4/637/Add.1 (n 24) 15.

[73] See Zwanenburg, *Accountability of Peace Support Operations* (n 16) 106–107.

[74] See Aurel Sari, 'Jurisdiction and International Responsibility in Peace Support Operations: The Behrami and Saramati Cases' (2008) 8(1) Human Rights LR 151, 158–59, who criticizes the European Court for failing to analyse whether the respondent States had jurisdiction, in advance of considering whether acts or omissions could be attributed to them.

[75] See *Banković and Others v Belgium and Others* (GC) App no 52207/99 (ECtHR, 12 December 2001) [46], [61]; *Loizidou v Turkey* (GC) App no 15318/89, (ECtHR, 28 July 1998); *Ilaşcu v Moldova and Russia* (GC) App no 48787/99 (ECtHR, 8 July 2004); IACommHR, 'Report on Terrorism and Human Rights', Doc no OEA/Ser.L/V/II.116, Doc 5 rev 1 corr (22 October 2002).

to the situation of the individual concerned,[76] effectively overruling *Banković* on this point.[77]

The same is arguably true for international organizations: factually, the extent of their control will depend upon the operating context and may vary over time. Invariably, any control they may enjoy will not be absolute: they may have control over certain functions and/or they may share authority or control with a variety of actors, both local and international. The UN Human Rights Committee has specifically mentioned 'forces constituting a national contingent of a State Party assigned to an international peace-keeping or peace-enforcement operation'[78] as being capable of exercising such control. The same would arguably be true for the international organization to whom the forces are assigned, depending on to whom conduct is attributed.[79]

The criterion of 'effective control' to attribute conduct also developed from the law of State responsibility; the ICJ jurisprudence consistently attributes unlawful acts to States said to have exercised effective control over the commission of the act.[80] A question arises as to how closely connected the operational aspects must be to the conduct. Certain cases dealing with State responsibility may shed light. In *Paramilitary Activities*, the ICJ, in deciding whether the conduct of Nicaraguan paramilitaries should be attributed to the United States, determined that the State must have 'effective control of the ... operations in the course of which the alleged violations were committed'.[81] This approach was confirmed in the *Bosnia Genocide* case.[82] For conduct to be imputed to the State, the ICJ has required that the State 'directed or enforced' it.[83] The European Court of Human Rights (ECtHR) has taken a different approach in several judgments, in which it held that the appropriate test is more about 'ultimate authority and control'.[84] However, this approach

76 *Al-Skeini v United Kingdom* App no 55721/07 (ECtHR, 7 July 2011) [137].

77 *Banković and Others v Belgium and Others* (n 75) [75].

78 UN Human Rights Committee, 'General Comment 31' Nature of the General Legal Obligation Imposed on States Parties to the International Covenant on Civil and Political Rights (26 May 2004) UN Doc CCPR/C/21/Rev.1/Add.13 para 10.

79 Suggested by John Cerone, 'Human Dignity in the Line of Fire: The Application of International Human Rights Law during Armed Conflict, Occupation, and Peace Operations' (2006) 39 Vand J Transnat'l L 1447, 1508–509.

80 *Military and Paramilitary Activities in and against Nicaragua (Nicaragua v USA)* (Merits) [1986] ICJ Rep 14 (*Nicaragua* case); *Application of the Convention on the Prevention and Punishment of the Crime of Genocide (Bosnia and Herzegovina v Serbia and Montenegro)* (Merits) [2007] ICJ Rep 43 (*Bosnia Genocide* case).

81 See *Nicaragua* case (n 80).

82 See *Bosnia Genocide* case (n 80) [403]–[404]. Note, however, the *Tadić* appellate ruling, which resurrected a test of overall control; however, this was not followed by the ICJ in the *Bosnia Genocide* case para 403. See *Prosecutor v Tadić* (Appeal Judgment) ICTY-94-1-T (ICTY, 15 July 1999) paras 120–44.

83 *Nicaragua* case (n 80) [115].

84 *Behrami and Behrami v France; Saramati v France, Germany and Norway* (GC) App nos 71412/01, 78166/01 (ECtHR, 2 May 2007) [133]–[144]. In the later case of *Al-Jedda* (*Al-Jedda v United Kingdom* (GC) App no 27021/08 (ECtHR, 7 July 2011) [9]–[15], relating to an Iraqi man who was unlawfully detained by British troops in Iraq, the European Court of Human Rights referred to both the 'ultimate authority and control' and 'effective control' tests and indicated that under both tests, the UK has the requisite level of control. See Mujezinović Larsen (n 3) 521, who refers to Sarooshi's

has largely been rejected by scholars,[85] by Rapporteur Gaja,[86] and by many domestic and international courts.[87]

The effective control standard has itself been criticized as artificial. Buchan has argued in relation to peacekeeping that use of the standard would divest the UN of responsibility even in those instances in which it 'played a crucial role in determining the objectives and tasks pursued by that military unit and, in addition, contributed substantially to the logistical support that this force needed in order to discharge the assigned tasks and realize the stipulated objectives'.[88] He sees more merit in the approach taken in *Tadić*,[89] wherein a test of 'overall control' was used.[90] He argues that unlawful acts committed by members of an organized group should be attributed to that group (which could be an international organization) even when the group did not specifically direct or enforce the commission of the unlawful acts.[91] However, many judges and commentators have sought to distinguish the *Tadić* ruling from other attribution cases, given that it concerned individual criminal responsibility; the determination on attribution was just a precondition to determining whether there was an international armed conflict.[92]

Even Buchan limits the application of the 'overall control' test to the specific context of organized groups. However, the way in which he applies the 'overall control' test to leaders of organized groups appears similar to the 'effective control' test. One of the factual contexts to consider as part of an overall assessment of the operating circumstances surrounding the conduct is the leadership structure. He seems to argue that for organized groups with a strong leadership structure, this would enable the organization with 'overall control' to prevent any act or appropriately forestall any omission. For the limited factual circumstances of organized groups, this would equate or significantly close the gap between the 'overall control' and 'effective control' standards. It is close to Dannenbaum's assessment of 'effective

analysis on delegation of powers which seems to have been persuasive for the Court. See Dan Sarooshi, *The United Nations and the Development of Collective Security* (OUP 1999) 163–5.

[85] See eg Mujezinović Larsen (n 3); Dannenbaum, 'Translating the Standard of Effective Control into a System of Effective Accountability' (n 3); Marko Milanović and Tatjana Papić, 'As Bad As It Gets: The European Court of Human Rights' Behrami and Saramati Decision and General International Law' (2009) 58 ICLQ 267.

[86] See DARIO (n 14) art 7 and commentaries thereto.

[87] *Mustafić-Mujić v Netherlands*, Court of Appeal in The Hague, LJN: BR 5386 (5 July 2011); *Nuhanović v Netherlands*, Court of Appeal in The Hague, LJN: BR 5388 (5 July 2011). Both of these judgments were upheld by the Supreme Court of the Netherlands on 6 September 2013. See *Netherlands v Nuhanović*, Supreme Court [HR] 12/03324, LZ/TT (6 September 2013); *Netherlands v Mustafić-Mujić*, Supreme Court [HR] 12/03329, LZ/TT (6 September 2013). See also *Mukeshimana-Ngulinzira v Belgium*, Brussels CFI, RG Nr 04 4807 A, 07 15547 A; ILDC 1604 (BE 2010) (8 December 2010); *Bosnia Genocide* case (n 80).

[88] Russell Buchan, 'UN Peacekeeping Operations: When Can Unlawful Acts Committed by Peacekeeping Forces be Attributed to the UN?' (2012) 32(2) Legal Studies 282, 298.

[89] *Prosecutor v Tadić* (Appeal Judgment) (n 82).

[90] See Buchan (n 88) 289.

[91] ibid 299. See also Antonio Cassese, 'The Nicaragua and Tadić Tests Revisited in Light of the ICJ Judgment on Genocide in Bosnia' (2007) 18(4) EJIL 649, 661, who Buchan cites in support of his position. See also Milanović and Papić (n 85) 278, who also show support for the ICTY approach.

[92] This point is raised by the ICJ in the *Bosnia Genocide* case (n 80) [406]. It is also raised by Dannenbaum, 'Translating the Standard of Effective Control' (n 3) 155.

control', which focuses on the agent or organ's ability to prevent,[93] a test which was taken up by the Hague Court of Appeal in the 2011 *Mustafić-Mujić* and *Nuhanović* cases.[94]

For peacekeeping, there will be a continuum between the international organization and the contributing State along which 'effective control' is situated. Understanding where the control lies will involve both formal and factual considerations.[95] Some have emphasised objective elements of control such as a State retaining disciplinary powers and criminal jurisdiction over members of the national contingent[96] and other resolutions, agreements and protocols that may be in place.[97]

Operations established under a UN mandate will differ from operations that are authorized or endorsed by the UN. In the former, the UN considers such missions as subsidiary UN organs in which it has 'exclusive command and control' and thus accepts attribution to the UN of relevant conduct.[98] In the latter cases, control may vest with a regional organization leading the operation, such as the AU or ECOWAS. Or, where the mission is led by one or several States, operational command and control will vest in the States conducting the operation.[99] However, the DARIO commentary sets out[100] and most commentators now agree[101] that the practical operational context is most relevant to the determination of control.

III.2.3 Conduct acknowledged and adopted by an international organization as its own

Conduct can also be considered to be an act of an international organization if the organization acknowledges and adopts the conduct as its own.[102] The same principle exists under the law of State responsibility.

[93] See Dannenbaum, 'Translating the Standard of Effective Control' (n 3). See also Tom Dannenbaum, 'Killings at Srebrenica, Effective Control, and the Power to Prevent Unlawful Conduct' (2012) 61 ICLQ 713.

[94] *Mustafić-Mujić v Netherlands* (n 87); *Nuhanović v Netherlands* (n 87).

[95] See DARIO (n 14) Official Commentary art 7(4).

[96] UNGA, 'Model Status-of-forces Agreement for Peace-Keeping Operations' (9 October 1990) UN Doc A/45/594 (Model SOFA). See the wording of the Model SOFA, which specifies that troop contributing countries retain exclusive criminal jurisdiction; see also ILC, Second Report on Responsibility of International Organizations (n 27) para 40. However, as is noted in the DARIO commentaries, such agreements focus on distribution of responsibility and not the attribution of conduct. See DARIO (n 14) Official Commentary art 7 para 3.

[97] See eg in the *Behrami* case (n 84) where, instead of focusing on the specifically challenged wrongful conduct, the court made a general application of its test to the entire operation, based upon UNSC Res 1244.

[98] The UN sets out its own view on attribution in peacekeeping contexts in UNGA, 'Financing of the United Nations Protection Force, the United Nations Confidence Restoration Operation in Croatia, the United Nations Preventive Deployment Force and the United Nations Peace Forces Headquarters' UN Doc A/51/389.

[99] Daphna Shraga, 'The United Nations as an Actor Bound by International Humanitarian Law' (1998) 5(2) Int'l Peacekeeping 64, 71.

[100] See DARIO (n 14) Official Commentary to art 7.

[101] Dannenbaum, 'Killings at Srebrenica' (n 93); Leck (n 55); Mujezinović Larsen (n 3).

[102] See DARIO (n 14) art 9.

In its comments to the ILC, the OLA noted that it was unaware of any case of acknowledgement or adoption, and that there was 'little likelihood that such admission would be made by an intergovernmental organ, or, if it were made, that it would be respected by the political organ having the budgetary authority to authorize the compensation'.[103] This suggests that OLA's view is that acts of acknowledgement and adoption must be express acts, incapable of being implied from the conduct of the organization, its organs, or agents. However, such an interpretation is out of keeping with the rest of DARIO, which takes a broad approach to the persons or entities who might engage the responsibility of the organization.[104] As is suggested by the OLA comments, an express acknowledgement and adoption would require formal approval by the official decision-making organs of the organization as a whole; however, the operating context in certain field locales may militate against such a formal approach.

The ARS commentaries make clear that 'acknowledgement and adoption' are cumulative, and are to be distinguished from cases of mere support or endorsement, which would be insufficient for attribution to the State.[105] The ILC refers to the *Lighthouses* arbitration[106] and the *Iran Hostages* case[107] to set out this principle. The *Lighthouses* arbitration concerned whether Greece was liable for the breach of a concession agreement to operate lighthouses, which was initiated by Crete when it had been an autonomous territory. After its assumption of sovereignty over Crete, it was held that Greece 'endorsed' the breaches and thus became liable for them. Thus, a State can 'adopt' the conduct *ex post facto* as its own, acquiring liability retroactively for that conduct. The *Iran Hostages* case concerned the attack on the US Embassy in Iran and subsequent hostage-taking of embassy officials. Here, even though the initial attack and hostage-taking were carried out by non-State actors on their own initiative, the subsequent actions of Iran led the ICJ to hold that: '[o]nce organs of the Iranian State had thus given approval to the acts complained of and decided to perpetuate them as a means of pressure on the United States, those acts were transformed into acts of the Iranian State: the militants became agents of that State, which itself became internationally responsible for their acts'.[108]

The ARS commentaries also refer to the abduction by Israeli citizens in Argentina and subsequent trial, conviction, and execution of Adolf Eichmann by Israel. Given the lack of clarity over Israel's role in the initial kidnapping, the commentaries are equivocal on whether the basis for attributing the conduct to Israel related to effective control or acknowledgement and adoption.[109] Absent clear evidence of effective control, the commentaries note that 'these may be resolved by the subsequent

[103] ILC, 'Comments and Observations Received from International Organizations' A/CN.4/637/Add.1 (n 24) art 8 para 2.

[104] See DARIO (n 14) art 6.

[105] See ARS (n 13) Official Commentary art 11 paras 6, 9.

[106] *Lighthouses Arbitration (France v Greece)* (1956) 12 RIAA 155, 198, discussed in ARS (n 13) Official Commentary art 11 para 3.

[107] *United States Diplomatic and Consular Staff in Tehran (United States of America v Iran)* [1980] ICJ Rep 3 (*Iran Hostages* case).

[108] ibid. [109] See ARS (n 13) Official Commentary art 11 para 5.

adoption of the conduct in question by the State'.[110] The question of whether the illegality of the transfer vitiated the legality of the eventual trial was not addressed in the related UN Security Council resolution.[111]

The impact of arbitrary or illegal arrests has arisen before the ad hoc criminal tribunals and the International Criminal Court (ICC). It has been argued that the international organization is responsible for the wrongful conduct of those effectuating the arrest because by proceeding with the criminal trial it has acknowledged and adopted the arrest as its own.[112] However, in *Nikolić*,[113] the International Criminal Tribunal for the former Yugoslavia Trial Chamber determined that the Stabilization Force in Bosnia and Herzegovina (SFOR) did not acknowledge and adopt the unlawful arrest and abduction (effectuated by private individuals) when it took custody of the accused and transferred him to the tribunal. It held that SFOR was a passive beneficiary of the 'fortuitous (even irregular) rendition to Bosnia', but this did not amount to an adoption and acknowledgement because once SFOR came into contact with the accused, it was bound, under other principles, to arrest and detain him.[114]

The Trial Chamber's ruling suggests that the very existence of the obligation to arrest/detain the accused once it came into contact with him negated the possibility for SFOR to have acknowledged and adopted the illegal conduct as its own; responsibility is negated on the ground that SFOR was enforcing its mandate. This seems to import into the test an exception: when the international organization has a conflicting obligation, this can serve as a ground to deny attribution. However, arguably the execution of SFOR's mandate should not have impacted on the determination of acknowledgement and adoption. If relevant at all, it could have been considered as an exception to liability under circumstances precluding wrongfulness under which SFOR could have argued that it was necessarily obliged to act as it did.[115]

Even if the Trial Chamber in *Nikolić* had correctly applied Article 9 DARIO, this would not have necessarily led to a different result, as the remedy for the wrongful act would not necessarily have been the release of the accused.[116] Some of these

[110] ibid. [111] UNSC Res 138/1960 (23 June 1960) S/4349.

[112] See Acquaviva, 'Human Rights Violations before International Tribunals' (n 11).

[113] *Prosecutor v Nikolić* (Decision on Challenge to Jurisdiction) ICTY-94-2-PT (ICTY, 9 October 2002) para 67.

[114] ibid.

[115] Note, however, the DARIO (n 14) Official Commentary to art 25 para 4, which suggest a narrow reading of the principle of necessity when applied to the conduct of international organizations. See also Robert Sloane, 'On the Use and Abuse of Necessity in the Law of State Responsibility' (2012) 106 AJIL 447, who emphasizes the exceptional character of necessity.

[116] The jurisprudence on this point is variable, with courts oscillating between *mala captus bene detentus* (courts will assert *in personam* jurisdiction without inquiring into the means by which the presence of the defendant was secured) and *ex injuria ius non oritur* (a legal right or entitlement cannot arise from an unlawful act or omission). The Appeals Chamber in *Nikolić* gave prominence to the *mala captus* maxim, placing significance on the heinousness of the crimes which the international community has a recognized interest in prosecuting. See Robert J Currie, 'Abducted Fugitives Before the International Criminal Court: Problems and Prospects' (2007) 18 Crim L Forum 349, 370–3, who criticizes the Appeals Chamber on its approach. See also *Jean-Bosco Barayagwiza v Prosecutor* (Appeals Chamber Decision) ICTR-97-19-AR72 (ICTR, 3 November 1999) paras 73–77, which emphasizes the abuse of process doctrine.

issues were raised by the defence on appeal; however, the Appeals Chamber upheld the Trial Chamber's decision without addressing the issue of attribution.[117]

Acknowledgement and adoption has also arisen in relation to ICPO-Interpol activities. As it indicated in its comments to the ILC, when it 'processes information on a person and issues Red Notices for their arrest, ICPO-Interpol can become involved in situations that are not in conformity with international law'.[118] It mentioned the *Yerodia* case, in which the ICJ determined that Belgium committed an internationally wrongful act when it issued an international arrest warrant against an acting Foreign Minister, contrary to obligations to respect his immunity.[119]

In that case, ICPO-Interpol had issued a Red Notice in response to Belgium's arrest warrant, thereby publishing and circulating information which the ICJ had later determined violated international law. Consequently, it changed its rules on processing information; the new rules 'contain a specific provision requiring the General Secretariat to verify whether information ... complies with the laws existing in its country and whether it is consistent with the international conventions to which the source country is a party (art. 10.1, para. (*a*) 5). It became necessary to explicate this rule, because in the *Yerodia* case, the General Secretariat issued Red Notices further to Belgian arrest warrants which were later found to be inconsistent with Belgian obligations under international law'.[120]

ICPO-Interpol publishes and circulates worldwide Red Notices to seek the location and arrest of wanted persons with a view to extradition or other lawful action. The notices are not legal instruments, but as Savino argues, they 'indicate to foreign police organizations that a national arrest warrant is pending on an individual. ... albeit "soft" (non-binding warrants), they *de facto* impinge upon the fundamental right to personal freedom insofar as they are widely enforced by national police forces'.[121] An arrest warrant which is politically motivated, discriminatory, and/or without proper legal foundation which is acted upon by Interpol can potentially lead to or encourage other States to act. In addition to falling foul of immunity principles, this may lead to the invasion of privacy, loss of liberty, ill-treatment, torture, or persecution of the subject of the notice thus breaching human rights and related *refoulement* prohibitions.[122]

Having regard to Article 9 DARIO, does ICPO-Interpol acknowledge and adopt the arrest warrants as its own? It publishes and circulates notices which in turn, aids in effectuating arrests. ICPO-Interpol has an arguably limited role in the chain. Nevertheless, many States honour the Notices as a matter of course, despite their non-binding status. ICPO-Interpol has knowledge of this practice which is a foreseeable consequence of issuing the Red Notice. As Savino notes

[117] *Prosecutor v Nikolić* (Interlocutory Appeal Concerning Legality of Arrest) ICTY-94-2-AR73 (ICTY, 5 June 2003).

[118] ILC, 'Comments and Observations Received from Governments and International Organizations' UN Doc A/CN.4/556 (n 33).

[119] *Arrest Warrant of 11 April 2000 (DRC v Belgium)* (Merits) [2002] ICJ Rep 3.

[120] ILC, 'Comments and observations received from Governments and international organizations' UN Doc A/CN.4/556 (n 33).

[121] See Savino, 'Global Administrative Law Meets "Soft" Powers' (n 10) 269.

[122] ibid.

in relation to the two time arrest of the former Kazakh Prime Minister following the issuance of a Red Notice, '[a]bsent such a captivating international wrapping, would Mr. Kazhegeldin have enjoyed a double stay in the Russian and Italian jails? Unlikely'.[123]

After the *Yerodia* ruling, the ICPO-Interpol rules were changed to require the General Secretariat to verify that processed information complied with, inter alia, international law.[124] However, there are insufficient control procedures to ensure, prior to the circulation of notices, that the information contained therein complies with such law.[125] It would arguably be administratively cumbersome, costly, and politically sensitive for ICPO-Interpol to put in place adequate and effective measures, which undoubtedly would require it to enquire into the foundations of arrest warrants it receives from States, prior to publishing and circulating them. However, the failure to do so and nevertheless to maintain the practice of publication and circulation, despite the seriousness of the risk, would arguably be sufficient to elevate ICPO-Interpol's actions to the level of acknowledgement and adoption.

In the alternative, assuming that ICPO-Interpol has a positive obligation to ensure that information it publishes and circulates does not offend human rights and international humanitarian law prohibitions,[126] it could be argued that ICPO-Interpol failed to honour due diligence obligations by failing to take all reasonable steps within its power to avoid such results.

III.3 Responsibility of an International Organization in Connection with the Act of a State or Another International Organization

An international organization may be responsible for acts or omissions which are connected with the conduct of a State or another international organization. Responsibility would reflect the degree of its causal contribution to the wrongful act.[127] This part of DARIO incorporates modes of accessorial liability, including aiding and assisting, directing and controlling, coercion, and circumvention of an international obligation through decisions and authorizations addressed to members.[128] The description of accessorial modes of liability makes clear that international organizations can be responsible for their role in the perpetration of internationally wrongful acts even if they are not the principal actors. The level of

[123] ibid 292.

[124] ILC, 'Comments and observations received from Governments and international organizations' UN Doc A/CN.4/556 (n 33) (comments on Draft Article 4).

[125] There is a Commission for the Control of INTERPOL's Files; however, most of its work is retrospective. See Savino (n 10) 303–15, who reviews ICPO-Interpol's 'Ex Ante Scrutiny' and 'Ex Post Review'. While both systems exist, they, and particularly the *ex ante* scrutiny, are arguably too weak to prevent any abuse through the Red Notice system. See Chapter V.

[126] ICPO-Interpol seems to recognize this, through its revision of its internal procedures.

[127] See DARIO (n 14) Official Commentary chap IV para 1.

[128] ibid arts 14–19.

responsibility will reflect the level of their action or inaction and its impact on the internationally wrongful act.

There are many examples of when international organizations' accessorial conduct may give rise to violations of human rights and international humanitarian law. International organizations regularly provide aid and assistance to States emerging from conflict as part of their humanitarian and peace-building functions, or in the context of refugee processing. They might contribute funds or equipment or second experts or personnel to States, which may go on to be instrumental in the perpetration of human rights or international humanitarian law abuses.[129]

The EU's funding and technical assistance to neighbouring countries to quell the flow of refugees and migrants into the EU, which foreseeably leads to *refoulement* or other abuses, is a case in point. Also, international organizations may adopt binding decisions that are mandatory for members, which result in the violation of human rights or international humanitarian law.[130] The adoption of sanctions on States, groups, or individuals has arguably led to or constituted wrongful acts.[131] According to Hirsch, the crucial factor in determining the attribution of conduct in such circumstances is the extent of discretion the implementer had in determining whether and how to implement the resolution.[132]

In order for the organization to incur liability, the conduct must have been carried out with knowledge of the circumstances of the internationally wrongful act and that the act would be internationally wrongful if committed by that organization. Thus, in principle, if the organization is duped by a State who uses the organization's good offices in a way unintended by the organization, this would not result in international organization liability.

III.4 Failure to Prevent and/or Respond to Violations

A State may be responsible for omissions when it is under a duty to act. It may also be responsible for the effects of the conduct of private parties, if it failed to take

[129] See eg the example provided in DARIO (n 14) Official Commentary art 14 para 6, whereby the UN Legal Adviser provided advice to the UN Mission in the DRC (MONUC) regarding the risks associated with MONUC's assistance to the DRC army. Some of these potentialities are covered in the UN's due diligence policy.

[130] DARIO (n 14) Official Commentary art 15 para 4; art 16 paras 4, 5.

[131] See eg *Nada v Switzerland* (GC) App no 10593/08 (ECtHR, 12 September 2012); Joined Cases C–402/05 P and C–415/05 P *Yassin Abdullah Kadi and Al-Barakaat International Foundation v Council of the European Union and Commission* [2008] ECR I–06351. See also UNGA, 'Report of the Special Rapporteur on the promotion and protection of human rights and fundamental freedoms while countering terrorism, Ben Emmerson' (26 September 2012) UN Doc A/67/396 para 48, in which he notes that the Office of the Ombudsperson on the 1267/1989 Al-Qaida sanctions regime has received and relied on intelligence obtained through torture, which 'involves complicity in the commission of an internationally wrongful act and is irreconcilable with the obligation *erga omnes* to cooperate in the eradication of torture'. See generally Antonios Tzanakopoulos, *Disobeying the Security Council: Countermeasures against Wrongful Sanctions* (OUP 2011).

[132] See Hirsch (n 31) 83.

adequate measures to prevent those effects.[133] However, this is only in a secondary sense. Private parties' conduct is not attributed to the State; the State is responsible for the failure to meet its own obligations to exercise due diligence. The issue arose in *British Claims in the Spanish Zone of Morocco*, where the arbitrator made clear that a State that failed to exercise due diligence in preventing or punishing the unlawful actions of armed groups could be held responsible for such failure.[134] It also arose in the *Iran Hostages*[135] case, wherein the ICJ determined that Iran failed to take adequate steps to protect the United States Embassy. The Court found that Iran was fully aware of the urgent need for action on its part, and that it had the means at its disposal to perform its obligations but had failed to do so.[136]

Both international humanitarian law[137] and human rights treaties[138] recognize the obligation to respect and ensure the rights contained therein, which in the latter case require States to 'adopt legislative, judicial, administrative, educative and other appropriate measures in order to fulfil their legal obligations'.[139] And, the even more robust 'undertake to prevent and to punish' language frames the positive obligations in the 1948 Convention on the Prevention and Punishment of the Crime of Genocide.[140] The determination of whether there is an obligation to take positive action and the nature of that action will depend on the content of the primary rule. Courts recognize an obligation on States to take reasonable steps to prevent human rights violations and to use the means at their disposal to investigate violations committed within their jurisdiction, to identify those responsible, impose appropriate punishments, and ensure the victim receives adequate compensation.[141]

Central to a finding of a State's failure to exercise due diligence is that the violations were foreseeable and that the State failed to take reasonable measures to prevent them, or having realized that the violations occurred, the State did not take adequate measures to protect victims, including by investigating, prosecuting

[133] ARS (n 13) Official Commentary ch II paras 3, 4. See also *Velásquez Rodriguez* case (Compensatory Damages) (n 22) para 172.

[134] *Spanish Zone of Morocco* case *(Great Britain v Spain)* (1925) 2 ILR 157, (1949) II RIAA 615. See also the *Zafiro* case *(D. Earnshaw and Others (Great Britain) v United States)* (1925) 6 RIAA 160, in which the United States was held responsible for looting committed ashore by a crew of a naval vessel, on the ground that the crew was permitted to go ashore uncontrolled in an evacuated area in circumstances in which looting might have been expected.

[135] *Iran Hostages* case (n 107).

[136] ibid [61]–[68].

[137] Common Article 1 of the 1949 Geneva Conventions stipulates that '[t]he High Contracting Parties undertake to respect and to ensure respect for the present Convention in all circumstances'.

[138] International Covenant on Civil and Political Rights (adopted 16 December 1966, entered into force 23 March 1976) 999 UNTS 171 (ICCPR) art 2(1); see European Convention for the Protection of Human Rights and Fundamental Freedoms (ECHR) (adopted 4 November 1950, entered into force 3 September 1953) art 1, which uses the language 'shall secure' to everyone within their jurisdiction the rights defined in the Convention; American Convention on Human Rights (ACHR, adopted 22 November 1969, entered into force 18 July 1978) art 1(1), whereby: '[t]he States Parties to this Convention undertake to respect the rights and freedoms recognized therein and to ensure to all persons subject to their jurisdiction the free and full exercise of those rights and freedoms'.

[139] See eg HRC, General Comment 31 (n 78) para 7.

[140] Convention on the Prevention and Punishment of the Crime of Genocide (adopted 9 December 1948, entered into force 12 January 1951) 78 UNTS 277 art 1.

[141] *Velásquez Rodriguez* case (Compensatory Damages) (n 22) para 174. See further Chapter IV.

and punishing those responsible and putting in place measures to guarantee non-recurrence. The reasonableness standard implies that the measures taken reflected the risks and were appropriate in light of the means available to the State. It is not an obligation of result.

Like States, international organizations have obligations to take positive action. The DARIO commentaries note that the obligation is context and fact-specific, contingent on the organization being in a position to prevent, which arguably would not always be the case,[142] even if in the same scenario, the organization may have been able to refrain from acting.

Examples of where international organizations have arguably failed to take adequate and sufficient actions to prevent human rights or international humanitarian law violations include the failure of the European Union to put in place adequate measures to protect refugees and other migrants seeking to access the EU from drownings at sea and from *refoulement* to torture and other abuses. A European Parliament study has concluded that 'boat migrants faced human rights violations in various phases of their migratory process',[143] yet the 'primary aim of existing EU policies and actions still seems to be the protection of the borders against "illegal" immigration and the return of illegally staying migrants, rather than the development of effective strategies to protect human rights of migrants and the saving of lives on the Mediterranean'.[144]

There is also the UN's paltry responses to prevent genocide in Srebrenica and Rwanda,[145] a charge which could also be laid in relation to its limited response to events in Sri Lanka,[146] and the continued failure of the organization to deal effectively with the situation in Syria, in accordance with its mandate to maintain international peace and security. And, there are examples of negligence and reckless indifference, in which individuals' rights to life and health have been violated by the failure of the UN to take appropriate measures to avoid the introduction of cholera in Haiti[147] and to avoid subjecting displaced persons to lead poisoning in Kosovo.[148]

In some circumstances, an organization's ability to act is predicated on a need for authority from the political organ of the organization—the Security Council in the

[142] ILC, Third Report on Responsibility of International Organizations by Giorgio Gaja, Special Rapporteur, 'Report of the International Law Commission on the Work of its 57th Session' (2 May–3 June and 11 July–5 August 2005) UN Doc A/CN.4/553 para 10.

[143] European Parliament, 'Migrants in the Mediterranean: Protecting Human Rights' (29 October 2015) EP/EXPO/B/DROI/2015/01, 59.

[144] ibid 60.

[145] UNGA, 'The Fall of Srebrenica' (15 November 1999) UN Doc A/54/549; UNSC, 'Report of the Independent Inquiry into the Actions of the United Nations during the 1994 Genocide in Rwanda' (15 December 1999) UN Doc S/1999/1257.

[146] UNGA, 'Report of the Secretary-General's Internal Review Panel on United Nations Action in Sri Lanka' (November 2012) https://www.un.org/News/dh/infocus/Sri_Lanka/The_Internal_Review_Panel_report_on_Sri_Lanka.pdf (last accessed 12 December 2016).

[147] UNGA, 'Report of the Special Rapporteur on Extreme Poverty and Human Rights' (26 August 2016) UN Doc A/71/367.

[148] *NM and Others v UNMIK* (HRAP, 26 February 2016) No 26/08.

case of the UN. Or, as might be argued in the case of the European Union's role in migrant management or in respect of the UN's role in ensuring that peacekeeper abuses are appropriately prosecuted,[149] the issue is the balance of responsibilities between the organization and its Member States.

To what extent is an international organization responsible when it fails to obtain the authority from its Member States to implement its obligations to prevent? Arguably, obtaining the authority is out of the organization's hands, and this may militate against its responsibility for failing to prevent. However, the issue is not clear cut. A failure of the political organs to take the necessary decisions to enable the organization to prevent human rights or international humanitarian law violations may properly engage the responsibility of the organization. Professor Gaja has noted, in relation to the duty to prevent genocide: 'Assuming that general international law requires States and other entities to prevent genocide in the same way as the Convention on the Prevention and Punishment of the Crime of Genocide, and that the United Nations had been in a position to prevent genocide, failure to act would have represented a breach of an international obligation. Difficulties relating to the decision-making process could not exonerate the United Nations'.[150]

Both the Dutch Supreme Court decision in *Mothers of Srebrenica*[151] and the ECtHR's consideration and dismissal of the later complaint brought by the claimants,[152] made much of the fact that entertaining claims against the UN would require Dutch courts to scrutinize the way in which the UN discharged its core function of protecting international peace and security,[153] which would 'interfere with the fulfillment of the key mission of the United Nations in this field'.[154] But while this may be a reason to preserve immunities before domestic courts,[155] it is a less compelling reason to avoid an independent process whereby the UN's responsibility can be ascertained.

But even without going this far, there may be questions about whether the executive side of an organization did all within its power to advise the decision-making body of the significant risks to the civilian population. Arguably, the duty and authority to act may be even greater when the organization operates 'safe areas' or otherwise has clear charge of vulnerable persons in need of protection, or where it already has an enforcement mandate but fails to apply that mandate adequately.

[149] See Chapters V and VIII.

[150] ILC, Third Report on Responsibility of International Organizations by Giorgio Gaja (n 142) para 10.

[151] *Stichting Mothers of Srebrenica v Netherlands and United Nations*, Supreme Court [HR] LJN: BW1999, ILDC 1760 (NL 2012) (13 April 2012).

[152] *Stichting Mothers of Srebrenica v Netherlands* App no 65542/12 (ECtHR, 11 June 2013) [152].

[153] ibid; *Mothers of Srebrenica v Netherlands and United Nations*, Supreme Court (n 151) paras 4.1.1, 4.3.4.

[154] *Stichting Mothers of Srebrenica v Netherlands* (n 152) [154].

[155] See Chapter VI.

III.5 Conclusion

With few exceptions, international organizations have sought to limit the instances in which conduct can or should be attributed to them. In contrast, States have sought to demonstrate international organizations' effective control, even when the State retains control over key functions such as discipline and criminal sanctions. The jurisprudence has heralded the 'effective control' standard, which has also been adopted in the DARIO. Yet, this standard will only be meaningful if and to the extent that it is based on factual operating contexts.

Some of the tension between the different approaches appears ill-placed, in that attribution of conduct should not be an 'either or' proposition in which conduct is only attributed to the State or to the organization. Essential, however, is the fact that multiple internationally wrongful acts may arise out of a single act, with different elements being appropriately attributed to the organization, the State or other entities.[156] This is because the vantage point of the organization will be different from other actors. It will have unique opportunities to act and to refrain from acting. It will also have limitations which may constrain its actions or limit the effectiveness of its interventions. Ensuring that these different layers of involvement enter into the analysis is essential to the appropriate assignation of responsibility and key to guarantee non-recurrence.

While this dual responsibility is evidenced by the facts, it does not translate to workable accountability structures. The problem is evidenced in the jurisprudence. There are too many cases when claims against States fail because the acts have been attributed to international organizations; at the same time, and as is set out in later chapters, mechanisms to obtain redress from international organizations remain inadequate.

[156] See Mégret (n 3), who refers to a 'simultaneous responsibility'.

IV

The Obligation to Afford Reparation to Injured Individuals

IV.1 Introduction

This chapter considers the consequences of breaches of human rights and international humanitarian law for the responsible international organizations. It concentrates on the obligations owed to injured individuals. Given the absence of rules in the Draft Articles on the Responsibility of International Organizations (DARIO) concerning this specifically and the limited relevant jurisprudence, I seek to determine where rules may lie, having regard to mainly indirect sources.

The obligation to make reparation arises automatically from a finding of responsibility and is an obligation of result. I analyse who has this obligation, to whom it is owed, and what it entails. I also consider the right of individuals to access procedures by which they may vindicate their right to a remedy and the right of access to a court that may be implied from certain human rights treaties. In tandem, I consider the relationship between those obligations and individuals' rights under international law. An overarching issue is how the law of responsibility intersects with the specialized regimes of human rights and international humanitarian law and, particularly, their application to individuals.

The jurisprudence concerning State obligations is limited by the nuances of claimant choices if and how to pursue a claim, and by the shortage of venues where claims can be pursued. There are also differences between human rights law and international humanitarian law, including the extent to which individuals are understood to possess an actionable 'right' to seek reparation and what this may entail. The law is particularly under-developed in contexts of mass victimization, given the emphasis in most treaties and related texts on individual recompense. Whilst international principles have been distilled,[1] it is debatable whether they constitute *lex lata* or *lex ferenda*.[2]

[1] See eg Basic Principles and Guidelines on the Right to a Remedy and Reparation for Victims of Gross Violations of International Human Rights Law and Serious Violations of International Humanitarian Law, UNGA Res 60/147 (16 December 2005) (Basic Principles and Guidelines).

[2] Christian Tomuschat, 'Reparation in Favour of Individual Victims of Gross Violations of Human Rights and International Humanitarian Law' in Marcelo G Kohen (ed), *Promoting Justice, Human Rights and Conflict Resolution through International Law: LiberAmicorum Lucius Caflisch* (Martinus Nijhoff 2007) 569–90.

These limitations regarding State-owed obligations also impact on what can be said about international organizations' obligations. This is because of the near total absence of practice concerning international organizations specifically. One must use the law on State responsibility to draw parallels to possible standards for international organizations, so unclear State obligations also influence what can be said about organizations' obligations.

I argue that the nature of the violation (as opposed to the type of entity responsible for the conduct) should frame reparation obligations. This is because the right to reparation is a secondary rule which arises when the primary obligation is breached; it has a symbiotic relationship with the primary obligation, from which it derives its status. It is also because special rules created by international organizations should not be capable of displacing the general ones (to the extent that these general rules are capable of being ascertained), when the latter afford higher protections.

I conclude that *de lege ferenda*, international organizations are obligated to afford reparation to injured individuals, both for human rights and international humanitarian law abuses. I argue further that implicit in this reparation obligation is the connected obligation on international organizations to ensure that adequate and effective procedures are in place to give the obligation effect.

IV.2 The Origin and Development of the Concept of Reparation

IV.2.1 Multidisciplinary origins

Reparation encompasses the various ways in which wrongdoers must answer for wrongdoing. It draws its meaning from disciplines including law,[3] psychology,[4] philosophy,[5] religion,[6] victimology,[7] sociology,[8] and political theory.[9] It incorporates the purposes of reconciliation, rehabilitation, strengthening the rule of law, compensation, restitution, deterrence, and punishment. These purposes are not

[3] Dinah Shelton, *Remedies in International Human Rights Law* (3rd edn, OUP 2015); Albrecht Randelzhofer and Christian Tomuschat (eds), *State Responsibility and the Individual—Reparation in Instances of Grave Violations of Human Rights* (Kluwer 1999).

[4] C Fred Alford, *Psychology and the Natural Law of Reparation* (CUP 2011).

[5] Aristotle, *The Ethics* (JAK Thompson tr, Penguin 1955) 148–49; Viktor Frankl, *Man's Search for Meaning* (Washington Square Press 1959).

[6] Abdullahi Ahmed An-Na'im, 'The Right to Reparation for Human Rights Violations and Islamic Culture(s)' in Theo van Boven and others (eds), *Seminar on the Right to Restitution, Compensation and Rehabilitation for Victims of Gross Violations of Human Rights and Fundamental Freedoms* (University of Limburg Human Rights Project Group, SIM 1992) 174, 180.

[7] Kieran McEvoy, 'Victimology in Transitional Justice: Victimhood, Innocence and Hierarchy' (2012) 9 Eur J Crim 527.

[8] Eric Yamamoto, 'Friend, or Foe or Something Else: Social Meanings of Redress and Reparations' (1991–1992) 20 Denv J Int'l L & Pol'y 223.

[9] Pablo de Greiff, 'Repairing the Past: Compensation for Victims of Human Rights Violations' in Pablo de Greiff (ed), *The Handbook of Reparations* (OUP 2006) 1–20; John Torpey, *Making Whole What Has Been Smashed: On Reparation Politics* (Harvard University Press 2006).

always compatible with each other given that some fulfil private interests whereas others serve societal ones.[10] Reparation is understood also as a process to respond to harm suffered by injured individuals and/or groups. However, particularly when negotiated in response to wide-scale wrongs, it can take on a political dimension and injured individuals may have little role in its conceptualization or outcome.

Increasingly, 'reparation' has been monopolized by lawyers, a practice that Torpey has termed a 'juridification of politics'.[11] Yet it is hard to fit all that reparation encompasses into the lens of the law.[12] It is complicated and at times beyond their jurisdiction for courts to rule on matters which extend to social policy. Reparation is also unachievable for the most egregious violations which forever change victims or in instances of mass victimization, owing to prohibitive administrative costs associated with assessing the harms suffered by individuals and limited evidence available to claimants. This introduces an ideational character to reparation. Yet, reparation that fits within the bounds of law is more predictable and transparent; there are standards that wrongdoers are obliged to meet and that injured individuals can expect. Extra-legal reparation processes can appear arbitrary. And, this 'arbitrariness' can become a negative rule whereby any measure, to the extent that it is termed 'reparation', may suffice to legitimize an award; this can further lessen the ability of injured individuals or groups to advocate that their particular legal rights are addressed. There is thus a challenge to ensure that reparation adheres to accepted principles, while at the same time responds adequately to the multidisciplinary context and the practical limitations.

IV.2.2 Legal origins

Reparation has a fundamental placement in law. Domestically, injured individuals can pursue public law or tort actions against persons or entities that wronged them, including officials and the State itself. Crime victims may also pursue civil claims against perpetrators, either alongside criminal trials or as separate tort actions. Some countries have established administrative programmes to indemnify victims as an extension of social welfare policies,[13] or to respond to mass victimization as part of political transitions.[14]

In international law, the obligation to afford reparation arises as a consequence of the breach of a primary obligation causing injury.[15] The Permanent Court of International Justice (PCIJ) held in *Chorzów Factory* that it is 'a principle of

[10] Dinah Shelton, 'Righting Wrongs: Reparations in the Articles on State Responsibility' (2002) 96 AJIL 833.

[11] See Torpey (n 9) 355.

[12] See de Greiff (n 9) 1–20.

[13] Andrew Ashworth, 'Punishment and Compensation: Victims, Offenders and the State' (1986) 6 Oxford J Legal Studies 86.

[14] See generally de Greiff (n 9).

[15] ILC, Articles on the Responsibility of States for Internationally Wrongful Acts, 'Report of the International Law Commission on the Work of its 53rd Session' (23 April–1 June and 2 July–10 August 2001) UN Doc A/CN.4/SER.A/2001/Add.1 (ARS) art 31, reflecting *Chorzów Factory (Germany v Poland)* (Jurisdiction) [1927] PCIJ Rep Series A No 9, 21.

international law, and even a general conception of law, that any breach of an engagement involves an obligation to make reparation'.[16] Reparation applies to any breached international obligation causing injury.[17] This should include breaches of human rights and international humanitarian law. However, consistent with classical notions of international law as a set of rules applicable to States in their relations to each other,[18] reparation first developed through inter-State claims applying the law of injury to aliens and diplomatic protection. The State of nationality would seek reparation from the offending State for the violation of its rights; the injured alien was not understood to possess rights separate from the State of nationality.[19] Nonetheless, the rights framework has progressively influenced how international law is perceived. Diplomatic protection is no longer understood only to relate to a State's own interest in injury to aliens; the concept now acknowledges that injured individuals are the beneficiaries of rights,[20] and that protection should be requested for their benefit.[21]

This classical framework underpins the approach of the International Law Commission (ILC) to reparation. There is no reference in either the Articles on the Responsibility of States for Internationally Wrongful Acts (ARS) or DARIO to obligations owed to individuals or rights belonging to individuals. Nonetheless, a rights framework is felt. Both texts explain that the approaches taken are without prejudice to any right which may accrue directly to any person or entity other than a State.[22] The DARIO commentaries note that one such area is that of 'breaches committed by peacekeeping forces and affecting individuals'.[23] In its rules on countermeasures, the DARIO specify that international organizations cannot breach obligations to refrain from the threat or use of force, to protect human rights, of a humanitarian character prohibiting reprisals, or other obligations under peremptory norms of general international law.[24] They also cite the 'not inconceivable' example of an organization committing aggression or infringing an obligation under a peremptory norm of general international law relating to the protection of human rights. Here, the commentaries indicate that: '[i]f a serious breach does occur, it calls for the same consequences as in the case of States'.[25]

16 *Chorzów Factory (Germany v Poland)* (Merits) [1928] PCIJ Rep Series A No 17, 29.

17 See ARS (n 15) art 31 and commentaries.

18 Lassa Oppenheim, *International Law: A Treatise*, vol I (Ronald Roxburgh ed, 3rd edn, Longmans Green & Co 1920) 18–19.

19 *Mavrommatis Palestine Concessions (Greece v United Kingdom)* (Merits) [1924] PCIJ Rep Series A No 2, 12; *Nottebohm Case* (Merits) [1955] ICJ Rep 4.

20 *Ahmadou Sadio Diallo (Republic of Guinea v DRC)* (Merits) [2010] ICJ Rep 639 [39].

21 ILC, Draft Articles on Diplomatic Protection, 'Report of the International Law Commission on the Work of its 56th Session' (3 May–4 June and 5 July–6 August 2004) UN Doc A/CN.4/L/647 art 19.

22 Article 33(2) of both texts.

23 ILC, Draft Articles on the Responsibility of International Organizations, 'Report of the International Law Commission on the Work of its 63rd Session' (26 April–3 June and 4 July–12 August 2011) UN Doc A/66/10 (DARIO) Commentary to art 33 para 5.

24 ibid art 53 and Commentary.

25 ibid Commentaries to art 41 para 5.

This move towards a more inclusive international law that takes into account individuals' rights has been heralded by some as a ground-breaking shift.[26] Yet, there is debate about the extent of the evolution. Some argue that the areas in which individual rights exist on the international plane remain confined to the instances in which States have created rights for individuals by treaty.[27] However, international law is not static or immutable; the question is whether the growing patchwork of jurisprudence, treaty law, and declarative instruments on reparation can provide a sufficiently solid and compelling foundation for wider understandings.

IV.3 Victims' Right to a Remedy and Reparation for Human Rights and International Humanitarian Law Violations

IV.3.1 General obligations

The State obligation to afford reparation is set out in human rights treaties[28] and their interpretive bodies,[29] in declarative texts,[30] by independent

[26] *Prosecutor v Tadić* (Decision on Motion for Interlocutory Appeal) IT-94-1-AR72 (ICTY, 2 October 1995) para 97.

[27] See Tomuschat, 'Reparation in Favour of Individual Victims' (n 2).

[28] See eg International Covenant on Civil and Political Rights (adopted 16 December 1966, entered into force 23 March 1976) 999 UNTS 171 (ICCPR) art 2(3); Convention for the Protection of All Persons from Enforced Disappearance (adopted 20 December 2006, entered into force 23 December 2010) 2716 UNTS 3 (CPPED) arts 18, 20(2), 24(4); Convention against Torture and Other Cruel, Inhuman or Degrading Treatment or Punishment (adopted 10 December 1984, entered into force 26 June 1987) 1465 UNTS 85 (UNCAT) art 14(1); Optional Protocol to the Convention on the Rights of the Child on the Sale of Children, Child Prostitution and Child Pornography (adopted 25 May 2000, entered into force 18 January 2002) 2171 UNTS 227 (CRC–OPSC) art 8; Convention on the Protection of the Rights of All Migrant Workers and Members of Their Families (adopted 18 December 1990, entered into force 1 July 2003) 2220 UNTS 3 (CPRMW) art 16(9); European Convention for the Protection of Human Rights and Fundamental Freedoms (ECHR) (adopted 4 November 1950, entered into force 3 September 1953) arts 13, 41; American Convention on Human Rights (ACHR, adopted 22 November 1969, entered into force 18 July 1978) arts 25, 63(1); African Charter on Human and Peoples' Rights (adopted 27 June 1981, entered into force 21 October 1986) (1982) 21 ILM 58 (ACHPR) art 21(2).

[29] UN Human Rights Committee, 'General Comment 31' Nature of the General Legal Obligation Imposed on States Parties to the International Covenant on Civil and Political Rights (26 May 2004) UN Doc CCPR/C/21/Rev.1/Add.13; Committee Against Torture, 'General Comment 3', Implementation of Article 14 by States Parties (13 December 2012) UN Doc CAT/C/GC/3; CEDAW Committee, 'General Recommendation 28' (16 December 2010) UN Doc CEDAW/C/GC/28 para 32; CESCR, 'General Comment 3' (14 December 1990) UN Doc E/C.12/1991/23; CESCR, 'General Comment 9' (3 December 1998) UN Doc E/C.12/1998/24 paras 2, 3, 8, and 9.

[30] See eg Universal Declaration of Human Rights, UNGA Res 217(A)(III) (10 December 1948) (adopted by 48 votes to none, eight abstentions) (UDHR) art 8; Basic Principles and Guidelines (n 1); Declaration of Basic Principles of Justice for Victims of Crime and Abuse of Power, UNGA Res 40/34 (29 November 1985) (adopted without vote) (Victims' Declaration) 4; Updated Set of Principles for the Protection and Promotion of Human Rights through Action to Combat Impunity (8 February 2005) UN Doc E/CN.4/2005/102/Add.1 (Impunity Principles) 31; Principles on the Effective Prevention and Investigation of Extra-legal, Arbitrary and Summary Executions, ESC Res 1989/65 (24 May 1989) UN Doc E/1989/89, 20; Declaration on the Rights of Indigenous Peoples, UNGA Res 61/295 (13 September 2007) (adopted by 144 votes to four; 11 abstentions) art 8(2); Nairobi Declaration on Women's and Girls' Right to a Remedy and Reparation (International Meeting

experts[31] in academic studies,[32] and as will be described, in judicial decisions. It is also reflected in international humanitarian law treaties, particularly Article 3 of the Hague Convention IV,[33] largely reproduced in Article 91 of Protocol I.[34] Declarative texts, such as the Basic Principles and Guidelines,[35] the Principles on Housing and Property Restitution,[36] and the International Law Association's Declaration of International Law Principles on Reparation for Victims of Armed Conflict,[37] also consider reparation for international humanitarian law violations and emphasize victims' 'right' to reparation. This differs from the treaty texts which refer simply to the obligation to compensate. Who must be compensated is not spelled out, nor whether any injury to individuals is subsumed by the injury to the State of nationality.

In human rights law, reparation entails two aspects: the right to a domestic remedy and the right to adequate and effective forms of reparation. Some texts focus on particularly heinous abuses,[38] whereas others specify that the rights apply to an array of violations.[39] The connection between the procedure by which reparation is

on Women's and Girls' Right to a Remedy and Reparation, Nairobi, 19–21 March 2007) 3(a) https://www.fidh.org/IMG/pdf/NAIROBI_DECLARATIONeng.pdf (last accessed 25 December 2016).

[31] See also UN Human Rights Council, 'Report of the Special Rapporteur on Violence against Women (Reparations for Women Subjected to Violence)' (23 April 2010) UN Doc A/HRC/14/22; UNGA, 'Report of the Special Rapporteur on Trafficking in Persons (The Right to an Effective Remedy for Trafficked Persons)' (9 August 2011) UN Doc A/66/283; UN Human Rights Council, 'Report of the Special Rapporteur on the Promotion and Protection of Human Rights and Fundamental Freedoms while Countering Terrorism' (4 June 2012) UN Doc A/HRC/20/14 paras 49–62; UN Human Rights Council, 'Report of the Special Rapporteur on the Promotion of Truth, Justice, Reparation and Guarantees of Non-recurrence' (9 August 2012) UN Doc A/HRC/21/46; UNGA, 'Interim Report of the Special Rapporteur on Torture' (11 August 2000) UN Doc A/55/290 paras 24–30; UNGA, 'Report of the Special Rapporteur on Torture' (3 July 2003) UN Doc A/58/120 paras 29–35; UNGA, 'Report of the Special Rapporteur on Torture' (15 January 2007) UN Doc A/HRC/4/33 paras 61–68; UN Commission on Human Rights, 'Report Submitted by the Special Rapporteur on Toxic Waste' (19 January 2001) UN Doc E/CN.4/2001/55 paras 74–83; CESCR, 'General Comment 14' The Right to the Highest Attainable Standard of Health (11 August 2000) UN Doc E/C.12/2000/4 para 59.

[32] See Shelton, *Remedies in International Human Rights Law* (n 3); Randelzhofer and Tomuschat (n 3).

[33] Convention Respecting the Laws and Customs of War on Land (adopted 18 October 1907, entered into force 26 January 1910).

[34] Protocol Additional to the Geneva Conventions of 12 August 1949, and relating to the Protection of Victims of International Armed Conflicts (adopted 8 June 1977, entered into force 7 December 1978) 1125 UNTS 3 (Protocol I).

[35] Basic Principles and Guidelines (n 1) 11.

[36] UN Commission on Human Rights, 'Principles on Housing and Property Restitution for Refugees and Displaced Persons' (28 June 2005) UN Doc E/CN.4/Sub.2/2005/17 para 2.1.

[37] International Law Association (ILA), 'Declaration of International Law Principles on Reparation for Victims of Armed Conflict' Res 2/2010 (74th Conference, The Hague, 15–19 August 2010) arts 6, 30.

[38] Basic Principles and Guidelines (n 1); Convention (I) for the Amelioration of the Condition of the Wounded and Sick in Armed Forces in the Field (adopted 12 August 1949, entered into force 21 October 1950) 75 UNTS 31 (GC1) art 51; Convention (II) for the Amelioration of the Condition of Wounded, Sick and Shipwrecked Members of Armed Forces at Sea (adopted 12 August 1949, entered into force 21 October 1950) 75 UNTS 85 (GC2) art 52; Convention (III) relative to the Treatment of Prisoners of War (adopted 12 August 1949, entered into force 21 October 1950) 75 UNTS 135 (GC3) art 131; Convention (IV) relative to the Protection of Civilian Persons in Time of War (adopted 12 August 1949, entered into force 21 October 1950) 75 UNTS 287 (GC4) art 148.

[39] ILA, 'Draft Declaration of International Law Principles on Reparation for Victims of Armed Conflict (Substantive Issues)' (Hague Conference 2010), Commentary to arts 4, 9.

sought and the ultimate award is understood as indivisible.[40] Under international humanitarian law, the emphasis has solely been on the latter aspect.

Tomuschat argues that the reciprocity which underpins the State obligation to repair the harm caused to another State is crucially absent from the scenario of the individual whose rights are breached by its State of nationality.[41] He thus argues that there is no basis to derive an international obligation to afford reparation for breaches of human rights or international humanitarian law outside of treaties which specifically provide for it. However, as a secondary rule, reparation should have no separate need for justification beyond the primary rule from which it derives its status; it is the natural and required consequence of the breach.[42] The ILC does not distinguish between types of internationally wrongful acts;[43] the requirement of reparation attaches to any such act. Shelton explains that some international courts have inferred 'an inherent power to afford remedies'.[44] She refers to *LaGrand* on breach of consular rights, where the International Court of Justice (ICJ) held that: 'no separate basis for jurisdiction is required by the Court to consider the remedies a party has requested for the breach of the obligation'.[45] Similarly, Gillard has argued in relation to international humanitarian law that: 'the obligation to make reparation arises *automatically* as a consequence of the unlawful act, without the need for the obligation to be spelled out in conventions'.[46] The ICJ takes this approach in its *Wall* Advisory Opinion, where it held that Israel was obliged 'to make reparation for all damage caused by the construction of the wall' 'to all the natural or legal persons concerned'[47] as a result of the various international obligations that Israel was said to have breached, which included violations of human rights and international humanitarian law.[48]

In *Difference Relating to Immunity from Legal Process of a Special Rapporteur of the Commission on Human Rights*, the ICJ pointed out that: '[t]he question of immunity from legal process is distinct from the issue of compensation for any damages incurred as a result of acts performed by the United Nations or by its agents acting in their official capacity. The United Nations may be required to bear responsibility

[40] Shelton, *Remedies in International Human Rights Law* (n 3); HRC, General Comment 31 (n 29) para 16.

[41] Tomuschat, 'Reparation in Favour of Individual Victims' (n 2) 577–81. See also Christian Tomuschat, 'Reparation for Victims of Grave Human Rights Violations' (2002) 10 Tulane J Int'l & Comp L 157 and Marten Zwanenburg, 'The Van Boven/Bassiouni Principles: An Appraisal' (2006) 24 Neth Q HR 654, 654–55.

[42] Menno Kamminga, 'Legal Consequences of an Internationally Wrongful Act of a State against an Individual' in Tom Barkhuysen, Michiel Leonard van Emmerik, and Piet Hein Kempen (eds), *The Execution of Strasbourg and Geneva Human Rights Decisions in the National Legal Order* (Martinus Nijhoff 1999) 65–74.

[43] See ARS (n 15) arts 1, 12; DARIO (n 23) arts 1, 10.

[44] See Shelton, *Remedies in International Human Rights Law* (n 3) 142.

[45] *LaGrand Case (Germany v United States of America)* (Merits) [2001] ICJ Reports 466 [48].

[46] Emanuela-Chiara Gillard, 'Reparation for Violations of International Humanitarian Law' (2003) 85(851) Int'l Rev Red Cross 532.

[47] *Legal Consequences of the Construction of a Wall in the Occupied Palestinian Territory* (Advisory Opinion) [2004] ICJ Reports 136 [152].

[48] ibid [114], [132]–[137].

for the damage arising from such acts'.[49] Thus, even when the UN is immune from legal process, this does not impact upon its responsibility or its obligation to afford reparations as a result of that responsibility. Immunities must be distinguished from responsibility for internationally wrongful acts and reparation for injury caused by such conduct. There is thus no general bar to reparation for international organizations on this basis, although the venues where such claims may be adjudicated may be limited by applicable privileges and immunities.

IV.3.2 Procedural aspects: the right to an effective remedy

(1) Human rights law

The right to reparation entails in part, the obligation to afford domestic remedies in response to human rights violations. All human rights treaties require, either explicitly or implicitly, States parties to provide remedies under national law.[50] The UN Basic Principles and Guidelines explain the obligation to respect, ensure respect for, and implement international human rights law and international humanitarian law as giving rise to a duty, inter alia, to '[p]rovide those who claim to be victims of a human rights or humanitarian law violation with equal and effective access to justice . . . irrespective of who may ultimately be the bearer of responsibility for the violation'.[51]

Because of the virtually uniform recognition of the right to an effective remedy in human rights treaties, some scholars have posited that it reflects customary international law.[52] But, and despite the arguments made by Shelton and Gillard referred to earlier concerning the inherent power to award reparation in the face of a breach of a primary obligation, components of the right to an effective domestic remedy such as the right to access a court may be restricted to the extent that the limitations pursue a legitimate aim and are necessary and proportionate to that aim, insofar

[49] *Difference Relating to Immunity from Legal Process of a Special Rapporteur of the Commission on Human Rights* (Advisory Opinion) [1999] ICJ Rep 62 [66] (*Cumaraswamy* case).

[50] See eg UDHR art 8 (n 30); art 2(3) ICCPR (n 28); art 83 CPRMW (n 28); Convention on the Elimination of All Forms of Racial Discrimination (adopted 21 December 1965, entered into force 4 January 1969) 660 UNTS 195 (CERD) art 6; Indigenous and Tribal Peoples Convention (adopted 27 June 1989, entered into force 5 September 1991) ILO No 169, 72 Official Bull 59 art 12; Convention on the Elimination of All Forms of Discrimination against Women (adopted 18 December 1979, entered into force 3 September 1981) 129 UNTS 13 (CEDAW) art 2(c); Protocol to Prevent, Suppress and Punish Trafficking in Persons, Especially Women and Children, supplementing the UN Convention against Transnational Organized Crime (adopted 15 November 2000, entered into force 25 December 2003) 2237 UNTS 319 art 6(6).

[51] Basic Principles and Guidelines (n 1) 3(c). See also Victims' Declaration (n 30) 4, Impunity Principles (n 30) 32, and Vienna Declaration and Programme of Action (World Conference on Human Rights, Vienna, 25 June 1993) UN Doc A/CONF.157/53 para 27.

[52] See Francesco Francioni, *Access to Justice as a Human Right* (OUP 2007) 1–56; Karel Wellens, 'Fragmentation of International Law and Establishing an Accountability Regime for International Organizations: The Role of the Judiciary in Closing the Gap' (2003–2004) 25 Mich J Int'l L 1162; M Cherif Bassiouni, 'International Recognition of Victims' Rights' (2006) 6 Hum R LR 203, 206–207; Riccardo Pisillo-Mazzeschi, 'International Obligations to Provide for Reparation Claims?' in Randelzhofer and Tomuschat (n 3) 164.

as they do not 'reduce the access left to the individual in such a way or to such an extent that the very essence of the right is impaired'.[53]

For instance, reasonable limitation periods can be lawful,[54] as can restrictions on vexatious claims. Certainly, these exceptions operate restrictively in the domestic sphere in relation to States' obligations to remedy those human rights violations they are directly responsible for perpetrating. But nevertheless, there is a modicum of contingency in how the right to a remedy has been framed. And, the exceptions to this right have been even more pronounced when a State is asked to provide access to a remedy for breaches which fall outside of its national remit which may conflict with other principles of international law, such as immunities.[55] Immunities, by extinguishing the claim impair the very essence of the right of access to court.[56] Yet, these immunities have been held to be lawful, on the basis that they pursue the legitimate aim of observing international law in the interest of good relations between States through respect of other States' sovereignty.[57]

But even with such contingencies, the right to a remedy is nonetheless required to the extent that it is necessary for the proper exercise of the primary obligation, even in the context of armed conflict and occupation[58] or states of emergency,[59] in the absence of any valid proportionality considerations. Thus, in a purely domestic context, the procedural remedy is understood to require States to afford effective access to fair processes in which arguable claims can be determined. The remedy should be prompt, accessible, and capable of offering a reasonable prospect of success.[60]

Jurisprudence and standard-setting texts also recognize the need to consider the quality of victims' access to and experience of justice processes. Victims must receive adequate information,[61] they must be treated with humanity and

[53] *Al-Adsani v United Kingdom* App no 35763/97 (ECtHR, 21 November 2001) [53].

[54] *Stubbings v United Kingdom* App nos 22083/93, 22095/93 (ECtHR, 22 October 1996) [50].

[55] *Jurisdictional Immunities of the State (Germany v Italy: Greece Intervening)* (Merits) [2012] ICJ Rep 143; *Jones v United Kingdom* (GC) App nos 34356/06, 40528/06 (ECtHR, 14 January 2014); *Stichting Mothers of Srebrenica v Netherlands* App no 65542/12 (ECtHR, 11 June 2013) [152] (finding the application inadmissible). These issues are discussed in Chapter VI.

[56] Lorna McGregor, 'State Immunity and Human Rights: Is There a Future after *Germany v. Italy*?' (2012) 11 J Int'l Crim J 125, 133–36.

[57] ibid 134, referring to *Al-Adsani v UK* (n 53) [54]. See Chapter VI.

[58] *Judicial Guarantees in States of Emergency* (Advisory Opinion) OC–9/87, Ser A no 9 (IACtHR, 6 October 1987) paras 22–24; *Al-Skeini v United Kingdom* App no 55721/07 (ECtHR, 7 July 2011) [164]–[167]; *Legal Consequences of the Construction of a Wall* (n 47) [106].

[59] UN HRC, 'General Comment 29' Derogations during a State of Emergency (31 August 2001) UN Doc CCPR/C/21/Rev.1/Add.11 para 14.

[60] *The Social and Economic Rights Action Center and the Center for Economic and Social Rights v Nigeria* Comm no 155/96 (ACommHPR, 30th Ord Sess, 13–27 October 2001); *Silver v United Kingdom* App nos 5947/72, 6205/73, 7052/75, 7061/75, 7107/75, 7113/75, and 7136/75 (ECtHR, 25 March 1983) [113(b)]; *Mayagna (Sumo) Awas Tigni Community v Nicaragua* (Merits, Reparations and Costs) Ser C no 79 (IACtHR, 31 August 2001) para 112.

[61] *Anguelova v Bulgaria* App no 38361/97 (ECtHR, 13 June 2002); See also Convention on Action against Trafficking in Human Beings (CATHB) (adopted on 16 May 2005, entered into force on 1 February 2008) CETS no 197 art 15; *Zontul v Greece* App no 12294/07 (ECtHR, 17 January 2012) [115]; Recommended Principles and Guidelines on Human Rights and Trafficking (20 May 2002) UN Doc E/2002/68/Add.1, 9.2.

dignity[62] and their privacy and safety, both physical and psychological, must be safeguarded.[63] Human rights violations that constitute crimes also give rise to an obligation to carry out prompt, impartial and thorough investigations capable of leading to the identification, and if appropriate, prosecution of the authors.[64] The most severe human rights violations require judicial remedies, however, the powers provided by a remedial mechanism and the guarantees it affords will determine whether it is effective.[65] Remedies must be available to all persons within a State's jurisdiction, which is understood to also include instances when a State exercises effective control over an area outside its national territory.[66]

(2) *State human rights obligations extrapolated to frame international organization obligations*

The human rights obligation to afford domestic remedies is only capable of direct application by States. An obvious limitation for international organizations is that they do not have sovereignty nor do they generally control territory and thus would not have the wherewithal to afford domestic remedies in the traditional sense. An exception is when international organizations administer territory, such as the temporary administration by the UN of Kosovo and East Timor. In such instances, the UN recognized to a limited degree the need to develop internal structures to give effect to the obligation to afford domestic remedies.

However, even when an international organization does not administer territory *in toto*, to the extent that conduct is capable of being attributed to it, one may still posit its obligation *de lege ferenda* to afford the equivalent of domestic remedies in response to human rights abuses and, as explained in the section below, in response to international humanitarian law violations. A central question is what standards should apply to organizations' internal mechanisms. Should these standards apply criteria under general international law or is it appropriate for them to be framed by international organizations within the context of their internal rules? In answering

[62] *AT v Hungary* UN Doc CEDAW/C/32/D/2/2003 (CEDAW Committee, 26 January 2005) para 9.6(II)(vi); HRC, General Comment 31 (n 29) para 15; UN Committee on the Rights of the Child (CRC Committee), 'General Comment 5' General Measures of Implementation of the Convention on the Rights of the Child (3 October 2003) UN Doc CRC/GC/2003/5 para 24; Basic Principles and Guidelines (n 1), 12(c); *Aksoy v Turkey* App no 21987/93 (ECtHR, 18 December 1996) [98].

[63] Basic Principles and Guidelines (n 1) 10, 12(b).

[64] *Barrios Altos v Peru* (Merits) [2001] Ser C no 75 (IACtHR, 14 March 2001) paras 42, 43; *Kaya v Turkey* App no 158/1996/777/978 (ECtHR, 19 February 1998); *Assenov v Bulgaria* App no 24760/94 (ECtHR, 28 October 1998); *Cantoral Benavides v Peru* (Merits) [2000] Ser C no 69 (IACtHR, 18 August 2000); *Güleç v Turkey* App no 21593/93 (ECtHR, 27 July 1998) [80]–[82].

[65] *Velásquez Rodríguez v Honduras* (Merits) Ser C no 4 (IACtHR, 29 July 1988) paras 62–68; *DRC v Burundi, Rwanda and Uganda*, Comm no 227/99 (ACommHPR, 20th Annual Activity Rep, May 2003); *Egyptian Initiative for Personal Rights and Interights v Egypt*, Comm no 334/06 (ACommHPR, 9th Extraordinary Sess, 23 February–3 March 2011) [96]–[98]; *De Souza Ribeiro v France* (GC) App no 22689/07 (ECtHR, 13 December 2012) [79].

[66] *Ilaşcu v Moldova and Russia* (GC) App no 48787/99 (ECtHR, 8 July 2004); *Al-Saadoon v United Kingdom* App no 61498/08 (ECtHR, 2 March 2010).

this question, it should be noted that there is little specific international law governing what international organizations are required to do.[67]

The dearth of international legal principles stems from the vagueness of the Convention on the Privileges and Immunities of the United Nations (CPIUN), the failure of the ILC to consider precisely this issue in the DARIO and the absence of other bilateral or multilateral treaties on the point. The CPIUN explains that appropriate modes of settlement shall be put in place,[68] which has been interpreted to mean that when the immunity of the UN bars domestic claims, the organization must use an alternative system to determine such claims. As has been argued by Reinisch, this 'obligation to provide for alternative dispute settlement in case of the Organization's immunity from legal process can be regarded as an acknowledgment of the right of access to court as contained in all major human rights instruments'.[69] Thus the intention of the Convention according to Reinisch was to ensure that immunities did not result in impunity; any exercise of immunity would need to be predicated on the provision of an 'appropriate mode of settlement'.[70] However, what constitutes an 'appropriate' mode of settlement is not set out in the Convention and the DARIO simply confirm that international organizations are responsible for their wrongful acts and obliged to afford reparation.[71]

There is also limited international jurisprudence that considers what constitutes 'appropriate modes of settlement'. This stems from the absence of legal forums capable of adjudicating disputes which interpret organizations' obligations, the limited advisory jurisdiction of the ICJ notwithstanding.[72] Indirectly, the European Court of Human Rights (ECtHR) in a line of cases has been called upon to assess whether organizations' internal procedures are sufficiently robust alternative means of redress, when States have upheld organizations' immunities, to determine whether this infringed individuals' right of access to court.[73] While the Court itself does not specify the standard, commentators have emphasized the importance for the alternate remedy to be capable of addressing the dispute, to be judicial in nature

[67] See Chapter V.

[68] Convention on the Privileges and Immunities of the UN (adopted 13 February 1946, entered into force 17 September 1946) 1 UNTS 15 (CPIUN) art VIII s 29(a). The Convention on the Privileges and Immunities of the Specialized Agencies (adopted 21 November 1947, entered into force 2 December 1948) 33 UNTS 261 art IX provides for the same framework.

[69] August Reinisch, 'Convention on the Privileges and Immunities of the United Nations / Convention on the Privileges and Immunities of the Specialized Agencies' (UN Audiovisual Library of International Law, undated) http://legal.un.org/avl/ha/cpiun-cpisa/cpiun-cpisa.html (last accessed 25 December 2016).

[70] See August Reinisch and Ulf Andreas Weber, 'In the Shadow of Waite and Kennedy: The Jurisdictional Immunity of International Organizations, the Individual's Right of Access to the Courts and Administrative Tribunals as Alternative Means of Dispute Settlement' (2004) 1 Int'l Org LR 59, 72; August Reinisch, 'The Immunity of International Organizations and the Jurisdiction of their Administrative Tribunals' (2008) 7(2) Chinese J Int'l L 285, 289. Note, however, that this goes beyond the literal wording of art 29 CPIUN, which only requires the UN to establish appropriate modes of settlement in relation to particular types of disputes. For further analysis of art 29 see Chapter V.

[71] DARIO (n 23) arts 3; 31(1).

[72] *Effects of Awards of Compensation Made by the United Nations Administrative Tribunal* (Advisory Opinion) [1954] ICJ Rep 47; *Cumaraswamy* case (n 49) [66].

[73] *Waite and Kennedy v Germany* (GC) App no 26083/94 (ECtHR, 18 February 1999) [67].

and that the adjudicators must be sufficiently qualified and independent.[74] This reference to the need for alternative means of redress has also proved important in the assessment by certain domestic courts of the immunity of international organizations, with some denying immunities when they determined that there was no appropriate alternative remedy.[75]

In a later series of cases concerning the immunity of States before foreign courts, the ECtHR determined that upholding immunities 'cannot in principle be regarded as imposing a disproportionate restriction on the right of access to court';[76] the immunity meant that there was no access to court the State could have given; it was not theirs to give.[77] This reasoning was adopted by the ICJ in *Germany v Italy*.[78] While the immunities of international organizations were not at stake in these decisions, in the *Mothers of Srebrenica* case, the ICJ's judgment in *Germany v Italy* featured prominently in the Dutch Supreme Court's rejection of an exception to the immunity of international organizations.[79] As McGregor argues, '[t]he cross-fertilization between the immunities of states and the immunities of international organizations in this case raises the question whether the ICJ decision will have a negative impact on the trend to deny international organizations immunity where no reasonable alternative to access justice exists'.[80]

In a study commissioned by the UN Office of Legal Affairs relating to the individual sanctions regime of the UN Security Council, Professor Fassbender notes that: 'there is a legitimate expectation that the UN, through its organs, observes standards of due process, or "fair and clear procedures" on which the person concerned can rely'.[81] He notes further that: '[d]ependent on the circumstances of a particular situation, appropriate standards must be determined, suited to that situation, paying due regard to the nature of the affected rights and freedoms and the extent to which action taken by the UN is likely adversely to affect those rights and freedoms'.[82] To the extent that procedural mechanisms also apply to international humanitarian law claims, the same would apply. This is so because human rights and international humanitarian law are mutually reinforcing and the one

[74] Matthias Kloth, *Immunities and the Right of Access to Court under Article 6 of the European Court of Human Rights* (Martinus Nijhoff 2010) 148–49.

[75] See Reinisch, 'The Immunity of International Organizations and the Jurisdiction of their Administrative Tribunals' (n 70), which refers to several domestic (mainly employment) cases which have begun to loosely consider whether the mode of settlement established by the international organizations is capable of providing an adequate remedy. See also Mizushima Tomonori, 'Denying Foreign State Immunity on the Grounds of the Unavailability of Alternative Means' (2008) 71 Modern LR 734, 743.

[76] *McElhinney v Ireland* App no 31253/96 (ECtHR, 21 November 2001) [37]; *Al-Adsani v United Kingdom* (n 53) [56].

[77] This issue is discussed in more detail in Chapter VI.

[78] *Germany v Italy* (n 55) [100], [101].

[79] *Stichting Mothers of Srebrenica v Netherlands and United Nations*, Supreme Court [HR] LJN: BW1999, ILDC 1760 (NL 2012) (13 April 2012) [4.3.14].

[80] See McGregor (n 56) 135.

[81] Reproduced in Bardo Fassbender, 'Targeted Sanctions Imposed by the UN Security Council and Due Process Rights: A Study Commissioned by the UN Office of Legal Affairs and Follow-up Action by the United Nations' (2006) 3 Int'l Org LR 437 para 6.6.

[82] ibid para 10.

may provide greater clarity to the obligations of the other, particularly where one body of law is silent. As human rights law is particularly instructive in regards to the standards for individual complaints procedures, as Roberts has indicated, it 'may not merely fill in gaps in the laws of war, but also provide procedures for assisting in the implementation of key provisions of those laws'.[83] Where the international organization is for whatever reason incapable of giving effect to the procedural obligation through its own procedures, arguably it must afford a route to external adjudication, eg through the insertion of arbitral clauses accessible to those whose rights have been adversely affected and/or through clear and transparent procedures to waive immunities.[84]

(3) International humanitarian law obligations

Unlike human rights law, international humanitarian law treaties do not oblige States to afford victims with a procedural remedy, nor are there specialized international complaints mechanisms.[85] This is due to the genesis of international humanitarian law as a set of rules applicable to States in their relations with each other. The International Committee of the Red Cross (ICRC) has made reference in its commentaries to this limitation, commenting that: '[t]he State is answerable to another contracting State and not to the former prisoner. On that point the recognised system was not in any way modified in 1949'.[86] It has expressed this view regarding the return of prisoners' valuables[87] and personal effects,[88] as well as for compensation for prisoners' work-related injuries.[89] This position has remained largely unchanged with Protocol I, although the ICRC has posited 'a growing tendency to recognise the exercise of rights by individuals',[90] although it has avoided asserting this tendency as evidence of an established rule of custom or even an emerging one. Furthermore, the examples it provides to evidence the trend do not demonstrate individuals' ability to seek reparation independently, but more the ability of victims to benefit individually from reparation programmes that States have on occasion decided to establish.[91]

[83] Adam Roberts, 'Transformative Military Occupation: Applying the Laws of War and Human Rights' (2006) 100 AJIL 580, 594.

[84] Considered in Chapter VI.

[85] See Jann Kleffner and Liesbeth Zegveld, 'Establishing an Individual Complaints Procedure for Violations of International Humanitarian Law' (2000) 3 YB Int'l Humanitarian L 384, who argue that a specialized procedure should be established.

[86] GC3 (n 38) Commentary to art 12. There is almost identical commentary for GC4 (n 38) art 29. See also GC3 (n 38), Commentary to art 131. See also Rudolf Dolzer, 'Settlement of War-Related Claims: Does International Law Recognize a Victim's Private Right of Action—Lessons after 1945' (2002) 20 Berkeley J Int'l L 296, 336.

[87] GC3 (n 38) Commentary to art 18(6); GC4 (n 38) art 97.

[88] GC3 (n 38) Commentary to art 68; GC4 (n 38) art 98.

[89] GC3 (n 38) art 68.

[90] See Protocol I (n 34) art 91, ICRC commentary to art 91, 1949 Conventions and Additional Protocols, and their Commentaries, www.icrc.org/applic/ihl/ihl.nsf/vwTreaties1949.xsp (last accessed 25 December 2016); ICRC, 'Customary International Law Database' (undated) rule 150 www.icrc.org/customary-ihl/eng/docs/home (last accessed 25 December 2016).

[91] ibid.

Some commentators have sought to imply procedural rights from the fact that victims are the ultimate beneficiaries of reparation.[92] The ARS commentaries to Article 33(2) recognize that reparation is owed not only to injured States but also to other injured parties, including individuals as the ultimate beneficiaries.[93] In the same sense, it has been suggested that the *travaux préparatoires* of Article 3 of the Hague Convention IV demonstrate that the victims of violations were the intended beneficiaries of compensation.[94] The ICJ has taken this approach by ordering States to afford reparation not only to injured States, but also to injured individuals.[95] The obligation to afford reparation to victims was also recognized by international commissions investigating wide scale human rights and international humanitarian law abuses.[96] Zegveld has implied an individual and directly enforceable procedural right under international law[97] from this understanding that victims are the ultimate beneficiaries of rights, arguing that individuals' rights *qua* beneficiaries necessarily imply procedural obligations. Others have considered that the progressive evolution of human rights has had an impact on the meaning of State responsibility and certain international humanitarian law provisions, including the recognition of procedural rights. For instance, Judge Jorda, then President of the ICTY, has implied from the universal recognition of the right to an effective remedy under human rights law, a similar right under international humanitarian law. He has written that: '[t]he integration of human rights into State responsibility has removed the procedural limitation that victims of war could seek compensation only through their own Governments, and has extended the right to compensation to both nationals and aliens'.[98] Similarly, Hoffmann has argued that: 'in view

[92] Liesbeth Zegveld, 'Remedies for Victims of Violations of International Humanitarian Law' (2003) 85(851) Int'l Rev Red Cross 497, 507; Michaela Frulli, 'When Are States Liable Towards Individuals for Serious Violations of Humanitarian Law? The *Markovic* Case' (2003) 1 J Int'l Crim J 406, 417. See also Yves Sandoz, 'Unlawful Damage in Armed Conflicts and Redress under International Humanitarian Law' (1982) 22(228) Int'l Rev Red Cross 131, 137; Frits Kalshoven, 'State Responsibility for Warlike Acts of the Armed Forces: From Article 3 of Hague Convention IV of 1907 to Article 91 of Additional Protocol I of 1977 and Beyond' (1991) 40 Int'l & Comp LQ 827, 835–36.

[93] See ARS (n 15) Commentary to art 33 para 3.

[94] Frulli (n 92) 417. See also Sandoz (n 92) 137; Kalshoven, 'State Responsibility for Warlike Acts of the Armed Forces' (n 92) 835–36.

[95] *Legal Consequences of the Construction of a Wall* (n 47) [152]–[153]; *Armed Activities on the Territory of the Congo (DRC v Uganda)* (Merits) [2005] ICJ Rep 168 [259]. See, however, *Application of the Convention on the Prevention and Punishment of the Crime of Genocide (Bosnia and Herzegovina v Serbia and Montenegro)* (Merits) [2007] ICJ Rep 43, in which the Court made no finding as to the ultimate beneficiaries, possibly as a result of its limited conclusion that in relation to the wrongful acts determined by the Court, satisfaction was a sufficient form of reparation.

[96] See eg International Commission of Inquiry on Darfur, 'Report of the International Commission of Inquiry on Darfur' (25 January 2005) www.un.org/News/dh/sudan/com_inq_darfur.pdf (last accessed 25 December 2016); UN Human Rights Council, 'Report of the United Nations Fact-Finding Mission on the Gaza Conflict' (25 September 2009) UN Doc A/HRC/12/48 para 1868; UN Human Rights Council, 'Report of the International Commission of Inquiry on Libya' (2 March 2012) UN Doc A/HRC/19/68 para 17.

[97] Zegveld, 'Remedies for Victims of Violations of International Humanitarian Law' (n 92) 503.

[98] UNSC, 'Letter Dated 12 October 2000 from the President of the ICTY Addressed to the Secretary-General' (3 November 2000) UN Doc S/2000/1063 Annex, 11 para 20. See also 'Report of the International Commission of Inquiry on Darfur' (n 96) para 593; Elke Schwager and Roland Bank, 'Is There a Substantive Right to Compensation for Individual Victims of Armed Conflicts against a State under International Law?' (2006) 49 German YB Int'l L 367, 378, 391.

of subsequent developments in international law ... it does seem possible to argue that this provision [Article 3 of Hague Convention IV], as interpreted in the light of current international law, now indeed provides for such a right'.[99]

It has also been argued that States' obligation to afford victims a procedural remedy when international humanitarian law obligations are breached can be implied from the wording of Article 1 common to the Geneva Conventions of 1949 and Protocol 1, in which States undertake to respect and ensure respect for compliance with international humanitarian law, which has been recognized to reflect a principle of customary international law, also applicable to non-international conflicts.[100] While the breadth of 'ensure respect' is contested,[101] even under a narrow reading it requires States to adopt all necessary measures within their jurisdiction (both positive and negative) to ensure respect for the Conventions. The *Basic Principles and Guidelines* specify that the obligation to respect, ensure respect for and implement human rights and international humanitarian law includes, inter alia, the duty to: 'provide those who claim to be victims of a human rights or humanitarian law violation with equal and effective access to justice, ... and provide effective remedies to victims, including reparation'.[102] However, this interpretation goes beyond the ICRC's general view as to the meaning of 'ensure respect'. The ICRC has not incorporated such an implied obligation into those model laws relating to treaties that do not expressly provide for such a right,[103] nor does it form part of

[99] Rainer Hoffmann, 'Reparation for Victims of War and Non-state Actors?' (2007) 32 S Afr YB Int'l L 291, 297. See also Paola Gaeta, 'Are Victims of Serious Violations of International Humanitarian Law Entitled to Compensation?' in Orna Ben-Naftali (ed), *International Humanitarian Law and International Human Rights Law* (OUP 2011) 310; Theo van Boven, 'Victims' Rights to a Remedy and Reparation: The New United Nations Principles and Guidelines' in Carla Ferstman, Mariana Goetz, and Alan Stephens (eds), *Reparations for Victims of Genocide, War Crimes and Crimes against Humanity: Systems in Place and Systems in the Making* (Martinus Nijhoff 2009) 19, 26.

[100] See *Military and Paramilitary Activities in and against Nicaragua (Nicaragua v USA)* (Merits) [1986] ICJ Rep 14 [220].

[101] The debate centres on whether the phrase obliges contracting States to take positive steps to ensure respect for the Convention outside of their jurisdiction. See Frits Kalshoven, 'The Undertaking to Respect and Ensure Respect in All Circumstances: From Tiny Seed to Ripening Fruit' (1999) 2 YB Int'l Humanitarian L 3; Carlo Focarelli, 'Common Article 1 of the 1949 Geneva Conventions: A Soap Bubble?' (2010) 21 EJIL 125.

[102] Basic Principles and Guidelines (n 1) 3. Note, however, the contrary view of the delegate from Germany: UN Commission on Human Rights, 'Summary Records of the 57th Meeting, 61st Session' (19 April 2005) UN Doc E/CN 4/2005/SR.57, 9 (Mr Koenigs, Germany). Germany expressed the same position before the ICJ in *Germany v Italy* (n 55). See *Reply of the Federal Republic of Germany* (5 October 2010) paras 40–42 www.icj-cij.org/docket/files/143/16650.pdf (last accessed 25 December 2016).

[103] ICRC, 'Legislation for Common Law States on the 1949 Geneva Conventions and their 1977 and 2005 Additional Protocols' (31 August 2008) www.icrc.org/eng/resources/documents/misc/geneva-conventions-protocols-model-law-310808.htm (last accessed 25 December 2016). Similarly, the ICRC has not read in to other conventions which do not have an express obligation to afford a domestic remedy. See ICRC, 'Legislation for Common Law States on the 2008 Convention on Cluster Munitions' (31 December 2008) www.icrc.org/eng/resources/documents/misc/cluster-munitions-model-law-010109.htm (last accessed 25 December 2016); ICRC, 'Model Legislation for Common Law States to Implement the 1997 Ottawa Convention on the Prohibition of the Use, Stockpiling, Production and Transfer of Anti-personnel Mines and on their Destruction' (August 2003) www.icrc.org/eng/assets/files/other/model_legislation_ottawa_convention.pdf (last accessed 25 December 2016); Christopher Harland and Angela Woodward, 'A Model Law: The Biological and

its understanding of the status of customary international law.[104] In contrast, the ICRC has understood international humanitarian law to provide for the right of access to remedial procedures only in relation to specific scenarios and persons. For instance, it has specified that such a right exists in relation to the missing or disappeared. In its commentary on its model law on the missing,[105] it specified that amnesties must not, inter alia, 'preclude the initiation of civil proceedings or have a legal effect on the victims' right to reparations'.[106] The right has also been recognized by the ICRC to a limited extent in relation to prisoners of war.[107]

Invariably, however, what is recognized is States' obligation to afford reparation and victims' right to *receive* it, not their independent right to *claim* it. This reflects the classical understanding that the right to receive reparation was capable of being given effect through diplomatic protection, however imperfect and discretionary that route may be. International humanitarian law claims lodged with domestic courts have usually failed on procedural grounds, because of the perceived incompatibility with peace settlements, sovereign immunity, act of State doctrine or the non-self-executing nature of the right to reparation under international humanitarian law; making reference to implied rights has not helped to overcome such blockages.[108] Those claims before domestic courts that have been successful are exceptional, and have mainly succeeded because of the existence of specific domestic legislation allowing for such claims. Nor does the administrative practice support such views. The instances in which claims procedures were established in response to international humanitarian law violations, such as pursuant to the Treaty of Versailles,[109] UN Compensation Commission,[110] Ethiopia Eritrea Claims Commission[111] or numerous property restitution commissions,[112] are not necessarily indicative of a pattern capable to give rise to an international rule regarding victims' procedural rights. The degree of claimant engagement within these bodies has also varied. In some processes, injured individuals have no procedural

Toxin Weapons Crimes Act: An Act to implement obligations under the 1972 Biological and Toxin Weapons Convention and the 1925 Geneva Protocol' (2005) 87(859) Int'l Rev Red Cross 573.

104 See CIL Database (n 90) rule 139 and associated commentary.

105 ICRC, 'Principles for Legislating the Situation of Persons Missing as a Result of Armed Conflict or Internal Violence: Measures to Prevent Persons from Going Missing and to Protect the Rights and Interests of the Missing and Their Families' (2009) www.icrc.org/eng/assets/files/other/model-law-missing-0209-eng-.pdf (last accessed 25 December 2016).

106 ibid Commentary to art 25.

107 See GC3 (n 38) art 14 and ICRC commentary; ICRC, 1949 Conventions and Additional Protocols, and their Commentaries, www.icrc.org/applic/ihl/ihl.nsf/vwTreaties1949.xsp (last accessed 25 December 2016).

108 See Chapter VI.

109 Treaty of Peace Between the Allied and Associated Powers and Germany (Treaty of Versailles) (adopted 28 June 1919, entered into force 10 January 1920) (1919) 225 CTS 188 art 297(e).

110 See UN Compensation Commission (UNCC), 'Arrangements for Ensuring Payments to the Compensation Fund' (2 August 1991) UN Doc S/AC.26/1991/1 para 14.

111 Agreement between the Government of the State of Eritrea and the Government of the Federal Democratic Republic of Ethiopia (adopted 12 December 2000, entered into force 12 December 2000) 2138 UNTS 94, 40 ILM 260 art 5.

112 IOM, 'Property Restitution and Compensation: Practices and Experiences of Claims Programmes' Ref no 978-92-9068-450-3 (IOM 2008).

involvement. In others, victims have been consulted usually in groups as to the harm suffered and their preferences for reparation. In yet other instances, more rigorous processes have been established in which injured individuals may make a claim to an administrative procedure established precisely for that purpose or a court. The recent practice of international or internationally supported criminal courts that allows victims to apply for reparation is an important procedural development, however restrictive.[113]

(4) *International humanitarian law obligations extrapolated to international organizations*

The inability for injured individuals to claim reparation for international humanitarian law abuses is a particularly serious limitation for international organization abuses. This is so, given the unlikelihood that the States of nationality will exercise their discretion in favour of diplomatic protection on behalf of their nationals, whether for reasons of lack of capacity or lack of interest,[114] or because of the failure to first exhaust the internal remedies of the international organizations.[115] It is feasible that troop contributing countries will take up troops' claims against an international organization through diplomatic protection. However, one can imagine the difficulties both practical and diplomatic for the authorities in failed or conflict-ridden States such as Somalia or Sudan to lodge a dispute with the AU or the UN for the treatment of their citizens.[116]

Thus, an individualized claims process may be the only means by which the result of reparation may be achieved. Does the obligation to afford the result of reparation necessarily require the offending organization to ensure that there are procedural modalities in place to give effect to it? To answer in the affirmative would be to ensure that the end result is capable of being achieved;[117] practical and effective for its ultimate beneficiaries.[118] It does not go so far as to imply a cause of

[113] Rome Statute of the International Criminal Court (adopted 17 July 1998, entered into force 7 July 2002) 2187 UNTS 90, UN Doc A/CONF.183/9 art 75; Internal Rules of the Extraordinary Chambers in the Courts of Cambodia (9 February 2009, amended 17 September 2010) Rule 23 *quinquies* (Civil Party Claim).

[114] A State's ability to exercise diplomatic protection against an international organization was not considered directly in *Reparation for Injuries*, although it was raised in Judge Krylov's dissenting opinion. See *Reparation for Injuries Suffered in the Service of the United Nations* (Advisory Opinion) [1949] ICJ Rep 174 219: 'the opposite—and possible—situation in which the said State may find it desirable and necessary to protect the agent against the acts of the Organization itself'.

[115] Whether there is an obligation to first exhaust domestic remedies in this way is disputed. See Chittharanjan Felix Amerasinghe, *Local Remedies in International Law* (2nd edn, CUP 2004) 371–72.

[116] This conundrum is raised by Tom Dannenbaum, 'Translating the Standard of Effective Control into a System of Effective Accountability: How Liability Should be Apportioned for Violations of Human Rights by Member State Troop Contingents Serving as United Nations Peacekeepers' (2010) 51 Harv Int'l LJ 113, 127–28.

[117] See Bassiouni 'International Recognition of Victims' Rights' (n 52) 217, who argues that States with deficient legal frameworks must establish procedures in order to ensure that they are capable of affording effective remedies, or else they would be implicitly violating their obligations.

[118] The ECtHR took this approach to recognize rights not explicitly provided in the Convention that are necessary by implication to give effect to stated rights. See eg *Golder v United Kingdom* App no 4451/70 (ECtHR, 21 February 1975); *Airey v Ireland* App no 6289/73 (ECtHR, 9 October 1979).

action—an unfettered right to claim reparation for international humanitarian law abuses in all instances, but the more limited proposition of implying an obligation on the wrongdoer to establish a procedural route where the one normally envisioned is not capable of practical application. Support for this approach is found in the practice of the UN Claims Commission, which allowed certain international agencies to submit claims on behalf of stateless persons, who unlike other individuals could not rely on their governments to put forward claims on their behalf.[119] Also, the ICJ recognized the ability for the UN to establish a Tribunal to deal with employment disputes,[120] based on the understanding that this was required to fulfil the UN's purposes.

IV.3.3 Forms of reparation

The reparation that is required will depend on the violation and the harm caused, and should not depend on the entity that caused the harm. The DARIO takes an almost identical approach to ARS in determining the required forms of reparation. Both texts describe reparation as needing to be 'full',[121] to wipe out all the consequences of the illegal act and re-establish the *status quo ante*. Both identify cessation, assurances and guarantees of non-repetition, and reparation, which may take the form of restitution, compensation, or satisfaction.[122] The approach of human rights treaties and their interpretive texts is similar, although with different emphases, mainly because the ILC understands cessation and assurances and guarantees of non-repetition to reflect inherent obligations resulting from wrongful acts, whereas human rights texts consider them as forms of reparation.[123] Similar to human rights texts, restitution is understood in most international humanitarian law treaties as the main obligation, failing which compensation or other forms of reparation should be afforded.[124] Yet, for many human rights and international humanitarian law violations, the concept of restoring the victim to the situation which pre-dated the violation (often a situation of marginalization) would not align

[119] UNCC, 'Guidelines Relating to Paragraph 19 of the Criteria for Expedited Processing of Urgent Claims' (23 October 1991) UN Doc S/AC.26/1991/5 paras 3–4, specifying that: 'A high number of individuals will most likely not be in a position to have their claims submitted by a Government . . . The international community, represented by the UNCC, bears the overall responsibility for protecting the interests of the above-mentioned individuals'.

[120] See *Effects of Awards of Compensation Made by the United Nations Administrative Tribunal* (Advisory Opinion) (n 72) 58.

[121] See ARS (n 15) arts 31(1), 34; DARIO (n 23) arts 31(1), 34. See also Basic Principles and Guidelines (n 1) 18, which describes 'full and effective' reparation for gross human rights and serious international humanitarian law violations.

[122] See ARS (n 15) arts 30(a), 30(b), 31; DARIO (n 23) arts 30(a), 30(b), and 31.

[123] For the approach in human rights texts see Basic Principles and Guidelines (n 1) 18.

[124] See eg GC1 (n 38) arts 34, 35; GC4 (n 38) art 55; Protocol for the Protection of Cultural Property in the Event of Armed Conflict (adopted 14 May 1954, entered into force 7 August 1956) 249 UNTS 358 art 3; UNCHR, 'Guiding Principles on Internal Displacement' Res 1998/50 (11 February 1998) UN Doc E/CN.4/1998/53/Add.2 (adopted without vote) principle 29(2); Convention for the Protection and Assistance of Internally Displaced Persons in Africa, AU (adopted 22 October 2009, entered into force 6 December 2012) art 12.

with other goals of guarantees of non-recurrence, which has led some to call for reparation with transformative potential.[125]

For human rights and international humanitarian law violations, restitution has been ordered most often to return property to individuals, restore identity, travel, or work permits,[126] vacate arrest warrants,[127] expunge criminal records,[128] release individuals from prison,[129] or issue stays of execution in death penalty cases.[130] International humanitarian law treaties emphasize the need to ensure that transferred detainees receive appropriate treatment, failing which the transferring authority must 'take effective measures to correct the situation or shall request the return of the prisoners of war'.[131] They also require the return of requisitioned property at the end of a war, failing which, compensation is required.[132] Similar obligations appear in the Convention for the Protection of Cultural Property and its first protocol.[133] With respect to refugees and displaced persons, the obligation to facilitate return and assist with the recovery of property, is also a primary objective, failing which compensation or other forms of reparation may be acceptable alternatives.[134]

Compensation is understood to cover any financially assessable damage both material and moral and loss of profit,[135] as well as the costs for legal or expert assistance, medicine, and psychological and social services.[136] Article 3 of the Hague Convention IV and Article 91 of Protocol I refer to compensation, 'if the case demands', which is understood to require compensation if restitution is impossible.[137] These provisions make clear that compensation is required for all breaches committed by persons forming part of armed forces (regardless of the context in which they were committed); a recently agreed declarative text has gone further, indicating that States are responsible for the acts of private contractors they employ

[125] An emphasis of the Nairobi Declaration (n 30).

[126] UN Commission on Human Rights 'Principles on Housing and Property Restitution' (n 36) para 2.1; *Institute for Human Rights and Development in Africa (on behalf of Esmaila Connateh and 13 Others) v Angola*, Comm no 292/04 (ACommHPR, 43rd Session, 7–22 May 2008) [85]–[86].

[127] *Arrest Warrant of 11 April 2000 (DRC v Belgium)* (Merits) [2002] ICJ Rep 3.

[128] *Cantoral Benavides v Peru* (Reparations and Costs) (n 64) para 78.

[129] *Loayza Tamayo v Peru* (Merits) Ser C no 33 (IACtHR, 17 September 1997) para 84.

[130] *Fermín Ramírez v Guatemala* (Merits, Reparations, Costs) Ser C no 126 (IACtHR, 20 June 2005) para 130(c).

[131] GC3 (n 38) art 12.

[132] See eg GC1 (n 38) arts 34, 35; GC4 (n 38) art 55.

[133] Convention for the Protection of Cultural Property in the Event of Armed Conflict (adopted 14 May 1954, entered into force 7 August 1956) 249 UNTS 240 art 18(b); Protocol for the Protection of Cultural Property in the Event of Armed Conflict (adopted 14 May 1954, entered into force 7 August 1956) 249 UNTS 358 art 3.

[134] UNCHR 'Guiding Principles on Internal Displacement' (n 124) principle 29(2); AU, Convention for the Protection and Assistance of Internally Displaced Persons in Africa (n 124) art 12.

[135] See ARS (n 15) art 36; CATHB (n 61) art 15(3).

[136] Basic Principles and Guidelines (n 1) 20; Model Law against Trafficking in Persons (5 August 2009) UN Office on Drugs and Crime, Doc No V.09-81990 (E) arts 28, 29; *Godínez Cruz v Honduras* (Interpretation of the Compensatory Damages) Ser C no 10 (IACtHR, 17 August 1990) para 27.

[137] See Protocol I (n 34) ICRC commentary to art 91, 1949 Conventions and Additional Protocols, and their Commentaries www.icrc.org/applic/ihl/ihl.nsf/vwTreaties1949.xsp (last accessed 25 December 2016).

during armed conflict.[138] While the Geneva Conventions do not contain similar wording, the obligation to compensate has been implied from the common provision[139] that parties cannot absolve themselves of liability they incur in respect of grave breaches.[140]

Rehabilitation includes measures for physical and psychological treatment[141] and scholarships and vocational training.[142] Certain specialist thematic international humanitarian law conventions emphasize the importance of targeted victim assistance and rehabilitation.[143]

Satisfaction, understood as an exceptional remedy in the ARS and DARIO,[144] has been frequently ordered in human rights jurisprudence to address injuries which involve breaches of trust, which acknowledgement and commemoration may help to remedy.[145] Criminal investigations have also been ordered as satisfaction.[146] Cessation, as a form of satisfaction, has been emphasized as a remedy for continuing violations such as disappearances, wherein full disclosure of the truth and the need to locate and identify remains is understood as central.[147]

Guarantees of non-repetition have included strengthening monitoring mechanisms and other procedural safeguards, changing policies or legislation, vetting public officials, and setting up commissions of inquiry.[148]

The standard of reparations first articulated by the PCIJ and which has thereafter framed the quantum and quality of inter-State claims is 'full', as needing to wipe out all the consequences of the illegal act and re-establish the *status quo ante*.[149] It is described in the ARS and DARIO in these same terms.[150] Human rights treaties tend to use descriptors such as fair, adequate, or effective, used either singly or grouped together,[151] appropriate,[152] proportionate to the

[138] Montreux Document on pertinent international legal obligations and good practices for States related to operations of private military and security companies during armed conflict (6 October 2008) UN Doc A/63/467–S/2008/636 para 8.

[139] GC1 (n 38) art 51; GC2 (n 38) art 52; GC3 (n 38) art 131; GC4 (n 38) art 148.

[140] GC1 (n 38) Commentary to art 51; GC4 (n 38) Commentary to art 29.

[141] *Plan de Sánchez Massacre v Guatemala* (Reparations) Ser C no 116 (IACtHR, 19 November 2004) paras 106–108.

[142] *Cantoral Benavides v Peru* (Reparations and Costs) (n 64) para 99(6); *Juvenile Reeducation Institute v Paraguay* (Preliminary Objections, Merits, Reparations and Costs) Ser C no 112 (IACtHR, 2 September 2004) para 340(13).

[143] See Convention on Cluster Munitions (adopted 30 May 2008, entered into force 1 August 2010) 2688 UNTS 39 art 3.

[144] Shelton, 'Righting Wrongs' (n 10) 838; ARS (n 15) Commentary to art 37 para 1.

[145] *Cantoral Benavides v Peru* (Reparations and Costs) (n 64) para 81; *Mack-Chang v Guatemala* (Merits, Reparations and Costs) Ser C no 101 (IACtHR, 25 November 2003) paras 8, 9, 11, and 12.

[146] See Bassiouni, 'International Recognition of Victims' Rights' (n 52) 263–64.

[147] *Neira-Alegría v Peru* (Reparations and Costs) Ser C no 29 (IACtHR, 19 September 1996) para 69.

[148] *Connateh v Angola* (n 126) para 87.

[149] *Chorzów Factory* (Merits) (n 16); *Legal Consequences of the Construction of a Wall* (n 47) [152].

[150] See ARS (n 15) arts 31, 34 and commentaries thereto; DARIO (n 23) arts 31(1), 34. See also Basic Principles and Guidelines (n 1) 18, which describes 'full and effective' reparation.

[151] Protocol on the Statute of the African Court of Justice and Human Rights, AU (adopted 1 July 2008, not yet in force) art 45; Victims' Declaration (n 30); ACHR (n 28) art 63(1); *Godínez Cruz v Honduras* (n 136) para 27; CERD (n 50) art 6; UNCAT (n 28) art 14; CPPED (n 28) art 24(4); CESCR, 'General Comment 9' (n 29) para 9; Basic Principles and Guidelines (n 1) 15.

[152] CRC, General Comment 5 (n 62) para 24.

harm,[153] and equitable.[154] These are not necessarily lesser standards; they help to clarify what is required, particularly when re-establishing the *status quo ante* is impossible and it is impractical to quantify the harm precisely.[155] There is therefore some consistency in what is understood to be required. Nonetheless, the practice of States is varied and inconsistent. More simplified approaches tend to be taken when there is a large number of injured individuals who would be entitled to significant reparation that would be overwhelming for a court to adjudicate claim by claim, and/or when the nature of the violations is such that victims would not have the requisite proof to satisfy a court of their injuries using typical standards of proof.[156] In other cases, there is a failure to resort to full reparation or a failure to enforce international orders to this effect, simply because of the absence of political will.

The ICRC has expressed the view that the State obligation to afford reparation for international humanitarian law abuses is a rule of custom, applicable in both international and non-international armed conflicts.[157] The same view was expressed in the final report of the International Commission of Inquiry on Darfur.[158] This is consistent with the approach taken by the ILC, which underscores that the reparations obligation attaches to all internationally wrongful acts, without distinguishing between international or non-international armed conflicts.[159] However, the status of the rule is controversial, owing to the limited and variable practice, typically contingent on States' interests and settlement prerogatives.

The rule has been particularly controversial for non-international conflicts, given that no compensatory obligation was included in Protocol II.[160] In its study on customary international law, the ICRC refers to 'an increasing amount of State practice from all parts of the world';[161] however, the references from practice do not appear

153 *Loayza Tamayo v Peru* (Reparations and Costs) Ser C No 42 (IACtHR, 27 November 1998) para 86; *AT v Hungary* (n 62) para 9.6(II)(vi); Basic Principles and Guidelines (n 1) 15, 18.

154 *Velásquez Rodríguez* (Compensatory Damages) Ser C no 4 (IACtHR, 21 July 1989) para 27, in which the IACtHR applied principles of equity. See also *Djot Bayi v Nigeria*, ECW/CCJ/JUD/01/09 (ECOWAS CCJ, 28 January 2009) paras 45–46.

155 *Aloeboetoe v Suriname* (Reparations and Costs) [1993] Ser C no 15 (IACtHR, 10 September 1993) para 49.

156 See generally Howard M Holtzmann and Edda Kristjánsdóttir (eds), *International Mass Claims Processes: Legal and Practical Perspectives* (OUP 2007); Michael Bazyler and Roger Alford (eds), *Holocaust Restitution: Perspectives on the Litigation and its Legacy* (NYU Press 2006); Priscilla Hayner, *Unspeakable Truths: Transitional Justice and the Challenge of Truth Commissions* (2nd edn, Routledge 2010); Marc Henzelin, Veijo Heiskanen, and Guénaël Mettraux, 'Reparations to Victims before the International Criminal Court: Lessons From International Mass Claims Processes' (2006) 17 Crim L Forum 317.

157 CIL Database (n 90) rule 150.

158 'Report of the International Commission of Inquiry on Darfur' (n 96) paras 76, 592, and 593. Note, however, that the recommended compensation commission was never established. For a contrary view on the law see Christian Tomuschat, 'Darfur—Compensation for the Victims' (2005) 3 J Int'l Crim J 579.

159 See ARS (n 15) art 31.

160 Protocol Additional to the Geneva Conventions of 12 August 1949, and relating to the Protection of Victims of Non-International Armed Conflicts (adopted 8 June 1977, entered into force 7 December 1978) 1125 UNTS 609.

161 See ICRC, CIL Database (n 90) rule 150.

to establish a clear pattern for non-international armed conflicts. Yet, a failure to recognize the reparations obligation in internal armed conflict may create discrepancies with other applicable law, given the significant if not complete overlap with non-derogable human rights obligations operating in such contexts.

With respect to international armed conflicts, compensation is typically dealt with at the inter-State level in multilateral or bilateral peace treaties or settlement agreements with token lump-sum amounts that have little or no correlation with the precise harm caused to individual victims, in spite of the general international law standard requiring *restitutio ad integrum*.[162] As Kalshoven has noted, 'the agreements usually lay an obligation on the vanquished State to pay a more or less random amount, determined more by its perceived financial capabilities than by any serious attempt to assess the damage caused by the unlawful acts of either party's armed forces; and the victor State may or may not distribute (part of) the money to individual claimants'.[163] The emphasis is on *cy-près* remedies, lump-sum payments to masses of individuals calculated along the line of specific beneficiary groups, symbolic and communitarian (as opposed to individual) forms of reparation determined by judicial, quasi-judicial, or non-judicial mechanisms. 'Full' reparation is not afforded because it is unrealistic—the compensable amount would be too high, there would be too many victims to repair, or because it is politically undesirable in the context of the end of the conflict.[164] At times, treaties deliberately exclude or settle claims.[165] Similarly, those international criminal courts and tribunals that allow reparation claims have not privileged the concept of 'full' reparation; quite the opposite, judgments to date have emphasized mainly that, given the specific statutory frameworks, and given the numbers of potential beneficiaries, a 'collective' or symbolic approach would be taken.[166]

IV.3.4 The impact of patchy enforcement

Thus, both for human rights and international humanitarian law, what the law says is required is disconnected from what happens in practice. A question arises as to how this state of exception impacts on the overall clarity of the rules pertaining to remedies and reparation for both human rights and international humanitarian law. It has been argued that the disconnect demonstrates the tenuousness or even absence of a right to reparation,[167] or the narrower point that it reveals the absence of a right to 'full' reparation.[168] Tomuschat, for example, has argued

[162] See ARS (n 15); DARIO (n 23).

[163] See Kalshoven, 'State Responsibility for Warlike Acts of the Armed Forces' (n 92) 836.

[164] ICRC, 'Strengthening Legal Protection for Victims of Armed Conflicts' (Draft Resolution and Report, 31st International Conference of the Red Cross and Red Crescent, Doc No 31IC/11/5.1.1, 28 November–1 December 2011) 27.

[165] Considered in Dolzer (n 86).

[166] *Prosecutor v Lubanga* (Appeal on Reparations) ICC-01/04-01/06-3129 (ICC, 3 March 2015); *Co-Prosecutors v Kaing Guek Eav alias Duch* (Appeal Judgment) 001/18-07-2007-ECCC/SC (ECCC, 2 February 2012) paras 630–717. Note, however, that the practice is evolving. In *Prosecutor v Katanga* (Order on Reparations) ICC-01/04-01/07-3728 (ICC, 24 March 2017) the Court ordered both individual and collective forms of reparation.

[167] Christian Tomuschat, 'Reparation for Victims of Grave Human Rights Violations' (n 41) 177–80.

[168] See *Germany v Italy* (n 55) [94].

that: '[w]henever chaos and anarchy set in, the magnitude of the sums required for effective reparation makes it imperative not only on economic, but also on legal grounds, to call into question the seemingly invincible proposition that reparation must wipe out all of the negative consequences of an injurious act'.[169] However, it can and has been argued that the exigencies of particular situations do not lower the overall standards; the overarching rules remain even if for practical reasons, the results are abridged.[170]

The DARIO takes this approach in Article 31, the commentary of which specifies that: 'It may be difficult for an international organization to have all the necessary means for making the required reparation. This fact is linked to the inadequacy of the financial resources that are generally available to international organizations for meeting this type of expense. However, that inadequacy cannot exempt a responsible organization from the legal consequences resulting from its responsibility under international law'.[171]As Judge Yusuf recognizes in his dissenting opinion in *Germany v Italy*: 'Such arrangements appear to have been resorted to for policy or practical reasons aimed at avoiding the prospect of innumerable private suits, or a delay in the conclusion of peace treaties and the resumption of normal relations between formerly belligerent States';[172] they do not imply an absence of individual rights.[173]

The Basic Principles and Guidelines also take this approach, by recognizing the importance for States to 'endeavour to develop procedures to allow groups of victims to present claims for reparation and to receive reparation', 'in addition to individual access to justice'.[174] The challenges do not give licence to a violating State to opt out of obligations to repair simply because to do so would be difficult, messy, politically sensitive or time-consuming. Just as amnesties were not capable of being justified for some of the worst crimes under international law, regardless of the potential political merits for recognizing them, one cannot absolve a State of its obligation to afford remedies and reparation, simply because it would not be expedient or in the State's perceived interest to so provide. The opposing view would lead to the counter-intuitive conclusion that the more widespread the violation, the less rights victims are entitled to.[175]

The ILC recognizes the challenges posed by mass victimization in the ARS and DARIO texts. While an earlier version of the ARS exempted debtors from the need to afford full reparation when to do so would 'result in depriving the population of a State of its own means of subsistence',[176] the final versions of both texts omit

169 Christian Tomuschat, 'Individual Reparation Claims in Instances of Grave Human Rights Violations: The Position under General International Law' in Randelzhofer and Tomuschat (n 3) 11. See *Germany v Italy* (n 55) [94].

170 See Schwager and Bank (n 98) 393; DARIO (n 23) Commentary to art 31 para 4.

171 DARIO (n 23) Commentary to art 31 para 4.

172 *Germany v Italy* (n 55) Judge Yusuf Dissenting Opinion [16].

173 ibid [19]. See also Basic Principles and Guidelines (n 1) 13.

174 Basic Principles and Guidelines (n 1) 13.

175 Joe Verhoeven, 'Comments in Discussion (Part 1)' in Randelzhofer and Tomuschat (n 3) 55.

176 Article 42(3) of a former version of the ARS (n 15) (not retained). ILC, 'Report of the International Law Commission on the Work of its 48th Session' (6 May–26 July 1996) UN Doc A/51/10 para 66.

this provision and instead introduce elements of equity and reasonableness. This is most evident with the reference to restitution, which is only required if it 'does not involve a burden out of all proportion to the benefit deriving from restitution instead of compensation'.[177] The commentaries make clear that the provision applies 'only where there is a grave disproportionality between the burden which restitution would impose . . . and the benefit which would be gained, either by the injured State or by any victim of the breach'.[178] Similarly, satisfaction 'shall not be out of proportion to the injury and may not take a form humiliating to the responsible international organization'.[179]

However, the texts never stray from the principle of 'full' reparation. Flexibility is introduced in how it may be achieved, and punitive or exemplary damages are not entertained;[180] however, there is no licence to restrict the quantum or quality of reparation that is owed should the amount prove difficult on the wrongdoer. Certainly, parties to a dispute may come to their own arrangements, although as will be canvassed in Chapter V, a key issue here is who may appropriately make such accommodations. DARIO makes clear that the 'rules of the organization' are capable of impacting the relations between the organization and its Member States and organizations,[181] and indeed that such 'rules' may 'modify the rules on the forms of reparation that a responsible organization may have to make towards its members'.[182] However, is the international organization capable of agreeing with its Member States rules modifying its obligations on reparation, when injured individuals (as opposed to Member States) are the ultimate beneficiaries? As will be explained in Chapter V, I argue that international organizations cannot agree modifications with Member States to the detriment of third parties.

Some might argue that extremely scarce international organizations funding necessarily requires them to skirt reparation obligations. However, as the International Law Association has noted, it is not clear whether necessity may be invoked to shield a debtor from responsibility under the ARS,[183] and the same would apply to DARIO. Article 25 of both texts focuses on the use of necessity to preclude wrongfulness, not to preclude reparation in response to behaviour determined to be internationally wrongful. To the extent that the failure to afford reparation constitutes its own separate internationally wrongful act, the principle of necessity arguably comes into play.[184] The ARS commentaries note that necessity may enable a State 'for the time being, not to perform some other international obligation',[185] and thus it would not be a licence to avoid reparation, at most to delay its implementation. However, in DARIO, the commentaries maintain that as a matter of policy, necessity should not be capable of being invoked by international organizations as widely as by States,[186] and nevertheless, the question of compensation is not

177 DARIO (n 23) art 35(b); the same provision appears in ARS (n 15) art 35(b).
178 ARS (n 15) Commentary to art 35 para 11.
179 DARIO (n 23) art 37(3).
180 ARS (n 15) Commentary to art 36 para 4.
181 DARIO (n 23) art 32(2).
182 ibid Commentary to art 32 para 3.
183 ILA, 'Reparation for Victims of Armed Conflict (Substantive Issues)' (n 39) 20–21.
184 See ARS (n 15) Commentary to art 25 para 7.
185 ibid para 1.
186 DARIO (n 23) Commentary to art 25 para 4.

extinguished by the preclusion of wrongfulness; even in such circumstances the State may be obliged to afford 'full' reparation.[187]

IV.4 Conclusions

Despite the ILC's statement that responsible international organizations must afford reparation for the injuries caused, this Chapter demonstrates the difficulty to extrapolate from this statement clear rules regarding reparation to injured individuals in the case of human rights and international humanitarian law breaches. This difficulty does not evidence an absence of rules or a legal vacuum. It simply evidences a haziness or lack of clarity with respect to those rules, as they have nowhere been cohesively spelled out, an unfortunate omission of the ILC. The very limited institutional practice on reparations for such violations is both a result of this lack of clarity as well as a factor contributing to the continued ambiguity. There is virtually no practice because the law is imprecise. There is a self-serving circularity in the comfort of this imprecision. The imprecision serves as a shield for organizations to hide behind, enabling them to maintain a position that they are not required to do more to facilitate access to remedial processes and adequate reparation, or that whatever special measures they put in place are superior to the absent obligations they have under general international law. Structures put in place by international organizations do not need to be measured against external standards because the latter are imprecise. The lack of access engendered by this shield of imprecision ensures that there are few examples to give evidence to any rule.

With those rather large caveats, international organizations are obligated to ensure that there are impartial and effective procedures in place to enable injured individuals to obtain reparation. This obligation does not depend for its existence on an enforcement regime, it has an independent existence. In relation to human rights law, this obligation derives from the State obligation to afford effective domestic remedies. In international humanitarian law, it derives from the need to make practical and effective the result of reparation, given the inability to rely on the traditional route of diplomatic protection. The failure by international organizations to establish effective procedural routes constitutes a further internationally wrongful act for which they incur responsibility. There is thus an implied obligation on international organizations to resolve any procedural gaps impeding access to procedures that may lead to reparation. As obligations are meant to be practical and effective, the absence of an effective enforcement structure cannot be an acceptable or static state of affairs; the enforcement structure must certainly catch up with the obligation.

International organizations are obligated to afford injured individuals with full reparation which corresponds to the harm suffered. What 'full' reparation entails and what forms of reparation will be appropriate will depend on the violation and

[187] ARS (n 15) art 27(b).

the harm caused. With respect to international humanitarian law, reparation is most clearly identified as required with respect to violations amounting to grave breaches; however, it is not limited to this. Regard must be had to the variety of discrete provisions setting out obligations to restitute, compensate, or rehabilitate; the particular circumstances and the overarching principle set out in DARIO that an internationally wrongful act automatically entails an obligation to afford reparation.

As is evident from the practice, there will be instances when full reparation may not be possible, given the nature of the violation, the large number of presumed victims or for other reasons. The rule, however, is one of full reparation, and there is thus no open licence to diverge from that general principle under the colour of any law. Necessity has not been recognized as a rationale for precluding full reparation. Nonetheless, there is a discord between the rigidity of the law and the practice. There is an absence of rules regarding 'second-best' remedies and reparation, particularly, how to assess when a State or other wrongdoer is justified even on a temporary basis in affording anything other than 'full' reparation, and what standards should be employed to assess such 'second-best' measures. Nonetheless, there are a range of approaches taken by administrative bodies as to how to realize adequate and effective reparation that corresponds to the greatest possible extent to the harm. Language such as 'appropriate', 'effective', 'capable of responding to the harm', suggest that 'second-best' measures must seek to approximate, to the greatest possible extent 'full' reparation.

PART II

THE IMPLEMENTATION OF THE REGIME OF RESPONSIBILITY

V

Internal Adjudication by International Organizations

V.1 Introduction

This chapter considers the nature, remit, and functioning of review mechanisms established by international organizations to address grievances concerning their conduct. Do these mechanisms serve as adequate modes of redress for injured individuals and can they result in effective reparation? The practice is diverse, although the mechanisms that address claims from individuals not connected to the organization remain few.

A review of the most relevant mechanisms reveals different understandings of, and degrees of adherence to, external rules and principles. For the most part, there has been little regard to the procedural and substantive rights of affected individuals explored in Chapter IV. But if reparation is a right belonging to victims or even an obligation owed to them as the ultimate beneficiaries, international organizations cannot restrict their procedures and claimants' entitlements in the pursuit of their own understanding of rules and obligations. However, the incentives to recognize these rights are low; the power relations between claimants and organizations are highly asymmetric. The victims have limited sway on organizational procedures and limited influence on their governments to pursue claims on their behalf.

V.2 The Rationale for Creating Internal Adjudicative Mechanisms

In municipal law, administrative bodies are designed to afford accountability for administrative conduct, by reviewing the decisions, rules, and practices of administrative actors. These bodies promote transparency and help ensure that officials act within their mandates with due regard to the fiduciary responsibilities created by those mandates. There is no exact equivalent under international law, yet some scholars have begun to map what they consider as the developing field of global administrative law.[1]

[1] Benedict Kingsbury, Nico Krisch, and Richard Stewart, 'The Emergence of Global Administrative Law' (2005) 68 Law and Contemporary Problems 15; Daniel Esty, 'Good Governance at the Supranational Scale: Globalizing Administrative Law' (2006) 115 Yale LJ 1490.

International organizations establish internal adjudicative mechanisms for some of the same reasons as municipal ones: to promote fairness, justice, and transparency, to provide oversight and address disputes which if not resolved could impact on the smooth running of the organization.

In municipal law, other rationales for administrative bodies are to provide flexible, more accessible, and less costly avenues for claimants, and to give the opportunity to the government department to rectify its own mistakes before external processes come into play. These rationales translate less well to the international organization because there are usually no external court processes for individuals to approach given operable immunities and problems of standing. Thus, international organizations create internal mechanisms because of the unavailability of more formal structures, rather than because the latter are cumbersome or ineffective. Indeed, internal adjudicative mechanisms can justify the immunities that many international organizations benefit from, which, aside from limited exceptions,[2] prevent claims from being resolved by domestic courts. There are usually no alternative forums to resolve disputes when internal remedies are exhausted or unavailable, ineffective, or unreasonably delayed.

V.3 International Organizations' Understanding of their Obligations—a *Lex Specialis*?

Chapter IV considered the content of international organizations' obligations to afford remedies and reparation for breaches attributable to the organizations. Those obligations form the basis for the assessment of the adequacy of organizations' internal adjudicative mechanisms. This is so because, unlike the equivalent under municipal law, organizations' internal processes are not subject to oversight by municipal courts. The use of abridged procedures to obtain paltry reparation that does not meet applicable standards might be justifiable if access to a court or other higher decision-making body is not prevented. When there is no such access, the abridged procedures and awarded reparation must satisfy the gamut of applicable standards; these must be fair, effective, and capable of leading to an adequate result.[3]

International organizations' own understanding of their obligations is one lens through which their practice can be understood. However, it is alone incapable of determining the law, given the limited practice and almost non-existent independent jurisprudence. Decisions which consider international organization obligations are mainly taken by bodies established and run by the organizations themselves. The few arm's-length bodies that have been established invariably have

[2] See Chapter VI.

[3] Bardo Fassbender, 'Targeted Sanctions Imposed by the UN Security Council and Due Process Rights: A Study Commissioned by the UN Office of Legal Affairs and Follow-up Action by the United Nations' (2006) 3 Int'l Org LR 437 paras 6.6, 10, and 12.10.

only recommendatory powers, and thus the decision whether to comply with the recommendations rests with the international organization.

The standards of fullness, adequacy, and effectiveness have not framed international organization approaches to reparations, despite the Draft Articles on the Responsibility of International Organizations (DARIO) requirement of 'full' reparation for internationally wrongful acts.[4] International organizations tend to be guided by internal rules and procedures only. As von Bernstorff argues, 'such mechanisms ... do not explicitly allow for the application of general international law. ...'.[5] The comments of the UN Office of Legal Affairs (OLA) on DARIO reveal its view that both the process and the result of claims against the organization form part of its *lex specialis* and, as such, the special rules it has created should exempt it from having to follow any general ones.[6] The range of limitations it has introduced 'prevails over the duty to provide full reparation under draft article 33 [of DARIO]'.[7] The International Monetary Fund has taken a similar approach.[8]

However, it is questionable whether UN practice has crystallized sufficiently to ground a *lex specialis* rule.[9] The DARIO does not address this. Article 32(1) emphasizes that '[t]he responsible international organization may not rely on its rules as justification for failure to comply with its obligations under this Part',[10] but Article 32(2) indicates that it is 'without prejudice to the applicability of the rules of an international organization to the relations between the organization and its member States and organizations'. The Commentary notes the irrelevance of internal law to such determinations,[11] but distinguishes this general rule from the particular relationship between an organization and its members, noting, inter alia, that: 'Rules of the organization could ... for instance, modify the rules on the forms of reparation that a responsible organization may have to make towards its members'.[12]

[4] ILC, Draft Articles on the Responsibility of International Organizations, 'Report of the International Law Commission on the Work of its 63rd Session' (26 April–3 June and 4 July–12 August 2011) UN Doc A/66/10 (DARIO) art 31(1). However, DARIO does not spell out obligations owed to injured individuals.

[5] Jochen von Bernstorff, 'Procedures of Decision-Making and the Role of Law in International Organizations' (2008) German LJ 1939, 1959.

[6] ILC, 'Comments and Observations Received from International Organizations' UN Doc A/CN.4/637/Add.1 (17 February 2011) para 16(8). See also paras 17(2), 20(3), and 25(2).

[7] ibid comments to draft art 63 para 2.

[8] ibid 9 para 2. See also its earlier statement in ILC, 'Responsibility of International Organizations: Comments and Observations Received from Governments and International Organizations, Report of the International Law Commission on the Work of its 57th Session' (2 May–3 June and 11 July–5 August 2005) UN Doc A/CN.4/556: 'the rules of an organization are lex specialis as between the organization and its members and agents and among its members. It is therefore not possible to suggest ... that in some cases (other than involving obligations of a peremptory nature) general international obligations might prevail over the rules of an organization. Such a suggestion ignores the international agreements between the organization's members regarding the exclusive application of the laws governing their relations and it suggests that lex generalis prevails over lex specialis'.

[9] See DARIO (n 4) arts 64, 32.

[10] ibid, referring to Pt 3.

[11] ibid paras 1–2 of the Commentary to art 32.

[12] ibid para 3. The statement is criticized in Christiane Ahlborn, 'The Rules of International Organizations and the Law of International Responsibility', Amsterdam Center for International Law Research Paper, 2011-03, SHARES Series (26 April 2011) 46.

While it might be possible for the organization and its members to agree rules to govern specific scenarios, and they have done so regularly, is it legitimate to develop abridged frameworks when the responsible organization owes reparation not to its members, but to injured individuals? Under classical international law, the rights of injured individuals are subsumed by their State of nationality but arguably this is an inadequate cover in the present circumstances. The injured individuals have not voluntarily agreed to the special regime.[13] Aspects of human rights and international humanitarian law are not subject to derogation even in a state of emergency, including as set out in Chapter IV, the obligation to afford a procedural remedy to victims of human rights breaches and the obligation to afford adequate and effective reparation in the case of both human rights and international humanitarian law violations.[14] As such, arguably neither international organizations nor States can derogate from such principles by way of any special rules.[15]

In his report on fragmentation, Koskenniemi considers the application of *lex specialis* and notes that: '[i]n regard to conflicts between human rights norms, for instance, the one that is more favourable to the protected interest is usually held overriding. At least derogation to the detriment of the beneficiaries would seem precluded'.[16] Elsewhere he lists among several 'concerns that may seem pertinent', 'prohibition to deviate from law benefiting third parties, including individuals or non-State entities'.[17] Arguably applying the UN's *lex specialis* would frustrate the purpose of the general law, which is to ensure that victims of violations receive adequate and effective reparation. Injured individuals would be affected by the operation of the *lex specialis*[18] and failure of the special regime could be inferred as a result of it having 'no reasonable prospect of appropriately addressing the objectives for which [it was] enacted'.[19]

As has been explained, opinions on the nature and extent of the obligations owed by international organizations to individuals will differ; the law is nowhere precisely spelt out. As will be shown, differing views about the law disadvantages individuals vis-à-vis the organization. Individuals' lack of standing before independent judicial or quasi-judicial bodies before which they can assert their view of the law means that the international organization's view will be incapable of challenge—it will simply trump.[20]

[13] ILC, 'Fragmentation of International Law: Difficulties Arising from the Diversification and Expansion of International Law, Report of the Study Group of the International Law Commission, Finalized by Martti Koskenniemi', Report of the International Law Commission on the Work of its 58th Session (1 May–9 June and 3 July–11 August 2006) UN Doc A/CN.4/L.682 para 61.

[14] UN HRC, 'General Comment 29' Derogations during a State of Emergency (31 August 2001) UN Doc CCPR/C/21/Rev.1/Add.11 para 14.

[15] ILC, Articles on the Responsibility of States for Internationally Wrongful Acts, 'Report of the International Law Commission on the Work of its 53rd Session' (23 April–1 June and 2 July–10 August 2001) UN Doc A/CN.4/SER.A/2001/Add.1 (ARS) Official Commentary arts 40, 41, and 48.

[16] See Koskenniemi, A/CN.4/L.682 (n 13) para 108.

[17] ibid para 109.

[18] ILC, 'Conclusions of the Work of the Study Group on the Fragmentation of International Law: Difficulties Arising from the Diversification and Expansion of International Law', Report of the International Law Commission on the Work of its 58th Session (1 May–9 June and 3 July–11 August 2006) UN Doc A/61/10 paras 251(8)–(10).

[19] ibid para 251(16).

[20] See Koskenniemi (n 13) para 52.

V.4 An Assessment of Internal Mechanisms

There are numerous examples of internal adjudicative practice; however, the mechanisms remain exceptional and they have limited competence.[21]

On one end of the spectrum, audit, evaluation, and inquiry mechanisms assess whether international organizations comply with institutional mandates, and that the work produced appropriate results in the most cost-effective manner. Usually, audits are performed at periodic intervals and/or at the end of a phase of work. Sometimes ad hoc investigations are undertaken in response to perceived problems or failings. While these mechanisms do not afford remedies to individuals, they can initiate reflection and serve as the catalyst for more targeted measures. Somewhat middle ground mechanisms include ombudsperson-like bodies that review complaints and provide informal dispute-resolution services for categories of persons usually, although not always, connected to the organization.[22] They can also provide upward feedback and make recommendations to rectify institutional failings, which may include reparation. There are then recommendatory and/or fact-finding bodies which, similar to Ombudsperson institutions, can receive individual complaints; however, they usually have more detailed procedures. Examples include the Kosovo Human Rights Advisory Panel (HRAP) which examined complaints of alleged human rights violations committed by or attributable to the UN Interim Administration Mission in Kosovo (UNMIK)[23] and the World Bank Inspection Panel.[24] In contrast, certain third party claims arising in the context of UN peace support operations are adjudicated through abridged administrative procedures; local claims review boards have been established by the UN for that purpose.[25] As a further category, certain organizations—mainly regional or sub-regional organizations—have taken a more judicial approach.[26]

[21] Armin von Bogdandy and Mateja Steinbrück Platise, 'ARIO and Human Rights Protection: Leaving the Individual in the Cold' (2012) 9 IO LR 67, 74.

[22] See eg UN Secretariat, 'Office of the Ombudsman—Appointment and Terms of Reference of the Ombudsman' (15 October 2002) UN Doc ST/SGB/2002/12; UNMIK Regulations 2000/38 (30 June 2000) 2003/8 (15 April 2003), 2006/6 (16 February 2006), 2007/15 (19 March 2007); *Law No.03/L–195 on the Ombudsperson (Kosovo)*. An Ombudsperson with a mandate relating to the listing and delisting procedures of the Al Qaida sanctions committee was created by UNSC Res 1904/2009 (17 December 2009) and extended by Res 1989 (17 June 2011) and Res 2083 (17 December 2012).

[23] UNMIK, 'Regulation 2007/3 amending Regulation 2006/12 on the Establishment of the Human Rights Advisory Panel' (12 January 2007).

[24] International Bank for Reconstruction and Development, International Development Association, 'The World Bank Inspection Panel' (22 September 1993) Res IBRD 93-10 and Res IDA 93-6.

[25] UNGA, 'Financing of the United Nations Protection Force, the United Nations Confidence Restoration Operation in Croatia, the United Nations Preventive Deployment Force and the United Nations Peace Forces headquarters' (20 September 1996) UN Doc A/51/389.

[26] See Chapter VII.

V.4.1 Employment disputes

Most internal mechanisms have been established to adjudicate employment disputes. The International Court of Justice (ICJ) recognized that such mechanisms are 'essential to ensure the efficient working of the Secretariat, and to give effect to the paramount consideration of securing the highest standards of efficiency, competence and integrity'[27] and vital to bring consistency with the wider principles of justice espoused by the Charter.[28]

In 1927, the statute for the League of Nations Administrative Tribunal was adopted with competence to adjudicate claims based on service contracts or staff regulations made by officials or ex-officials of the League of Nations Secretariat or the International Labor Office (ILO). This was the precursor to the ILO Administrative Tribunal, which is open to officials, former officials and their heirs of the ILO, or other organizations which have recognized the jurisdiction of the Tribunal for employment matters.[29] Similarly, UN employees can resort to the UN Dispute Tribunal, with appeals to the UN Appeals Tribunal.[30] Other international organizations have instituted similar processes. Illustrative examples include the administrative tribunals of the Council of Europe;[31] European Union;[32] Organization of American States;[33] World Bank;[34] Asian Development Bank[35] and African Development Bank.[36] Judges tend to be independent to the organizations.

These models apply only to employees and deal only with employment matters. As such, they are unavailable to other individuals with human rights or international humanitarian law grievances against the organizations, although the tribunals have considered cases concerning discrimination and the dismissal or non-renewal of contracts of whistle blowers for making public claims of international organization

[27] *Effects of Awards of Compensation Made by the United Nations Administrative Tribunal* (Advisory Opinion) [1954] ICJ Rep 47, 57.

[28] ibid. This rationale is maintained in UN employment judgments. See eg *Buendia v UNSG* UNDT/2011/008 (UN Dispute Tribunal, 12 January 2011) para 4.

[29] Statute of the Administrative Tribunal of the International Labour Organization (adopted and entered into force 9 October 1946, as amended) art 6(a), (b).

[30] UNGA, 'Administration of Justice at the United Nations' Res 62/228 (6 February 2008) and 63/253 (17 March 2009); UNGA, 'Administration of Justice at the United Nations: Report of the Secretary-General' (1 August 2014) UN Doc A/69/227; UNGA, 'Procedures in Place for Implementation of Article VIII, Section 29, of the Convention on the Privileges and Immunities of the United Nations' (24 April 1995) UN Doc A/C.5/49/65.

[31] Staff Regulations of the Council of Europe (25 September 1981) COM Res(81) 20, as amended art 60.

[32] Protocol (No 3) on the Statute of the Court of Justice of the European Union (30 March 2010) C 83/210 Annex 1.

[33] Statute of the OAS Administrative Tribunal, AG/RES 35 (I-O/71) (22 April 1971).

[34] Statute of the Administrative Tribunal of the International Bank for Reconstruction and Development, International Development Association and International Finance Corporation (adopted and entered into force 30 April 1980 as amended) art II.

[35] Statute of the Administrative Tribunal of the Asian Development Bank (adopted and entered into force February 2006) art II.

[36] Statute of the Administrative Tribunal of the African Development Bank (adopted and entered into force 16 July 1997).

misconduct.[37] Nonetheless, the model illustrates that where there is will to develop adjudicative systems, these can provide a measure of accessible and relatively independent justice for eligible claimants.[38]

V.4.2 Finance and development

International organizations with development remits have established adjudicative mechanisms that accord standing to individuals and/or groups. The World Bank Inspection Panel was the first in a line of bodies[39] established to ensure that the international organizations concerned implemented faithfully their own policies when supporting development projects, and it has had occasion to consider human rights impacts.[40] The idea for the Inspection Panel arose from the failure of the Bank to consult local populations about its investment in the Sardar Sarovar dam and irrigation projects in India. As was determined, the Bank did not adequately consider the need to resettle and rehabilitate displaced people or mitigate the projects' environmental effects, contrary to the internal policies developed specifically for those purposes.[41] The Sarovar dam commission findings led to an internal review of other Bank projects, which confirmed that the Bank disregarded its own social and environmental policies and tolerated its borrowers' violation of same.[42] This ultimately led to the establishment of the Inspection Panel in 1994.

The Panel can receive complaints by groups of individuals who represent a commonality of interests (single claimants are ineligible) and whose rights or interests have been or are likely to be directly and adversely affected. Claimants must show that they took steps 'to bring the matter to the attention of [Bank] Management with a result unsatisfactory to the Requester'.[43] The Panel has a degree of independence; however, it is the Bank management that decides whether to authorize the

[37] *Hunt-Matthes v UNSG* UNDT/2013/085 (UN Dispute Tribunal, 28 May 2013). See also *CP v ICC* No 2757 (ILOAT, 9 July 2008).

[38] Olufemi Elias, 'Remarks by Olufemi Elias' (2012) 106 Am Soc'y Int'l L Proc 355, 356.

[39] Other bodies include the Office of the Compliance Advisor, which can receive complaints about International Finance Corporation and/or Multilateral Investment Guarantee Agency projects (Article 2.1.2, Compliance Advisor Ombudsman Guidelines (adopted 2000, revised 2013), and each of the regional development banks (African Development Bank Independent Review Mechanism Operating Rules and Procedures (adopted and entered into force 16 June 2010); Asian Development Bank Accountability Mechanism Policy (2012); European Bank for Reconstruction and Development Project Complaint Mechanism Rules of Procedure (adopted 7 May 2014, entered into force 7 November 2014); Inter-American Development Bank Independent Consultation and Investigation Mechanism (undated)).

[40] See generally Daniel Bradlow, 'Private Complainants and International Organizations: A Comparative Study of the Independent Inspection Mechanisms in International Financial Institutions' (2004–2005) 36 Geo J Int'l L 403; Dana Clark, Jonathan Fox, and Kay Treakle (eds), *Demanding Accountability: Civil Society Claims and the World Bank Inspection Panel* (Rowman & Littlefield 2003).

[41] Bradford Morse and Thomas Berger, 'Sardar Sarovar—Report of the Independent Review' (Resource Futures International 1992).

[42] Willi Wapenhans (ed), *Effective Implementation: Key to Development Impact: Report of the World Bank's Portfolio Management Task Force* (World Bank 1992).

[43] World Bank Inspection Panel, 'Operating Procedures' (1995) 34 ILM 510.

claims, and determines whether Panel recommendations will be implemented and lead to reparation of any kind. While general consultation can take place, the claimants are not afforded the right to comment on any response received from the Bank management nor will they have access to the Panel's report of its findings prior to the Board's decision.[44]

The Panel has considered World Bank and the recipient countries' compliance with human rights standards in a number of cases.[45] While some of these cases have resulted in only cursory and indirect consideration and remediation of human rights impacts, others such as the *Uganda Transport Sector Development Project case*[46] have been more transformative. Arguably the work of the Panel has been most important in underscoring the need for community consultations particularly in cases involving indigenous peoples,[47] and the implementation of fair resettlement policies, although some of the Panel's approaches have provoked controversy.[48]

In the *Chad–Cameroon Pipeline and Petroleum* case, which involved an array of environmental concerns,[49] the requesters (one of whom had been tortured) raised human rights concerns even though there is no specific bank policy on the issue, and this was taken up by the Panel in an arguably overly measured way; it simply indicated that the situation was 'far from ideal', 'raises questions about compliance with the Bank's policies' and 'warrants renewed monitoring by the Bank'.[50] Bank management argued that human rights concerns are only relevant for the Bank if they have direct economic effects on a Bank financed project.[51] In follow up, the management report justified consultative actions already taken and reiterated its lack of mandate over human rights.[52] In the *Honduras: Land Administration Project Case*, in which the Garifuna people claimed the Project would impede their

[44] Fatma Marouf, 'Holding the World Bank Accountable for Leakage of Funds from Africa's Health Sector' (2013) Health and Human Rights J, nn 76–80, http://www.hhrjournal.org/2013/08/27/holding-the-world-bank-accountable-for-leakage-of-funds-from-africas-health-sector/ (last accessed 25 December 2016).

[45] See generally Steven Herz and Anne Perrault, 'Bringing Human Rights Claims to the World Bank Inspection Panel' (2009) http://www.bankinformationcenter.org/en/Document.101841.pdf (last accessed 27 December 2016).

[46] *Uganda: Transport Sector Development Project—Additional Financing (P121097)* (Investigation Report) Case no 98, 106710-UG (World Bank Inspection Panel, 4 August 2016).

[47] See eg *Kenya: Natural Resource Management Project (Investigation Report)* Case no 84, Rep 88065-KE (World Bank Inspection Panel, 22 May 2014); *Honduras: Land Administration Project (IDA Credit 3858-HO)* (Investigation Report) Case no 38 (World Bank Inspection Panel, 12 June 2007).

[48] See Amnesty International, 'Nigeria: The World Bank Inspection Panel's early solutions pilot approach: the case of Badia East, Nigeria' (2 September 2014) AFR 44/018/2014, and the Panel's response to Amnesty International, *Nigeria: Lagos Metropolitan Development and Governance Project* 'First Pilot on Early Solutions: Lagos Metropolitan Development and Governance Project (LMDGP) Response To Amnesty International's Concerns Raised In Its Briefing Note On Badia East (Sept 2014)' Case no 91, Rep P071340 (World Bank Inspection Panel, 12 September 2014).

[49] *Chad–Cameroon Petroleum Development and Pipeline Project, Management of the Petroleum Economy Project, and Petroleum Sector Management Capacity Building Project* (Investigation Report) Case no 22, Rep 23999 (World Bank Inspection Panel, 17 July 2002).

[50] ibid para 214. [51] ibid para 212.

[52] See *Chad–Cameroon Petroleum Development and Pipeline Project, Management of the Petroleum Economy Project, and Petroleum Sector Management Capacity Building Project* (Management Report and Recommendation) Case no 22, Rep 24667 (World Bank Inspection Panel, 21 August 2002) para 51 and Annex 1 No 28.

access to ancestral lands and that they had not benefited from genuine participation in decision-making processes, the Panel expressed concern that the Bank did not adequately consider whether the Project would comply with the ILO Indigenous Peoples' Convention.[53] Again, the Panel recommendations were vaguely framed, although the follow-up reports of Bank management appear to take seriously in this particular case the recommendations made,[54] because of the clear Bank policy concerning indigenous rights.[55]

In the *Uganda Transport Sector Development Project Case*, the Panel determined inter alia that there had been poor community consultations, inadequate and untimely compensation for involuntary resettlement, and many instances of child sexual abuse and teenage pregnancies by Project road workers.[56] The Panel report elicited a strong response from Bank management, who agreed with the bulk of the Panel's findings. In addition to cancelling the project, the Bank set in motion and funded a plan to meet the immediate material and psychosocial needs of victims in coordination with local NGOs, expressed its commitment to following up with the Government on efforts to investigate and prosecute the sexual violence cases; Bank support to the affected community to carry out gender based violence prevention and response work and a reconfiguration of other Bank project work in Uganda better to incorporate measures for addressing social risks.[57] Thus, the Panel is capable of having a transformative effect in certain cases.

V.4.3 Peacekeeping and territorial administrations

There is significant scope for international organizations to cause harm to local populations during peacekeeping operations. The key ways in which accountability has been dealt with in respect to peacekeeping operations, are considered in turn:

(1) Inquiries

Several large-scale inquiries have considered crucial questions concerning respect for human rights and international humanitarian law, including the (in)adequacy of measures taken to protect the civilian population in response to foreseeable

[53] *Honduras: Land Administration Project (IDA Credit 3858-HO)* (Investigation Report) (n 47) para 258.

[54] *Honduras Land Administration Project (CREDIT NO. 3858-HO)* (Management Report and Recommendation) INSP/39933-HN (World Bank Inspection Panel, 3 August 2007); *Honduras Land Administration Project (CREDIT NO. 3858-HO)* (Progress Report: Implementation of Management's Action Plan) (World Bank Inspection Panel, 9 March 2009).

[55] World Bank, 'Operation Policy 4.10—Indigenous Peoples' (July 2005, revised April 2013).

[56] *Uganda: Transport Sector Development Project—Additional Financing (P121097)* (Investigation Report) (n 46) para 359.

[57] *Uganda: Uganda Transport Sector Development Project—Additional Financing (P121097)* 'Management Report and Recommendation in Response to the Inspection Panel Investigation Report' (13 October 2016) INSP/106710-UG, 44–46.

dangers,[58] the response to sexual exploitation and abuse,[59] and the investigation of claims concerning the introduction of disease.[60]

For the most part, both internal and independent inquiries have been helpful in identifying problem areas and positing solutions; occasionally they have engendered lessons-learned which have impacted on later policies and practice and at times, qualified apologies to the victims and communities most affected have been proffered. However, typically these mechanisms have failed to take the corresponding step and determine adequate and effective reparations for the injuries caused. The Independent Inquiry established by the UN following the peacekeeping mission in Rwanda found clear failings in the response of the UN before and during the 1994 genocide in Rwanda, and attributed responsibility to a number of UN bodies and agencies, including the Secretary-General, the UN Secretariat, the Security Council, and the UN peacekeeping mission operating in Rwanda, in addition to the broader State membership of the United Nations. Despite the grievous consequences of this responsibility, it finds that what is warranted is 'a clear apology by the Organization and by Member States concerned to the Rwandese people'.[61] Nowhere does the Independent Inquiry indicate that additional forms of reparation should follow.

(2) Local claims review boards

Claims procedures have been instituted to deal with losses incidental to UN peacekeeping and peace support operations.[62] Virtually identical procedures are in place in African Union missions.[63] In contrast, North Atlantic Treaty Organization (NATO) operations emphasize the responsibilities of troop-contributing States

[58] UNSC, 'Report of the Independent Inquiry into the actions of the United Nations during the 1994 genocide in Rwanda' (n 358); UNGA, 'The Fall of Srebrenica' (15 November 1999) UN Doc A/54/549; UNGA, 'Report of the Secretary-General's Internal Review Panel on United Nations Action in Šri Lanka' (November 2012) https://www.un.org/News/dh/infocus/Sri_Lanka/The_Internal_Review_Panel_report_on_Sri_Lanka.pdf (last accessed 12 December 2016).

[59] Marie Deschamps, Hassan Jallow, and Yasmin Sooka, 'Taking Action on Sexual Exploitation and Abuse by Peacekeepers: Report of an Independent Review on Sexual Exploitation and Abuse by International Peacekeeping Forces in the Central African Republic' (17 December 2015) http://www.un.org/News/dh/infocus/centafricrepub/Independent-Review-Report.pdf (last accessed 25 December 2016); Prince Zeid Ra'ad Zeid Al-Hussein, 'A Comprehensive Strategy to Eliminate Future Sexual Exploitation and Abuse in United Nations Peacekeeping Operations' (24 March 2005) UN Doc A/59/710 para 76; OIOS, 'Investigation by the Office of Internal Oversight Services into allegations of sexual exploitation and abuse in the UN Mission in the Democratic Republic of the Congo' (5 January 2005) UN Doc A/59/661.

[60] Alejandro Cravioto and others, 'Final report of the independent panel of experts on the cholera outbreak in Haiti' (4 May 2011) http://www.un.org/News/dh/infocus/haiti/UN-cholera-report-final.pdf (last accessed 27 December 2016).

[61] 'Report of the Independent Inquiry into the actions of the United Nations during the 1994 genocide in Rwanda' (15 December 1999) UN Doc S/1999/1257 30.

[62] UNGA, 'Model Status-of-forces Agreement for Peace-Keeping Operations' (9 October 1990) UN Doc A/45/594 (UN Model SOFA) art 51; UNGA, 'Administrative and Budgetary Aspects of the Financing of the United Nations Peacekeeping' (21 May 1997) UN Doc A/51/903 para 8.

[63] See eg Status of Mission Agreement on the Establishment and Management of the Ceasefire Commission in the Darfur Area of the Sudan (adopted and entered into force 4 June 2004).

to compensate for any harm caused during the mission.[64] The Model Status of Forces Agreement, which is a template for the agreements the UN signs with host States, provides for the establishment of a standing claims commission,[65] with one member appointed by the Secretary-General, one by the host Government and a chairman appointed jointly. However, no such commission has ever been established.[66] Not all missions take place in countries where governments are willing or able to participate in a claims commission, nor will it always be clear who may legitimately represent the Government in volatile conflict contexts, thus alternative mechanisms would in any event be needed.[67]

Local claims review boards that have been established in their stead 'as the need arises'[68] are deficient in a number of respects.[69] First, they are not automatically in place at the start of a mission[70] which means aggrieved individuals would need to use general channels to contact the mission, and the mission would then decide whether the grievance 'merits' the establishment of a claims procedure. Second, the decisions are not made public and the review boards are comprised solely of UN staff, thus not meeting basic requirements for independence and impartiality.[71] Third, review boards experience backlogs and delays, with many claims remaining unresolved at the end of the mission period.[72] And, there has been no attempt to introduce procedural safeguards for third-party claimants and aggrieved individuals do not have an obvious way to appeal. In contrast, the model SOFA provides that: 'any appeal which the UN or the host State agree to allow from the award of the claims commission, shall, unless otherwise agreed by the parties, be submitted to an arbitral tribunal. The decisions of the claims commission and the arbitral tribunal shall be binding on both parties'.[73] There is no such framework for local claims review boards. Even if such a model were made applicable to decisions taken by review boards, the aggrieved individual is not a party to the SOFA, and would

[64] NATO, 'NATO Claims Policy for Designated Crisis Response Operations' (5 May 2004) AC/119-N (2004) 0058.

[65] UN Model SOFA (n 62) art 51.

[66] UNGA, 'Administrative and Budgetary Aspects of the Financing of the United Nations Peacekeeping' (n 62) para 8.

[67] Andrew Clapham, *Human Rights Obligations of Non-State Actors* (OUP 2006) 115.

[68] UNGA, 'Financing of the United Nations Protection Force' (n 25) para 22.

[69] See Guglielmo Verdirame, *The UN and Human Rights: Who Guards the Guardians?* (CUP 2011) 225–26; Tom Dannenbaum, 'Translating the Standard of Effective Control into a System of Effective Accountability: How Liability Should be Apportioned for Violations of Human Rights by Member State Troop Contingents Serving as United Nations Peacekeepers' (2010) 51 Harv Int'l LJ 113 126–28; Frédéric Mégret, 'The Vicarious Responsibility of the United Nations for "Unintended Consequences" of Peacekeeping Operations' in Chiyuki Aoi, Cedric de Cooning, and Ramesh Thakur (eds), *The 'Unintended' Consequences of Peace Operations* (UN University Press 2007) 262–63.

[70] UNGA, 'Third-party Claims: Reform of the Procedures for Determining Reimbursement to Member States for Contingent-owned Equipment, Death and Disability Benefits' (1 October 1997) UN Doc A/52/410 para 15.

[71] UNGA, 'Administrative and Budgetary Aspects of the Financing of the United Nations Peacekeeping' (n 62) para 10.

[72] UNGA, 'Financing of the United Nations Protection Force' (n 25) paras 26, 28.

[73] See UN Model SOFA (n 62).

need to rely on his or her State of nationality to pursue an appeal on his or her behalf.

The funding to implement successful awards tends to come from funds specifically authorized for the particular peacekeeping mission. As was indicated in a 2001 legal opinion, 'the current practice is for the budgets of peacekeeping operations to contain a line item, "claims and adjustments", to cover potential third-party claims. In addition, we have been informed that the budgets for the pre-liquidation phase of peacekeeping operations typically include a line item to cover outstanding or anticipated third-party claims. ... To the extent that the amounts of such payments exceed the amounts budgeted, additional funds would have to be obtained'.[74] It is unclear from where any needed additional funds would be located; however, the legal opinion does not suggest that the obligation to pay is somehow contingent on the location of funds: 'the fact that funds have not been appropriated to pay legal obligations is not an excuse for failing to pay these obligations. This has been recognized in two advisory opinions of the International Court of Justice and it follows from general principles of law'.[75]

Owing to concerns over the financing of claims, restrictions were eventually put in place to limit the recoverable amounts,[76] including a usual cap of US$50,000; a bar on compensation in the event of 'operational necessity'; a bar on compensation for non-economic loss, such as pain and suffering or moral anguish, as well as for punitive or moral damages. Aside from punitive damages which are not a well-recognized feature of international responsibility,[77] the other across the board limitations on the quantum and quality of reparation can significantly impede local review boards from affording adequate and effective reparation which corresponds to the nature of the violation and the injuries caused. As Wellens has noted, 'one could question whether the restriction imposed by the public policy of the organization on the remedies available is not going beyond the minimum, which, ... should ensure that as far as possible the extent of the compensation and the nature of the remedy should be governed by the *lex causae*'.[78]

Also, the UN introduced a temporal limitation whereby claims must be lodged within six months 'from the time the damage was sustained, or from the time the injury was discovered, and in any event not later than one year after the termination of the mandate of the operation'.[79] This derived from the UN's practice of imposing temporal limits for staff claims relating to personal injury, incapacitation, or death. But third party claims are different from staff claims, the terms of which

[74] UN OLA, 'Memorandum to the Controller' (23 February 2001) UN Juridical Y pt 2 ch VI 381 para 15.

[75] ibid para 16.

[76] UNGA, 'Resolution on Third-party Liability: Temporal and Financial Limitations' (17 July 1998) UN Doc A/RES/52/247.

[77] The ARS (n 15) and DARIO (n 4) both reject the notion of punitive or exemplary damages.

[78] Karel Wellens, *Remedies Against International Organisations* (CUP 2002) 163–64.

[79] UNGA, 'Administrative and budgetary aspects of the financing of the United Nations peacekeeping' (n 62) para 20.

are inevitably agreed by contract in which employees, and by extension their family members, are put on notice as to applicable procedures.

While time limits are arguably important in light of the short-term nature of many peacekeeping operations and the need to investigate claims *in situ*, it has been recognized that for certain human rights and international humanitarian law violations there should be no limitation period, and for others, the limitation period should not be unduly restrictive so as to inhibit claims.[80] Prescription periods should also be considered against the information the claimants receive about where and how to file a claim, their situation and potential vulnerability in light of the spectre of the conflict or post-conflict environment, as well as the public interest in the claims being resolved.

Local claims review boards have not been capable of, nor are they necessarily appropriately designed for, dealing with wide-scale problems identified in a number of missions, such as mass liability stemming from systemic organizational failings or incidents involving large numbers of victims. As is later described, the UN has limited the remit of such review boards to 'private claims' concerning official conduct[81] without establishing a separate forum to deal with claims which fall outside its own interpretation of this remit.

(3) Arbitration

In principle, the State of nationality could espouse an individual's claim and use negotiation, conciliation, or arbitration. This was the approach employed by Belgium and other sending States following the deaths of their citizens in the UN Operation in the Congo in the 1960s.[82] However, as the UN Secretary-General has acknowledged, this approach 'is largely dependent on the State's willingness to espouse the claims of its nationals'.[83] The few diplomatic negotiations have been undertaken by States whose nationals served on peacekeeping missions, and not the States hosting those missions. Yet the majority of injured individuals are citizens of the host State where the mission operates. It will rarely be in the host State's power or interests to pursue such claims, and to distribute any award received fairly and equitably to the individuals concerned, given the disarray of the conflict or post-conflict context. As Verdirame notes, '[f]or Congolese citizens who suffered the brunt of the conflict, no such fund was created, partly because of the failure of their authorities to advocate their case'.[84]

80 Liesbeth Zegveld, 'Victims' Reparations Claims and International Criminal Courts: Incompatible Values?' (2010) 8 J Int'l Crim J 79, 107–108; Updated Set of Principles for the Protection and Promotion of Human Rights through Action to Combat Impunity (8 February 2005) UN Doc E/CN.4/2005/102/Add.1 (Impunity Principles) Principle 23 para (c).

81 See section V.4.3(6) and (7).

82 UNSG, 'Exchange of Letters Constituting an Agreement between the United Nations and Belgium Relating to the Settlement of Claims Filed Against the United Nations in the Congo by Belgian Nationals' (20 February 1965) (1965) UN Juridical Y 39.

83 UNGA, 'Financing of the United Nations Protection Force' (n 25) para 37.

84 See Verdirame (n 69) 338. See also Dannenbaum, 'Translating the Standard of Effective Control into a System of Effective Accountability' (n 69) 127–28.

(4) Assistance policies and trust funds

Special assistance policies and trust funds have occasionally been used. In accordance with a 2007 strategy on peacekeeper sexual exploitation and abuse,[85] 'complainants' are supposed to receive basic assistance and support which corresponds to their needs, with 'victims' and 'children born as a result of sexual exploitation and abuse' to receive additional assistance. No specific funding structure is set out despite suggestions appearing in earlier drafts of the strategy;[86] the 2007 strategy simply providing that '[a]ssistance and support should be provided through existing services, programmes and their networks' through 'implementing partners'.[87] An Office of Internal Oversight Services (OIOS) review of support provision in this area has noted significant problems.[88] According to its 2015 findings, 'only 26 out of 217 identified victims (12 per cent) identified by its victim assistance architecture have been referred for assistance and of those referred, little is known what assistance, in reality, was provided to them'.[89] The main reasons cited for this neglect were lack of budget and the need to rely on local service providers. 'One interviewee who typified the sentiments said that they had "a mandate to give assistance that cover[ed] every possible type of assistance and not been given a penny" '.[90]

A trust fund to better address the particular harms caused by sexual exploitation and abuse was proposed by the Secretary-General and has now been established,[91] to be serviced by withheld payments to peacekeepers against whom claims of sexual exploitation and abuse have been substantiated and additionally through voluntary payments from Member States.[92] The precise details of how it operates have yet to be made public, although it was reported to have become fully operational in March 2016.[93] As the independent Panel indicated in respect of the Central African Republic, the trust fund is an imperfect solution. 'As a matter of principle, victims of conflict related sexual violence should be compensated. In an armed conflict, however, individual remedies are often illusory. Furthermore, in many countries emerging from conflicts, domestic judicial systems can be dysfunctional. Recourse

[85] UNGA, 'United Nations Comprehensive Strategy on Assistance and Support to Victims of Sexual Exploitation and Abuse by United Nations Staff and Related Personnel' (7 March 2008) UN Doc A/RES/62/214, Annex.

[86] UNGA, 'Draft United Nations policy statement and draft United Nations comprehensive strategy on assistance and support to victims of sexual exploitation and abuse by United Nations staff or related personnel' (5 June 2006) A/60/877, Annex paras 5, 39–47.

[87] ibid paras 6–10, 12.

[88] UN OIOS, 'Evaluation of the Enforcement and Remedial Assistance Efforts for Sexual Exploitation and Abuse by the United Nations and Related Personnel in Peacekeeping Operations' (15 May 2015) IED-15-001.

[89] ibid para 57.

[90] ibid para 60; see also para 64.

[91] UNGA, 'Special Measures for Protection from Sexual Exploitation and Sexual Abuse: Report of the Secretary-General' (13 February 2015) A/69/779 para 66; UNGA, 'Special Measures for Protection from Sexual Exploitation and Sexual Abuse: Report of the Secretary-General' (16 February 2016) UN Doc A/70/729 paras 76–79.

[92] UN Doc A/70/729 (n 91) para 76.

[93] UNGA, 'Special Measures for Protection from Sexual Exploitation and Sexual Abuse' (n 91) paras 65, 66; this is also repeated in UNGA, "Combating Sexual Exploitation and Sexual Abuse', Report of the Secretary-General (23 June 2016) UN Doc A/71/97.

against foreign perpetrators in their own domestic courts is most of times unrealistic as victims do not have the resources to pursue accountability and to obtain a remedy. In recognition of the difficulty faced by victims in accessing a remedy in such circumstances, victims should have access to the common trust fund proposed by the Secretary-General'.[94]

Following the introduction of cholera to Haiti which reportedly led to more than 10,000 deaths, the UN eventually issued a qualified apology after a long period in which it denied its role and refused to afford victims a venue in which to assert their claims of harm.[95] The Secretary-General unveiled a remediation plan which includes efforts to eliminate the disease from Haiti, and material assistance and support.[96] As part of the plans, victims and their families and affected communities would receive assistance and support through community projects and initiatives and there is consideration to pay the families of those individuals who died of cholera. In order to finance the planned interventions, the 'UN Haiti Cholera Response Multi-Partner Trust Fund' was established.[97]

The use of assistance frameworks and trust funds can be important ways in which to deliver services to victims; however, the reliance on voluntary contributions introduces a contingency into victims' entitlements and is inconsistent with their rights to reparation flowing from the commission of an internationally wrongful act. Reparation to victims becomes contingent on the whims of donors and is separated from the wrongdoing of the organization. This differs substantially from processes in which binding decisions which determine liability are taken and are understood by the organization as a legal requirement to implement.[98]

(5) Territorial administrations

When an international organization serves as a territorial administrator—in effect, the *de facto* government, the need for mechanisms to address grievances from the local population is stark.[99] In Kosovo, the lack of accountability of the international territorial administration was raised by the Council of Europe.[100] It recommended setting up a human rights court to adjudicate alleged human rights violations attributable to the international organization administration, and with competence to annul any decisions and acts that were incompatible with human rights obligations and to allocate appropriate redress or compensation.[101] The court was never

[94] See Deschamps, Jallow, and Sooka (n 59) 84.

[95] UN News Centre, 'UN's Ban Apologizes to People of Haiti, Outlines New Plan to Fight Cholera Epidemic and Help Communities' (1 December 2016).

[96] UNGA, 'A New Approach to Cholera in Haiti' (25 November 2016) UN Doc A/71/620.

[97] ibid para 61.

[98] UN OLA, 'Memorandum to the Controller' (n 74) para 16.

[99] Ralph Wilde, *International Territorial Administration: How Trusteeship and the Civilizing Mission Never Went Away* (OUP 2008) 450–53; Carsten Stahn, *The Law and Practice of International Territorial Administration. Versailles to Iraq and Beyond* (CUP 2008) 760; Simon Chesterman, *You, the People: The United Nations, Transitional Administration, and State-building* (OUP 2004) 145–52.

[100] European Commission for Democracy through Law (Venice Commission) 'Opinion No 280/2004 on Human Rights in Kosovo—Possible Establishment of Review Mechanisms' (11 October 2004) CDL-AD (2004) 033 para 2.

[101] ibid paras 104, 106.

established, although the Kosovo Ombudsperson Institution and Human Rights Advisory Panel (HRAP)[102] were eventually set up.

The Ombudsperson institution was established in 2000. It had authority to receive and investigate complaints from any person or entity in Kosovo concerning human rights violations and actions constituting an abuse of authority by UNMIK or any emerging central or local institution.[103] Its jurisdiction was limited temporally to cases arising after 30 June 2000 and excluded cases involving the Kosovo Force (KFOR), the military presence[104] 'placing one of the most significant areas of potential complaints outside the reach of the ombudsperson's jurisdiction'.[105] The Ombudsperson had only recommendatory powers[106] and observers have indicated that UNMIK frequently failed to implement the recommendations.[107] In 2006, UNMIK replaced the international ombudsperson with a national one appointed by the Kosovo Assembly, who had jurisdiction only over indigenous Kosovo institutions.[108] An ombudsperson office was also established in East Timor within UNTAET.[109] However, its mandate was more limited in scope than the one in place in Kosovo.[110]

HRAP was mandated to 'examine complaints from any person or group of individuals claiming to be the victim of a violation by UNMIK of their human rights'.[111] HRAP could receive claims relating to alleged violations that had occurred from 23 April 2005 or which arose prior to this date where these facts give rise to a continuing violation of human rights.[112] This is despite the fact that the international organization administration was in place since 1999.[113] The deadline to submit new complaints to the Panel was set at 31 March 2010, which coincided with the scaling down of UNMIK following Kosovo's declaration of independence.

There were three Panel members,[114] none of whom were UN employees; indeed, the Panel has been comprised of academics, judges, and lawyers specialized in

[102] UNMIK, 'Regulation 2006/12 on the Establishment of the Human Rights Advisory Panel (23 March 2006).

[103] UNMIK, 'Regulation 2000/38 on the Establishment of the Ombudsperson Institution in Kosovo' (n 22), s 3.1; UNMIK, 'Regulation 2006/6 on the Ombudsperson Institution in Kosovo' (16 February 2006) s 3.1.

[104] UNMIK Regulation 2006/6 (n 22) ss 3.2–3.5; See also Chesterman, *You, The People* (n 99) 147–48.

[105] Duncan French and Richard Kirkham, 'Complaint and Grievance Mechanisms in International Law: One Piece of the Accountability Jigsaw?' (2009) 7 NZ YB Int'l L 179, 198, although they argue that this did not prevent the Ombudsperson from considering issues relating to the security presence.

[106] UNMIK Regulation 2000/38 (n 22) s 4.

[107] Rebecca Everly, 'Reviewing Governmental Acts of the United Nations in Kosovo' (2007) 8(1) German LJ 21, 32.

[108] UNMIK Regulation 2006/6 (n 22).

[109] Frederick Rawski, 'To Waive or not to Waive: Immunity and Accountability in U.N. Peacekeeping Operations' (2002–2003) 18 Connecticut J Int'l L 103, 116, 125; UNGA, Advisory Committee on Administrative and Budgetary Questions, 'Financing of the UN Transitional Administration in East Timor' (30 October 2000) UN Doc A/55/531 para 33.

[110] Amnesty International, 'East Timor, Justice Past, Present and Future' (2001) AI Index: ASA 57/001/2001, 29 ff.

[111] UNMIK, Regulation 2006/12 (n 102) ss 1.1, 1.2.

[112] ibid s 2.

[113] UNSC Res 1244/1999 (10 June 1999).

[114] UNMIK, 'Administrative Direction 2009/1 Implementing UNMIK Regulation No. 2006/12 on the Establishment of the Human Rights Advisory Panel' (17 October 2009) s 3.1.

international law.[115] The Panel was deemed to be 'non-adversarial',[116] and could hold public hearings limited to clarifying the facts.[117] The decisions were advisory only, and the Special Representative of the Secretary-General has often failed to implement them. Similar to the limitations imposed on the Ombudsperson's office, the Panel had no jurisdiction over KFOR. KFOR has not followed the recommendation to set up a similar Advisory Board.[118]

When the Panel was first established, claims to HRAP could be filed if all other available avenues for review had been exhausted, and within a period of six months from the date on which the final decision pertaining to the claim was taken. As part of its review, HRAP assessed whether the availability of UN local claims review boards could be considered a remedy requiring exhaustion. However, in mid-course UNMIK decided the issue itself; it introduced a new Administrative Direction which set out an additional admissibility requirement that: 'any complaint that is or may become in the future the subject of the UN Third Party Claims process or proceedings ... shall be deemed inadmissible for reasons that ... [this process or proceedings] are available avenues'.[119] Thus, subsequent to the Direction, the Panel was only in a position to consider whether the UN Third Party Claims Process was capable in principle, by virtue of the limited scope of the claims considered by that process, of addressing the claim.[120] In its 2009 Report, HRAP clarified that: '[c]omplaints about violations of human rights attributable to UNMIK will be deemed inadmissible under Section 2.2 of UNMIK Administrative Direction no. 2009/1 to the extent that they have resulted either in personal injury, illness or death, or in property loss or damage. Complaints about violations of human rights that have not resulted in damage of such a nature will normally not run counter to the requirement of exhaustion with the UN Third Party Claims Process'.[121] Professor Chinkin, a member of HRAP, commented that: '[i]nternally, it seems that UNMIK had failed to appreciate the implications of what the establishment and

115 www.unmikonline.org/hrap/Eng/Pages/Members-of-the-Panel.aspx (last accessed 27 December 2016).

116 HRAP has taken issue with this, noting that: 'On this point, the Panel is of the opinion that it is hard to reconcile the Administrative Direction with the spirit, if not the wording, of UNMIK Regulation No. 2006/12'. See HRAP, 'Annual Report' (2009) para 41.

117 UNMIK Administrative Direction 2009/1 (n 114) ss 1.1, 1.2, 1.4. See also HRAP Annual Report 2009 (n 116) paras 41, 42.

118 Venice Commission, Opinion No 280/2004 (n 100) paras 125–33.

119 UNMIK Administrative Direction 2009/1 (n 114) s 2 para 2.2.

120 In the *Balaj* case, which concerned the killing and/or serious injury of individuals who participated in a demonstration, the effectiveness of the criminal investigation that followed, and the impossibility for the complainants to bring a claim against UNMIK before any court or other body capable of providing redress. See *Balaj and Others v UNMIK*, Case no 04/07, Decisions of 6 June 2008, 31 March 2010 and 11 May 2012. HRAP initially determined the claim admissible. It then determined that it was no longer admissible on the basis of para 2.2 of Administrative Direction 2009/1 (n 114). However, it ultimately admitted the claim when it was clear that the UN Third Party Claims Process had come to an end and would not be capable of serving as a remedy. See similarly *NM and Others v UNMIK*, Case No 26/08 (HRAP, 31 March 2010 and final decision 26 February 2016), which concerned members of the Roma community in Kosovo who were living in UNMIK administered camps, who suffered lead poisoning as a result of the soil contamination in the camp sites.

121 HRAP Annual Report 2009 (n 116) para 61.

functioning of an independent complaints mechanism would entail; namely that there would in fact be investigations and questions asked of UNMIK with respect to alleged human rights violations raised by complainants'.[122]

The EU Rule of Law Mission in Kosovo (EULEX)[123] established a Human Rights Review Panel (HRRP), which operates similarly to HRAP. It has jurisdiction over alleged human rights violations by EULEX[124] and can make non-binding recommendations and follow up on the implementation of its recommendations with the Head of EULEX. HRRP complements the EULEX Internal Investigation Unit and the EULEX Third Party Liability Insurance Scheme. It has decided a range of cases, including ones that consider violations of the right to life, prohibition of torture, liberty and security, fair trial, respect for private and family life, freedom of expression, and the right to an effective remedy.[125]

In several territorial administrations, acts of the international organization were also capable of challenge before domestic courts. In Bosnia and Herzegovina, for instance, the Constitutional Court deemed itself competent to examine the compatibility of laws enacted by the High Representative with the constitutional provisions and human rights guarantees under the Dayton Peace Agreement.[126] In East Timor, the UN Transitional Administration in East Timor (UNTAET) introduced a *habeas corpus* procedure to challenge unlawful arrest or detention,[127] and allowed for certain of its decisions to be challenged in domestic courts.[128] These, however, are exceptional occurrences; most administrations rely on the *sui generis* status of their mandates and decisions as well as their institutional immunities to avoid having decisions so challenged.

(6) *The characterization of claims: private disputes vs. claims involving public policy*

Article VIII(29)(a) of the CPIUN requires the UN to make provisions for appropriate modes of settlement of disputes arising out of contracts or other disputes of a private law character to which it is a party. The UN has recognized that it 'is duty-bound' to provide for such alternative modes of settlement.[129] However, it has taken a narrow view of what it considers as 'private', with all else falling into

[122] Chatham House, 'The Kosovo Human Rights Advisory Panel' (International Law Meeting Summary, 26 January 2012) 5.

[123] Council Joint Action 2008/124/CFSP on the EU Rule of Law Mission in Kosovo (adopted and entered into force 4 February 2008) (2008) OJ L42/92 amended by Council Joint Action 2009/445/CFSP (adopted and entered into force 9 June 2009) (2009) OJ L148/33.

[124] EULEX Human Rights Review Panel Rules of Procedure (15 January 2013) rule 25(2).

[125] Described in its Annual Reports www.hrrp.eu/annual-report.php (last accessed 27 December 2016).

[126] Andrew Mitchell and John Farnik, 'Global Administrative Law: Can it Bring Global Governance to Account?' (2009) 37 Federal LR 237, 248–49.

[127] Carsten Stahn, 'Justice under Transitional Administration: Contours and Critique of a Paradigm' (2005) 27 Houston J Int'l L 311, 334.

[128] ibid 334, 335.

[129] ILC, 'Comments and Observations Received from International Organizations' (17 February 2011) A/CN.4/637/Add.1 para 18(2).

a wide chasm of non-receivable claims and, the organization contends that it *only* has the obligation to afford alternative modes of settlement in relation to private claims.

In the peacekeeping context, the UN has indicated that most 'private law' disputes concern claims for compensation for personal injury or death and/or property loss or damage or claims arising out of commercial agreements that the UN has entered into to meet the requirements of a peacekeeping operation.[130] It has recognized that there may be other kinds of claims; however, these have been dismissed outright:

> The Organization does not agree to engage in litigation or arbitration with the numerous third parties that submit claims (often seeking substantial monetary compensation) based on political or policy-related grievances against the United Nations, usually related to actions or decisions taken by the Security Council or the General Assembly in respect of certain matters. Such claims, in many instances, consist of rambling statements denouncing the policies of the Organization and alleging that specific actions of the General Assembly or the Security Council have caused the claimant to sustain financial losses. The Secretary-General considers that it would be inappropriate to utilize public funds to submit to any form of litigation with the claimants to address such issues.[131]

On one reading, the UN appears to suggest that these 'other' types of claims cannot be considered as 'private' because they contain 'political or policy-related grievances against the United Nations'. Yet it is unclear why the existence of political or policy aspects of any grievances is sufficient to displace the private law character of a claim.[132] The OLA discounted the claims concerning the UN Mission in Haiti's responsibility for the introduction of cholera in Haiti on this precise basis. In dismissing the claimants' request for the establishment of a standing claims commission or other appropriate mode of settlement, OLA indicated that the claims were not receivable as they would necessarily include a review of political and policy matters.[133] The CJEU took an analogous approach in its determination of the meaning of 'civil matters' in Article 1 of the Brussels Convention.[134] Yet as the plaintiffs' counsel have said the argument is untenable because 'it implies that the UN's

[130] UNGA, 'Procedures in Place for Implementation of Article VIII(29) CPIUN' (n 30) para 15.

[131] ibid para 23.

[132] See IDI's 1957 statement, which notes that the right of access to an independent court also applies specifically to international organizations '(...) for *every* particular decision of an international organ or organization which involves private rights or interests, there be provided appropriate procedures for settling by judicial or arbitral methods juridical differences which might arise from such a decision'. IDI, Statement (1957) 47(II) Annuaire de l'Institut de Droit International 478.

[133] Letter from Patricia O'Brien, UN Under Secretary-General for Legal Affairs to Brian Concannon (21 February 2013) (on file with the author).

[134] Convention on Jurisdiction and the Enforcement of Judgments in Civil and Commercial Matters (Brussels Convention) as amended (adopted 27 September 1968, entered into force 1 February 1973) OJ 1972 No L299/32; 1262 UNTS 153; (1968) 8 ILM 229. Case C–292/05 *Lechouritou v Germany* [2007] ECR I–01519 CJEU para 41: 'The fact that the proceedings brought before the referring court are presented as being of a civil nature in so far as they seek financial compensation for the material loss and non-material damage caused to the plaintiffs in the main proceedings is consequently entirely irrelevant'.

tortious dumping of raw sewage into rivers of vulnerable countries where it operates is a matter of UN policy'.[135]

It is unclear where the outer limits of the distinction lie between 'private' and 'public'. Traditional private law regulates civil or commercial relationships between private individuals, with private international law regulating such relationships with a cross-border element. Public law usually denotes the relationship between a State and its citizens, and at the international level, the relationship between States. In the Haiti claim, the government of Haiti is not participating in the dispute; the matter has been brought by private Haitians under the law of tort and they are seeking to recover monetary damages for their personal injuries. The UN has regularly committed itself to resolving claims relating to death and personal injury which occur in a peacekeeping context, when they concern for instance, motor vehicle accidents. It is unclear why other forms of death and personal injury which in principle may give rise to the responsibility of the organization are understood as not receivable. The only difference appears to be the numbers of potential claimants.

In a similar case, Roma claimants in Kosovo who were lodged in several internally displaced camps in northern Mitrovica sought to invoke UNMIK's responsibility as a result of the lead poisoning in the soil and consequent serious health ailments including deaths they suffered. They sought to claim before the local claims review board, however due to a lengthy delay without substantive response the claimants filed their grievance with the HRAP, whose mandate is discussed earlier in this chapter. Initially, the Panel dismissed the claims, because it held that they were precisely the types of claims which should come within the ambit of the UN claims review board process:

> The substantive complaints . . . are all directly linked to the initial operational choice to place the IDPs in the camps in question and/or the failure to relocate them, and the subsequent effects which resulted in personal injury, illness or death. The Panel considers that these parts of the complaint fall *prima facie* within the ambit of the UN Third Party Claims Process and therefore are deemed inadmissible.[136]

Thus, according to the HRAP, operational choices which may indeed involve questions of policy which result in death or personal injury should not escape the attention of the UN's claims process;[137] these are not simply 'rambling statements denouncing the policies of the Organization'.[138] The Roma claimants did go back

[135] Letter from Brian Concannon Jr and Ira Kurzban to Patricia O'Brien, UN Under Secretary-General for Legal Affairs (7 May 2013) (on file with author).

[136] See *NM and Others v UNMIK* (n 120) para 40.

[137] Note, however, that s 7 of UNMIK, 'Regulation 2000/47 on the Status, Privileges and Immunities of KFOR and UNMIK and Their Personnel in Kosovo' (18 August 2000), which refers to third party claims, is worded differently, and arguably somewhat broader than the CPIUN (see Chapter 2 n 120) art VIII(29)(a). It provides that: 'Third Party claims for property loss or damage and for personal injury, illness, or death arising from or directly attributed to KFOR, UNMIK, or their respective personnel and which do not arise from "operational necessity" of either presence, shall be settled by Claims Commissions established by KFOR and UNMIK, in the manner provided for'.

[138] UNGA, Resolution 63/253 (n 30).

to the claims process to pursue further their grievances; five years after their initial complaint was lodged they were told their claim was non-receivable.[139]

On another reading, OLA is simply stating its approach to contentious cases involving these 'other' issues. It does not find it appropriate to use public funds to submit to litigation for these 'other' matters when 'often' or 'usually' they relate 'to actions or decisions taken by the Security Council or the General Assembly in respect of certain matters', or consist in 'rambling statements'.[140] The difficulty with this approach is that when the UN decides not to submit to any form of litigation, the claimants have no forum. They are fully reliant on the UN's goodwill to develop alternative modes of settlement when immunity forecloses other avenues.[141]

It is also questionable whether 'public' claims should inevitably be non-receivable. It is difficult to generalize as to the merits of any prospective claim, and on that basis to rule out an entire category of possible disputes (and particularly problematic when the body taking the decision to rule out the category of claims is the would-be respondent). The OLA's quoted statement does not anticipate the UN's role in the administration of territory involving extensive governance functions,[142] nor does it reflect an understanding of the organization's secondary obligations flowing from *any* internationally wrongful act whether 'public' or 'private'.[143]

In peacekeeping operations with a protection mandate, there will be instances when the policies, decisions, and actions of international organizations, properly construed as 'public' will significantly impact on individuals' lives and well-being. On one end of the spectrum, decisions of the Security Council to upgrade (or not) a particular mission, reinforce troop contingents and/or expand the types of activities that troops may engage in, may all have significant impacts on local populations.[144] At the other end of the spectrum, peacekeeping contingents may become involved in discrete aspects of governance such as detention or the transfer and relocation of civilian populations. The OLA comment refers to 'actions or decisions taken by the Security Council or the General Assembly in respect of certain matters'.[145] It thus emphasizes a narrow subset of what might be termed 'public'—and those which necessarily involve the political organs which must take decisions to maintain international peace and security. Whether and the extent to which the Security Council is bound to respect international law, and/or should be so bound, has been extensively canvassed by other authors.[146] It suffices to state for the purposes here

[139] See *NM and Others v UNMIK* (n 120) para 8. HRAP re-instituted the proceedings and decided the matter in favour of the claimants (HRAP, 28 February 2016).

[140] UNGA, Resolution 63/253 (n 30).

[141] UN Human Rights Council, 'Report of the Independent Expert on the Situation of Human Rights in Haiti, Gustavo Gallón' (7 February 2014) UN Doc A/HRC/25/71 para 77. See also UNGA, 'Report of the Special Rapporteur on Extreme Poverty and Human Rights' (26 August 2016) UN Doc A/71/367.

[142] See Wellens, *Remedies Against International Organisations* (n 78) 89.

[143] See DARIO (n 4).

[144] The UN's failure to (adequately) intervene to protect the local populations in Rwanda and in Srebrenica are oft-cited examples.

[145] UNGA, Resolution 63/253 (n 30).

[146] See generally August Reinisch, 'Developing Human Rights and Humanitarian Law Accountability of the Security Council for the Imposition of Economic Sanctions' (2001) 95(4) AJIL

that one cannot treat all 'public acts' with the same brush: even if Security Council political decisions could not be subject to reparation claims by affected individuals because of their central nature to the functioning of the Organization,[147] or because they cannot be distinguished from the will of the States who take the decisions, this would and should not impact on other operational or policy-based decisions of international organizations which directly impact individuals.

The CPIUN, from which this 'private' 'public' distinction derives, was agreed in 1946, and arguably the types of claims envisioned at that time reflect a different, much simpler era of UN activity. Article 29(a) focuses on 'disputes arising out of contracts or other disputes of a private law character to which the United Nations is a party'. The emphasis on 'private' acts only is presumably because the possibility for the UN to act in a 'public' way was much more confined in 1946.[148] Sub-section (b) relates to instances when the UN may be held responsible for the conduct of one of its officials when acting in its official capacity, where that official enjoys immunity and immunity has not been waived. It thus concerns those instances when the acts of an official may implead the Organization. The CPIUN does make reference to the possibility for the Organization to waive its institutional immunity,[149] although unlike Article 29(b), there is no explicit requirement in the Convention for the UN to provide appropriate modes of settlement when it decides not to waive it.[150] However, consistent with Reinisch's view on the purpose of Article 29, such a requirement could arguably be implied, in order to avoid the result of impunity.[151] This view was also affirmed by the ICJ in relation to the UN Administrative Tribunal: as the UN enjoyed immunity before national courts, it would be 'hardly consistent' with the goals of the UN and its Charter if it did not provide a legal remedy for staff disputes.[152]

851; Vera Gowlland-Debbas, 'Security Council Enforcement Action and Issues of State Responsibility' (1994) 43 Int'l & Comp LQ 55; Jose Alvarez, 'Judging the Security Council' (1996) 90(1) AJIL 1; Antonios Tzanakopoulos, *Disobeying the Security Council: Countermeasures against Wrongful Sanctions* (OUP 2011).

[147] This was part of the argument of the Third Chamber of the European Court in its decision to find the Srebrenica claim inadmissible: 'since operations established by United Nations Security Council resolutions under Chapter VII ... are fundamental to the mission of the United Nations to secure international peace and security, the Convention cannot be interpreted in a manner which would subject the acts and omissions of the Security Council to domestic jurisdiction without the accord of the United Nations. To bring such operations within the scope of domestic jurisdiction would be to allow individual States, through their courts, to interfere with the fulfilment of the key mission of the United Nations in this field, including with the effective conduct of its operations ...'. See *Stichting Mothers of Srebrenica and Others v Netherlands* App no 65542/12 (ECtHR, 11 June 2013) [154].

[148] Eric De Brabandere, 'Immunity of International Organizations in Post-conflict International Administrations' (2010) 7 IO LR 79.

[149] Convention on the Privileges and Immunities of the UN (adopted 13 February 1946, entered into force 17 September 1946) 1 UNTS 15 (CPIUN) art II(2).

[150] Unless the claim also involves an official whose immunity was not waived, the liability of which could be imputed to the organization.

[151] August Reinisch, 'Convention on the Privileges and Immunities of the United Nations / Convention on the Privileges and Immunities of the Specialized Agencies' (UN Audiovisual Library of International Law, undated) http://legal.un.org/avl/ha/cpiun-cpisa/cpiun-cpisa.html (last accessed 25 December 2016). See also Cheah Wui Ling, 'Policing Interpol: The Commission for the Control of Interpol's Files and the Right to a Remedy' (2010) 7 IO Law Rev 375.

[152] See *Effects of Awards* (n 27).

Nonetheless, the most straight-forward reading of the text is that it was meant to be an exhaustive requirement. Appropriate mechanisms for the resolution of disputes are required in precise circumstances, and not for all those circumstances in which institutional immunities prevent aggrieved individuals from accessing justice. International jurisprudence in this general area has taken such an approach. The availability of immunity has been considered separately and distinctly from any other obligations, including the obligation to afford victims with access to a remedy.[153]

However, even with such a narrow reading, the ability for the UN to create appropriate settlement mechanisms would be permissive in other areas beyond those contemplated by Article 29 to the extent that mechanisms are understood to be required by virtue of the operational needs of its mandate.[154] International organizations' *responsibility* is not circumscribed to the limited circumstances set out in the CPIUN; immunity does not impact on responsibility and the concomitant obligations that stem from such responsibility to afford reparation.[155] As the DARIO spells out, an international organization is responsible for any breach of an international obligation attributable to it.[156] As such, and in keeping with international organizations' forays into areas not anticipated at the time of the adoption of the CPIUN, the UN *should* put in place appropriate settlement procedures to deal with matters which may engage its responsibility. Arguably, it *must* do so in order to ensure its continued ability to carry out its functions faithfully in accordance with the UN Charter. As the UN Special Rapporteur for Haiti puts it, 'The United Nations should be the first to honour these principles'.[157]

(7) The characterization of conduct

Consistent with understandings of the immunity from legal process of individual officials, which is limited to conduct performed by them in their official capacity (immunity *ratione materiae*), *ultra vires* acts and omissions which may implead the organization will only be attributed to the organization if they are carried out in an official capacity.[158] As the DARIO commentaries indicate, this is intended to make clear that actions which took place in a purely private capacity are not attributable to the organization.[159] As is set out in Chapter III, the OLA has taken a wide approach to the 'off duty' (and thereby non-official) acts of peacekeepers, and a narrow characterization of the *ultra vires* conduct that is 'on duty'. Under such

[153] *Jurisdictional Immunities of the State (Germany v Italy: Greece Intervening)* (Merits) [2012] ICJ Rep 143; *Jones v United Kingdom* (GC) App nos 34356/06, 40528/06 (ECtHR, 14 January 2014); *Stichting Mothers of Srebrenica v Netherlands* App no 65542/12 (ECtHR, 11 June 2013) [152] (finding the application inadmissible).

[154] See *Effects of Awards* (n 27).

[155] *Difference Relating to Immunity from Legal Process of a Special Rapporteur of the Commission on Human Rights* (Advisory Opinion) [1999] ICJ Rep 62 [66] (*Cumaraswamy* case).

[156] See DARIO (n 4).

[157] See Gallón (n 141).

[158] See DARIO (n 4) art 6(1).

[159] ibid Official Commentary art 6 para 7.

readings, the private conduct exception might exempt a wide range of conduct amounting to internationally wrongful acts.

When damages are caused 'from the necessary actions taken by a peacekeeping force in the course of carrying out its operations in pursuance of its mandate', existing UN frameworks specify that the UN incurs no liability.[160] Part of the rationale for the exception is that the State receiving the peacekeeping operation should bear the costs of the operation, since the peacekeeping efforts are undertaken at its request or on its behalf. This is misleading because it is highly improbable that the host Government will assume responsibility for an internationally wrongful act attributable to the organization, given the absence of a legal obligation to do so, the exigencies of the conflict or immediate post-conflict context as well as the absence of means to oblige enforcement. As Prescott has noted, the denial of these claims 'will disproportionately impact the citizens of the receiving states. Typically, states receiving UN peacekeeping missions are in a shambles, and lack the resources and infrastructure to make their nationals whole for damages their governments waived when the UN was invited in. The wholesale exclusion of damages on grounds of operational necessity can only detract from the legitimacy of the UN mission in the eyes of the people whom the UN is ostensibly there to assist'.[161]

The Secretary-General has also suggested that the troop contributing country (or the individual troop member as appropriate) should bear the responsibility for affording reparation in full in cases of 'gross negligence or wilful misconduct'.[162] In such cases, the UN bears the full liability for compensation, while retaining the right to seek reimbursement from the member of the force or his troop contributing country.[163] While in a way the UN's approach positively enables those harmed to seek 'full' reparation, the notion that it will seek to recover such amounts from the troop contributing country necessarily implies that the UN accepts no real liability for such acts, even though they occurred on its watch and when it exercised effective control. Thus, the worst abuses are relegated to instances of abuse of a few 'bad apples' and do not consider the potential role of the institution in fostering the climate in which the acts were able to take place.

V.4.4 Asylum and migration

The human rights impact of international organizations' conduct also pervades asylum and migration policies. The Office of the UN High Commissioner for Refugees can take binding refugee status determination decisions in several countries; these decisions impact on the lives of vulnerable applicants. As Pallis argues,

[160] See UNGA, 'Resolution on Third-party Liability: Temporal and Financial Limitations' (n 76) para 6. See also Daphna Shraga, 'UN Peacekeeping Operations: Applicability of International Humanitarian Law and Responsibility for Operations-related Damage' (2000) 94(2) AJIL 450, 453.

[161] Jody Prescott, 'Claims' in Dieter Fleck (ed), *The Handbook of the Law on Visiting Forces* (OUP 2001) 173.

[162] UNGA, 'Administrative and budgetary aspects of the financing of the United Nations peacekeeping' (n 62) para 14.

[163] ibid para 14.

'[a] procedural failure can leave refugees at risk of return to the country from which they fled *(refoulement)*, can deny them a durable solution—and it may cost them their lives'.[164] Unlike the United Nations High Commissioner for Refugees (UNHCR) recommended procedures for refugee status determination carried out by States,[165] status determination by the UNHCR contains fewer safeguards for applicants, and does not afford the same possibilities for review.

The OIOS has issued a number of reports concerning UNHCR, including ones which chronicled corruption in its Nairobi office[166] and the sexual exploitation of refugees in West Africa.[167] OIOS recommended UNHCR to set up an 'external reporting process for refugees or asylum-seekers who are victimized or otherwise mistreated by UNHCR or its partner non-governmental organization staff members'.[168] UNHCR set up the Inspector General's Office (IGO) to strengthen its own internal oversight capacity[169] and following on from the OIOS recommendations access by alleged victims to the IGO was facilitated, leading to a significant increase in claims. The IGO can receive individual complaints, including allegations of staff misconduct raised by refugees.[170] The office's mandate concerns professional misconduct,[171] and thus it tends to deal with issues such as fraud or abuse as opposed to problems which may arise in the course of refugee status determination. Furthermore, it does not address the crucial question of remedies to the aggrieved parties.

Concerns have equally been raised about the structures in place to oversee the European Agency for the Management of Operational Cooperation at the External Borders of the Member States of the European Union (FRONTEX),[172] an agency

[164] Mark Pallis, 'The Operation of UNHCR's Accountability Mechanisms' (2004–2005) 37 NYU J Int'l L & Pol 869, 878. See also Michael Alexander, 'Refugee Status Determination Conducted by UNHCR' (1999) 11 Int'l J Refugee L 251 (1999); Michael Kagan, 'The Beleaguered Gatekeeper: Protection Challenges Posed by UNHCR Refugee Status Determination' (2006) 18 Int'l J Refugee L 1, 9–12.

[165] UNHCR, 'Determination of Refugee Status' (12 October 1977) 8 (XXVIII)—1977; UNHCR, 'Global Consultations on International Protection/Third Track: Asylum Processes (Fair and Efficient Asylum Procedures)' (31 May 2001) UN Doc EC/GC/01/12.

[166] UNGA, 'Investigation into allegations of refugee smuggling at the Nairobi Branch Office of the Office of the United Nations High Commissioner for Refugees' (21 December 2001) UN Doc A/56/733.

[167] UNGA, 'Report of the Office of Internal Oversight Services on the Investigation into Sexual Exploitation of Refugees by Aid Workers in West Africa' (11 October 2002) UN Doc A/57/465.

[168] UNGA, 'Investigation into allegations of refugee smuggling at the Nairobi Branch Office of the Office of the United Nations High Commissioner for Refugees' (n 166) para 87.

[169] UNHCR, 'Relationship between the Inspector General's Office (IGO) and the United Nations Office of Internal Oversight Services (OIOS)' (Informal Consultative Meeting, 21 July 2005) www.unhcr.org/42de51652.pdf (last accessed 27 December 2016).

[170] See Pallis (n 164) 892–98.

[171] UNHCR, 'How to Report Misconduct and What to Expect?' (undated) www.unhcr.org/4a1278f06.html (last accessed 27 December 2016).

[172] Amnesty International, 'The Human Cost of Fortress Europe: Human Rights Violations against Migrants and Refugees at Europe's Borders' (2014) AI Index EUR 05/001/2014. See also Elspeth Guild and others, 'Implementation of the EU Charter of Fundamental Rights and its Impact on EU Home Affairs Agencies Frontex, Europol and the European Asylum Support Office' (2011) European Parliament Study, Directorate General For Internal Policies, Policy Department C: Citizens' Rights And Constitutional Affairs, Civil Liberties, Justice And Home Affairs, EU Doc PE 453.196, 105;

that was established in 2004,[173] and expanded in 2016.[174] The Parliamentary Assembly of the Council of Europe has recognized that: 'although ... [FRONTEX] plays an ever increasing role in interception at sea, there are inadequate guarantees of respect for human rights and obligations arising under international and European Union law, in the context of the joint operations it coordinates' and it 'is concerned about the lack of clarity regarding the respective responsibilities of European Union States and Frontex and the absence of adequate guarantees for the respect of fundamental rights and international standards in the framework of joint operations coordinated by that agency'.[175] FRONTEX typically operates through Member States, but there remain instances in which responsibility may be attributed to FRONTEX, although the allocation of liability between the Agency and Member States is ambiguous.[176]

Since its establishment, concerns have been raised about the liability of FRONTEX for human rights violations which have been said to have occurred under the guise of its joint operations,[177] and the lack of clarity regarding its responsibility.[178]

In 2011, reforms to FRONTEX underscored the Agency's commitment to carry out its work 'fully respecting applicable Union law, including the Charter of Fundamental Rights of the European Union; applicable international law, including the Geneva Convention relating to the Status of Refugees ... and obligations relating to access to international protection, particularly the principle of non-return'.[179] In 2012, FRONTEX appointed a Fundamental Rights Officer and set up a Consultative Forum on Fundamental Rights to monitor compliance with the Strategy. It has developed internal procedures to report possible violations and can follow up reports of violations. On 6 March 2012, the European Ombudsman initiated an inquiry into FRONTEX operations and underscored the importance

PACE, 'Frontex: Human Rights Responsibilities' Doc 13161 (Committee on Migration, Refugees and Displaced Persons, 8 April 2013).

173 Regulation (EU) No 1168/2011 of the European Parliament and of the Council of 25 October 2011 amending Council Regulation (EC) No 2007/2004 establishing a European Agency for the Management of Operational Cooperation at the External Borders of the Member States of the European Union, EU Doc L 304/2 (22 November 2011).

174 Regulation No 2016/1624 on the European Border and Coast Guard (adopted 14 September 2016, entered into force 6 October 2016) [2016] OJ L 251/1.

175 PACE, The interception and rescue at sea of asylum seekers, refugees and irregular migrants (21 June 2011) Res 1821 (2011) paras 5.4 and 10 respectively.

176 Regulation No 2016/1624 on the European Border and Coast Guard (n 174) art 5.

177 Ska Keller and others, '*Frontex Agency: Which Guarantees for Human Rights?*' (2011) Migreurop, European Free Alliance; Human Rights Watch, 'The EU's Dirty Hands Frontex Involvement in Ill-Treatment of Migrant Detainees in Greece' (2011) 46; Human Rights Watch, 'Pushed Back, Pushed Around: Italy's Forced Return of Boat Migrants and Asylum Seekers, Libya's Mistreatment of Migrants and Asylum Seekers' (2009).

178 PACE Resolution 1821 (n 175) para 10.

179 Regulation (EU) No 1168/2011 of the European Parliament and the Council amending Council Regulation (EC) No 2007/2004 establishing a European Agency for the Management of Operational Cooperation at the External Borders of the Member States of the European Union, OJ 2011 L 304 (25 October 2011) art 1.2.2.

of granting effective access to a complaints mechanism for infringements of fundamental rights in all FRONTEX activities submitted by persons individually affected by the infringements and also in the public interest.[180] The Ombudsman also initiated an inquiry into the means through which FRONTEX ensures respect for fundamental rights in joint return operations.[181]

The 2016 reforms introduce a new complaint mechanism to monitor and ensure respect for human rights in all activities of the agency.[182] It is open to anyone who alleges to be the victim of a human rights violation committed by staff during an operation coordinated by the Agency. The Fundamental Rights Officer who 'shall be independent in the performance of his or her duties'[183] decides on admissibility and ensures 'appropriate follow-up' by the agency or by a Member State when the latter's responsibility is engaged.[184] The nature of what may constitute 'appropriate follow-up' is not spelled out.

In principle, following the Lisbon Treaty[185] FRONTEX's actions could be the subject of proceedings before the Court of Justice of the EU. If it had jurisdiction, the CJEU could review the legality of FRONTEX acts and annul them if it had acted unlawfully,[186] and rule on allegations relating to the failure to act.[187] Possible violations of human rights could result in non-contractual liability if the conduct is attributable to an EU action. But, it will be difficult to attribute conduct to FRONTEX given its primary role of coordinating Member States' actions, although this would turn on the facts in any given case. Nonetheless, access of irregular migrants to the CJEU is extremely limited.[188]

V.4.5 Policing, criminal record keeping, and transfer of data

Cross-border policing and intelligence sharing in the detection of crime and the pursuit of alleged offenders have also given rise to human rights concerns for the institutions involved. A key question is the extent to which conduct can be attributed to the international organizations involved in such work.

[180] Decision of the European Ombudsman Closing Own-initiative Inquiry OI/5/2012/BEH-MHZ concerning the European Agency for the Management of Operational Cooperation at the External Borders of the Member States of the European Union (Frontex) (12 November 2013) paras 79–83.

[181] European Ombudsperson, 'Ensuring Respect for Fundamental Rights in Joint Operations for the Forced Return of Irregular Third-country Migrants' OI/9/2014/MHZ (20 October 2014).

[182] Regulation No 2016/1624 on the European Border and Coast Guard (n 174) art 72.

[183] ibid art 71.

[184] ibid art 72.

[185] Treaty of Lisbon, Consolidated Versions of the Treaty on European Union (TEU) and the Treaty on the Functioning of the European Union (TFEU) (adopted 13 December 2007, entered into force 1 December 2009) [2008] OJ C115/01; PACE Resolution 1821 (n 175) art 3.1.

[186] Treaty of Lisbon (n 185) arts 263, 265.

[187] ibid art 267. Elspeth Guild and Florian Geyer (eds), *Security Versus Justice?: Police and Judicial Cooperation in the European Union* (Ashgate Publishing 2008) 44.

[188] For an analysis of the limited standing of individuals to pursue claims before the CJEU see Chapter VII.

(1) Policing

Interpol publishes 'red notices' regarding persons wanted by States for prosecution or to serve a sentence based on an arrest warrant or court decision. These notices are based on information supplied by States and while not binding, they are used to seek the location and arrest of wanted persons with a view to extradition or similar lawful action. This can lead to arrests, which in turn can cause situations which 'are not in conformity with international law'.[189] Arrests may be unlawful or arbitrary. Extraditions or transfers which follow may violate the political offences exceptions under extradition law and/or breach the prohibition on *refoulement*. Given Interpol's role in circulating such information and the consequences of such circulation, it has devised a procedure to allow individuals who are the subject of the notice to approach an internal Commission for the Control of Interpol's Files[190] to review what personal information is held and to ensure that the processing of that information conforms with Interpol's rules and does not infringe the basic rights of the persons concerned.[191]

This Commission is charged with reviewing individual complaints and ensuring that Interpol facilities are used in compliance with relevant legal rules. In the past, any review would only occur after the information is stored and circulated, and thus it did not serve an initial preventive function.[192] However, changes to this review process have been instituted; all red notices are now reviewed by the General Secretariat prior to their publication.[193] However, the precise nature of the *ex ante* review, including the criteria and standards which are applied, remains unclear. Also, Interpol issued new guidance which enables it to remove a red notice if it can verify that the person has been recognized as a refugee under the 1951 Refugee Convention.[194]

The Commission's power to release the data it holds to individuals is severely limited by member sovereignty; it must receive the permission of the data supplier before data can be released to the individual.[195] This is understood as necessary to preserve the integrity of police investigations.[196] In some cases, the result of its investigation may itself remain classified,[197] which can prove problematic for the

[189] ILC, 'Comments and Observations Received from Governments and International Organizations', Report of the International Law Commission on the Work of its 57th Session' (n 8) 20. See Chapter III, where Interpol's 'acknowledgement and adoption' of conduct as its own, is discussed.

[190] Interpol, 'Rules relating to the Control of Information and Access to Interpol's Files' (RCI), (ICPO-International General Assembly, Cancún, 73rd Session, 5–8 October 2004) Res AG-2004-RES-08. See Interpol, 'Composition of the Commission for the Control of INTERPOL's Files (the Commission)—Amendment to Article 2 of the Rules on the Control of Information and Access to INTERPOL's Files (RCI)' (ICPO-INTERPOL General Assembly, Singapore, 11–15 October 2009, 78th Session) Res AG-2009-RES-13, that amended arts 2.a and 2.b of the RCI. See generally Wui Ling (n 151); Mario Savino, 'Global Administrative Law Meets "Soft" Powers: The Uncomfortable Case of Interpol Red Notices' (2010) 43 NYU J Int'l L Pol 263, 299–336.

[191] RCI (n 190) arts 1(a), 4(a), 9(a).

[192] See Savino (n 190) 313–14.

[193] Interpol, *Rules on the Processing of Data* (ICPO-Interpol General Assembly, 85th Session, 2016) Res AG-2016-RES-06 III/IRPD/GA/2011 art 86.

[194] https://www.fairtrials.org/wp-content/uploads/INTERPOL-TEXT-ON-REFUGEE-POLICY.pdf (last accessed 27 December 2016).

[195] RCI (n 190) art 11(b).

[196] See Wui Ling (n 151) 401.

[197] See RCI (n 190) art 18(4).

claimant. As Wui Ling notes, 'the Commission may not be able to explain to the individual the kind of violation that took place or the remedial steps that have been taken. With such limited information, the individual is often unable to verify if the Commission's recommendations have been complied with'.[198] Furthermore, the Commission is only empowered to recommend the release to the individual and/or the altering or removal of data; the ultimate decisions on what action should be taken rests with the General Secretariat of Interpol,[199] and/or the Executive Committee,[200] as appropriate. Accordingly, when the Commission takes a final view, its report and recommendations are forwarded to the General Secretariat, who ultimately decides whether data should be deleted or amended, with permission of the data source.

Europol has a similar body, the Joint Supervisory Body, which handles requests for personal information held by Europol and for such information to be corrected or deleted.[201] Unlike the Interpol Commission, Europol has instituted an appeals process, whereby concerned individuals can appeal decisions of the Joint Supervisory Body to the Appeals Committee,[202] and the decisions are made public.[203] Furthermore, the European Ombudsperson has also taken up issues concerning Europol's handling of requests for access to documents.

(2) Listing procedures

The UN Security Council has instituted an administrative procedure as a result of the impact of the listing procedures of its Al-Qaeda/Taliban Sanctions Committee on individuals' freedom of movement and access to personal bank accounts. The use of mandatory sanctions is intended to apply pressure on a State or entity to comply with the objectives set by the Security Council without resorting to the use of force. Sanctions thus offer the Security Council an important instrument to enforce its decisions. The listing procedures stem from Security Council resolution 1267,[204] adopted under Chapter VII of the Charter which requires States to freeze, inter alia, funds and other financial resources and to take steps to restrict the entry into or transit through their territory of individuals, groups, undertakings, and other entities associated with Al-Qaeda designated by the Committee. As a result, affected individuals' bank accounts have been frozen and they have been unable to travel. When the resolution was adopted, there was no formal procedure through which affected individuals could challenge their inclusion on a list. Individuals

[198] See Wui Ling (n 151) 401.

[199] See RCI (n 190) art 6(b), art 5(e)(3)–(4), and art 6(a).

[200] Interpol Constitution art 22.e, as argued by Wui Ling (n 151) 391.

[201] See website of the Joint Supervisory Body http://europoljsb.consilium.europa.eu/opinions/rules.aspx?lang=en (last accessed 27 December 2016).

[202] Act No 29/2009 of the Joint Supervisory Body of Europol of 22 June 2009 laying down its rules of procedure (adopted 22 June 2009, entered into force 1 December 2009) (2010) OJ C 45/2 arts 12–29.

[203] Available on the website of the Appeals Committee http://europoljsb.consilium.europa.eu/appeals-committee/appeals-committee---decisions.aspx?lang=en (last accessed 27 December 2016).

[204] The Committee was first established by UNSC, Res 1267/1999 (15 October 1999).

could request their government under the guise of diplomatic protection to request the Sanctions Committee to review the case; however, States were not obliged to take up such cases, nor was the Sanctions Committee obliged to review the case.

Pursuant to SC Resolution 1730, the Security Council established a focal point within the Secretariat (Security Council Subsidiary Organs Branch) to receive delisting requests directly from aggrieved individuals.[205] This provided a direct route for individuals to seek a measure of redress. The mechanism was established to ensure fair and clear procedures for removing individuals and entities from sanctions lists,[206] however it is not independent; it was simply a structure tasked with receiving petitions from individuals or through their State of residence or citizenship, and ensuring that such requests were duly placed before the Committee. Individual petitioners had no right to consideration of their request, nor any right to be heard by the Sanctions Committee. Similarly, they were not provided with reasons for the Committee's decisions which were taken by consensus without clear standards of review to guide decision-making,[207] nor with any opportunity to appeal an unfavourable decision.

In 2009, the Security Council established an Ombudsperson to assist with delisting requests.[208] Under the revised procedure, petitioners can submit delisting requests through the Ombudsperson.[209] Additionally, Member States may at any time submit directly to the Committee requests for delisting of individuals, groups, undertakings, and/or entities inscribed on the Al-Qaida Sanctions List. Under the two procedures, designating States and States of citizenship and residence are entitled to review delisting requests and indicate whether they support or oppose the request in order to facilitate the Committee's review. The Committee also carries out an annual review of the names on the Consolidated List to ensure the list is accurate.

While the introduction of the mandate of the Ombudsperson provided several new safeguards for individuals, and in a subsequent resolution reversed the need for Committee consensus to allow a delisting request,[210] the Committee, a political body, was still vested with the sole authority to overturn its decisions.[211] The Ombudsperson was not privy to information States did not wish to disclose.

[205] UNSC Res 1730/2006 (19 December 2006) para 1.

[206] ibid 5th recital; see also UNSC, 'Statement of the President of the Security Council' (22 June 2006) UN Doc S/PRST/2006/28.

[207] Clemens Feinfaugle, 'The UN Security Council Al-Qaida and Taliban Sanctions Committee: Emerging Principles of International Institutional Law for the Protection of Individuals?' (2008) 9 German LJ 1513, 1532.

[208] UNSC Res 1904/2009 (17 December 2009).

[209] UNSC Res 2083/2012 (17 December 2012).

[210] UNSC Res 1989/2011 (17 June 2011). A delisting recommendation by the Ombudsperson takes effect automatically 60 days after the Committee completes its consideration of the comprehensive report, unless the Committee decides otherwise by consensus. If there is no consensus, any member of the Committee may refer the delisting request to the Security Council (the 'trigger mechanism' procedure).

[211] UNGA, 'Report of the Special Rapporteur on the Promotion and Protection of Human Rights and Fundamental Freedoms while Countering Terrorism, Ben Emmerson' (26 September 2012) UN Doc A/67/396 para 32.

Petitioners' access to information, including exculpatory information, was similarly confined to States' discretion.[212] Furthermore, evidence obtained by torture has allegedly been used to justify designations and the Ombudsperson office has not automatically rejected such evidence from her considerations.[213]

In order to address these challenges, the UN Special Rapporteur on Counter-Terrorism recommended the Security Council to establish an 'independent adjudicator at the United Nations level with jurisdiction to review and overturn a designation by the Committee'.[214]

V.5 Conclusions

Of the mechanisms surveyed, none has the capacity to afford adequate and effective reparation in the manner envisioned in Chapter IV. Most of the bodies surveyed only have recommendatory powers, and thus the decision on whether to provide reparation, and if so the form it should take is left to executive bodies, which have often failed to heed recommendations where these have been made and left victims without a substantial remedy. The Kosovo HRAP has on numerous occasions recommended UNMIK to afford reparation for the human rights breaches found by the Panel however adequate compensation has not been paid.[215]

Part of the difficulty stems from UNMIK's position that it is bound by the UN General Assembly instruction, which seeks to limit the organization's liability in peacekeeping operations, the terms of which have since been incorporated into agreements with States.[216] This is despite the fact that the UN agreed to establish the specialist HRAP body distinct from the UN claims process, which has the authority to recommend the appropriate remedy in the case of a finding of a human rights violation. This significantly undercuts HRAP's mandate.[217] While some HRAP applicants have received *ex gratia* payments, 'the compensation is limited to economic loss, including in particular loss of earnings. No compensation has been paid for pain and suffering, moral anguish, punitive or moral damages or other types of loss which are not directly related to the injury'.[218] In its final Annual Report, HRAP wrote: 'Due to UNMIK's failure to follow the Panel's recommendations, the HRAP process has obtained no compensation for the complainants. As such, they have been victimized twice by UNMIK: by the original human rights

[212] ibid para 39–41, 45. *Yassin Abdullah Kadi v European Commission*, General Court (Seventh Chamber), 30 September 2010 [2011] CMLR 24 para 128; CJEU, *European Commission and Others v Yassin Abdullah Kadi* (GC), Joined Cases C–584/10 P, C–593/10 P and C–595/10 P (18 July 2013); *Her Majesty's Treasury v Mohammed Jabar Ahmed* [2010] UKSC 2, [78], [80]–[81], [239].

[213] See Emmerson (n 211) paras 46–49.

[214] ibid para 23.

[215] See Chatham House (n 122) 10.

[216] UNGA, 'Resolution on Third-party liability: temporal and financial limitations' (n 76).

[217] European Commission for Democracy Through Law (Venice Commission), 'Opinion on the Existing Mechanisms to Review the Compatibility with Human Rights Standards of Acts by UNMIK and EULEX in Kosovo' (21 December 2010) 545/2009, CDL-AD(2010)051 para 46.

[218] *Balaj and Others v UNMIK* Case no 04/07 (HRAP, 27 February 2015) paras 113, 271–74. See also HRAP, 'Annual Report' (2014) paras 75–79.

violations committed against them and by not receiving compensation through this process'.[219]

Very few mechanisms are able to afford compensation, and of those that do, often there are restrictions with respect to quantum, or the factual scenarios that may qualify. The EULEX HRRP in Kosovo specifically excludes compensation from its remit. The Venice Commission, when commenting on this limitation, noted that it 'is of the opinion that, in principle, *restitutio in integrum* is the most suitable manner of redress of human rights violations. The possibility for the HRRP to recommend remedial action removing the effects, and the causes, of the violation is therefore crucial. However, in some cases the most effective remedy is financial compensation, which instead the HRRP cannot recommend'.[220]

Other forms of reparation aside from compensation are equally unavailable or inaccessible. Few mechanisms allow individuals to seek restitution or specific performance. For instance, individuals who are affected by Interpol's inclusion of certain data in its files have the right to file a complaint with the independent Commission for the Control of Interpol's Files. However, they do not have a right to the removal of such data in case the Commission finds in their favour. Such removal remains within the discretion of the Secretary General.

Very few of the mechanisms afford victims that have suffered physical or psychological harm the ability to seek rehabilitation. As is evidenced by the 2015 OIOS report on sexual exploitation and abuse responses, service provision remains aspirational due to a lack of funds and poor coordination.[221]

Few mechanisms afford victims with satisfaction or guarantees of non-repetition. The fact that some adjudicative mechanisms have made findings of responsibility is itself a form of satisfaction, however depending on the harm suffered, this may ring hollow for many victims. Also, decisions of adjudicative bodies are often not made public, impeding transparency, disadvantaging claimants, and limiting their value as forms of satisfaction.[222] The World Bank Inspection Panel investigations have prompted certain changes to a number of high-profile projects, however adequate and effective reparations to aggrieved individuals have not always followed.

In summary, the current framework does not afford a realistic prospect for human rights and international humanitarian law abuses to be adequately resolved. The reasons for this are many and interlinked as described above. With respect to the UN, the most problematic of these stem from its broad understanding of its ability to apply a *lex specialis* to remedial claims and forms of reparation; the failure to characterize anything other than private claims against the organization as receivable; and the inability for injured individuals to challenge these understandings, which affords the UN a monopoly over the law and its procedures.

219 HRAP, 'Annual Report' (2016) para 255.

220 Venice Commission 2010 Opinion (n 100) para 67.

221 UN OIOS, 'Evaluation of the Enforcement and Remedial Assistance Efforts for Sexual Exploitation and Abuse by the United Nations and Related Personnel in Peacekeeping Operations' (n 88).

222 See Wellens, *Remedies Against International Organisations* (n 78) 104.

Some commentators have indicated that one should be happy with what we have and shouldn't expect more. French and Kirkham, for example, have argued that international organizations would never have accepted 'more intrusive procedures—with greater legal enforcement powers—over the same subject matter. This is not a viable political alternative'.[223] They contend that it would be unrealistic to expect more, or to think that the international organizations themselves would allow for more.[224] However, on a rights based analysis, the question is not whether international organizations would have been willing to do something more but whether as a matter of law, they must do so. If the latter is true then the question becomes how to move towards a legally compliant model. Indeed, should it be accepted that international organizations must afford reparation for breaches of human rights and international humanitarian law that correspond to the standards that exist in those specialized fields, there is a corresponding obligation for them to establish the framework for that to be achieved, which might include strengthening the internal adjudicative framework.

As identified, the most critical gap concerns the absence of an independent route for disagreements as to the state of the law to be addressed. Currently, human rights and international humanitarian law claims will not be necessarily or typically, taken up by international organizations for the reasons already cited, nor are they likely to be espoused by States on behalf of their nationals. Victims will thus have no route to assert their view as to the law, the position of the international organization will simply trump unless the individual has access to a formal decision-making body before which they can state their case.

[223] French and Kirkham (n 105) 205–206. [224] ibid 182.

VI
Challenging the Conduct of International Organizations before Domestic Courts

VI.1 Introduction

This chapter is about domestic courts. Victims often have no other option than to seek a remedy against an international organization before domestic courts. This is so even though the domestic character of such courts does not lend well to them playing this particular adjudicative role and organizational immunities from the jurisdiction of domestic courts are near absolute.

The rules governing domestic courts' ability to adjudicate claims involving conduct that took place outside their territory resemble the jurisdictional considerations for domestic courts when faced with claims against international organizations. Even more so, the extent to which domestic courts may adjudicate claims concerning the conduct of a foreign sovereign State is somewhat analogous to the considerations governing domestic courts' jurisdiction over international organizations. These two areas of exception are somewhat relevant when determining domestic courts' jurisdiction over international organizations. However, international organizations are fundamentally different to States and the underlying rationales for the jurisdictional rules that have developed to determine 'horizontal allocations of authority among sovereign states'[1] are not easily transposed to them. The possession of territory and sovereign equality, neither of which apply to international organizations, underpin the rationale for rules relating to the allocation of jurisdiction between States.

Arguably, it is time for absolutist principles that domestic courts are *always* barred from adjudicating claims concerning international organizations to give way to a more nuanced approach which takes into account the particular context. Domestic adjudication impacts the independence of the organization; however, this does not mean that there are necessarily no instances in which such intrusions are warranted. Invariably, there will be institutional costs associated with the forays of domestic courts into such areas. However, this should not imply necessarily and in all circumstances that such costs are not warranted.

[1] Chimène Keitner, 'State Courts and Transitory Torts in Transnational Human Rights Cases' (2013) 3 UC Irvine L Rev 81, 92.

While domestic courts may not be ideal forums to resolve disputes concerning international organizations, at times they will be the only available forum. And, the limited practice suggests that the engagement of domestic (and international) courts in disputes concerning international organizations—and even the threat of such engagement—creates incentives for the organizations to establish and strengthen their own internal claims processes. Thus, in addition to the direct impact access to domestic courts will have on aggrieved individuals, such access can also serve an indirect regulating function on the behaviour of international organizations. Reinisch refers to this as 'a subsidiary control tool'.[2]

This chapter outlines the limited ways in which domestic courts have overcome jurisdictional and procedural barriers to entertain claims against international organizations and in contrast, the avoidance techniques some courts have used to entrench those same barriers. It ends by outlining the areas in which further inroads may be made, focusing in particular on the relationship between immunities and the need for international organizations to develop appropriate modes of settlement, as well as the criteria to determine whether immunities should be waived by international organizations.

VI.2 The Ability of Domestic Courts to Adjudicate Claims Involving International Organizations

Courts require jurisdiction to adjudicate claims. Generally, domestic courts have jurisdiction over persons and property and acts occurring within their territory. Territorial competence derives from State sovereignty—States' authority to act within their borders and to regulate internal affairs freely.[3] Adjudication of claims where the evidence is located will usually be most efficient and serves the interest of showing up close to those most affected by the acts that justice was done. For all these reasons, the court where the wrongs took place will normally have the strongest claim to jurisdiction.

Yet, territorial competence is anomalous when considering claims against international organizations. Organization's conduct naturally impacts States and their citizens.[4] International organizations operate on the territory of one or many States and their employees will be nationals of a State. However, the place where the wrong occurred can straddle several countries. The site of responsibility may be the country office, but particularly in a peacekeeping or development context, it is

[2] August Reinisch (ed), *Challenging Acts of International Organizations before National Courts* (OUP 2010) 8.

[3] Charter of the United Nations and Statute of the International Court of Justice (adopted 26 June 1945, entered into force 24 October 1945) 1 UNTS XVI art 104 (UN Charter) art 2 para 1; UNGA, 'Declaration on Principles of International Law Concerning Friendly Relations and Cooperation Among States in Accordance with the Charter of the United Nations' (24 October 1970) UN Doc A/RES/25/2625.

[4] *Interpretation of the Agreement of 25 March 1951 between the WHO and Egypt* (Advisory Opinion) [1980] ICJ Rep 73, Separate Opinion of Judge Ago [155].

foreseeable that host State courts will be ill-equipped to adjudicate.[5] If the wrong stemmed from policies or directives taken by the headquarters, the site of responsibility may be construed more aptly as the headquarters. Regardless, by virtue of the organization's status and independence, this activity will place it outside the usual competence of the territorial State. There is thus no domestic court that has inherent or natural authority over the conduct of international organizations.

There are two main exceptions to territorial competence. The first concerns a domestic court's competence over acts which took place outside its territory: extraterritorial jurisdiction. The second is the court's competence over actors typically understood as immune from the jurisdiction of domestic courts. Largely because of the dearth of jurisdictional rules specific to international organizations and because the decisions whether to adjudicate claims against international organizations have proceeded on similar if not identical grounds, principles are extrapolated by reference to these two areas of exception.

VI.2.1 Extraterritorial jurisdiction and principles of restraint

Extraterritorial bases for exercising jurisdiction[6] reflect the variety of ways in which a claim's subject matter or the plaintiff or defendant interact with a particular country, even when the conduct does not fall neatly within the confines of that territory. These rules differ depending on the area of law. The rules governing the exercise of extraterritorial jurisdiction over crimes occurring wholly or primarily outside a State's own territory are relatively clear and are reflected in a number of international treaties.[7] In contrast, there is no universal treaty governing the allocation of jurisdiction in civil matters between States or the mutual recognition of bases for exercising extraterritorial civil jurisdiction.[8] Nor is there an accepted uniform basis for determining domestic court jurisdiction over claims concerning international organizations.

Extraterritorial competence in civil cases exists when plaintiffs are nationals of the State exercising jurisdiction and/or where defendants habitually reside or are domiciled in the jurisdiction, or in more limited cases, when property or assets are

[5] See, however, UNGA, 'Report of the Group of Legal Experts on Ensuring the Accountability of UN Staff and Experts on Mission with Respect to Criminal Acts Committed in Peacekeeping Operations' (16 August 2006) UN Doc A/60/980 10–14, which recommends greater resort to host State jurisdiction in criminal matters, despite the practical challenges posed by the post-conflict environment.

[6] International Bar Association, 'Report of the Task Force on Extraterritorial Jurisdiction' (6 February 2009) http://tinyurl.com/taskforce-etj-pdf (last accessed 27 December 2016).

[7] ibid 133–200.

[8] The efforts which led to the 2001 draft Hague Convention on Jurisdiction and Foreign Judgments in Civil and Commercial Matters were aborted due to a lack of consensus on the text. See Hague Conference on Private International Law, 'Summary of the Outcome of the Discussion in Commission II of the First Part of the Diplomatic Conference' (Interim text, 6–20 June 2001) www.hcch.net/upload/wop/jdgm2001draft_e.pdf (last accessed 27 December 2016). In Europe, a more uniform framework exists, although jurisdiction for civil claims related to the exercise of public powers are outside the framework's scope and thus are left to States' national law. See Case C–292/05 *Lechouritou v Germany* [2007] ECR I–01519 CJEU paras 38–43.

located there. Domicile is the predominant basis for jurisdiction over multinational corporate defendants, including claims against parent companies for acts carried out by foreign subsidiaries.[9] In some countries, jurisdiction follows from service of defendants present within the jurisdiction. Jurisdiction may also exist by way of agreement between the parties.

As will be described, domestic courts also apply restraint principles to avoid exercising jurisdiction. The decision to refrain from exercising jurisdiction over international organizations stems from many of the same rationales employed to refrain from exercising jurisdiction over extraterritorial claims and claims concerning the acts of foreign States. Examples of avoidance and jurisdictional restraint are canvassed by Reinisch.[10] Some courts refuse to hear claims against international organizations when there is no express grant of competence,[11] thereby introducing absolutist principles that go beyond what has been set out for foreign States. More frequently, jurisdiction is denied when a claim concerns an organization's compliance with its internal rules.[12] This form of rejection is often accompanied by an assessment that the organization has its own means to resolve the claim and thus there is no need for the forum State to adjudicate in order to ensure claimants' access to justice.

(1) Forum non conveniens *and* lis pendens

In mostly common law countries, the *forum non conveniens* doctrine affords judges discretion to disallow or stay a case or transfer it to another court when it would be significantly more convenient for it to be heard elsewhere.[13] The doctrine is designed to reduce the costs of litigation and avoid plaintiff 'forum shopping'. While there are different approaches, for the doctrine to apply the court must be 'satisfied that there is some other available forum, having competent jurisdiction, which is the appropriate forum for the trial of the action'.[14] Courts will also consider the extent to which the more convenient jurisdiction is actually so in practice—its accessibility to the parties, the costs of doing so and the ability to compel witnesses. In contrast, many civil law countries apply the *lis pendens* rule, which gives priority to the first jurisdiction seized, thus favouring efficiency and predictability. Inside Europe, a *lis pendens* rule has been adopted in the Brussels Regime, which regulates which

[9] *Lubbe v Cape Plc* [2000] UKHL 41, [2000] 1 WLR 1545. In contrast, other cases against domiciled parent companies have been disallowed on the basis of the principle of *forum non conveniens.* See *Anvil Mining Ltd v Association canadienne contre l'impunité*, 2012 QCCA 117, leave to appeal denied (1 November 2013).

[10] August Reinisch, *International Organizations before National Courts* (CUP 2000) 84–168, 233–51.

[11] ibid 123. [12] ibid 114–15.

[13] Alexander Reus, 'Judicial Discretion: A Comparative View of the Doctrine of forum non conveniens in the United States, the United Kingdom, and Germany' (1994) 16 Loyola of Los Angeles Int'l and Comp LR 455, 459; *Spiliada Maritime Corpn v Cansulex Ltd* [1987] AC 460.

[14] *Spiliada Maritime Corpn v Cansulex Ltd* (n 13) 476–78.

courts have jurisdiction in civil or commercial disputes.[15] The rule usually turns on whether it can be shown that the cause of action is the same in both jurisdictions.

These jurisdictional principles may help determine whether a forum State should adjudicate a claim against an international organization that is brought before it. Domestic courts will need to assess whether there is a significantly more appropriate forum. There is the place where the impugned acts took place or where the impacts of those acts were felt (often this will entail multiple jurisdictions), the place convenient to the complainants by reason of their nationality or residence, or the location of the headquarters. If the organization has its own internal dispute resolution mechanism, a domestic court may use *forum non conveniens* type arguments to refrain from exercising jurisdiction, to the extent that the internal mechanism has a realistic prospect of affording an adequate remedy. In contrast, the State where the acts took place may be understood as most appropriate, given that most plaintiffs are located there and it is the site of the evidence. However, that assumption may be displaced if that State is adjudged to be unable to afford fair and equitable proceedings, owing to the breakdown of the rule of law or related reasons.

There may be difficulties to apply such principles to actions involving multiple plaintiffs in an array of jurisdictions. Some may be present in the jurisdiction where the claim is lodged, others may be elsewhere and may have no knowledge of the proceedings and it could be difficult to bind them to any settlement or judgment. These issues have arisen in relation to a class action claim brought against the UN and certain UN officials in New York on the basis that certain plaintiffs (although not all) are citizens and residents of the USA and residents in New York and given the presence of the UN Headquarters in New York.[16] Domestic courts have had to navigate such challenges in class action claims brought against corporate defendants.[17] While this can complicate proceedings, solutions such as requiring opt-in clauses for foreign plaintiff classes could be pursued to promote fairness.[18]

(2) Political questions and act of State doctrines

Domestic suits may also be stayed or quashed pursuant to 'political questions' and act of State doctrines. Government acts can be non-justiciable under the separation of powers principle; as political decisions, their merits should not be scrutinized by the judiciary. The political questions doctrine is often used to avoid courts' scrutiny of foreign policy or national security considerations, which are understood to be

[15] Convention on jurisdiction and the recognition and enforcement of judgments in civil and commercial matters (adopted 30 October 2007, entered into force 1 January 2010) OJ 2007 L 339/3 art 28,; EU Regulation No 1215/2012 on jurisdiction and the recognition and enforcement of judgments in civil and commercial matters (adopted 12 December 2012, entry into force 9 January 2013) art 22.

[16] *Georges v United Nations* 13 Civ 7146(JPO) (SDNY) 9 January 2015, which concerns the UN's responsibility for the cholera epidemic in Haiti.

[17] See eg *Phillips Petroleum v Shutts* 472 US 797 (1985). Note, however, that the court's handling of foreign members of the class has been criticized. See Debra Lyn Bassett, 'U.S. Class Actions Go Global: Transnational Class Actions and Personal Jurisdiction' (2003) 72(1) Fordham LR 41.

[18] Bassett (n 17) 87.

more appropriately addressed by the executive.[19] The act of State doctrine stems from some of the same separation of power rationales, particularly regarding the need to ensure the primacy of the executive in the conduct of foreign relations.[20] Courts should avoid ruling on the legitimacy of a foreign government's actions or laws as to do otherwise 'might hinder rather than further [this country's] pursuit of goals both for itself and for the community of nations as a whole in the international sphere'.[21]

Political questions and act of State doctrines are discretionary tools which have been interpreted flexibly.[22] The doctrines are not applied uniformly as there has rarely been a clear line drawn between executive acts (containing non-justiciable elements) and those taken to implement executive decisions (which should in principle be justiciable).[23] Franck noted that when the political interests are to avoid certain issues from being litigated, there is a tendency for over-broad interpretations of the scope of the doctrine,[24] and the opposite has also been asserted: when political interests align with litigation, judges have been more 'activist' in asserting jurisdiction.[25]

There is no international law requirement to deny jurisdiction,[26] unlike, arguably and as is later described in this chapter, for State immunity. That there are political aspects to questions before a court does not necessarily negate jurisdiction.[27] Courts may find it appropriate to assess the legality and constitutionality of governmental action, even in sensitive cases.[28] Domestic courts routinely investigate the lawfulness of foreign State conduct, particularly in regards to *refoulement* claims.[29] Furthermore, the act of State doctrine permits exceptions where the impugned act

[19] See generally Thomas Franck, *Political Questions / Judicial Answers: Does the Rule of Law Apply to Foreign Affairs?* (Princeton University Press 1992).

[20] ibid 105; Prosper Weil, '*Le contrôle par les tribunaux nationaux de la licéité des actes des gouvernements étrangers*' (1977) 23 Annuaire Français de Droit International 9, 30.

[21] *Banco Nacional de Cuba v Sabbatino* 376 US 398 (1964).

[22] Thijmen Koopmans, *Courts and Political Institutions: A Comparative View* (CUP 2003) 98–104. See also *Buttes Gas and Oil Co v Hammer (No 3)* [1982] AC 888.

[23] Michaela Frulli, 'When Are States Liable Towards Individuals for Serious Violations of Humanitarian Law? The *Markovic* Case' (2003) 1 J Int'l Crim J 406, 417 411–12.

[24] See Franck (n 19) 79.

[25] Sharon Weill, *The Role of National Courts in Applying International Humanitarian Law* (OUP 2014) 100, who takes a similar view to Franck (n 19) but argues that the same principle could also apply in reverse when political interests align with the plaintiffs.

[26] Hazel Fox QC and Philippa Webb, *The Law of State Immunity* (3rd edn, OUP 2013) 71. See *Regina v Bow Street Metropolitan Stipendiary Magistrate, ex p Pinochet Ugarte (No 3)* [2000] 1 AC 147, 269 (Lord Millett); *Sabbatino* (n 21) pt V; *Belhaj v Straw* [2014] EWCA Civ 1394 [122], affirmed [2017] UKSC 3. See also Dominique Carreau and Fabrizio Marrella, *Droit International* (11th edn, Pedone 2012) 1: '[*la*] *politique de retenue que les tribunaux américains ont longtemps pratiquée au nom de la théorie de "l'Act of State" est étrangère au droit international et n'est nullement dictée par lui. Elle relève de considérations tenant à une certaine conception de l'ordonnancement constitutionnel interne, en l'espèce au désir de respecter une stricte séparation des pouvoirs entre le "judiciaire" et "l'exécutif"*'.

[27] *Legal Consequences of the Construction of a Wall in the Occupied Palestinian Territory* (Advisory Opinion) [2004] ICJ Reports 136 [41].

[28] *Canada (Justice) v Khadr* [2008] 2 SCR 125, 2008 SCC 28 [36]–[37]; *Hamdan v Rumsfeld* 548 US 557 (2006); *Boumediene v Bush* 553 US 723 (2008).

[29] *RB (Algeria) v Secretary of State for the Home Department* [2010] 2 AC 110.

is contrary to public policy,[30] including breaches of international law such as gross violations of human rights.[31] As the English Court of Appeal held in *Yukos Capital v OJSC Rosneft*, the act of State doctrine will not apply to 'a breach of international law which is a matter of deep concern to the worldwide community'.[32] Similarly, the Canadian Supreme Court in *Canada (Justice) v Khadr* held that: 'the deference required by the principle of comity ends where clear violations of international law and fundamental rights begin'.[33] This is also the position taken by the Institut de droit international in its 1993 resolution.[34]

As these restraint doctrines are not 'required' under international law, the basis for applying them to bar a claim or restrain the course of proceedings should satisfy wider considerations. In *Habib v Commonwealth of Australia*, the Australian Federal Court in deciding to exercise jurisdiction took into account that the claim was brought by an Australian and concerned Australian officials' aiding and abetting torture allegedly committed by foreign officials. If the complaint was disallowed, State immunity would bar courts in other jurisdictions from adjudicating Australian officials' role in the crimes; there would be no adequate alternative means of redress.[35] Similar considerations were at play in *Belhaj*.[36] This approach approximates the jurisprudence of the European Court of Human Rights (ECtHR) whereby access to court restrictions must be proportionate.[37] Given that the political questions and act of State doctrines do not constitute absolute bars to proceedings, proportionality considerations apply, as they did in *Habib v Commonwealth of Australia*.

The European Court diverged from this approach in *Marković v Italy*,[38] which concerned Italian officials' role in the aerial bombing by the North Atlantic Treaty Organization (NATO) of a Belgrade radio station. The Italian Court of Cassation had ruled that the conduct of war was an 'act of government'—a political, non-justiciable question,[39] and thus prevented the case from being adjudicated. The Grand Chamber in a slim majority held that there had been no violation of the Convention. The applicants were not denied access to court but only failed to satisfy the conditions for their claim to be adjudicated under domestic law.[40]

[30] See Fox and Webb (n 26) 71.

[31] James Crawford, *Brownlie's Principles of Public International Law* (8th edn, OUP 2012) 72–77. *Oppenheimer v Cattermole* [1976] AC 249, 278, (Lord Cross of Chelsea); *Kuwait Airways Co v Iraqi Airways Co* [2002] UKHL 19; *Abbasi v Secretary of State for Foreign and Commonwealth Affairs* [2002] EWCA Civ 1598 [53]; *Habib v Commonwealth of Australia* [2010] FCAFC 12 [112]. See also *Belhaj v Straw* (n 26) [81], [114], [121], affirmed at [2017] UKSC 3.

[32] *Yukos Capital v OJSC Rosneft* [2012] EWCA Civ 855 [69].

[33] *Canada (Justice) v Khadr* (n 28) [17]–[18]. Note the nearly identical conclusion in *Habib v Commonwealth of Australia* (n 31) para 37.

[34] IDI, 'The Activities of National Judges and the International Relations of their State' (Milan, 7 September 1993) art 2.

[35] *Habib v Commonwealth of Australia* (n 31) paras 118, 119, 129, and 130.

[36] See *Belhaj v Straw* (n 26).

[37] *Waite and Kennedy v Germany* (GC) App no 26083/94 (ECtHR, 18 February 1999) [68]–[74].

[38] *Markovic v Italy* App no 1398/03 (ECtHR, 14 December 2006).

[39] *Presidency of the Council of Ministers v Markovic*, Corte Costituzionale, Cass Sez 8157/02 (8 February 2002) 85 Rivista di diritto internazionale (2002) 799, ILDC 293 (IT 2002) referred to in Frulli (n 23) 407.

[40] See *Markovic v Italy* (n 38) [114]–[115].

That the bar of their claims made access to justice 'theoretical and illusory' was inconsequential.[41] The majority decision held, similar to *Jones v United Kingdom* on immunities,[42] that the political questions doctrine does not constitute a bar on the domestic courts' ability to determine a substantive right, but is a limitation on the scope of the substantive law of the State concerned. The dissent argued that the Court of Cassation and the majority had gone 'beyond any legitimate aim the political-act doctrine may be recognized as furthering and far beyond the bounds of proportionality'.[43]

Not only did the court exercise restraint in relation to 'political' decisions, it also extended that restraint to the lawfulness of actions taken pursuant to those political decisions.[44] Furthermore, the majority seemed to suggest that the court had no other option but to deny the claims (similar to the rationales used in State immunity cases). This is plainly not the case; given the absence of an international rule requiring such restraint, the court of cassation's decision was taken in the exercise of its discretion which should have led to a proportionality analysis.

Certain courts have applied extended versions of the political questions and 'act of State' doctrines to avoid considerations of acts of or attributable to international organizations.[45] Versions of the political questions doctrine have entered into the consideration of whether domestic courts should be able to review the legality of key political decision-making organs of the UN, on the basis that to allow review would inappropriately limit the organization's independence. Yet, as Tzanakopoulos argues, when courts are requested to determine the legality of Security Council resolutions and States' obligations flowing from those resolutions, they have tended to restrict their analysis to the measures taken by States to implement the resolutions, and have refrained from reviewing the legality of the resolutions themselves.[46]

Thus, cases have turned on whether States have breached national or international law when taking such measures. Most courts have read in an obligation on States to implement the resolution of the international organization consistently with wider human rights obligations,[47] and thereby avoided finding that a particular resolution breached States' other human rights obligations. On other occasions,

[41] ibid Concurring Opinion of Judge Costa [12].

[42] *Jones v United Kingdom* (GC) App nos 34356/06, 40528/06 (ECtHR, 14 January 2014). Request for referral to the Grand Chamber was rejected on 2 June 2014. See ECtHR Press notice 158 (3 June 2014).

[43] See *Markovic v Italy* (n 38), Dissenting Opinion of Judge Zagrebelsky joined by Judges Zupančič, Jungwiert, Tsatsa-Nikolovska, Ugrekhelidze, Kovler, and Thór Björgvinsson.

[44] ibid, also raised by Frulli (n 23) in her analysis of the cassation decision. See also Sangeeta Shah, 'Seeking Remedies for Violations of International Humanitarian Law: Markovic v Italy' (2007) 7(2) Human Rights LR 412.

[45] Antonios Tzanakopoulos, 'Domestic Court Reactions to UN Security Council Sanctions' in August Reinisch (ed), *Challenging Acts of International Organizations before National Courts* (OUP 2010) 54, 64–69.

[46] ibid.

[47] *Nada v Switzerland* (GC) App no 10593/08 (ECtHR, 12 September 2012) [170], [171], [197]; *Al-Jedda v United Kingdom* (GC) App no 27021/08 (ECtHR, 7 July 2011) [102].

courts implicitly exercised restraint or exercised only cursory review[48] or employed presumptions of legality, which the courts have only been prepared to rebut in exceptional circumstances.[49] Thus, the cases are not barred from proceeding but the subject matter impacts the methods and extent of the review.[50]

As will be explored under immunities, the need for international organizations' absolute independence from domestic courts has been challenged. But even so, some courts appear to conflate the discretionary political questions and act of State analyses (with no or limited consideration of proportionality) with the rationale for the application of an absolute immunities regime, and thereby make the political considerations regarding domestic courts' jurisdiction over international organizations impermeable. In the Dutch Supreme Court decision *Mothers of Srebrenica*[51] and the ECtHR's consideration and dismissal of the later complaint brought by the claimants,[52] both courts made much of the fact that entertaining claims against the UN would require Dutch courts to scrutinize the way in which the UN discharged its core function of protecting international peace and security,[53] which would 'interfere with the fulfillment of the key mission of the United Nations in this field'.[54] Had the courts determined jurisdiction separately from immunity, the consideration of the political aspects of the cases may have been more measured, drawing inspiration from the discretionary act of State and political questions doctrines as appropriate. The assessment of immunities should have focused solely on the operable international law framework and the application of the Convention on the Privileges and Immunities of the United Nations (CPIUN).[55]

The courts were careful to limit their analyses to the narrow set of circumstances where courts are asked not only to assess the legality of Security Council action under Chapter VII but to determine liability and assess consequential damages. Nonetheless, there is a risk that this jurisprudence will lead to wider, unwarranted

[48] *Prosecutor v Tadić* (Decision on Motion for Interlocutory Appeal) IT-94-1-AR72 (ICTY, 2 October 1995) paras 18–22. Jose Alvarez, 'Judging the Security Council' (1996) 90 AJIL 1, 11–12; *Ntakirutimana v Reno* 184 F 3d 419 (5th Cir) 5 August 1999 pt V.

[49] *Rukundo v Federal Office of Justice*, Federal Supreme Court, Nos 1A.129/2001, 1.A.130/2001 (3 September 2001). Referred to in Jean d'Aspremont and Catherine Brölmann, 'Challenging International Criminal Tribunals Before Domestic Courts' in August Reinisch (ed), *Challenging Acts of International Organizations before National Courts* (OUP 2010) 111. See also August Reinisch, 'Should Judges Second-guess the UN Security Council?' (2009) 6 Int'l Org LR 257, 264–66.

[50] This is similar to the rationale used by courts to adjudicate claims despite comity and/or separation of powers arguments. Some courts limit themselves to reviewing the extent to which the executive appropriately exercised its discretion (eg *Abbasi v Secretary of State for Foreign and Commonwealth Affairs* (n 31)), or will review the legality or constitutionality of the act of the executive, but will refrain from ordering anything other than declaratory relief (eg *Canada (Justice) v Khadr* (n 28), *Abbasi v Secretary of State for Foreign and Commonwealth Affairs* (n 31)).

[51] *Stichting Mothers of Srebrenica v Netherlands and United Nations*, Supreme Court [HR] LJN: BW1999, ILDC 1760 (NL 2012) (13 April 2012).

[52] *Stichting Mothers of Srebrenica v Netherlands* App no 65542/12 (ECtHR, 11 June 2013) [152].

[53] ibid; *Stichting Mothers of Srebrenica v Netherlands and United Nations* (n 51) paras 4.1.1, 4.3.4.

[54] *Stichting Mothers of Srebrenica and Others v Netherlands* (n 52) [154].

[55] Convention on the Privileges and Immunities of the UN (adopted 13 February 1946, entered into force 17 September 1946) 1 UNTS 15 (CPIUN).

interpretations—that any ancillary act stemming from a Security Council resolution would be out of bounds. In this regard, the argument put forward on behalf of the UN in the Haiti cholera litigation before US courts, is that any act of the UN Mission in Haiti established by UN Security Council resolution would be outside the jurisdiction of the courts.[56]

VI.2.2 A procedural bar par excellence: immunities of international organizations before domestic courts

'Immunities' are procedural rules which exempt certain individuals and/or entities from the adjudicative or enforcement jurisdiction of courts. They belong to the entity benefiting from the immunity: 'Immunity from jurisdiction is the absolute privilege of whoever enjoys it'.[57]

The law on the immunity of international organizations remains in development. The International Law Commission (ILC) had attempted to assemble the core principles, leading in part to the finalization of the 1975 Vienna Convention on the Representation of States in their Relations with International Organizations of a Universal Character.[58] However, it never entered into force and the ILC abandoned the topic in 1992 because of lack of interest from Member States.[59] Thus there is no universal treaty concerning organizational immunities. For the UN and affiliated agencies, immunities are set out in the UN Charter, the CPIUN and the similar treaty for affiliated agencies.[60] Aside from these, the status of organizational immunities can be gleaned from organizations' constituent agreements, headquarters agreements[61] and regulations.[62] These have also been analysed in academic texts and jurisprudence. Certain elements of these immunities may constitute customary international law, although this is limited by the divergent approaches taken by domestic courts. Fox and Webb explain that 'the extent of such "organizational immunities" is debated'.[63]

The CPIUN is silent on who determines whether the UN is immune in a given case, notwithstanding the final judicial determination that might be made by the

56 *Georges v United Nations* 13 Civ 7146(JPO) (SDNY) Statement of Interest filed by the US State Dept (7 March 2014).

57 *Manderlier v Organisation des Nations Unies (Ministre des Affaires Etrangères)* Brussels CT, 11 May 1966 (1966) JT 721, (1972) 45 ILR 446, 453.

58 UN Doc A/CONF.67/16 (adopted 14 March 1975, not yet in force).

59 UNGA, 'Report of the International Law Commission on the Work of its 44th Session' (25 November 1992) GA res 47/33, UN Doc A/RES/47/33 para 7. See also Peter Bekker, 'The Work of the International Law Commission on "Relations between States and International Organizations" Discontinued: An Assessment' (1993) 6(1) Leiden J Int'l L 3.

60 Convention on the Privileges and Immunities of the Specialized Agencies (adopted 21 November 1947, entered into force 2 December 1948) 33 UNTS 261.

61 *A v UN Economic Commission for Latin America*, Supreme Court of Chile, 8 November 1969 (1969) UN Juridical Y 237.

62 See eg UNMIK, 'Regulation 2000/47 on the Status, Privileges and Immunities of KFOR and UNMIK and Their Personnel in Kosovo' (18 August 2000).

63 See Fox and Webb (n 26) 572.

International Court of Justice (ICJ).[64] The UN Office of Legal Affairs (OLA) considers that the determination of immunities is made exclusively by the Secretary-General, and that such determination has conclusive effect and therefore must be accepted by domestic courts.[65] Certain commentators have agreed.[66] The ICJ's position is more nuanced, holding, somewhat consistently with the US[67] and UK[68] statements in the *Cumaraswamy* case, that the Secretary-General's finding 'creates a presumption which can only be set aside for the most compelling reasons and is thus to be given the greatest weight by national courts'.[69]

As will be argued later in this section, there is a need to ensure some appropriate mode of adjudication to assess responsibility and determine reparations. This reasoning stems from the fact that immunities are distinct from responsibility; an organization or any other actor may be responsible for damages arising from unlawful behaviour, even though operable immunities may bar a particular court from adjudicating the claim.[70] It also stems from the language of Article VIII(29) of the CPIUN, which requires in certain circumstances that the UN make provisions for appropriate modes of settlement of disputes when it fails to waive its immunity.[71] Appropriate modes of settlement could be an internal adjudicative mechanism or recourse to some form of arbitration. Yet as described, such mechanisms have their own limitations and are not always available or adequate.[72] The extent to which the absence of an adequate alternative forum, or the failure by the organization to provide recourse to another forum, impacts on domestic courts' ability to override organizations' immunities is contested, and the jurisprudence in this regard is variable. The ICJ's pronouncement in *Germany v Italy*,[73] and comparable jurisprudence at the ECtHR,[74] while focusing on State immunity, arguably has a chilling effect on domestic courts' ability to ignore or override immunities when faced with competing objectives.

[64] Anthony Miller, 'Privileges and Immunities of United Nations Officials' (2007) 4 Int'l Org LR 169, 196.

[65] See *Difference Relating to Immunity from Legal Process of a Special Rapporteur of the Commission on Human Rights* (Advisory Opinion) [1999] ICJ Rep 62 (*Cumaraswamy* case), Written Statement submitted on behalf of the Secretary-General of the UN (2 October 1998) [44], [46].

[66] See eg Peter H E Bekker, *The Legal Position of Intergovernmental Organizations: A Functional Necessity Analysis of their Legal Status and Immunities* (Martinus Nijhoff 1994) 173–78; Miller (n 64) 199. In *Manderlier v Organisation des Nations Unies et l'État Belge (Ministre des Affaires Etrangères)* Brussels CA, 15 September 1969; (1969) 69 ILR 139, the Court held that it would be acting *ultra vires* if it were to assess the essential nature of immunities granted by the General Convention to the UN. See also the Separate Opinion of Judge Weeramantry in the *Cumaraswamy* case (n 65) 97, in which he sets out the rationale for this determination to be within the sphere of the Secretary-General's authority, but for compelling reasons.

[67] See *Cumaraswamy* case (n 65) Statement of the United States (7 October 1998) [22].

[68] ibid Statement of the United Kingdom (October 1998) [6].

[69] ibid Advisory Opinion [61].

[70] ibid [66].

[71] Discussed in Chapter V.

[72] ibid.

[73] *Jurisdictional Immunities of the State (Germany v Italy: Greece Intervening)* (Merits) [2012] ICJ Rep 143.

[74] See *Jones v United Kingdom* (n 42).

(1) *The history, rationales, and scope of the immunities of international organizations*

International organization immunity developed from the law of State immunity, which itself developed from sovereign immunity. The sovereign was understood as absolutely immune from the jurisdiction of his or her own courts, and this was extended to the jurisdiction of foreign courts.[75] The principle of *par in parem non habet imperium*[76]—that one equal (sovereign) cannot sit in judgment of another—underpinned classical notions of immunity. State immunity reflects the principles of comity, reciprocity, and sovereign equality. Originally, it provided States with immunity from suit in their own territorial courts and was also understood as affording them absolute immunity from the jurisdiction of foreign courts.

Over time, State immunity has evolved into a more restrictive formulation.[77] States are no longer recognized as being immune from the jurisdiction of their own courts and there are a number of recognized exceptions to their immunity before foreign courts.[78] State immunity is understood to cover only those acts which are of a public, governmental, or sovereign nature (*acts jure imperii*); immunity does not extend to acts *jure gestionis* (private or commercial acts).[79] Other recognized exceptions include certain torts committed by States or their officials within the jurisdiction of the forum State,[80] although the tort exception has not been held to extend to personal injury caused by 'matters relating to the core area of State sovereignty such as the acts of a soldier on foreign territory which, of its very nature, may involve sensitive issues affecting diplomatic relations between States and national security'.[81]

There have been attempts to read in additional exceptions to State immunity, on the basis of the nature of the impugned conduct[82] or by implying a waiver to immunity.[83] Other attempts have been made to argue that immunity should not be recognized in those instances when to grant it would result in the foreclosure of all remedies to victims.[84] However, the ICJ in *Germany v Italy* made clear that immunity was not made contingent on the nature of the acts or the impact that

75 Malcolm Shaw, *International Law* (5th edn, CUP 2003) 698.

76 *Al-Adsani v United Kingdom* App no 35763/97 (ECtHR, 21 November 2001) [54].

77 *Cudak v Lithuania* (GC) App no 15869/02 (ECtHR, 23 March 2010) [64]; *Trendtex Trading Corporation Ltd v The Central Bank of Nigeria* [1977] 1 QB 529.

78 See eg *Trendtex Trading Corporation Ltd v The Central Bank of Nigeria* (n 77); *Schooner Exchange v McFadden* 11 US 116 (1812) 136.

79 See Fox and Webb (n 26) 413–34. See also Hersch Lauterpacht, 'The Problem of Jurisdictional Immunities of Foreign States' (1951) 28 Brit YB Int'l L 220, 227; Convention on Jurisdictional Immunities of States and Their Property (adopted 2 December 2004, not yet in force).

80 See eg *Fogarty v United Kingdom* App no 37112/97 (ECtHR, 21 November 2001); *McElhinney v Ireland* App no 31253/96 (ECtHR, 21 November 2001).

81 See *McElhinney* (n 80) [38].

82 See eg *Ferrini v Germany*, Corte Costituzionale, Cass Sez Un 5044/04 (11 March 2004) 87 Rivista diritto internazionale (2004) 539, 128 ILR 659 (where the Italian Court of Cassation determined that immunity was unavailable for acts which violate *jus cogens* norms).

83 *Prefecture of Voiotia v Germany*, Greek Areios Pagos, Cass Nr 11/2000 (288933) (4 May 2000) 129 ILR 514

84 See *Jones v United Kingdom* (n 42).

the application of immunity would have on the availability of a remedy.[85] Thus, under the current state of the law, a State enjoys jurisdictional immunity from legal proceedings in the domestic courts of another State with respect to its *acta jure imperii*, regardless of the gravity of the acts alleged and irrespective of the impact such immunity may have on victims' access to justice.

(2) *The differing rationales for the immunity of international organizations*

The traditional understanding of the absolute inviolability of the State was transposed to the domain of international organizations. The rationale for organizational immunities is, however, different from that for State immunity. International organization immunity is not so concerned with the status, equality, or dignity of the organization. The notion of sovereign equality and the related principle of reciprocity do not apply to international organizations because they are not sovereign; there is no sovereign that their agents personally represent and organizations have no jurisdiction comparable to that of a State from which they could establish reciprocal rules and relations.[86]

The rationale for international organization immunities relates to the need to preserve their independence.[87] Indeed, immunities are understood to be the main, and perhaps the only way in which to protect their independence and enable them to carry out their functions.[88] International organizations can be particularly vulnerable to interference because they do not possess the power of a State but ultimately need to operate on or within the territory of States. If international organizations were capable of being sued before national courts, they would arguably be under the control and influence of the States in which they operate, which would impede them from discharging effectively their mandates.[89]

One could imagine an international organization carrying out sensitive peacekeeping within a State or monitoring a ceasefire between a State and non-State

[85] *Jurisdictional Immunities of the State (Germany v Italy: Greece Intervening)* (Merits) (n 73) paras 92–97. Note, however, the Italian Constitutional Court's later decision in *Sentenza no 238 del 2014*, Corte Costituzionale, Cass Sez 238/14 (22 October 2014), in which it held that the legislation that Italy had enacted to give effect to the ICJ judgment was unconstitutional. See Anne Peters, 'Let Not Triepel Triumph—How to Make the Best out of Sentenza No. 238 of the Italian Constitutional Court for a Global Legal Order' (*VerfBlog*, 23 December 2014) http://www.verfassungsblog.de/en/let-not-triepel-triumph-make-best-sentenza-no-238-italian-constitutional-court-global-legal-order/ (last accessed 15 January 2017).

[86] Alice Ehrenfeld, 'United Nations Immunity Distinguished from Sovereign Immunity' (1958) 52 Am Soc'y Int'l L Proc 88, 92–93.

[87] Jan Klabbers, *An Introduction to International Institutional Law* (2nd edn, CUP 2009) 132–37; *Applicability of Article VI, Section 22, of the Convention on the Privileges and Immunities of the United Nations (Mazilu case)* (Advisory Opinion) [1989] ICJ Rep 177, [44]–[55]; Eric De Brabandere, 'Immunity of International Organizations in Post-conflict International Administrations' (2010) 7 IOLR 79, 87–89.

[88] ILC, Report by Leonardo Díaz-González, Fourth Report on Relations between States and International Organizations (Second Part of the Topic), 'Report of the International Law Commission on the Work of its 26th Session' (6 May to 26 July 1974) UN Doc A/CN.4/424, paras 32–33.

[89] Clarence Wilfred Jenks, *International Immunities* (Stevens 1961) 17.

armed actors. If the organization was subject to the jurisdiction of local courts this could jeopardize its independence. Also, immunities help ensure that no State derives an unfair advantage from its association with an international organization.[90] As De Brabandere has argued,[91] freeing organizations from the control of domestic courts is an essential means by which to preserve States' sovereign equality. If one State—typically the Host State—had the ability to exert undue influence over an international organization, this would undermine the ability of the organization to act fairly and neutrally to all States.

Yet, there are counter-arguments to the need for international organization immunity. The first is that the ultimate objective for the international organization is the ability to function effectively to achieve its mandate. Independence is one of the important conditions for this objective to be met; however, it is not the only condition, and arguably not the only way in which it can be achieved. If an international organization's immunity leads to a gap in accountability for acts over which it has responsibility, this gap may be the greatest detriment to the ability of the organization to achieve its mandate, given the centrality of respect for human rights and the rule of law to the mandates of many international organizations and the UN in particular. As Miller recounts, the Preparatory Commission of the UN study on privileges and immunities affirmed that: 'any excess or abuse of immunity and privilege is as detrimental to the interests of the international organization itself as it is to the countries that are asked to grant such immunities'.[92]

Wellens has similarly contended that: 'the principle of fairness towards parties dealing with an IO and to other third parties seems to require a more circumscribed immunity, in the same way as that principle underpins restricted State immunity'.[93] The second is that the scenario of the weak organization needing to be defended from the unchecked and capricious power of a State on whose territory it operates is not always the reality. When the UN is operating as the territorial administrator, its powers are significant vis-à-vis the host State, and a 'blanket lack of accountability paves the way for impunity'.[94]

But even where the international organization is strong vis-à-vis the host State, the change in balances of power still may not override the need for organizational immunities. Other rationales continue to apply. Organizational immunities remove the need for the organization to defend itself before local courts with diverse understandings of the law in each country in which it operates and the associated inconsistencies in the characterization of acts of the organization.[95] As Ehrenfeld

[90] See Díaz-González (n 8) para 28; Miller (n 64)182.

[91] See De Brabandere (n 87) 87–89.

[92] See Miller (n 64)180.

[93] Karel Wellens, 'Fragmentation of International Law and Establishing an Accountability Regime for International Organizations: The Role of the Judiciary in Closing the Gap' (2003–2004) 25 Mich J Int'l L 1162 1176.

[94] Special Report No. 1 on the Compatibility with Recognized International Standards of UNMIK Regulation No. 2000/47 on the Status, Privileges and Immunities of KFOR and UNMIK and their Personnel in Kosovo (18 August 2000) and on the Implementation of the Above Regulation 2001 (Ombudsperson Institution of Kosovo, 26 April 2001) para 23 www.ombudspersonkosovo.org/repository/docs/E4010426a_874491.pdf (last accessed 27 December 2016).

[95] *Broadbent v OAS* 628 F 2d 27 (DC Cir) 8 January 1980.

has argued, 'it would be a serious burden were the Organization to defend itself in the local courts of the diverse countries in which it operates or maintains an office. There is also the real possibility of a local prejudice against certain programs or a lack of understanding on the part of local courts of the Organization's substantive immunities from certain local laws'.[96] Immunities also shield organizations from vexatious litigation. The UN has placed emphasis on both these arguments, 'not only to preserve its independence in principle, but because exercise of local jurisdiction seriously interferes with effective working of the relief programs'.[97]

Thus, the immunities of international organizations serve a range of purposes. However, as will be described, this does not require them to be absolute.

(3) *The articulation of international organization immunities*

The UN Charter specifies that the UN is only accorded the privileges and immunities necessary to fulfil its purposes.[98] However, the later 1946 CPIUN confers on the UN, its property and assets, wherever located and by whomsoever held, 'immunity from every form of legal process',[99] subject only to an express waiver by the organization. A similar provision appears in the Specialized Agencies' Convention.[100] The Council of Europe, African Union, and Organization of American States (OAS)' provisions all refer to 'immunity from every form of legal process'.[101] By contrast, the Charter of the OAS[102] provides that the Organization shall have 'such legal capacity and privileges and immunities necessary for the exercise of its functions and the accomplishment of its purposes'.[103]

The differences in the framing of immunities in the UN Charter and the later CPIUN have led to debate as to the precise scope of the immunity. Authors have interpreted this discrepancy in different ways. For some there is an inconsistency between the two texts and the Charter should prevail. Others argue that the treaty prevails. In *Manderlier*, the Belgium Court of Appeals held in 1969 that the signatories of the UN Charter had determined the privileges and immunities necessary in adhering to the CPIUN. As a consequence, courts would be acting *ultra vires* if they assessed the essential nature of the immunities granted by the CPIUN.[104] The most commonly held view is that the more precise and detailed rules of the

[96] See Ehrenfeld (n 86) 90. [97] ibid 91–92.

[98] Charter of the United Nations and Statute of the International Court of Justice (adopted 26 June 1945, entered into force 24 October 1945) 1 UNTS XVI art 105(1).

[99] CPIUN (n 55) art II.

[100] Convention on the Privileges and Immunities of the Specialized Agencies (n 60) s 4.

[101] General Agreement on Privileges and Immunities of the Council of Europe (adopted 2 September 1949, entered into force 10 September 1952) CETS No 2 art 3; General Convention on the Privileges and Immunities of the Organization of African Unity, OAU CAB/LEG/24.2/13 (adopted and entered into force 25 October 1965) art 1; Agreement on Privileges and Immunities of the Organization of American States (C-13) (adopted 15 May 1949, entered into force 4 June 1951) art 2.

[102] Charter of the Organization of American States (adopted 30 April 1948, entered into force 13 December 1951).

[103] ibid art 133.

[104] *Manderlier v Organisation des Nations Unies (Ministre des Affaires Etrangères)* (A) (n 66).

CPIUN must be respected as an interpretation of what the 'functional' standard in the Charter means in respect to jurisdictional immunity;[105] in other words, that the later text is an interpretation of the first. Under this approach, UN immunities are functional in nature but absolute in character.[106] Yet, does the functional nature of international organizations whose sphere of activity depends on their mandates, introduce a contingency or relativism into international organization immunities, and if so how does or how should this impact on the adjudicative jurisdiction of domestic courts? Arsanjani, formerly of the UN Office of Legal Affairs, has written that:

> Immunity ... does not necessarily mean 'absolute' immunity, for not all activities undertaken by IOs are within their principal functions. IOs may conduct activities of a so-called private nature that only minimally affect their major functions, but that may have adverse impact on the public order of a particular State. The appropriate degree of immunity of IOs from suits in local courts should depend on (1) the nature of the IOs (the degree of universality), (2) the purpose of the IOs (the extensiveness of the function), (3) the intention of IO members as expressed in the constituent instruments of IOs and subsequent agreements, (4) practice, and (5) the particular acts in question.[107]

The first way in which international organizations' immunities have been framed focuses on organizations' limited international legal personality. Some argue that the fact that organizations can only act in pursuit of their purposes means that the functional immunity they possess is inevitably absolute—all international organization acts are official acts to which functional immunity extends.[108] As Reinisch and Weber have noted, 'since international organizations can only act within the scope of their functional personality there is no room left for non-functional acts for which immunity would be denied'.[109] Yet, as Reinisch has argued, 'the idea of functional immunity is rather imprecise in so far as it could refer both to the rationale for granting immunity at all ... as well as to a certain content of immunity to be accorded'.[110] Article 105 of the UN Charter provides that immunities apply to 'functions in connexion with the Organization', which some commentators

[105] The UN Office of Legal Affairs has stated that the 'detailed application' of the principle contained in art 105 of the Charter 'was effected inter alia through the [General Convention]'. UN Office of Legal Affairs, 'Opinion prepared at the request of the Committee on Relations with the Host Country' (1983) UN Juridical YB 222. Others regard the multilateral instruments as 'implementation of the brief and general provisions of the constituent instrument of the organization'.

[106] See *Cumaraswamy* case (n 65) [66]. The failure of the law of IOs to embrace a theory of restrictive immunity (unlike for State immunity) is discussed in Emmanuel Gaillard and Isabelle Pingel-Lenuzza, 'International Organisations and Immunity from Jurisdiction: to Restrict or Bypass' (2002) 51 ICLQ 1, 1–4. See also Michael Singer, 'Jurisdictional Immunity of International Organizations: Human Rights and Functional Necessity Concerns' (1995) 36 Va J Int'l L 53, 135; De Brabandere (n 87) 87.

[107] Mahnoush Arsanjani, 'Claims against International Organizations: *Quis Custodiet Ipsos Custodes*' (1981) 7(2) Yale J World Public Order 131, 163.

[108] See Reinisch, *International Organizations before National Courts* (n 10) 127 ff.

[109] August Reinisch and Ulf Andreas Weber, 'In the Shadow of Waite and Kennedy: The Jurisdictional Immunity of International Organizations, the Individual's Right of Access to the Courts and Administrative Tribunals as Alternative Means of Dispute Settlement' (2004) 1 Int'l Org LR 59, 63. See also De Brabandere (n 87) 88.

[110] See Reinisch, *International Organizations before National Courts* (n 10) 331.

have argued is broader than simply those acts which are official,[111] requiring an examination of both the acts themselves and the context in which they were carried out.[112] In *Spaans*, the Dutch Supreme Court determined that for functional immunity to be recognized, it was necessary to demonstrate that the acts in question are 'immediately connected to the tasks entrusted to the organisation',[113] whereas in *De Luca*, the question of whether the case 'relates to' acts performed by the defendants in their official capacity was determined on the basis of whether the acts alleged occurred in the course of an official's exercise of functions, and not on the nature of the underlying conduct.[114] The jurisprudence is equivocal, with an equal, if not greater number of cases taking a very expansive approach to the definition of function.

Human rights and international humanitarian law violations attributable to the international organization may be *ultra vires* acts and nonetheless the conduct could constitute an act of the organization, depending on the context. 'Official' acts would benefit from immunity to the extent that the acts were taken pursuant to organizational policies, however they would not necessarily benefit from the proviso in Article 29 of the CPIUN for appropriate modes of settlement to be put in place, as arguably they do not arise out of contracts or other disputes of a private law character, nor do they necessarily involve any official of the UN for which immunity is waived.[115] Similarly, certain offensive conduct of individual officials would not be in the performance of official functions and immunity would not apply. Nevertheless, there are instances when the UN is unprepared nevertheless to enable a host State to exercise jurisdiction.[116]

But, as this would not be a case of an official who enjoys immunity that the organization decides not to waive, Article 29(b) is inapplicable. Without the requirement of Article 29 pressing the UN to establish appropriate modes of settlement, which it has interpreted as an exhaustive requirement, no appropriate mode of settlement for such types of claims exists. Thus, it is not the functional nature of international organizations that results in absolute immunity; it is more so the narrow interpretation of the need for appropriate modes of settlement that serves as a practical bar. Immunity does not equate with a lack of responsibility. The responsibility of the international organization for internationally wrongful acts remains intact, even if access to remedies appears to be foreclosed.

[111] See eg Miller (n 64) 193, who posits that it also covers activities that are reasonably connected with those acts.

[112] The ICJ in both the *Mazilu* (n 87) [56]–[60] and the *Cumaraswamy* (n 65) [50] cases looked to the particular circumstances in which the acts were carried out.

[113] *Spaans v Iran-US Claims Tribunal*, Supreme Court [HR], LJN: AC 9158, NJ 1986, 438 (1987) 18 NYIL 357, ILDC 1759 (NL 1985) (20 December 1985), referred to in Thomas Henquet, 'International Organisations in the Netherlands: Immunity from the Jurisdiction of the Dutch Courts' (2010) Netherlands Int'l LR 268, 274–75.

[114] *De Luca v United Nations* 841 F Supp 531 (SDNY) (10 January 1994) 534–35.

[115] The meaning of art 29 is considered in Chapter V.

[116] See UNSG, 'Ensuring the Accountability of United Nations Staff and Experts on Mission with Respect to Criminal Acts Committed in Peacekeeping Operations' UN Doc A/60/980 paras 21–22.

The second approach has been to contend that, because the rationales that have led to a more restrictive understanding of State immunity do not seamlessly apply to international organization immunity, one cannot transpose the trend from one to the other. The distinction between public and private acts, which underpins the trend towards a more restrictive understanding of State immunity 'has little direct relevance in determining the scope of immunities'[117] of an organization. The issue was canvassed in a case concerning the scope of immunities of the East African Development Bank, in relation to its lending transactions.[118] The judges determined that the 'restrictive theory of State immunity as a principle of common law has no application in the present case'.[119] They place significant weight on what they understood to be the clear construction of immunities in the constituent agreements. In such instruments, 'member States have full sovereignty to grant such privileges and immunities to the organization as they deem it proper for the purpose of achieving its objectives. The courts should always be loath to interfere with the States' transparent exercise of their sovereign powers or impose constrained interpretations on such treaties on the basis of fanciful reasons'.[120]

The language in the *East African Development Bank Act*[121] is clear in its provision of absolute immunity to the Bank. The language is almost identical to the CPIUN, although in the latter case there is the need to interpret in light of the more nuanced language of the UN Charter. Jurisprudence has tended to recognize the absolute immunity of international organizations (and the UN in particular) on the basis of a textual reading of the CPIUN.[122] Even with the CPIUN wording in place however, some US judgments have incorporated a restrictive understanding of UN immunities, given the precise language of domestic implementing legislation.[123]

The third approach has been to argue that absolute immunity is required in order to enable international organizations to function in accordance with their mandates. De Brabandere, for instance, has noted that: 'to allow the organization to function properly, the only result can be to give the organizations full immunity from the jurisdiction of national courts and tribunals. The opposite would clearly compromise the independence of the organization if it could be subjected to pressure for the official (judicial) institutions of the host state'.[124] This has been the

[117] See Fox and Webb (n 26) 574.

[118] *East African Development Bank v Blueline Enterprises Ltd* (Civil Appeal No 110 of 2009) [2011] TZCA 1 (22 December 2011).

[119] ibid 14. [120] ibid 29.

[121] See in particular the East African Development Bank Act, Act No 7 of 1984 (Cap 231) (Tanzania), as amended by the Finance Act 2005 (No 13) arts 44, 45.

[122] This has been confirmed expressly by the ICJ in the *Cumaraswamy* case (n 65) [66]: 'any such claims against the United Nations shall not be dealt with by national courts'.

[123] In *Dupree v OAS* 76-2335 (US Distr Ct DC) 31 May 1977, 22 June 1977 (1982) 63 ILR 92 (1977) UN Juridical Yearbook 260, 261, the Court held that since foreign sovereigns were only entitled to restricted immunity, international organizations too were entitled only to restricted immunity. However, the case can be distinguished by the particularities of the US Act on organization immunities which provides that international organizations should benefit from the same immunity enjoyed by foreign sovereigns.

[124] See De Brabandere (n 87) 87–88.

position taken by the UN Legal Office.[125] Ehrenfeld, formerly of OLA has argued that: '[n]othing short of complete immunity from process can give the necessary protection from this kind of litigation and from a variety of interpretations of the nature of the Organization's operations and the applicability of substantive law'.[126] In this sense, absolute immunity is justified as necessary to fulfil international organizations' functions. But, are international organizations as frail as is perhaps suggested?[127]

The main arguments of De Brabandere and others appear to be that the purpose for granting immunity is ever present and vital. They focus much less on why *absolute immunity* is necessary, more so on why immunity is *absolutely necessary*. There is a failure to distinguish between the need for immunity on functional grounds, and the character of that immunity, in those cases in which it is deemed necessary. In contrast to De Brabandere's position, some scholars have argued that a restrictive approach 'should' apply to international organization immunities because absolute immunity is not necessary to allow organizations to function. Something less than 'absolute' immunity is required, although determining how best to approximate this nuanced test has been difficult. Reinisch and Weber argue that there is no 'workable and practicable test for a functional immunity'.[128] Others have emphasized that while something less than absolute may be desirable, it is simply inconsistent with the practice.[129]

(4) The impact of immunities on claimants' ability to access justice

A constant question has been if, and if so how, immunities relate to and interact with other principles of international law. When immunity is upheld, claimants' ability to access courts can be detrimentally affected particularly if there are no alternative avenues for justice. Does this correlative fact have any bearing on the way in which immunity is determined and/or recognized? As indicated in Chapter V, Article 29 of the CPIUN can be understood as intending to ensure that international organization immunity does not have the result of negating the prospects for justice, however these intentions are not always borne out by the practice. Neither the CPIUN, nor any other treaty which recognizes the obligation on States or other duty bearers to ensure access to courts, creates a direct reciprocal or conditional relationship between the immunity afforded to the UN and the right of aggrieved individuals to access court. The absence of an avenue to access courts does not

[125] *Broadbent v OAS* Brief for the UN as *Amicus Curiae* (1980) UN Juridical Yearbook 227, 230. The UN argues that, by virtue of its functions, it requires absolute immunity, 'complete protection from national jurisdiction'.

[126] See Ehrenfeld (n 86) 92.

[127] See Gaillard and Pingel-Lenuzza (n 106) 2: 'Just as the reinforcement of the authority of the State made possible its submission to the rule of law, so international organisations have achieved a sufficiently solid foundation in the international legal order for private persons to be able to have their disputes with those organisations heard, when this is required by the imperatives of justice'.

[128] See Reinisch and Weber (n 109) 63.

[129] See Gaillard and Pingel-Lenuzza (n 106) 2.

necessarily impinge on the recognition of immunities, which are considered on their own terms. However, the failure to afford an effective remedy may constitute a separate violation for which the international organization bears responsibility.

There are two trends in the jurisprudence which analyse the relationship between immunities and access to justice. Some would argue that the second trend has overtaken the first. However, arguably there remains a narrow space in which the first trend remains relevant.

The first trend is to affirm that the recognition by a domestic court of State or international organization immunity can be an unjustifiable restriction on the claimant's ability to access justice. Whether the restriction on access to justice is justifiable will depend on whether it is proportionate and restricts the right in the least possible way. This type of analysis has been prevalent in the Article 6 jurisprudence of the ECtHR.[130] It has also been applied in a number of domestic cases.[131] The availability of alternative means of dispute settlement will be one element in the assessment of whether the application of immunity is proportionate, but this availability has never served as a *precondition* to upholding immunity.[132]

One might posit that the possibility of recourse to administrative tribunals for staff members with employment grievances, or the recourse to arbitration for commercial contractors or to local claims commissions might constitute alternative remedies, but as is clear from *Waite and Kennedy*, it is not enough for these forums to exist, they must be adequate and effective to redress the harm, and in a matter of speaking, must constitute a form of equivalent protection to the recourse that would otherwise had been available had access to courts not been curtailed.[133] In that case, it was determined that an alternative remedy did exist and thus Article 6 was not breached, although as some have criticized, the Court did not enter into a substantive assessment of the availability of that remedy to the applicant.[134]

Waite and Kennedy concerned the European Space Agency and some have posited that the type of analysis which guided the ECtHR in that case may have been shaped by the specificities of a European agency, and would not necessarily extend to universal organizations. Reinisch notes these difficulties, holding that, '[i]t is clear that the high level of integration within the EC/EU differs markedly from the UN system'.[135] These differences were picked up upon by an English High Court

[130] See *Waite and Kennedy v Germany* (n 37); *Beer and Regan v Germany* App no 28934/95 (ECtHR, 18 February 1999).

[131] *Western European Union v Siedler*, Cass Nr S 04 0129 F, ILDC 1625 (BE 2009) (21 December 2009); *African Development Bank v Haas*, French *Cour de Cassation* (soc) 25 January 2005 (2005) JT 454, 138 ILM 198; *General Secretariat of the ACP Group v Lutchmaya*, Cass Nr C 03 0328 F, ILDC 1573 (BE 2009) (21 December 2009).

[132] *Waite and Kennedy v Germany* (n 37) [59], [68].

[133] Note, however, that this jurisprudential trend has mainly been limited to Europe. See, in contrast, *Brzak v United Nations* 551 F Supp 2d 313 (SDNY) 29 April 2008, 318–19, where the Court held that the UN possessed absolute immunity.

[134] Matthias Kloth, *Immunities and the Right of Access to Court under Article 6 of the European Court of Human Rights* (Martinus Nijhoff 2010) 142–44. See also *Chapman v Belgium* App no 39619/06 (ECtHR, 5 March 2013).

[135] See Reinisch, 'Should Judges Second-guess the UN Security Council?' (n 49).

in *Entico v UNESCO*, which concerned a claim brought by a publishing company for breach of contract.[136] There, the Court distinguished *Waite and Kennedy* on the basis that the European Convention had been adopted after the 1947 Specialized Agencies Convention and was limited to Europe.

The Dutch Supreme Court adopted similar reasoning when distinguishing the *Mothers of Srebrenica* claim against the UN from the considerations at play in *Waite and Kennedy*, and 'opted not to engage in the increasingly accepted balancing act in which upholding immunity of an international organization is made dependent on certain human rights factors, in particular on the right to access to court, [which] is not a test that applies to the UN'.[137] The claimants in *Georges* sought to argue that in the narrow context of peacekeeping, the requirement that the UN establish a claims commission is an essential component of the status of forces agreements which recognizes the UN's immunity. The failure to establish the commission (as opposed to the ineffectiveness of a mechanism so established) constituted a material breach of the status of forces agreement, which essentially prevented the Organization's immunity from kicking in.[138] This argument was ultimately not accepted by the District Court,[139] although the case is under appeal.

The second trend emphasizes that only the beneficiary of the immunity may choose to waive it; a domestic court cannot decide whether to recognize it regardless of whether other appropriate modes of settlement are available. Under this reasoning, as a procedural rule, immunity only determines access to a particular jurisdiction; any substantive consideration of its impact on access to justice is immaterial.[140] This second trend aligns with recent jurisprudence on State immunity. The ECtHR in *Al-Adsani v United Kingdom* determined that when a State complies with a public international law rule like State immunity, its actions cannot be said to be disproportionate. Thus, it recognized the applicability of a proportionality analysis as a matter of principle, but the act of compliance with a public international law rule exempted the Court from the need to carry out a thorough analysis: it would 'clearly' be proportionate. The position shifted somewhat further with *Jones v United Kingdom*, where the ECtHR made clear that the proportionality test was never arrived at: immunity meant that there was no access to court the UK could have given; it was not theirs to give. This approach is mirrored in *Germany v Italy*.[141]

[136] *Entico v UNESCO* [2008] EWHC 531 (Comm) [24].

[137] Aleksandar Momirov, 'Dutch Courts and Srebrenica: Ascribing Responsibilities and Defining Legally Relevant Relationships' (2012) 43 Neth Y Int'l L 233, 245. *Stichting Mothers of Srebrenica v Netherlands and United Nations* (n 51) para 4.3.5.

[138] *Georges v United Nations* 13 Civ 7146(JPO) (SDNY) Oral Argument (23 October 2014) (on file with author).

[139] See *Georges v United Nations* (n 16).

[140] *Holland v Lampen-Wolfe* [2000] 1 WLR 1573, [2000] UKHL 40. See also *Jones v Saudi Arabia* [2007] 1 AC 270 [64] (Lord Hoffmann): '[t]here is not even a prima facie breach of Article 6 if a State fails to make available a jurisdiction which it does not possess'.

[141] *Jurisdictional Immunities of the State (Germany v Italy: Greece Intervening)* (Merits) (n 73) para 101.

It is relevant to consider the extent to which this more recent jurisprudence impacts on the *Waite and Kennedy* line of cases relating to the immunity of international organizations. In effect, *Waite and Kennedy* itself overruled prior jurisprudence. In *Spaans*, the European Commission found no incompatibility with the Convention in recognizing and upholding the immunity of the Iran-US Claims Tribunal.[142] The *Waite and Kennedy* bench did not refer to this prior jurisprudence. Before domestic courts, in *Manderlier*, an early Belgian case which concerned damages the claimant suffered as a result of abuses committed by UN troops in the Congo, the Brussels Court of Appeal made clear that international organization immunities did not depend on the existence of another appropriate mode of settlement: '[i]t must be admitted that in the present state of international institutions there is no court to which the appellant can submit his dispute with the United Nations; and although this situation, which does not seem to be in keeping with the principles proclaimed in the Universal Declaration of Human Rights, may be regrettable, it must be recognized that the judge of first instance was correct in declaring that the action brought against the United Nations was inadmissible'.[143]

The Dutch Supreme Court decision in the *Mothers of Srebrenica* case distinguished the *Waite and Kennedy* analysis on the basis that the latter court was not faced with a case concerning the UN, and particularly Article 103 of the UN Charter.[144] The ECtHR later made clear in its rejection of the *Mothers of Srebrenica* applicants that even in the absence of an alternative remedy, the recognition of immunity is not *ipso facto* constitutive of a violation of the right of access to a court. It thus applied *Waite and Kennedy*, but finds the case inadmissible for a combination of reasons—particularly that the dispute concerns the use by the Security Council of its powers under Chapter VII of the United Nations Charter, and the fact that Article 6 does not require the Netherlands to provide a remedy against the United Nations in its own courts.[145]

As such, the *Waite and Kennedy* line of analysis appears to narrowly survive *Germany v Italy*. The facts of the *Mothers of Srebrenica* case, which concerned the key decision-making responsibilities of the UN in maintaining international peace and security, easily met the proportionality considerations. Indeed, this is the reasoning taken by the Dutch Court of Appeal in its consideration of the immunities from jurisdiction of the European Patent Organization.[146] It will be interesting to see how American courts operating outside of the frame of the European Court ultimately assess the different facts of the cholera claims, which arguably do not

[142] See *Spaans v Iran-US Claims Tribunal* (n 113) and *Spaans v Netherlands* (Decision on Admissibility) App no 12516/86 (ECommHR, 12 December 1988), where the European Commission regarded the grant of immunity from suit to the Iran–United States Claims Tribunal by the Netherlands as a restriction of national sovereignty which did not give rise to an issue under the Convention.

[143] *Manderlier v Organisation des Nations Unies (Ministre des Affaires Etrangères)* (n 66) para 69.

[144] *Stichting Mothers of Srebrenica v Netherlands and United Nations* (n 51).

[145] *Stichting Mothers of Srebrenica v Netherlands* (n 52).

[146] *VEOB and SUEPO v EPO*, Court of Appeal in The Hague, 200.141.812/01 (17 February 2015) paras 3.3–3.7.

raise those same decision-making responsibilities of the UN; at issue is how the organization carried out its day-to-day operations on the ground.

It is also relevant to consider whether any of the differences between State and international organization immunities impacts on the seamlessness of the jurisprudence. As Reinisch has argued, in State immunity cases, there is always another forum—the courts of the territorial State.[147] Whilst the ECtHR in *Jones v United Kingdom* paid little attention to this issue, it was canvassed in *Germany v Italy*. In the latter case, it was argued that Germany was not entitled to immunity because those acts involved the most serious violations of rules of international law of a peremptory character for which no alternative means of redress was available. The majority was not persuaded.[148]

However, Yusuf in his dissent, focusing on the exceptional circumstances of the case, argues that:

'[T]he assertion of jurisdiction by domestic courts for a failure to make reparations for serious breaches of the law of armed conflict admitted by the responsible State, particularly where no other means of redress is available, could not, in my view, harm the independence or the sovereignty of another State. It simply contributes to the crystallization of an emerging exception to State immunity, which is based on the principles underlying human rights and IHL on the widely held *opinio juris* of ensuring the realization of those rights, including the right to an effective remedy, in those circumstances where the victims would have no other means of redress'.[149] While the Dutch Supreme Court in *Mothers of Srebrenica* recognizes the distinction between State immunity (and thus the *Germany v Italy* approach) and international organization immunities, it notes that the difference is not so great to justify a different approach: 'The UN is entitled to immunity regardless of the extreme seriousness of the accusations on which the Association et al. base their claims'.[150]

A third trend, taken up mainly by theorists, concerns the application of the principle of countermeasures to justify the denial by domestic courts of international organization immunity. Under international law, States may be entitled to respond to a breach of an international obligation by taking countermeasures to ensure cessation of the wrongful act and reparation for its consequences. The ILC has set this out in the Articles on the Responsibility of States for Internationally Wrongful Acts (ARS),[151] and this principle has equally been incorporated into the Draft Articles on the Responsibility of International Organizations (DARIO) in regards to breaches of an international obligation by the international organization. Only those countermeasures that meet certain substantive and procedural

[147] See Reinisch and Weber (n 109) 85–86.

[148] See *Jurisdictional Immunities of the State (Germany v Italy: Greece Intervening)* (Merits) (n 73) para 101.

[149] ibid Judge Yusuf dissent para 51.

[150] *Stichting Mothers of Srebrenica v Netherlands and United Nations* (n 51) para 4.3.14.

[151] ILC, Articles on the Responsibility of States for Internationally Wrongful Acts, 'Report of the International Law Commission on the Work of its 53rd Session' (23 April–1 June and 2 July–10 August 2001) UN Doc A/CN.4/SER.A/2001/Add.1 (ARS) art 22.

conditions may be legitimate.[152] Thus, it has been raised whether the breach of an international obligation in relation to human rights and/or international humanitarian law and the concomitant failure to afford reparations in response to the breach, provides a State with the ability to take the countermeasure of not recognizing immunities which would otherwise apply before its courts.

The issue has been raised in relation to States' breach of the international prohibition of torture. As Moser has pointed out,[153] the UN Committee Against Torture, when examining Canada's State party report, raised in general terms the issue of countermeasures as a possible route for Canada to override immunity before Canadian courts: 'as a countermeasure permitted under international public law, a State could remove immunity from another State—a permitted action to respond to torture carried out by that State'.[154] In principle, the breach of an individual's human rights constitutes an internationally wrongful act against that individual's State of nationality. The taking of countermeasures by that State would be as a matter of principle a justifiable response, at least after that State sought to resolve the matter by other lawful means of diplomatic protection.[155] This is Moser's argument. She contends that outside of the enumerated exceptions in the ARS, 'there are no other established restrictions that delimit which norms may be affected by countermeasures.... there is nothing in the nature of State immunity that prevents the potential of its non-recognition as a countermeasure'.[156]

Tzanakopoulos recognizes the possibility for domestic courts to apply countermeasures. He notes that: '[t]his response will sometimes not be limited simply to reciprocal non-application of a treaty against another State, as described above; it may involve other measures as well, such as for example the denial of sovereign immunity'.[157] As is explained by Fox and Webb, the issue of countermeasures was mentioned by Italy in its oral pleadings in *Germany v Italy*, although it was not the main basis upon which Italy argued its case[158] nor was it referred to in the judgment.[159] Yet, Fox and Webb note that the relevance of the law of countermeasures to State immunity 'seems questionable'.[160]

152 ILC, Draft Articles on the Responsibility of International Organizations, 'Report of the International Law Commission on the Work of its 63rd Session' (26 April–3 June and 4 July–12 August 2011) UN Doc A/66/10 (DARIO) art 22.

153 Patricia Tarre Moser, 'Non-recognition of State Immunity as a Judicial Countermeasure to *Jus Cogens* Violations: The Human Rights Answer to the ICJ Decision on the *Ferrini* Case' (2012) 4 Göttingen J Int'l L 809, 811.

154 UN Committee Against Torture, 'Consideration of Reports Submitted by States Parties under Article 19 of the Convention' (1 May 2005) UN Doc CAT/C/SR.646/Add.1 para 67.

155 Rosanne van Alebeek, *The Immunity of States and Their Officials in International Criminal Law and International Human Rights Law* (OUP 2008) 344: 'An exception to immunity rules based on the rules on countermeasures should hence be contingent on the fruitless result of the fulfilment of the obligations resting on the executive of the forum state as well as the fulfilment of the requirements of the local remedies rule'.

156 See Moser (n 153) 832.

157 See Tzanakopoulos, 'Disobeying the Security Council' (n 45) 194.

158 Italy's arguments focused on there being an exception to State immunity for serious violation of human rights and IHL, which the ICJ ultimately rejected.

159 See Fox and Webb (n 26) 16.

160 ibid.

Taking this argument one step further, a State could just as easily deny the immunity of an international organization as a countermeasure where the organization fails to afford reparations in response to a breach of human rights and/or international humanitarian law attributable to it. Yet it is nonetheless difficult to justify in light of the ICJ jurisprudence in *Germany v Italy*. If the immunity belongs to the offending State (or international organization), it is not within the power of a domestic court to decide not to recognize it, it is outside its competence. Indeed, the argument on the availability of countermeasures is similar in its core to that of an implied waiver of immunity: if a State carries out an internationally wrongful act, a domestic court is entitled to hold that the State has, as a direct consequence, waived its entitlement to immunities.[161] Yet, this argument, which persuaded the Court in the *Prefecture of Voiotia* case,[162] was later resolutely rejected.[163]

(5) Waivers of immunity

Constituent agreements allow international organizations to waive immunity. The CPIUN provides that the UN's immunity from every form of legal process may be 'expressly waived' in 'any particular case'.[164] The same wording is used in the Specialized Agencies Convention,[165] the Council of Europe General Agreement,[166] the OAU General Convention[167] and the OAS Agreement.[168]

To be accepted, the waiver must come from the Secretary-General or similar head of the organization, not the official or office implicated in the proceedings. This is because immunities are given in the interests of the organization, and do not constitute a personal benefit to any individual or group.[169] The need for an express waiver by the organization is more onerous a requirement than what is needed for a waiver of immunity by a State. In the latter case, consent to jurisdiction may be implied from conduct consistent with consent, such as taking a positive step in the proceedings other than simply to plead immunity.[170] Domestic courts have by and large followed this approach, refusing to imply waivers for international organization immunities.[171]

161 See van Alebeek (n 155) 345, who makes oblique reference to this argument, citing Willem Riphagen, 'State Responsibility: New Theories of Obligation in Interstate Relations' in Ronald St John MacDonald and Douglas Millar Johnston (eds), *The Structure and Process of International Law* (Martinus Nijhoff 1983) 581, 606.

162 See *Prefecture of Voiotia v Germany* (n 83).

163 See *Jurisdictional Immunities of the State (Germany v Italy: Greece Intervening)* (Merits) (n 73).

164 CPIUN (n 55) art II s 2.

165 Convention on the Privileges and Immunities of the Specialized Agencies (n 60) art III, s 4.

166 General Agreement on Privileges and Immunities of the Council of Europe (n 101) Pt II, art 3.

167 General Convention on the Privileges and Immunities of the Organization of African Unity (n 101) art II(1), although it does not qualify the term waiver with the word 'express'.

168 Charter of the Organization of American States (adopted 30 April 1948, entered into force 13 December 1951) art 2.

169 See eg CPIUN (n 55) s 20.

170 See Fox and Webb (n 26) 373, 575.

171 *Mendaro v World Bank* 717 F2d 610 (DC Cir) 27 September 1983; *Georges v United Nations* 13 Civ 7146(JPO) (SDNY) 9 January 2015.

The waiver stipulations in constituent agreements provide no guidance as to when it would be appropriate for international organizations to waive the immunity of the organization, providing what would seem to be an absolute discretion. This differs from the references in such agreements to the waiver of immunities of officials and other categories of personnel benefiting from some form of functional immunity. The distinction between cases brought against a named official and those cases brought against the organization as such are perhaps overstated, given the typical practice of claimants to name in their actions both types of defendants. Nonetheless, the CPIUN treats these two categories differently.

The Secretary-General has 'the right and the duty to waive the immunity of any official or expert in any case where, in his opinion, the immunity would impede the course of justice and can be waived without prejudice to the interests of the United Nations'.[172] The African Union and Council of Europe agreements similarly refer to the right and duty to waive in such instances.[173] In contrast, the OAS formulation is obligatory, setting out that in the circumstances described, the Secretary-General 'shall waive' the privileges and immunities of any official or member of the staff.[174] The European Union formulation also requires a waiver, although this is muted by the vagueness of the framing of the circumstances in which EU institutions 'shall waive', which is set out as 'wherever that institution considers that the waiver of such immunity is not contrary to the interests of the Union'.[175]

The language of 'duty to waive' seemingly obligates the organizations concerned to do more than consider whether they simply wish to waive immunity. As Miller sets out, the importance for the UN to waive immunities of officials so as to prevent abuses was a clearly articulated principle already from the Preparatory Commission responsible for drafting the General Convention. Its minutes set out that:

> It is ... most desirable that both the United Nations and all specialized agencies should adopt the principle that privileges and immunities are only given to their officials in the interests of the Organization in whose service they are, and in no way for the benefit of the individual concerned, and that, in consequence, the Secretary-General both can waive immunity and will in fact do so in every case where such a course is consistent with the interests of the United Nations. This rule has long been in force in the International Labour Organization.[176]

Arguably, the *duty* to waive operates as a presumption in favour of a waiver in the absence of any compelling reason not to waive, taken in good faith.[177] Any

[172] CPIUN (n 55) arts 20, 23.

[173] General Convention on the Privileges and Immunities of the Organization of African Unity (n 101) art VI(4); Additional Protocol to the OAU General Convention on Privileges and Immunities, OAU CM/1034(XXXV) Rev 3, Annex 1 (adopted 1 June 1980, entered into force 6 August 2012) (OAU Additional Protocol).

[174] Agreement on Privileges and Immunities of the Organization of American States (n 101) art 17; General Agreement on Privileges and Immunities of the Council of Europe (n 101) art 19.

[175] Protocol on the Privileges and Immunities of the European Union, C 310/261 (16 December 2004) art 17.

[176] See Miller (n 64) 236.

[177] See Bekker, *The Legal Position of Intergovernmental Organisations* (n 66) 192; see also Jenks (n 89) 170.

discretion in the decision-making process should not be fettered.[178] However, the difficulty to independently review waiver decisions, limits the practical impact of any such duty.[179]

A question which follows is what criteria, if any, are used to determine whether the organization will waive immunity, and whether such criteria, if they exist, need to be considered subjectively or objectively. For example, it is unclear whether the availability of an alternate justice process would suffice as a matter of principle to satisfy the test of not impeding the course of justice, or whether implied in the language of the constituent agreements is a need to ensure that the justice process is adequate and effective in light of the alleged act, or whether it is a more limited statement relating to whatever domestic processes of justice are underway—an obligation to ensure that these are not impeded. If the latter were the case, this would significantly widen the balance in favour of waiver. It would seem clear, at the least, that the obligation of the organization to assess whether maintenance of the immunity impedes the course of justice requires a case by case consideration of the facts.

It is also difficult to assess what circumstances might *not* lead a waiver of immunity to prejudice an organization, in one way or another. Miller says that: 'it is difficult to envisage when immunity could properly be maintained if there was no UN interest to support such a result, only the personal interests of the official concerned'.[180] But, aside from parking tickets, spousal maintenance claims and perhaps motor vehicle injuries, most claims to be adjudicated in national courts against officials in relation to the performance of their official functions will evidently not be in the interests of the organization. This is certainly the case if the organizations' independence and freedom from domestic processes are seen as vital to the very essence of the organization. This general statement with somewhat circular reasoning is indeed asserted by the Secretary-General in his written statement in the *Cumaraswamy Case*, in which it is noted that: '[t]he adjudication of United

[178] See in contrast, the *Cumaraswamy* case (n 65) Written Comments of the Government of Costa Rica, 5, in which it is argued that: 'the plain language of Section 23 [of the CPIUN] requires the Secretary-General to make subjective determinations about the likely effects of waiver based on his specialized institutional knowledge and his personal evaluation of facts. The fact that the Secretary-General's "duty" is to act only in accordance with "his opinion" renders the exercise of that duty unreviewable by a third party, and, therefore, non-justiciable. This is in stark contrast to the Secretary-General's decisions under Section 22 as to whether or not immunity exists, which are not similarly authorized to be made "in his opinion", but instead require the application of objective criteria and, thus, may be reviewed by the Court'.

[179] In principle, the Secretary-General's decision could be reviewed by the ICJ in the course of Advisory Opinion proceedings. See *Cumaraswamy* case (n 65), Oral Statement of the United Nations (7 December 1998) [59]; Written Statement of the Government of Federal Republic of Germany. However, there is no forum before which an aggrieved individual can seek to have the decision of the Secretary-General independently reviewed. In contrast, there are examples of employees using the ILOAT to complain indirectly about a decision of an organization to waive the employee's immunity. As the mandate of ILOAT is restricted to employment matters, it has no competence to assess the validity of a decision taken to waive immunity, an assessment can only be made as whether any aspect of the employee's rights were violated in that process. See eg *JAT v IOM*, Judgment No 2302 (ILOAT, 4 February 2004) paras 7, 8; *GM v UNESCO*, Judgment No 2222 (ILOAT, 16 July 2003).

[180] See Miller (n 64) 237.

Nations privileges and immunities in national courts would be certain to have a dangerous effect on the independence of officials and experts, who would then have to fear that at any time, whether they were still in office or after they had left it, they could be called to account in national courts, not necessarily their own, civilly or criminally, for their words spoken or written, or acts performed, as officials or experts'.[181]

When a case is brought against the organization (as opposed to a named official), not only is there no obligation to waive the organization's immunity, there is also no obligation to provide an alternate method of settlement; in the case of the UN the Secretary-General simply decides.

VI.3 Conclusions

Domestic courts have rarely entertained claims against international organizations because of the limits of their jurisdiction and the near absolute immunities. Unlike the progressive recognition of restrictions to the immunity of States and their agents, there have been only limited parallel developments in the domain of organizational immunity. What is most concerning is the denial in some cases of any recourse to justice.

[181] See *Cumaraswamy* case (n 65), written statement of the UN Secretary-General (2 October 1998) [54].

VII
Adjudication before Regional and International Courts

VII.1 Introduction

International and regional courts provide a degree of oversight over the conduct of international organizations. In some instances, these courts have played an important, albeit indirect, role in assessing the validity of international organization conduct in the course of proceedings against States, or in assessing the acts of regional integration organizations (RIOs).

International courts would be the most appropriate complement to international organizations' internal adjudicative mechanisms, if such courts were to be available. They would be more independent and impartial than organizations' internal processes. They would be fitting venues in light of organizations' international character and having regard to the desirability of a model that has the potential to influence organization practice, arguably better than municipal courts could do. For similar reasons, international courts are arguably superior forums to adjudicate claims concerning international organizations than regional courts. Not least, adjudication by international courts is better suited to claims which concern international organizations with universal mandates and could help avoid conflicting jurisprudence emanating from regional courts.

But, international courts are no panacea. There are challenges, most notably having regard to the difficulty for individuals in remote areas to access them, even if rules on standing did not present formal obstacles. Beyond physical access, other practical challenges include the difficulty for international courts to engage with large numbers of potential claimants—borne out by the recent experience of the International Criminal Court (ICC).[1] International court procedures tend to be complex, cumbersome, expensive, and time-consuming.

Individuals face numerous impediments to have their claims against international organizations adjudicated by international or regional courts. These include limited subject matter and personal jurisdiction; limited or no *locus standi*; short limitation periods within which to commence proceedings and requirements to exhaust local remedies or to take steps to consult or negotiate a claim prior to

[1] Carla Ferstman, 'The Participation of Victims in International Criminal Court Proceedings: A Review of the Practice and Consideration of Options for the Future' (REDRESS, 2012).

bringing an international claim. Typically, at least one or more of these or the way in which they operate in combination, will bar proceedings. The chapter focuses on the first three impediments, as they represent the most consistent and severe barriers to justice within this field of inquiry.

VII.2 Subject Matter Jurisdiction—Human Rights and International Humanitarian Law

Subject matter jurisdiction, or jurisdiction *rationae materiae*, concerns a court's competence to adjudicate particular subjects or sources of law. International courts can only adjudicate matters which are in keeping with their constitutive instruments. This stems from the limited personality of the organizations that establish these courts, which is tied to their functions. Subject matter jurisdiction may be stipulated expressly in constituent agreements or implied from those instruments and interpreted and progressively developed by courts. As will be explained, many of these courts recognize their competence over human rights and to a lesser extent international humanitarian law violations. However, these areas are usually narrowly construed as State acts only, regardless of any wider understandings applicable in law or practice. This has impacted several courts' procedures, which in turn has restricted individuals from having their claims concerning international organizations adjudicated.

VII.2.1 International courts

No universal court has a subject-specific mandate to adjudicate human rights and/or international humanitarian law violations. There have been proposals to establish an international human rights court and to afford individuals direct standing before it, but so far these have not been heeded.[2] Nor is there an international court with a specific mandate over international humanitarian law violations.[3] The ICC has jurisdiction over certain international humanitarian law breaches but is restricted to determining individual criminal responsibility. And, its limited reparations

[2] See Australia's proposal for an international court of human rights. UN CHR, 'Draft Proposals for an International Court of Human Rights/Australia', Drafting Committee on an International Bill of Human Rights, 2nd Session (10 May 1948) UN Doc E/CN.4/AC.1/27; Julia Kozma, Manfred Nowak, and Martin Scheinin, 'A World Court of Human Rights—Consolidated Statute and Commentary' (2010) www.eui.eu/Documents/DepartmentsCentres/Law/Professors/Scheinin/ConsolidatedWorldCourtStatute.pdf (last accessed 28 December 2016); Martin Scheinin, 'Towards a World Court of Human Rights' (2009) Research report within the framework of the Swiss Initiative to commemorate the 60th anniversary of the Universal Declaration of Human Rights www.enlazandoalternativas.org/IMG/pdf/hrCourt_scheinin0609.pdf (last accessed 28 December 2016). Kozma, Nowak, and Scheinin's proposal includes jurisdiction over international organizations.

[3] Jann Kleffner and Liesbeth Zegveld, 'Establishing an Individual Complaints Procedure for Violations of International Humanitarian Law' (2000) 3 YB Int'l Humanitarian L 384; Dieter Fleck, 'The Law Applicable to Peace Operations' in Andrew Clapham and Paula Gaeta (eds), *The Oxford Handbook of International Law in Armed Conflict* (OUP 2014) 246.

mandate does not extend beyond this; there is no possibility for the Court to award reparations against States, international organizations, or other legal persons.[4]

The International Court of Justice (ICJ) has a wide and general subject matter jurisdiction for contentious proceedings,[5] whereas other international courts have mandates restricted to interpreting specific treaties[6] or subject matters,[7] none of which concern human rights or international humanitarian law specifically. The ICJ can adjudicate disputes concerning 'any question of international law' and 'the existence of any fact which, if established, would constitute a breach of an international obligation'.[8] It has considered many human rights and international humanitarian law matters in contentious cases including unlawful arrest, detention and expulsion,[9] consular rights,[10] failure to extradite or prosecute,[11] racial discrimination,[12] and mass violations of human rights during conflict.[13] It has also held that States breached international humanitarian law,[14] the principle of non-intervention,[15] and the obligation to prevent genocide.[16]

In advisory proceedings, the ICJ's jurisdiction *rationae materiae* is restricted to legal questions put forward by UN organs or specialized agencies authorized to make such requests. Article 96 of the Charter authorizes the General Assembly and Security Council to request advisory opinions on 'any legal question'. Other UN organs or specialized agencies can request opinions on legal questions arising within the scope of these bodies' activities, provided that the requests were authorized by the General Assembly. Human rights and international humanitarian law have been considered in many opinions.[17]

[4] Rome Statute of the International Criminal Court (adopted 17 July 1998, entered into force 7 July 2002) 2187 UNTS 90, UN Doc A/CONF.183/9 arts 25(4), 75.

[5] Statute of the International Court of Justice (adopted 26 June 1945, entered into force 24 October 1945) 1 UNTS XVI art 36(1).

[6] Statute of the International Tribunal for the Law of the Sea, Annex VI of the Convention on the Law of the Sea (adopted 10 December 1982, entered into force 16 November 1994) 1833 UNTS 3 art 21.

[7] Statute of the UN Dispute Tribunal, UNGA Res 63/253, 24 December 2008 art 2, as amended.

[8] ICJ Statute (n 5) arts 36(2)(b), (c).

[9] *Ahmadou Sadio Diallo (Republic of Guinea v DRC)* (Merits) [2010] ICJ Rep 639 [73], [74], and [80].

[10] ibid [97]; *Case Concerning Avena and Other Mexican Nationals (Mexico v United States of America)* (Merits) [2004] ICJ Rep 128 [106]; *LaGrand Case (Germany v United States of America)* (Merits) [2001] ICJ Reports 466 [77], [91]; *United States Diplomatic and Consular Staff in Tehran (United States of America v Iran)* [1980] ICJ Rep 3 (*Iran Hostages* case) [67], [77].

[11] *Questions relating to the Obligation to Prosecute or Extradite (Belgium v Senegal)* (Merits) [2012] ICJ Rep 422 [88], [117].

[12] *Application of the International Convention on the Elimination of All Forms of Racial Discrimination (Georgia v Russian Federation)* (Preliminary Objections) [2011] ICJ Rep 70 [113], [184].

[13] *Armed Activities on the Territory of the Congo (DRC v Uganda)* (Merits) [2005] ICJ Rep 168 [207], [219]–[220].

[14] ibid [207]–[211], [219], [220], and [249]–[50].

[15] *Military and Paramilitary Activities in and against Nicaragua (Nicaragua v USA)* (Merits) [1986] ICJ Rep 14 [292].

[16] *Application of the Convention on the Prevention and Punishment of the Crime of Genocide (Bosnia and Herzegovina v Serbia and Montenegro)* (Merits) [2007] ICJ Rep 43 (*Bosnia Genocide* case) [449], [450].

[17] *Legal Consequences of the Construction of a Wall in the Occupied Palestinian Territory* (Advisory Opinion) [2004] ICJ Reports 136 [114]–[137] (*Legal Consequences of the Construction of a Wall*); *Legality of the Threat or Use of Nuclear Weapons* (Advisory Opinion) [1996] ICJ Rep 226 [105(2)(c)],

VII.2.2 Regional courts

There are several courts in Europe, the Americas, and Africa with human rights specific mandates. These courts have jurisdiction over rights reflected in the courts' founding treaties and additional protocols thereto.[18] If the treaties are sufficiently broad, jurisdiction can extend to other treaties not explicitly listed to the extent that they are in force between the parties, without valid reservations.[19] Invariably however, human rights courts are unable to also independently address breaches of international humanitarian law[20] or treaties such as the Genocide Convention,[21] although this would not prevent the treaties from serving as interpretive tools.[22] Human rights courts regularly recognize the application of human rights law to situations of armed conflict.[23]

Most regional human rights treaties require States Parties to secure to everyone within their jurisdiction or all persons subject to their jurisdiction, the rights defined therein.[24] The American Convention on Human Rights (ACHR) and the European Convention on Human Rights (ECHR) contain explicit rules to this effect, but the African Charter and the American Declaration (applicable to Organization of American States (OAS) Member States that have not ratified the ACHR) are silent on this point.[25] Nonetheless, both the African and Inter-American commissions have recognized their competence over breaches occurring outside of the territory of the Respondent, if it exercised effective control.[26] So far, these commissions

[105(2)(d)]; *Legal Consequences for States of the Continued Presence of South Africa in Namibia (South West Africa) notwithstanding Security Council Resolution 276 (1970)* (Advisory Opinion) [1971] ICJ Rep 16 [118], [131].

18 European Convention for the Protection of Human Rights and Fundamental Freedoms (ECHR) (adopted 4 November 1950, entered into force 3 September 1953) art 32(1); American Convention on Human Rights (ACHR, adopted 22 November 1969, entered into force 18 July 1978) art 62(1), (3); Protocol to the African Charter on Human and Peoples' Rights on the Establishment of the African Court on Human and Peoples' Rights, OAU/LEG/EXP/AFCHPR/PROT(III) (adopted 10 June 1998, entered into force 25 January 2004) art 3 (ACHPR Protocol).

19 See art 3 of the ACHPR Protocol (n 18), which affords competence over any instrument, including international human rights treaties, which have been ratified by the State party in question. This is replicated in the Protocol on the Statute of the African Court of Justice and Human Rights, AU (adopted 1 July 2008, not yet in force) (2009) 48 ILM 317 (ACJHR Protocol) art 28.

20 *Las Palmeras Case* (Preliminary Objections) Ser C no 67 (IACtHR, 4 February 2000) para 34.

21 *Plan de Sánchez Massacre v Guatemala* (Merits) Ser C no 105 (IACtHR, 29 April 2004) para 51.

22 *Bámaca-Velásquez v Guatemala* (Merits) Ser C no 70 (IACtHR, 25 November 2000) paras 208–209.

23 *Serrano-Cruz Sisters v El Salvador* (Preliminary Objections) Ser C no 118 (IACtHR, 23 November 2004) paras 111–13; *Al-Skeini v United Kingdom* App no 55721/07 (ECtHR, 7 July 2011) [164].

24 See ECHR (n 18) art 1; ACHR (n 18) art 1. See also *Al-Skeini* (n 23); *Loizidou v Turkey* (Preliminary Objections) (GC) App no 15318/89 (ECtHR, 23 March 1995) [60]–[64].

25 African Charter on Human and Peoples' Rights (adopted 27 June 1981, entered into force 21 October 1986) (1982) 21 ILM 58 (ACHPR) art 1; American Declaration of the Rights and Duties of Man (adopted by the Ninth International Conference of American States April 1948) (American Declaration).

26 *Coard v United States*, Case 10.951, Rep no 109/99 (IACommHR, 29 September 1999) para 37; *DRC v Burundi, Rwanda and Uganda*, Comm no 227/99 (ACommHPR, 20th Annual Activity Rep, May 2003); *Egyptian Initiative for Personal Rights and Interights v Egypt*, Comm no 334/06 (ACommHPR, 9th Extraordinary Session, 23 February–3 March 2011); *Association pour la sauvegarde de la paix au Burundi v Kenya, Uganda, Rwanda, Tanzania, Zaire (DRC), Zambia*, Comm no 157/96 (ACommHPR, 33rd Ordinary Session 15–29 May 2003) [52]. See generally Marko Milanović,

have only considered conduct occurring within the territorial scope of the relevant treaty. It is thus unclear whether actions outside the territorial space would also be covered. This is relevant for conduct taking place in overseas operations. If conduct is attributed to the sending State, are host State citizens able to avail themselves of regional human rights mechanisms applicable to the sending State? The answer is affirmative for the European Court of Human Rights (ECtHR)[27] with some limitations,[28] although less clear for other regional courts.

Several, although not all,[29] RIO courts can adjudicate human rights claims.

In Africa, owing to the absence of a functioning Africa-wide RIO court,[30] sub-regional courts have a particularly important role. While the East African Court of Justice (EACJ) has no jurisdiction over human rights violations per se, it can consider such cases if they fall within its overall jurisdictional framework.[31] It interpreted its mandate in this way, even though the operative treaty refers to the possibility for the Court to have jurisdiction over human rights cases *at some future date*.[32] The Southern African Development Community (SADC) Tribunal held similarly in the *Mike Campbell* case.[33] There, the Zimbabwe Government contended that the SADC treaty did not concern human rights or agrarian land reform and thus those matters could not form the basis of a claim before the Tribunal. The Tribunal held otherwise. Referencing general obligations in the Treaty,[34] it recognized its jurisdiction over the issues raised.

The fallout from this and related SADC cases led the Zimbabwe Government to stop cooperation with the Tribunal. This ultimately led SADC heads of State to review the terms of the Tribunal,[35] effectively halting its operations.[36] In 2012,

Extraterritorial Application of Human Rights Treaties: Law, Principles, and Policy (OUP 2011); Takele Bulto, 'Patching the "Legal Black Hole": The Extraterritorial Reach of States' Human Rights Duties in the African Human Rights System' (2011) 27 S Afr J Hum Rts 249.

27 See *Al-Skeini* (n 23).

28 See *Banković and Others v Belgium and Others* (GC) App no 52207/99 (ECtHR, 12 December 2001) [80].

29 *Shanique Myrie v Barbados*, CCJ 3 (OJ) (CCJ, 4 October 2013) para 10; *Ricardo Duarte Moncada v Gobierno de Nicaragua, Alcaldía de Managua y Banco Centroamericano de Integración Económica (BCIE)*, Case no 1-01-12-1994 (CACJ, 21 February 1995).

30 The African Court of Justice is not operational. Shortly after the entry into force of the Protocol of the Court of Justice of the African Union (adopted 11 July 2003, entered into force 11 February 2009), it was decided to merge it with the ACtHPR. The protocol on the establishment of this merged court put out of force the Protocol of the Court of Justice of the African Union. See ACJHR Protocol (n 19) arts 1, 2. See Gino Naldi and Konstantinos Magliveras, 'The African Court of Justice and Human Rights: A Judicial Curate's Egg' (2012) 9 Int'l Org LR 383, 387.

31 *James Katabazi v Secretary General of the EAC*, Ref no 1 (EACJ, 20 November 2007).

32 Treaty for the Establishment of the East African Community as Amended (adopted 30 November 1999, entered into force 7 July 2000) 2144 UNTS I-37437 art 27(2) (EAC Treaty).

33 *Mike Campbell (Pvt) Ltd & 78 Others v Zimbabwe* 02/07 JUD (SADC Tribunal, 28 November 2008).

34 Treaty of the Southern African Development Community (adopted 17 August 1992, entered into force 30 September 1993) art 4(c) (SADC Treaty).

35 SADC, Communiqué (30th Jubilee Summit of SADC Heads of State and Government, Windhoek, 16–17 August 2010) para 32.

36 SADC, Communiqué (Extraordinary Summit of SADC Heads of State and Government, Windhoek, 20 May 2011) paras 7, 8. See also Laurie Nathan, 'The Disbanding of the SADC Tribunal: A Cautionary Tale' (2013) 35(4) Human Rights Q 870, 878–79; Frederick Cowell, 'The

SADC resolved to negotiate a new Protocol on the Tribunal and determined that its mandate should be confined to interpreting the SADC Treaty and Protocols relating to disputes between Member States.[37] Some have argued that this retreat evidences a privileging of State sovereignty over and above community values.[38] Others like Nkhata see the pushback as a response to perceived judicial activism in the face of a vague and fragile mandate,[39] although EAC governments did not have the same response to the EACJ's arguably similar expansive judicial interpretations. The Economic Community of West African States (ECOWAS) took a different approach. In an early case, the ECOWAS Community Court of Justice (ECOWAS CCJ) determined that the Protocol establishing the Court did not afford it with the necessary competence to adjudicate human rights cases.[40] However, that finding spurred efforts to revise the Protocol.[41] The result of the revision process is a Court which now has a wide competence over any treaty adopted by the Respondent State, including the African Charter.[42]

Similarly, the founding treaties on the European Union (EU) did not expressly reference human rights; however, these have been recognized progressively in the jurisprudence of the Court of Justice of the European Union (CJEU) and predecessor courts[43] and now form a core part of EU law. With the coming into force of the Treaty of Lisbon,[44] the Charter of Fundamental Rights of the European Union[45] binds all EU bodies and Member States,[46] including the CJEU. The CJEU also applies the ECHR, and Charter rights which correspond to rights already guaranteed by the ECHR are given the same meaning and scope as, and no lesser degree

Death of the Southern African Development Community Tribunal's Human Rights Jurisdiction' (2013) 13(1) Human Rights LR 153, 161–64.

[37] SADC, Final Communiqué (32nd Summit of SADC Heads of State and Government, Maputo, 18 August 2012) para 24.

[38] See Nathan (n 36) 879.

[39] Mwiza Jo Nkhata, 'The Role of Regional Economic Communities in Protecting and Promoting Human Rights in Africa: Reflections on the Human Rights Mandate of the Tribunal of the Southern African Development Community' (2012) 20 Afr J Int'l & Comp L 87, 99.

[40] *Jerry Ugokwe v Nigeria*, ECW/CCJ/JUD/03/05 (ECOWAS CCJ, 7 October 2005) paras 29–33.

[41] Supplementary Protocol Amending the Protocol Relating to the ECOWAS Community Court of Justice (adopted 19 January 2005, entered into force 19 January 2005) ECOWAS Doc A/SP.1/01/05 (ECOWAS 2005 Protocol).

[42] Article 9(4) of the ECOWAS 2005 Protocol enables the Court to entertain cases that concern 'violation of human rights that occur in any Member State'; and article 10(d) affords the Court the possibility to hear cases from individuals on application for relief for violation of their human rights. See Solomon Ebobrah, 'Critical Issues in the Human Rights Mandate of the ECOWAS Court of Justice' (2010) 54(1) J Afr L 1, 14–19.

[43] Case 26/62 *NV Algemene Transporten Expeditie Onderneming van Gend en Loos v Nederlandse Administratie der Belastingen* [1963] ECR 1.

[44] Treaty of Lisbon, Consolidated versions of the Treaty on European Union (TEU) and the Treaty on the Functioning of the European Union (TFEU) (adopted 13 December 2007, entered into force 1 December 2009) [2008] OJ C115/01.

[45] 2000/C 364/01 (adopted 7 December 2000, entered into force 1 December 2009) (EU Charter).

[46] Consolidated version of the Treaty on European Union (TEU), 13 December 2007, 2008/C 115/01 art 6(1). Stelios Andreadakis and Sonia Morano-Foadi, 'Reflections on the Architecture of the EU after the Treaty of Lisbon: the European Judicial Approach to Fundamental Rights' (2011) 17 Eur LJ 595, 610.

of protection than, provided under the ECHR.[47] Nonetheless, gaps remain. The CJEU has minimal jurisdiction over acts adopted within the EU's Common Foreign and Security Policy (CFSP),[48] with the exception of sanctions.[49] Accountability is thus restricted for the EU's military, anti-piracy and external border control actions.

It is likely that certain acts undertaken by Member States under the guise of the EU will be attributed to the EU.[50] Without access to the CJEU for areas linked to CFSP, the prospects for EU accountability are slim, despite the EU's own obligation to compensate for damages caused by its institutions or servants in the performance of their duties.[51] The EU has established only one mechanism to assess alleged human rights violations attributable to an EU Common Security and Defence Policy mission—the Human Rights Review Panel (HRRP), which can review alleged human rights violations by EULEX Kosovo.[52] But, it can only issue non-binding recommendations for remedial action (other than compensation) by the Head of Mission. Thus, without access to the CJEU, the victims of these violations have no recourse to a court, nor any ability to ensure the recommendations are heeded.[53]

A possible solution lies with the EU's planned accession to the ECHR, which would afford ECtHR oversight over the conduct of the EU and its institutions.[54] Accession was recommended as early as 1979, given the increasing impact of the Community's activities on citizens, and the need to counterbalance its powers 'by their formal subjection to well-defined fundamental rights'.[55] Discussions have continued ever since. A draft accession treaty was agreed in 2013.[56] However, the CJEU determined that it was incompatible with EU law, one of the reasons being that it allowed the ECtHR to assess the human rights compatibility of CFSP

[47] See Case C–400/10 PPU *J McB v LE* [2010] ECR I–08965 para 53.

[48] See art 24(4) TEU (n 46) and Consolidated Version of the Treaty on the Functioning of the European Union (TFEU), 2008 OJ C 115/47 art 275.

[49] TFEU (n 48) art 275.

[50] Applying the rationale of the ECtHR's decision in *Behrami and Behrami v France* and *Saramati v France, Germany and Norway* (GC) App nos 71412/01, 78166/01 (ECtHR, 2 May 2007), which attributed conduct to UNMIK. Stefano Piedimonte Bodini, 'Fighting Maritime Piracy under the European Convention on Human Rights' (2011) 22(3) EJIL 829, 845–46. See also the draft explanatory report to the accession agreement of the EU to the ECHR, which envisions that acts of EU institutions, bodies, offices, or agencies, or persons acting on their behalf, will be attributed to the EU. Draft Explanatory report to the Agreement on the Accession of the European Union to the ECHR (2 April 2003) COE Doc 47+1(2013)007 art 21(a).

[51] See TFEU (n 48) art 340(2).

[52] See Chapter V.

[53] Gentian Zyberi, 'The Applicability of General Principles and Instruments of International Law to Peace Missions of the European Union' in Aurel Sari and Ramses Wessel (eds), *Human Rights in EU Crisis Management Operations: A Duty to Respect and to Protect?* (CLEER Working Papers 2012/6, TMC Asser Institute 2012) 21, 33.

[54] See TEU (n 48) art 6(2). See also Sionaidh Douglas-Scott, 'The European Union and Human Rights after the Treaty of Lisbon' (2011) 11 HRLR 645.

[55] European Commission, 'Memorandum on the Accession of the European Communities to the Convention for the Protection of Human Rights and Fundamental Freedoms' (2 May 1979) COM(79) 210 final.

[56] Draft Revised Agreement on the Accession of the European Union to the ECHR (5th Negotiation Meeting between the CDDH Ad Hoc Negotiation Group and the European Commission on the Accession of the EU to the ECHR, Final Report to the CDDH) (10 June 2013) COE Doc 47+1(2013)008rev2 Appendix I.

decisions without prior scrutiny by the CJEU, potentially jeopardizing the autonomy of EU law.[57] As such, changes to the accession agreement would need to be agreed, if accession is still to be pursued.[58]

VII.3 Personal Jurisdiction—Claims Concerning International Organizations

Aside from RIO courts, most international or regional courts with subject matter competence over human rights and/or international humanitarian law cannot adjudicate claims against international organizations.

VII.3.1 International courts

General international courts such as the ICJ can only adjudicate contentious cases against States, and then only in specified circumstances.[59] International organization conduct can be considered as part of advisory proceedings, albeit in limited and usually indirect ways. The ICJ can also use its advisory procedure to 'review' decisions of certain international administrative tribunals,[60] or provide an opinion on a difference between the UN and a Member State arising out of the interpretation or application of a convention which designates the ICJ for this purpose.[61] These 'reviews' or treaty-based opinions, which may have binding effect in accordance with the treaties, headquarters agreements or other texts which accord them that status,[62] nevertheless must comply with the procedures for Advisory Opinions set out in the Charter.[63]

The procedure is imbalanced. Advisory proceedings can only be lodged by the organizations themselves, not by those who have grievances with them.[64] Only the international organization is 'represented', although the ICJ has adopted

[57] Opinion 2/13, *Request for an Opinion pursuant to Article 218(11) TFEU, made on 4 July 2013 by the European Commission* ECLI:EU:C:2014:2454 (Grand Chamber, 18 December 2014) paras 95–100.

[58] Eva-Maria Poptcheva, 'Human Rights Applied to CSDP Operations and Missions' (European Parliamentary Research Service Briefing, 21 January 2014).

[59] ICJ Statute (n 5) arts 34–36.

[60] The Administrative Tribunal of the International Labour Organization affords this possibility. The UN Administrative Tribunal previously had this system in place, but this was abolished with the establishment of the internal appeals mechanism. Paolo Vargiu, 'From Advisory Opinions to Binding Decisions: The New Appeal Mechanism of the UN system of Administration of Justice' (2010) 7(2) Int'l Organizations L 261.

[61] Convention on the Privileges and Immunities of the UN (adopted 13 February 1946, entered into force 17 September 1946) 1 UNTS 15 (CPIUN) art VIII s 30.

[62] Roberto Ago, '"Binding" Advisory Opinions of the International Court of Justice' (1991) 85 AJIL 439.

[63] *Judgment No 2867 of the Administrative Tribunal of the International Labour Organization upon a Complaint Filed against the International Fund for Agricultural Development* (Advisory Opinion) [2012] ICJ Rep 10 [21]–[27].

[64] ibid [65]; UN Charter (n 5) art 96.

procedures to assist the 'party' that does not benefit from standing.[65] International organizations tend to bring proceedings to seek legal advice to resolve a matter before one of the organs of the UN or to support a particular position. This limits the capacity of proceedings to serve as a check on international organization actions or as a route whereby the grievances of natural or legal persons unaffiliated with the organization may be aired and resolved; those types of advisory opinions are simply not sought. Even when there is a treaty right for a State to insist upon a 'binding' Advisory Opinion, there is no obligation on the State to seek enforcement of it. For instance, Haiti has not insisted in accordance with Article 30 of the CPIUN that the UN bring a request for an Advisory Opinion in relation to the differences arising out of the interpretation and application of Article 29 of the Convention. This is despite the fact that Office of Legal Affairs' interpretation has scuppered efforts of Haitians affected by the cholera epidemic to obtain an effective resolution of their disputes with the UN. Under the law of diplomatic protection, Haiti is not obliged to take up the disputes of its citizens.

The ICJ has assessed various matters concerning international organizations in the course of its rulings. It recognized that the UN's international personality gives rise to both rights and duties, and UN competence to present an international claim.[66] It also determined that, in relation to 'acts performed by the United Nations or by its agents acting in their official capacity' that '[t]he United Nations may be required to bear responsibility for the damage arising from such acts'.[67] The ICJ affirmed that the UN can establish a tribunal to deal with staff disputes[68] in order to fulfil its purposes. While it has made clear that the Charter does not enable it to review decisions of UN organs,[69] in a number of its proceedings the ICJ has carried out limited inquiries into the validity of the actions of UN organs,[70] as did the ICTY, at least for the purposes of confirming its own jurisdiction.[71]

65 *Judgment No 2867 of the Administrative Tribunal of the International Labour Organization upon a Complaint Filed against the International Fund for Agricultural Development* (Advisory Opinion) (n 63) [3], [6], [7], [12], and [45].

66 *Reparation for Injuries Suffered in the Service of the United Nations* (Advisory Opinion) [1949] ICJ Rep 174, 179 (*Reparation for Injuries*).

67 *Difference Relating to Immunity from Legal Process of a Special Rapporteur of the Commission on Human Rights* (Advisory Opinion) [1999] ICJ Rep 62 [88]–[89] (*Cumaraswamy* case) [66].

68 *Effects of Awards of Compensation Made by the United Nations Administrative Tribunal* (Advisory Opinion) [1954] ICJ Rep 47, 58.

69 *Questions of Interpretation and Application of the 1971 Montreal Convention arising from the Aerial Incident at Lockerbie (Libyan Arab Jamahiriya v United States of America)* (Provisional Measures) [1992] ICJ Rep 114, [42]–[46]; *Legal Consequences for States of the Continued Presence of South Africa in Namibia (South West Africa) notwithstanding Security Council Resolution 276 (1970)* (Advisory Opinion) [1971] ICJ Rep 16 [89].

70 See eg *Certain Expenses of the United Nations (Article 17, paragraph 2, of the Charter)* (Advisory Opinion) [1962] ICJ Rep 151 [20]–[23]; *Legal Consequences for States of the Continued Presence of South Africa in Namibia (South West Africa) notwithstanding Security Council Resolution 276 (1970)* (Advisory Opinion) [1971] ICJ Rep 16 [89]–[95]; *Legal Consequences of the Construction of a Wall* (n 17) [25]–[35].

71 *Prosecutor v Tadić* (Decision on Jurisdiction) IT-94-1-T (ICTY, 10 August 1995) paras 16, 40; ICTY, *Prosecutor v Tadić* (Decision on Motion for Interlocutory Appeal) (n 395); Jose Alvarez, 'Judging the Security Council' (1996) 90 AJIL 1, 11–12.

These assessments of international organization conduct are noteworthy. Nonetheless, they are relatively few and are not evidence of a burgeoning process of substantial or coherent review by the ICJ, nor do they resolve its lack of competence to resolve contentious claims concerning international organizations.[72] Sir Robert Jennings has noted 'the extraordinary anomaly of an international community in which international organizations play an increasing role and yet, even interstate organizations cannot be parties, or be made parties, to contentious cases before the supreme court of that community'.[73]

Other international courts with subject specific mandates cannot adjudicate claims against international organizations that are not parties to the agreements relevant to those courts. In this sense, the World Trade Organization (WTO) Appellate Body cannot rule on any actions or inactions of the WTO; however, it can consider claims made against the EU which is a WTO member since 1995.[74] Similarly, the International Tribunal on the Law of the Sea can consider claims made against the EU, which ratified the UN Convention on the Law of the Sea.[75] Other international organizations may in future become parties to the Convention which would enable claims to be lodged against them.[76] The Seabed Disputes Chamber can also hear claims against the EU as a party. Claims can also be lodged against the International Seabed Authority which administers the resources of the deep seabed and the Enterprise, which once established will serve as the Seabed Authority's operator on mining issues.[77]

VII.3.2 Regional courts

Most RIO courts can adjudicate claims against those organizations that form part of their internal system. These tend not to be full-fledged contentious procedures but instead help ensure the proper interpretation and valid application of the acts of the internal system. Annulment, reference, or review proceedings can be lodged before many RIO courts.[78] These same courts can adjudicate cases where it is alleged that

[72] The inability to sue NATO forced Yugoslavia to bring its claim related to the NATO aerial bombing campaign against individual NATO members only. See *Legality of Use of Force (Yugoslavia v United States of America)* (Application Instituting Proceedings) 1999 General List No 114, filed with ICJ Registry (29 April 1999). At the same time, an application instituting proceedings was filed against Belgium, Canada, France, Germany, Italy, Netherlands, Portugal, Spain, and the United Kingdom.

[73] Robert Jennings, 'The United Nations at Fifty: The International Court of Justice After Fifty Years' (1995) 89 AJIL 493, 504–505.

[74] At the time of writing, more than 80 disputes had been filed against the EU as respondent. See WTO, 'The European Union and the WTO' www.wto.org/english/thewto_e/countries_e/european_communities_e.htm (last accessed 28 December 2016).

[75] UN Convention on the Law of the Sea (adopted 10 December 1982, entered into force 16 November 1994) 1833 UNTS 3. It was ratified by the European Community on 7 December 1984.

[76] ibid arts 20(2), 305. [77] ibid Part XI s 5 art 187.

[78] Agreement Establishing the CCJ (adopted 14 February 2001, entered into force 23 July 2002) arts XII(1)(c), (d), XIII, XIV; Statute of the CACJ (adopted 10 December 1992, entered into force 2 February 1994) (1995) 34 ILM 923 arts 22(b), (k), 23; Treaty Creating the Court of Justice of the Cartagena Agreement (Amended by the Cochabamba Protocol) (adopted 28 May 1996, entered into force 25 August 1999) (1979) 18 ILM 1203 (Treaty Creating the CJAC) arts 17–20, 32–34; TFEU (n 48) arts 19(b), 218(11), 263, 267, 269; EAC Treaty (n 32) arts 27(1), 28(2), 30(1); ECOWAS 2005 Protocol (n 41) art 9(1)(a), (b), and (c).

the RIO failed to fulfil an obligation or infringed a legal provision binding upon it.[79] Additionally, some courts are mandated to resolve employment disputes.[80]

In contrast, regional human rights courts have not exercised jurisdiction over international organizations given their limited competence under their constituent agreements and the restrictive interpretations they have given to these agreements. The European Commission confirmed the lack of personal jurisdiction over the European Community in its 1978 *Confedération Française Démocratique Du Travail* decision.[81] The ECtHR has equally affirmed that it had no jurisdiction over acts of universal international organizations.[82] And, as indicated above, the planned accession of the EU to the ECHR has been stymied by an opinion of the CJEU.[83] Until such time as the EU accedes, claims against it and its institutions are inadmissible *ratione personae.*

Both the African Commission and Court on Human and Peoples' Rights have refrained from exercising jurisdiction against AU and sub-regional institutions in Africa. Following the suspension of the work of the SADC Tribunal, several recipients of judgments impacted by the suspension claimed to the African Commission.[84] Their initial claim was brought against SADC institutions and SADC Member States. The Commission admitted the case against the fourteen States, but not against the SADC institutions, because it has 'no jurisdiction over intergovernmental organizations and their organs'.[85] Civil society groups also sought to encourage the African Court on Human and Peoples' Rights (ACtHPR) to issue an advisory opinion on the matter; however, it declined to do so given that the matter was pending before the Commission.[86]

79 See Agreement Establishing the CCJ (n 78) art XII(1)(b); Statute of the CACJ (n 78) art 22(g); Treaty Creating the CJAC (n 78) arts 37, 38; TFEU (n 48) arts 263, 265, 271(b), (c), (d), 272; EAC Treaty (n 32) art 28(1); ECOWAS 2005 Protocol (ibid art 9(1)(g), (2)); Protocol on SADC Tribunal (adopted 7 August 2000, entered into force 14 August 2001) arts 17, 18.

80 EAC Treaty (n 32) art 31; ECOWAS 2005 Protocol (n 41) art 9(1)(f); Protocol on SADC Tribunal art 19; TFEU (n 48) art 270; Treaty Creating the CJAC (n 78) art 40.

81 *Confedération Française Démocratique du Travail v European Communities, alternatively: their Member States a) jointly and b) severally* (Decision on Admissibility) App no 8030/77 (ECommHR, 10 July 1978) para 3. See also *M & Co v Germany* (Decision on Admissibility) App no 13258/87 (ECommHR, 9 February 1990) 144; *Matthews v United Kingdom* App no 24833/94 (ECtHR, 18 February 1999) [32].

82 See eg the ECtHR cases *Behrami v France* (n 50); *Galić v Netherlands* (Decision on Admissibility) App no 22617/07 (ECtHR, 9 June 2009); *Blagojević v Netherlands* (Decision on Admissibility) App no 49032/07 (ECtHR, 9 June 2009); *Berić v Bosnia and Herzegovina* (Decision on Admissibility) App nos 36357/04, 36360/04, 38346/04, 41705/04, 45190/04, 45578/04, 45579/04, 45580/04, 91/05, 97/05, 100/05, 101/05, 1121/05, 1123/05, 1125/05, 1129/05, 1132/05, 1133/05, 1169/05, 1172/05, 1175/05, 1177/05, 1180/05, 1185/05, 20793/05, and 25496/05 (ECtHR, 16 October 2007); *Kalinić and Bilbija v Bosnia and Herzegovina* (Decision on Admissibility) App nos 45541/04, 16587/07 (ECtHR, 13 May 2008); *Gajic v Germany* (Decision on Admissibility) App no 31446/02 (ECtHR, 28 August 2007).

83 Opinion 2/13 (n 57).

84 *Luke Munyandu Tembani and Benjamin John Freeth v Angola and Thirteen Others*, Comm no 409/12 (ACommHPR, 54th Ordinary Session, 22 October–5 November 2013).

85 ibid paras 15, 80.

86 *Request for an Advisory Opinion by Pan African Lawyers' Union and the Southern Africa Litigation Centre* App no 002/2012 (ACtHPR, 15 March 2013).

The ACtHPR has denied competence over cases brought against the AU and its institutions, although its rulings used other rationales for dismissal.[87] However, the Protocol establishing the Court and its jurisdiction only outline subject matter jurisdiction; personal jurisdiction is not set out.[88] If this approach were adopted by the merged African Court of Justice and Human Rights, then claims against AU institutions would only be capable of being made to the General Affairs section, and these could not involve human or peoples' rights.[89] Thus, the merging of the two courts and the strict demarcations of competencies would have the effect of narrowing jurisdiction. Unlike some other RIO courts which are competent to address human rights claims against RIOs, the merged AU court would appear not to have this possibility, absent creative interpretation.

VII.3.3 Limited indirect review by regional courts?

Like the ICJ, some regional human rights courts have exercised limited review over acts of international organizations. Several RIO courts have done similarly in respect of international organizations outside their regional remit. These reviews of acts of the organization are incidental to the assessment of State responsibility.

The jurisprudence does not follow a linear or chronological trajectory. One is left with an overall impression of the need for an international court with a mandate to assess directly international organization responsibilities. To focus attention on the State implementers of acts originating from organization decisions ensures a measure of accountability for what would otherwise be unaccountable acts of the organization. Yet, State responsibility does not displace the need for international organization responsibility. As the DARIO makes clear, '[e]very internationally wrongful act of an international organization entails the international responsibility of that organization'.[90] Focusing exclusively on State responsibility may also undermine the notion that international organizations have distinct and separate legal personalities from the Member States that establish them. Co-mingling these two responsibilities in effect pierces the veil of the separate personality of the international organization, which may undermine organizations' independence in the longer-term.

The jurisprudence can be separated into four main categories:

[87] *Femi Falana v African Union* App no 001/2011 (ACtHPR, 26 June 2012), dismissed on the basis of lack of standing; *Efoua Mbozo'o Samuel v Pan African Parliament* App no 010/2011 (ACtHPR, 13 September 2011), dismissed for lack of subject matter jurisdiction. In the latter case, Judge Fatsah Ouguergouz issued a Separate Opinion in which lack of personal jurisdiction over the Pan African Parliament is addressed [7]–[11].

[88] ACHPR Protocol (n 18) art 3(1).

[89] See art 17 of the ACJHR Protocol (n 19) which explains the competencies of the General Affairs and Human Rights sections. See also Naldi and Magliveras (n 30) 398–400.

[90] ILC, Draft Articles on the Responsibility of International Organizations, 'Report of the International Law Commission on the Work of its 63rd Session' (26 April–3 June and 4 July–12 August 2011) UN Doc A/66/10 (DARIO) art 3.

(1) *The primacy of Article 103 of the UN Charter*

In several cases in which responsibility was attributed to international organizations, these same courts determined that they could not ascertain also States' and/or RIO's separate responsibility arising from their implementation of the impugned acts, because to do so would constitute an unwarranted intrusion with the fulfilment of the organization's key mission.

The 2005 *Yusuf and Kadi* decisions take this approach.[91] The applicants requested an annulment of the EC regulation imposing Community-wide restrictions on legal and natural persons suspected of terrorism, which was put in place to comply with UN Security Council sanctions. The Court of First Instance of the European Communities (CFI) determined that UN Member States' obligations under the Charter which extend to the implementation of Security Council decisions prevail over any other obligation, including those under the ECHR and EC Treaty.[92] As the purpose of the European regulation was to give effect to Security Council resolutions, any review of its lawfulness would necessarily require the Court to examine the lawfulness of the Security Council resolutions,[93] which it had no authority to do.

Somewhat at odds with the first part of its ruling, the CFI set out a limited exception. It considered itself competent to assess the lawfulness of the regulation and, indirectly, of the Security Council resolutions implemented by that regulation in the light of the higher rules of general international law comprising *jus cogens*, from which neither the Member States nor the bodies of the UN may derogate.[94] It proceeded upon this review[95] and determined that no principles of *jus cogens* are impacted by the resolution. The lacuna in the judicial protection available to the applicants is not in itself contrary to *jus cogens*, because the right to access courts is not absolute.[96]

The *Behrami and Saramati* cases[97] take the same approach. The cases concerned the conduct of French and Norwegian military personnel in Kosovo, who served under the KFOR NATO military mission. Mr Behrami alleged a violation of the right to life, following the killing of one son and serious injury of another, due to

[91] Case T 306/01 *Ahmed Ali Yusuf and Al-Barakaat International Foundation v Council and Commission* [2005] ECR II–03533; Case T 315/01 *Yassin Abdullah Kadi v Council and Commission* [2005] ECR II–03649. The decisions were overruled by the Court of Justice of the European Communities in Case C–415/05 P *Yassin Abdullah Kadi and Al-Barakaat International Foundation v Council of the European Union and Commission* [2008] ECR I–06351.

[92] Case T 306/01 *Ahmed Ali Yusuf and Al-Barakaat International Foundation v Council and Commission* (n 91) paras 233–34, 240, 249.

[93] ibid para 266. [94] ibid para 277.

[95] Marko Milanović, 'Norm Conflict in International Law: Whither Human Rights?' (2009) 20 Duke J Comp & Int'l L 69, 91; Mielle Bulterman, 'Fundamental Rights and the United Nations Financial Sanction Regime: The Kadi and Yusuf Judgments of the Court of First Instance of the European Communities' (2006) 19(3) Leiden J Int'l L 753, 769–72; Christina Eckes, 'Judicial Review of European Anti-Terrorism Measures—The *Yusuf* and *Kadi* Judgments of the Court of First Instance' (2008) 14(1) European L J 74, 90–91.

[96] Case T 306/01 *Ahmed Ali Yusuf and Al Barakaat International Foundation v Council and Commission* (n 91) para 341.

[97] See *Behrami v France* (n 50).

French KFOR troops' failure to mark and defuse undetonated cluster bombs. Mr Saramati's claim concerned his unlawful detention in a KFOR camp. At the time of the incidents, Kosovo was under the authority of UNMIK and the ECtHR attributed the conduct to UNMIK 'exclusively'.[98] This conclusion was criticized not least because it implied that attribution of responsibility to UNMIK necessarily prevented an inquiry into States' distinct liability for their specific roles in relation to the events.[99]

The ECtHR determined that it cannot scrutinize State conduct that is covered by Security Council resolutions, because the acts 'were directly attributable to the UN, an organisation of universal jurisdiction fulfilling its imperative collective security objective'.[100] To embark on a review would 'interfere with the fulfilment of the UN's key mission ... [and] would also be tantamount to imposing conditions on the implementation of a UNSC Resolution which were not provided for in the text of the Resolution itself'.[101] It distinguished its *Bosphorus* ruling on the need for 'equivalent protection', because the acts in question were not carried out by France and Norway on their territories or as a result of a decision by their authorities.[102] Article 103 of the Charter prevails over all other obligations in the event of a conflict between them. *Bosphorus* was thus inapplicable because the UN 'was acting in pursuit of its "fundamental mission ... to secure international peace and security", the efficacy of which would be undermined if troop-contributing States could scrutinize orders given to their troops'.[103]

(2) *A presumption of harmony*

The ECtHR took a more nuanced approach in several post *Behrami* cases.[104] *Nada*[105] concerned an Egyptian national living in an Italian enclave surrounded by Switzerland who was effectively prevented from travelling as a result of Switzerland's implementation of UN sanctions. *Al-Jedda*[106] concerned the lawfulness of UK detention practices in Iraq, under the cover of UN Security Council resolutions. In both cases, the ECtHR determined that there was a presumption that: 'the Security Council does not intend to impose any obligation on Member States to breach fundamental principles of human rights. In the event of any ambiguity in the terms of a Security Council Resolution, the Court must therefore choose the interpretation which is most in harmony with the requirements of the Convention and which avoids any conflict of obligations'.[107] Both these cases also turned on the fact that

[98] The rationale for the attribution of conduct to UNMIK is discussed in Chapter III.

[99] Aurel Sari, 'Jurisdiction and International Responsibility in Peace Support Operations: The Behrami and Saramati Cases' (2008) 8(1) Human Rights LR 151, 159.

[100] See *Behrami v France* (n 50) [151]. [101] ibid [149]. [102] ibid para 151.

[103] Tom Dannenbaum, 'Translating the Standard of Effective Control into a System of Effective Accountability: How Liability Should be Apportioned for Violations of Human Rights by Member State Troop Contingents Serving as United Nations Peacekeepers' (2010) 51 Harv Int'l LJ 113, 124.

[104] *Behrami v France* (n 50) [149].

[105] *Nada v Switzerland* (GC) App no 10593/08 (ECtHR, 12 September 2012) [121]–[122].

[106] *Al-Jedda v United Kingdom* (GC) App no 27021/08 (ECtHR, 7 July 2011) [101]–[102].

[107] ibid [102]; cited affirmatively in *Nada v Switzerland* (n 105) [171].

the respective Respondent States were understood to have discretion in how they were to implement the resolutions. Yet, in both cases there was no more than cursory consideration of the legal protections within the UN system.

(3) Limited review or presumption of validity

The African Commission on Human and Peoples' Rights was called upon to assess the compatibility of an embargo imposed against Burundi by States of the Great Lakes region following a coup d'état by the Burundian army. The decision to impose the embargo was taken by the States of the Great Lakes Region in 1996, but was thereafter endorsed by the OAU and UN Security Council. The Commission noted that, once endorsed by the Security Council, the embargo was no longer the act of a few States but imposes obligations on all UN Member States. It then went on to assess the validity of the embargo as endorsed, holding that:

> '[t]he critical question and one which may affect the legitimacy of the action is whether such action as has been determined is excessive and disproportionate, is indiscriminate and seeks to achieve ends beyond the legitimate purpose. Sanctions therefore cannot be open-ended, the effects thereof must be carefully monitored, measures must be adopted to meet the basic needs of the most vulnerable populations or they must be targeted at the main perpetrators or authors of the nuisance complained of ... We are satisfied that the sanctions imposed were not indiscriminate, that they were targeted in that a list of affected goods was made'.[108]

Another area of review concerns allegations that States breached applicants' rights when surrendering them to international criminal tribunals. In *Naletilic*, the ECtHR exercised limited review over the ICTY when it determined that the Tribunal afforded defendants sufficient procedural guarantees. It declared the claim inadmissible, one of the reasons being that the Tribunal 'in view of the content of its Statute and Rules of Procedure, offers all the necessary guarantees including those of impartiality and independence'.[109]

(4) The presumption of 'equivalent protection'

The ECtHR's doctrine of equivalent protection is set out in *Bosphorus*.[110] The case concerned Ireland's alleged responsibility for implementing the sanctions regime against the Federal Republic of Yugoslavia to the detriment of a Turkish charter company, whose leased aircraft Ireland impounded because it was owned by the Yugoslav national airline. The ECtHR recognized that States Parties retain responsibility for their conduct whether it stems from domestic law or acts taken to comply with international obligations.[111] It would not be compatible with the ECHR

[108] *Association pour la sauvegarde de la paix au Burundi* (n 26) [75]–[76].

[109] *Naletilic v Croatia* (Decision on Admissibility) App no 51891/99 (ECtHR, 4 May 2000) para 1(b).

[110] *Bosphorus v Ireland* App no 45036/98 (ECtHR, 30 June 2005) [152]–[153].

[111] ibid para 153.

to absolve States completely for any actions taken in pursuit of international obligations. State action in these areas is justified:

> [a]s long as the relevant organisation is considered to protect fundamental rights, as regards both the substantive guarantees offered and the mechanisms controlling their observance, in a manner which can be considered at least equivalent to that for which the Convention provides. By 'equivalent' the Court means 'comparable'; any requirement that the organisation's protection be 'identical' could run counter to the interest of international cooperation pursued . . . . However, any such finding of equivalence could not be final and would be susceptible to review in the light of any relevant change in fundamental rights protection.
>
> If such equivalent protection is considered to be provided by the organisation, the presumption will be that a State has not departed from the requirements of the Convention when it does no more than implement legal obligations flowing from its membership of the organisation. However, any such presumption can be rebutted if, in the circumstances of a particular case, it is considered that the protection of Convention rights was manifestly deficient. In such cases, the interest of international cooperation would be outweighed by the Convention's role as a 'constitutional instrument of European public order' in the field of human rights.[112]

The ECtHR made clear that the presumption of equivalent protection can only apply when the Member State had no discretion in implementing the international obligation. When there is discretion, States' responsibility is fully engaged. The ECtHR has applied this assessment in several cases, although it has only rarely determined that an international organization does not afford equivalent protection. In *Bosphorus*, the ECtHR held that the protection afforded by the EU was not 'manifestly deficient' and thus the presumption of equivalent protection was not displaced.[113]

The *Bosphorus* principle concerned the ECtHR's relationship with the EU, ostensibly as a tool to respect complementary legal regimes. But, the principle has since been applied to other international organizations. It was applied to the ICC in *Djokaba Lambi Longa v Netherlands*,[114] which concerned a detained defence witness from the DRC who was brought to the Netherlands to testify in ICC proceedings. While in the Netherlands, he claimed asylum, and asked the ICC to defer his removal to the DRC until that claim was decided. During this time he was held in the ICC's Detention Unit. He challenged the lawfulness of his detention on the basis that the term for his imprisonment in the DRC had already expired, and therefore the ICC had no basis to detain him. The ECtHR determined that the ICC's detention of Mr Longa was not a sufficient basis to attract Dutch jurisdiction.[115]

In this respect it followed its earlier jurisprudence in several ICTY fair trial and abuse of process cases.[116] But, the applicants, pursuant to *Bosphorus*, argued that the presumption of equivalent protection was rebutted, because the protection offered by the ICC to defence witnesses was insufficient. This was rejected, but in so doing, the ECtHR carried out a rudimentary review of ICC procedures. It affirmed that

112 ibid paras 155, 156. 113 ibid paras 159–66.
114 *Djokaba Lambi Longa v Netherlands* App no 33917/12 (ECtHR, 9 October 2012).
115 ibid para 80. 116 See *Galić* (n 82); *Blagojević* (n 82).

Longa's detention had a basis in the provisions of international law governing the functioning of the ICC, observed that there were provisions in the ICC's rules to protect witnesses, and indicated that it was not evident that Longa would be kept in detention by the DRC authorities by the operation of those rules.[117]

The *Bosphorus* principle was also the basis upon which the African Commission accepted that it had jurisdiction to consider whether SADC Member States violated the African Charter by acts they undertook under the guise of SADC institutions.[118]

Bosphorus was also central to the analysis in the 2008 and 2013 *Kadi* judgments before the CJEU. The 2008 judgment annulled Regulation 881/2002 in so far as it concerned Mr Kadi, distinguished *Behrami* and affirmed that it was competent to review the legality of EU regulations, even though these stemmed from Security Council resolutions. The Court recognized that the Community needed to attach special importance to Security Council resolutions adopted under Chapter VII which reflect the Council's primary purpose to maintain international peace and security.[119] However, the Charter does not dictate how these resolutions should be transposed into domestic law; States have discretion as to how to implement. Because of the absence of judicial protection, the UN Sanctions Committee's de-listing procedure does not satisfy the presumption of equivalent protection.[120] Thus, the Community judicature must 'ensure the review, in principle the full review, of the lawfulness of all Community acts in the light of the fundamental rights forming an integral part of the general principles of Community law, including review of Community measures which, like the contested regulation, are designed to give effect to the resolutions adopted by the Security Council under Chapter VII of the Charter of the United Nations'.[121] The Court held that for a review to be effective, the EU must be in a position to explain why a person appears on a sanctions list and to give that person an opportunity to be heard. Persons should be informed that they appear on a list when the listing decision is taken or as swiftly as possible thereafter.[122] These requirements were not met in Mr Kadi's case, resulting in the infringement of his rights.

The Court maintained the effects of the annulled regulation in so far as it concerned Mr Kadi for three months in order to allow the Council to remedy the infringements. Thereafter, the Sanctions Committee provided a summary of the rationale for the listing, which was shared with Mr Kadi, who was afforded the opportunity to respond. Before the expiry of the three month term, Mr Kadi was re-listed under a new EU regulation. Consequently, he lodged a new action for annulment.[123] With respect to the level and intensity of the review, the General Court in its 2010 judgment determined that there was a need to respect 'the principle of a full and rigorous judicial review of [freezing measures such as those at issue in this instance]', which were taken to require indirectly, the substantive

[117] *Djokaba Lambi Longa* (n 114) [78], [80].

[118] *Luke Munyandu Tembani and Benjamin John Freeth v Angola and Thirteen Others* (n 84) [134].

[119] See Case C–415/05 P *Yassin Abdullah Kadi and Al Barakaat International Foundation v Council of the European Union and Commission* (n 91) paras 294, 310–13.

[120] ibid paras 298, 321–25. [121] ibid para 326. [122] ibid paras 336–41.

[123] Case T–85/09 *Yassin Abdullah Kadi v Commission* [2010] ECR II–05177 (Kadi 2010).

assessments of the Sanctions Committee itself and the evidence underlying the listing.[124] This was understood as necessary, 'at the very least, so long as the re-examination procedure operated by the Sanctions Committee clearly fails to offer guarantees of effective judicial protection'.[125] The Court further determined, *inter alia*, that the lack of proper access to information and evidence used against him, and without giving him proper opportunity to be heard, has meant that Mr Kadi was unable to adequately defend his rights and thus compromised his right to effective judicial review and effective judicial protection.[126] That decision was then appealed by the Commission and others, but was ultimately dismissed.[127]

The *Bosphorus* analysis was also applied to the UN sanctions regime in the Chamber decision of *Al-Dulimi and Montana Management Inc v Switzerland*,[128] which concerned Switzerland's freezing and confiscation of an Iraqi national's assets in accordance with UN Security Council resolutions. The ECtHR concluded that Switzerland had no discretion whether to implement the sanctions,[129] thus the Court considered whether the UN afforded sufficient human rights protections as compared to ECHR standards. It held that it did not. Even though the Sanctions Committee had introduced a range of safeguards including a de-listing procedure, these did not afford equivalent protection.[130] The case is controversial in that it makes a clear break from *Behrami* (which had distinctly rejected the *Bosphorus* reasoning from cases which concerned obligations stemming from Article 103 of the UN Charter).[131] The consequence of the ruling is unequivocal; it affirms that ECHR Member States will violate their ECHR obligations if they comply with the UN sanctions regime.

Arcari argues that the equivalent protection doctrine is better able (than for instance the *Behrami* approach of pure primacy of the UN Charter) to balance the range of interests at stake, both legal and political.[132] But as he notes, this will depend on how rigorously the doctrine is applied. He suggests that the progressive strengthening of the judicial review requirement—from a rather lax and flexible standard of 'equivalent protection'[133] to the more rigid and precise requirement of 'effective and independent judicial review'[134] has perhaps swung the pendulum too far.[135] But, clearly the strengthening of the EC's review model has played an instrumental role in galvanizing attention to the deficiencies in the Sanctions Committee's procedures, as no other court could do, and in the absence of a specially mandated international court. It thus not only has helped to safeguard fundamental human

[124] ibid paras 126, 129. [125] ibid paras 127, 128. [126] ibid paras 181, 183, 184.

[127] Joined Cases C-584/10 P, C-593/10 P, and C-595/10 P *European Commission and Others v Yassin Abdullah Kadi* ECLI:EU:C:2013:518 (Grand Chamber, 18 July 2013) (Kadi 2013).

[128] *Al-Dulimi and Montana Management Inc v Switzerland* App no 5809/08 (ECtHR, 26 November 2013).

[129] ibid [90]; *Nada v Switzerland* (n 104) [121], [122].

[130] *Al-Dulimi* (n 128) para 106.

[131] Maurizio Arcari, 'Forgetting Article 103 of the UN Charter? Some perplexities on "equivalent protection" after Al-Dulimi' (2014) 6 Questions of Int'l Law 31, 35–36.

[132] ibid 36–38. [133] See *Bosphorus v Ireland* (n 110). [134] *Al-Dulimi* (n 128).

[135] See Arcari (n 131) 39.

rights protections for the individuals concerned, but has contributed indirectly to the progressive strengthening of the system.

Dulimi was referred to the Grand Chamber, and in its 2016 judgment, the pendulum swings back.[136] The Grand Chamber majority determined that the applicants' right of access to a court under Article 6(1) of the Convention was clearly restricted. Switzerland's refusal to examine on the merits the applicants' complaints about the confiscation of their assets could be explained by its concern to implement the Security Council Resolution. This pursued a legitimate aim, namely to maintain international peace and security. Citing *Nada*,[137] the Grand Chamber determines that when there are two seemingly competing obligations, these must 'be harmonised as far as possible so that they produce effects that are fully in accordance with existing law'.[138]

The Grand Chamber affirms that under the terms of the Resolution, Switzerland was not precluded from embarking upon judicial scrutiny of the measures taken to implement it. Thus, Switzerland was not faced with a real conflict of obligations. Therefore, it finds that Switzerland violated the applicants' rights pursuant to Article 6(1).

This reasoning was criticized in several of the concurring separate opinions and dissents. Judge Keller puts it succinctly: 'the Court has missed an opportunity to clarify to States what is required of them when they have no discretion in the application of a Security Council resolution that is incompatible with the ECHR system. By skirting round the issue, it has instead given States no additional guidance—zero, zilch, *Nada*—on how to proceed in such situations'.[139]

Judge Pinto de Albuquerque, joined by judges Hajiyev, Pejchal, and Dedov, argues that a more robust *Bosphorus*-style analysis should have been undertaken. He argues that:

> '[t]here is no plausible reason not to apply the human rights standards of the United Nations to its own decisions. As a matter of principle, nothing hinders the adoption of adequate substantive and procedural safeguards by the United Nations bodies, in conformity with the Charter and the ICCPR themselves, when they take binding decisions which impose sanctions on individuals and entities. The Office of the Ombudsperson is not an insignificant development, which shows that incremental changes in the system are possible. It can be further strengthened, if the political will is there. Second, the issues addressed by Security Council resolutions imposing sanctions, like genocide, crimes against humanity and terrorism, are not per se strictly political or excluded from any legal considerations. On the contrary, these issues warrant a robust but lawful response from the international community'.[140]

[136] *Al-Dulimi and Montana Management Inc v Switzerland* (Grand Chamber) App no 5809/08 (ECtHR, 21 June 2016).

[137] See *Nada v Switzerland* (n 105).

[138] See *Al-Dulimi* (Grand Chamber) (n 136) paras 138, 140.

[139] ibid Concurring Opinion of Judge Keller para 27.

[140] ibid Concurring Opinion of Judge Pinto de Albuquerque, joined by Judges Hajiyev, Pejchal, and Dedov para 66.

Judge Pinto de Albuquerque issues a final plea:

'The way out of the present deadlock is clear: either the United Nations faces up to the challenge of the times and seizes this opportunity to go ahead with the creation of a World Human Rights Court, opening up this legal avenue to the individuals and entities targeted by conduct of UN bodies and officials, such as the listing of suspected terrorists, transfer of their property and restriction of their freedom of movement; or it acknowledges alternative judicial avenues, for example, by extending and strengthening the Ombudsperson Office's mandate and powers to such an extent that it takes on a judicial nature. Since the present State-oriented UN architecture is unprepared to protect the rights and freedoms of those subject to non-forcible Chapter VII Security Council sanctions, a new human rights accountability mechanism is definitively needed'.[141]

VII.4 *Locus Standi* of Individuals before International and Regional Courts

Standing, or *locus standi*, refers to whether a person or entity has the right to be heard in court. This term can apply to potential plaintiffs who wish to lodge proceedings and to those who wish to be heard by a court in ongoing proceedings brought by others. The focus of this section is on the ability of individuals to lodge proceedings. Some international and regional courts afford a modicum of standing to individuals; however, the rules tend to be more onerous than what is in place for other parties. Furthermore, the way rules of standing interact with other rules on jurisdiction can combine to impede individuals from accessing courts.

A court will usually determine standing in accordance with explicit rules, only allowing certain types of parties to lodge proceedings: for example, only States, or Parties to a Treaty, certain types of individuals such as employees or persons recognized as victims under the treaty regime. For instance, before the ICJ, only States may lodge contentious claims.[142] This underpins the purpose of the ICJ to regulate disputes between sovereign States and underscores the traditional conception of international law which gives pre-eminence to the role of States in international affairs.

Some rules on standing are silent or vague and contextual, requiring judicial interpretation and discretion. Assessments tend to involve whether there is an identifiable dispute concerning the applicant raising a legal question that can be properly answered by the court. Courts will consider the degree of connection of the applicant to the dispute, such as whether the issue to be addressed is causing harm to the applicant or that the applicant has a sufficient interest in the matter to which the application relates. Criteria will depend on the court and the purpose for which standing is sought. Overly restrictive interpretations of these or related principles can greatly reduce the number and type of persons eligible to bring an action.

[141] ibid para 73. [142] ICJ Statute (n 5) arts 35, 36.

Proposals have been made to grant international organizations standing as plaintiffs and defendants before international tribunals and the compulsory jurisdiction of the ICJ in particular.[143] But even if those proposals were heeded, this would only tackle part of the problem. Without standing for natural and legal persons, these would have to rely on States to espouse the claims through diplomatic protection. States have rarely brought claims against other States for the violation of their citizens' rights,[144] and there is no indication that they would be more willing to bring contentious claims against international organizations. Alter notes that in the limited instances in which States have espoused their nationals' claims, they have refrained from raising sensitive issues which fall outside their political interests.[145] Furthermore, real or *de facto* stateless persons, refugees and others without normal relations with their States of nationality are disadvantaged by diplomatic protection regimes.[146] Persons coming from failed States, States in conflict or political or economic turmoil will be similarly disadvantaged by the disinterest or lack of capacity of their States of nationality.

While some might argue that increasing individuals' access to international adjudication may affect State sovereignty, impede international courts' efficiency and effectiveness; these courts may drown in a flood of frivolous, malicious, and unmeritorious applications, others including Lauterpacht have countered those suggestions.[147]

VII.4.1 Regional human rights courts

Regional human rights courts have an inconsistent approach to standing. The Inter-American and African systems rely heavily on commissions to vet individuals' access to courts, whereas the access of States Parties to those courts is direct. Individuals must file a claim with the Inter-American Commission before their claim can be presented by the Commission to the Court.[148] This system is also in

[143] Anastasia Telesetsky, 'Binding the United Nations: Compulsory Review of Disputes Involving UN International Responsibility before the International Court of Justice' (2012) 21 Minn J Int'l L 75, 96–103.

[144] Stefan Trechsel, 'A World Court for Human Rights' (2003) 1 Nw Univ J Int'l HR (unpaginated).

[145] Karen Alter, 'Private Litigants and the New International Courts' (2006) 39(1) Comparative Political Studies 22, 24.

[146] Note, however, art 8 of the ILC's Draft Articles on Diplomatic Protection, 'Report of the International Law Commission on the Work of its 58th Session' (1 May–9 June and 3 July–11 August 2006) UN Doc A/CN.4/L.684, which allows States to exercise diplomatic protection in favour of stateless persons and refugees who at the date of injury were lawfully resident in those States, except in respect of injury caused by an internationally wrongful act of the State of nationality of the refugee. This provision is permissible, not obligatory. Furthermore, it does not extend to the vast majority of situations involving individuals with unregulated residential status and persons who have become stateless or acquired refugee status subsequent to their injuries.

[147] Hersch Lauterpacht, *International Law and Human Rights* (FA Praeger 1950) 186–94.

[148] See ACHR (n 18) arts 44, 51(1), and 61(1). While individuals cannot lodge independent proceedings before the Court and formally it is the Commission that takes forward the proceedings before the Court, it has been recognized that the victims have full and autonomous standing before the Court. See art 25 of the Rules of Procedure of the Inter-American Court of Human Rights, Approved by the Court during its LXXXV Regular Period of sessions (16–28 November 2009).

place for the ACtHPR, although individuals may institute cases directly before the Court if the State concerned has accepted the competence of the Court to receive cases in this way.[149] The ECtHR initially had a similar procedure; however, it has since been streamlined.[150] In addition to the inevitable delays caused by multiple tiers, dual processes also introduce contingency into individuals' access, given commissions' discretion whether to introduce an individual's claim before the court.[151]

For the most part, regional human rights courts specify in their constituent agreements the jurisdictional bases for claims and the limitations on same. As set out in the prior section, the personal jurisdiction of regional human rights courts tends to be restricted to States. However, the ACHPR Protocol is silent on the issue, which has impacted on an individual's standing before the Court in a case directed at the African Union. In the *Femi Falana* case, which concerned a challenge by a Nigerian lawyer of the validity of Article 34(6) of the ACHPR Protocol, the Court determined that while its statute afforded limited ability for claims to be brought against AU institutions, individuals were only entitled to lodge such claims if the State (presumably of their nationality) consented to the Court's jurisdiction. The Court's reasoning stemmed from its reading of the jurisdictional provisions of the Statute which provide that individuals may have access to the court when the State in question submits a declaration to that effect. The majority held that the fact that the AU is not a State does not automatically mean that no declaration is necessary to found jurisdiction.[152] Article 34(6) of the Protocol which requires States to make a declaration to accept the competence of the Court to hear and determine human rights cases filed by individuals and NGOs was also deemed necessary to enable individuals to make claims against non-State respondents. The decision provoked several separate and dissenting opinions. Judges Ouguergouz and Mutsinzi understood that the Court had no mandate whatsoever to consider human rights claims against the AU.[153] Judges Akuffo, Ngoepe, and Thompson in their dissent argued that Article 34(6)

> only requires that State Parties make the declaration, and not non-State Parties. The law is not against an individual *per se*, but is aimed at protecting a State Party which has not made the declaration; that is why even a foreign individual can sue a State Party that has made the declaration.[154]

Before the ECtHR, persons with standing need not be citizens of the Respondent State nor of any State Party, nor do they need to be resident or present in the territory of any State Party. This enables the Court to consider claims concerning the

[149] ACHPR (n 25) art 55; ACHPR Protocol (n 18) arts 5, 34(6).

[150] See arts 25(1), 48 of the original ECHR and art 34 of the current text. The merging of the functions of the Commission and Court occurred in 1998 by virtue of the adoption of Protocol No 11 to the Convention for the Protection of Human Rights and Fundamental Freedoms, restructuring the control machinery established thereby (adopted 11 May 1994, entered into force 1 November 1998) CETS No 155.

[151] See ACHPR (n 25) art 55; ACHR (n 18) art 62.

[152] *Femi Falana* (n 87) [59]–[61], [63].

[153] ibid Separate Opinion of Judge Fatsah Ouguergouz [11], [12]; Separate Opinion of Judge Jean Mutsinzi [7], [8].

[154] ibid Dissenting Opinion of Judges Sophia Akuffo, Bernard Ngoepe, and Elsie Thompson [8.5].

actions of States Parties outside of their territorial jurisdiction.[155] The American Convention is similarly broad, referring to 'any person or group of persons'.[156] The African Charter and ACHPR Protocol are silent on any nationality requirements for applicants. However, as described in *Femi Falana*, the applicant sought to claim against the AU (and not his State of nationality), but the Court used the failure of the applicant's State of nationality to ratify the Protocol as a means to dismiss the claim,[157] thereby confounding the need for a potential respondent to have accepted the jurisdiction of the court to adjudicate claims lodged by individuals against it, and the nationality of the applicant, which should be an irrelevant consideration. The Inter-American Commission has a vague *locus standi* clause, and it is thus not clear whether claims can be brought from citizens outside the region.[158] Certain RIO courts also restrict *locus standi* to nationals from the States of the respective regions. This is the case with the Caribbean Court of Justice.[159]

In addition to these differences in standing, there are further distinctions in regards to the various regional human rights mechanisms' understanding of 'which' individuals may have standing, or who might be the object of a human rights claim. Article 34 of the ECHR envisages applications to the Court from those claiming to be the victim of a violation of a Convention right by one of the contracting States. In its jurisprudence, the Court has held that only direct victims of a violation acting in their personal capacity have standing,[160] although claims of violations of the right to life may be brought on behalf of those who died (or disappeared) by their next-of-kin, recognized as 'indirect victims' for those purposes.[161]

In contrast, neither the African Charter or ACHPR Protocol, nor the American Convention, contains similar restrictions. To the contrary, they explicitly allow for *actio popularis*, allowing claims to be brought by certain organizations, recognizing that it will not always be possible for victims to file claims directly. However, the ACJHR Protocol specifies that only 'Individuals or relevant Non-Governmental Organizations accredited to the African Union or to its organs, subject to the provisions of Article 8 of the Protocol' may have standing.[162] Naldi and Magliveras interpret this limitation as affording standing to 'African individuals and African NGOs' only,[163] although the term 'individuals' is not prefaced in the text by 'African', and thus whether individuals too must necessarily be African is unclear. However, taking into account the ACtHPR's ruling in *Femi Falana*,[164] which interpreted the standing requirement as connected to the nationality of the applicant, their concerns are justified. If indeed standing is limited to African nationals only, this impedes the Court from adjudicating extra-African violations of human rights. A near identical

[155] See *Al-Skeini* (n 23). [156] See ACHR (n 18) art 44.
[157] See *Femi Falana* (n 87). [158] American Declaration (n 25) art 1.
[159] Agreement Establishing the CCJ (n 78) art XXIV.
[160] *Amuur v France* App no 19776/92 (ECtHR, 25 June 1996) [36]; *Tănase v Moldova* (GC) App no 7/08 (ECtHR, 27 April 2010) [104]–[111]; *Aksu v Turkey* (GC) App nos 4149/04, 41029/04 (ECtHR, 15 March 2012) [50]–[54].
[161] *Gakiyev and Gakiyeva v Russia* App no 3179/05 (ECtHR, 23 April 2009) [165]; *Çakici v Turkey* (GC) App no 23657/94 (ECtHR, 8 July 1999) [98]–[99].
[162] ACJHR Protocol (n 19) art 30(f). [163] See Naldi and Magliveras (n 30) 405 fn 86.
[164] See *Femi Falana* (n 87).

provision appears in the Rules of Procedure and Evidence of the Inter-American Commission on Human Rights. Article 23 specifies that those eligible to submit petitions comprise of '[a]ny person or group of persons or nongovernmental entity legally recognized in one or more of the Member States of the OAS'.[165]

There is no known case in which the Inter-American or African commissions considered whether nationals from other continents would be eligible pursuant to these rules. If these rules were to be construed narrowly, this would pose a significant limitation on accountability, given the extent of both African and American States' involvement in global peace operations, and the potential impacts of those operations on nationals from other regions.

VII.4.2 RIO courts—individuals' standing to pursue claims

Neither has the approach of RIO courts been uniform. Most RIO courts afford a modicum of standing to natural and legal persons; however, the rules tend to be more onerous for such applicants than for other parties. Furthermore, some RIO courts only afford standing to individuals from the respective region.[166] Most of such courts allow for some form of annulment, reference, or review proceedings concerning the applicable regional organizations. However, not all of these allow individuals to lodge such proceedings. And, of the ones that do, some have placed significant restrictions on standing.

(1) The Court of Justice of the European Union (CJEU)

The CJEU has served as a model for many other RIO courts. While it is known for the breadth of its cases and relatively wide subject matter jurisdiction, the standing of natural and legal persons is quite restrictive.

Natural and legal persons are able to bring a direct action against any EU body or institution for acts which are of direct and individual concern to them. They can bring actions for annulment to void a directive or decision adopted by an EU body.[167] In addition, they can challenge the failure of an EU body or institution to act, where there was a duty to act. In order for such actions to be lodged, the individual must first call upon the institution to act.[168]

Natural and legal persons face heavy burdens to institute proceedings before the CJEU. Article 263(4) of the TFEU allows them to bring actions for annulment to the CJEU General Court against EU institutions only to the extent that the acts complained of:

i) are addressed to them specifically;

ii) are of direct and individual concern to them (it is not enough for it to be a measure of general application, the applicants need to show that the measure

[165] Rules of Procedure of the Inter-American Commission on Human Rights (entered into force 1 August 2013) rule 23.

[166] See eg Agreement Establishing the CCJ (n 78) art XXIV; EAC Treaty (n 32) art 30(1).

[167] See TFEU (n 48) art 263. [168] ibid art 265.

targets them specifically by reason of certain attributes which were peculiar to them or by reason of circumstances which differentiated them from all other persons); or

iii) in relation to regulatory as opposed to legislative acts, so long as it does not entail implementing measures (which would be a matter for national courts), they can challenge such acts if they can show direct concern, but need not demonstrate individual concern.

Article 263(4) TFEU has been interpreted narrowly. For instance, seal hunters who brought a claim to annul the basic regulation prohibiting the marketing of seal products on the EU internal market, were prevented by the CJEU from so doing, because the seal hunters lacked the required direct and individual connection to challenge a legislative act.[169] This is in contrast to the less onerous requirements for States or EU institutions to seek review of EU acts.[170]

One of the rationales for the CJEU's narrow and rigid standing rules is that the system preserves the preeminent role of national courts. The system encourages would-be applicants to address themselves to national courts, which if appropriate, could initiate a reference application to the CJEU for a preliminary ruling.[171] In the *Area Cova SA* case, legal persons sought to challenge this rationale and the cumbersome reference procedure.[172] After all, States are not obliged to agree to pursue references; often they do not. When Dutch courts denied the *Mothers of Srebrenica* claim against the UN because of the UN's immunity before Dutch courts, the stichting requested that the Supreme Court seek a preliminary ruling from the CJEU on the relationship between UN immunities and the principle of effective judicial protection. The Supreme Court refused to do so.[173] As has been noted by the ECtHR, the reasons for the refusal may well have been justified.[174] Nevertheless, in practice there is no sanction if a reference is not made so the effectiveness of the system is not guaranteed.

Area Cova SA's arguments on the reference procedure were not accepted.[175] In a later case, a First Instance Court (now General Court) disagreed with the *Area Cova SA* ruling, and held that: '[T]he fact that an individual affected by a Community measure may be able to bring its validity before the national courts by violating the rules it lays down and then asserting their illegality in subsequent judicial proceedings brought against him does not constitute an adequate means of judicial protection'.[176] Nonetheless this later ruling was reversed on appeal.[177]

[169] Case C–583/11 P *Inuit Tapiriit Kanatami and Others v Parliament and Council* ECLI:EU:C:2013:625 (Grand Chamber, 3 October 2013).

[170] See TFEU (n 48) art 263(2) and (3).

[171] This procedure is set out in art 267 TFEU (n 48).

[172] Joined Cases C–300/99 P and C–388/99 P *Area Cova SA and Others v Council* [2001] ECR I–00983.

[173] See *Stichting Mothers of Srebrenica v Netherlands* App no 65542/12 (ECtHR, 11 June 2013) [171].

[174] ibid. [175] *Area Cova SA* (n 172) para 54.

[176] Case T–177/01 *Jégo-Quéré et Cie v Commission* [2002] ECR II–02365 para 45.

[177] Case C–263/02 P *Commission of the European Communities v Jégo-Quéré & Cie SA* [2004] ECR 2004 I–03425 paras 30–39.

These cases were decided before the entry into force of the Lisbon Treaty and thus before the Fundamental Rights Charter became directly applicable before the CJEU. Nevertheless, the post-Lisbon practice does not appear to have evolved significantly. Thus far, CJEU judges have refrained from giving a more expansive reading to standing rules in light of the Charter.[178] If the EU were to become party to the ECHR as planned, *locus standi* before the CJEU would be but one further area where the ECtHR might have greater influence. To date, given the limitations of the ECtHR's mandate with respect to acts of the EU or any other international organization, judgments which have considered these or related issues have focused on the need for the applicant to rebut the presumption of 'equivalent protection', which is a relatively weak test. However, it is questionable whether this will be a sustainable argument going forward.

(2) RIO courts in the Americas

The Andean Court of Justice affords the widest standing to individuals of all RIOs. Largely mirrored on the CJEU, in many respects it surpasses the CJEU in respect to access by natural and legal persons, although its subject matter jurisdiction is more restricted. Natural and legal persons can bring suits to nullify decisions or acts adopted by the Andean Community that affect their subjective rights or legitimate interests.[179] This gives wider scope for standing, when compared to the CJEU's requirement that individuals show that the acts are of direct and individual concern to them.[180]

Mirroring the CJEU provisions,[181] individuals whose rights and interests are affected can also challenge an Andean institution's failure to carry out an activity for which it is expressly responsible, first through a procedure to demand fulfilment of the obligation and thereafter, as needed, to seek recourse before the Court.[182] Individuals are also able to appeal directly to the Court if they disagree with the Secretariat's prior disposition on a non-compliance complaint against a Member State[183] (which goes beyond what is available for individuals at the CJEU).[184] The Andean Court can also arbitrate disputes involving the application of Andean law, including those involving natural and legal persons.[185]

The Central American Court of Justice also affords standing to natural and legal persons. Any party, including a natural or legal person can approach the Court regarding a State's non-compliance with any Conventions, Treaties, or rules of the Central American integration system; any matters regarding actions by Central American institutions that affect anyone; any grievance concerning the disregard of local court orders by a branch or office of government, or to rule on any matter, arbitrate, mediate, or decide on matters *ex aequo et bono*.[186] However, as indicated, it

[178] European Praesidium of the Convention, 'Updated Explanations Relating to the Text of the Charter of Fundamental Rights' (9 July 2003) CONV 828/03, 41.
[179] Treaty Creating the CJAC (n 78) art 19.
[180] TFEU (n 48) art 263(4).
[181] ibid 265.
[182] Treaty Creating the CJAC (n 78) art 37.
[183] ibid arts 24, 25.
[184] TFEU (n 48) art 258.
[185] Treaty Creating the CJAC (n 78) arts 38, 39.
[186] Statute of the CACJ (n 78) arts 22, 39.

has specifically determined that its mandate does not extend to human rights. This is stipulated in the Statute and has been confirmed in its jurisprudence.[187]

The Caribbean Court of Justice operates on the basis of a presumption of no standing for natural or legal persons, which may be rebutted with special leave of the Court.[188] In applying its discretion, the Court considers whether the interest of justice requires that standing be granted, and whether the persons seeking standing have suffered prejudice in respect of a benefit owed to them directly that the State has failed to espouse.[189] Individuals are only entitled to apply for standing to pursue claims concerning the interpretation and application of the Treaty.[190] The Court has granted special leave to individuals alleging *inter alia* discriminatory immigration laws[191] and breach of CARICOM rules on free movement.[192] Unlike States, individuals cannot request advisory opinions.[193] The presumption of no standing also applies to natural and legal persons who wish to bring claims against CARICOM institutions.

(3) RIO courts in Africa

Somewhat exceptionally, the initial framework of the ECOWAS CCJ provided exclusive competence to States to lodge contentious proceedings. The Protocol on the Court provided that only the Authority of Heads of State and Government and the Member States acting individually could initiate contentious cases.[194] Despite this, a Nigerian businessman who suffered losses as a result of Nigeria's closure of the border with Benin sought to bring a claim against Nigeria for violating ECOWAS laws and his right to freedom of movement. He argued that the absence of a clear statutory basis for the *locus standi* of individuals did not prevent the Court from exercising its inherent jurisdiction in his favour. Given that Nigeria was the defendant, it was not realistic to expect Nigeria to espouse its national's claim.[195] The Court dismissed the case for lack of standing, but the dismissal led to a discussion on the need to amend the Protocol to give standing to legal and natural persons. A revised Protocol was adopted in 2005,[196] which provides now arguably the widest direct access to natural and legal persons of any international or regional court.[197]

Similar to the CJEU, the EACJ allows individuals to bring reference proceedings to challenge the legality of the acts of EAC Member States or Community institutions,[198] as does the ECOWAS CCJ.[199] However, the EACJ limits access

[187] The CACJ has likewise excluded human rights from its competence in accordance with art 25 of its Statute. See also CACJ, *Ricardo Duarte Moncada v Gobierno de Nicaragua, Alcaldía de Managua y Banco Centroamericano de Integración Económica (BCIE)* (n 29).

[188] See Agreement Establishing the CCJ (n 78) art XXIV.

[189] ibid.

[190] ibid art XXII(1)(d).

[191] *Maurice Tomlinson v Belize and Trinidad and Tobago* CCJ 2 (OJ), (CCJ, 8 May 2014).

[192] See *Shanique Myrie v Barbados* (n 29).

[193] Agreement Establishing the CCJ (n 78) art XXIII (2).

[194] Protocol on the ECOWAS Community Court of Justice (adopted 6 July 1991, entered into force 5 November 1996), ECOWAS Doc A/P.1/7/91 art 8.

[195] *Olajide Afolabi v Nigeria*, ECW/CCJ/APP/01/03 (ECOWAS CCJ, 27 April 2004) para 15.

[196] See ECOWAS 2005 Protocol (n 41).

[197] ibid art 10(c), (d), (f). See generally Ebobrah (n 42).

[198] EAC Treaty (n 32) art 30.

[199] ECOWAS 2005 Protocol (n 41) art 10(c).

to individuals who are resident in the sub-region. And, for both courts, the ability of individuals to bring reference proceedings is predicated on them being able to demonstrate a sufficient direct and personal connection to the act in question. The ECOWAS CCJ had occasion to consider this issue in several cases. *Odafe Oserada v ECOWAS Council of Ministers* concerned the Applicant's attempt to declare unlawful the ECOWAS regulation that allocated the post of Secretary General of the Community Parliament to Guinea. In arriving at its decision, the court referred to CJEU jurisprudence on standing and determined that: 'there should exist, as an additional condition, a sufficiently direct relationship of cause and effect. The act made by the Council of Ministers, i.e. the Regulation complained of, must affect the legal status of the Applicant'.[200] This was later confirmed in the *Oluwatosin Rinu Adewale* case.[201] The Court affirmed that to have access to the Court under that provision the claimant must be 'the person whose interest is directly and immediately affected by the act or inaction that is being contested'.[202]

As indicated, the SADC Tribunal is currently non-functional, largely as a result of Zimbabwe's reaction to human rights rulings and SADC's decision to revise its operating procedures. The planned revisions are set to end the *locus standi* of natural and legal persons.[203]

The future merged African Court of Justice and Human Rights has a split standing requirement. Individuals or relevant non-governmental organizations[204] are eligible to submit claims to the human rights section of the court only. This bifurcated structure has the effect of impeding individuals from pursuing annulment claims as is the practice before some other RIO courts. Naldi and Magliveras consider this to be 'a serious omission'.[205] Individuals' lack of standing means that they would have to rely on States to bring any matters they have to the General Affairs section, on their behalf. But as Naldi and Magliveras have noted, 'having to rely on the traditional principle of diplomatic protection is simply wholly inadequate for this sort of situation. Unfortunately, the impression is given of a lack of "joined-up" thinking'.[206] The rules on standing may also have the effect of preventing individuals from pursuing claims against AU institutions, although this is not precisely set out in the text.[207]

VII.5 Conclusions

Out of all the courts surveyed, not one enables individuals to make a direct claim against a universal international organization, other than in the contexts of

[200] *Odafe Oserada v ECOWAS Council of Ministers*, ECW/CCJ/JUD/01/08 (ECOWAS CCJ, 16 May 2008) para 33.
[201] *Oluwatosin Rinu Adewale v ECOWAS Council of Ministers*, ECW/CCJ/JUD/07/12 (ECOWAS CCJ, 16 May 2012).
[202] ibid para 45. [203] See section VII.II.2.
[204] ACJHR Protocol (n 19) art 30(f). [205] See Naldi and Magliveras (n 30) 399, 400.
[206] ibid 400. [207] See *Femi Falana* (n 87).

specialized regimes like the *UN Convention on the Law of the Sea*, or staff employment claims. Nor is there a single court where States may espouse their nationals' claims against universal international organizations. While regional human rights courts provide a useful venue for indirect claims against States for their role in the acts of international organizations, as was explored in Chapter III, at times these courts attribute responsibility solely to the international organization and thus the case against the State will be dismissed for lack of competence. Similarly, RIO courts have no jurisdiction against universal organizations. Also, RIO courts invariably do not provide adequate access for victims of human rights or international humanitarian law violations attributable to international organizations, for a combination of access limitations, whether these stem from the CJEU's narrow rules on standing, the bifurcated rules of the African Court of Justice and Human Rights, the limited subject matter jurisdiction before the Central American Court of Justice or the impact of the various planned revisions to the SADC Tribunal's competence.

The courts are not human rights courts and do not incorporate many of the procedural rules common to human rights courts that foster access to justice and take cognizance of the nature of particular kinds of violations. The CJEU has thus far not felt it necessary to ensure that all its remedies are effective or enforceable. As was held in *Area Cova SA*, even if it could be established that there was no effective remedy, this 'cannot constitute authority for changing, by judicial action, the system of remedies and procedures established by [the Treaty]'.[208] The EACJ has produced other challenges for applicants with human rights and international humanitarian law claims. In a case concerning widespread torture and killings that the applicants allege the Respondent government knew about but did nothing to investigate, the Court refused to extend its inordinately short limitation periods, even though the facts arguably constituted continuing human rights violations,[209] and despite the widely accepted jurisprudence of other courts on this point.[210]

Without doubt, the most significant challenge is access. Nonetheless, there are additional problems of result. Of the few courts that allow individuals to bring proceedings against regional or sub-regional organizations, these tend to be restricted to judicial review or nullity proceedings. Enforcement of judgments constitutes an additional barrier. While the legal frameworks of many courts make clear that rulings are binding upon the parties, this has not always led them to be enforced. Even without accounting for Zimbabwe's extreme reaction to the SADC tribunal following several contentious rulings against it, the traditional tools for enforcement of domestic judgments are unavailable in the regional and international spheres. The powers of suasion and the pull of Community cohesion and integration may be enough in some cases, but usually fall short in the most sensitive ones.

[208] See *Area Cova SA* (n 172) para 55.

[209] *Independent Medical Legal Unit v the Attorney General of the Republic of Kenya and 4 Others*, Ref Appeal no 1 of 2011 (EACJ, 15 March 2012).

[210] See eg *Moiwana Community v Suriname* (Preliminary Objections, Merits, Reparations and Costs) Ser C no 124 (IACtHR, 15 June 2005) para 39; *Varnava v Turkey* (GC) App nos 16064/90, 16065/90, 16066/90 (ECtHR, 18 September 2009).

Given the challenges to bring claims against international organizations, particularly universal ones, those claims that have addressed the responsibility of universal organizations are necessarily indirect, as are the remedies. Nevertheless, the pressure placed on universal organizations as a result of RIO judgments against RIO institutions or regional human rights courts against States, may lead to important changes within the universal organizations. This is best evidenced with the sanctions de-listing cases before the CJEU and ECtHR. The UN Sanctions Committee has progressively strengthened its procedures and following the *Kadi* CJEU litigation, Mr Kadi was ultimately de-listed. As Patricia O'Brien, the former Under-Secretary-General for Legal Affairs and UN Legal Counsel has noted, there were a variety of factors which caused the UN Sanctions Committee to progressively amend its procedures. She has surmised, in relation to the *Kadi* litigation that: '[t]his Judgment has undoubtedly marked an important development in the consideration of the legal regime of sanctions. It would, however, be an unfair assessment to consider that adaptations of the sanctions regime developed by the Security Council have *only* been triggered by such external elements'.[211]

Nonetheless, one cannot discount the role played by the CJEU and to a lesser extent, the ECtHR. One can question whether the impact of the sanctions cases is a one-off quasi-success. The ECtHR's attribution of conduct to UNMIK in the *Behrami and Saramati* cases should have had a corresponding impact on the strengthening of the UN's operational procedures or internal accountability structures. O'Brien has said in regard to this and other like cases: 'Following the *Behrami* decision, I have actually engaged my Office in a thorough internal review of the past and current practice of the Organization regarding issues of international responsibility. In none of the instances I have just referred to has the UN been held accountable. We cannot, however, satisfy ourselves with such myopic reasoning. As I have striven to demonstrate today, the United Nations needs to lead by example'.[212] As I have argued elsewhere, while the UN indeed *needs* to do so, it is not yet doing so.[213] Thus, all one can posit is that indirect suasion has the potential for a modest influence on the procedures of universal organizations. The case for an international court with the mandate to adjudicate directly the acts of international organizations, especially the universal ones, is all the more important.

[211] Patricia O'Brien, 'Legal Challenges Facing the United Nations: An Appraisal from the Legal Counsel's Perspective' (Sean Lester Lecture of the Irish Society of International Law, 11 March 2010) 27 (emphasis added) http://legal.un.org/ola/media/info_from_lc/53-ISIL-11-March-2010.pdf (last accessed 30 December 2016).

[212] ibid 31–32. [213] Chapter V.

VIII
The Direct Responsibility of Organization Employees, Contractors, and Troop Contingents

VIII.1 Introduction

Organization employees, experts on mission, contractors, and troop contingents may have direct responsibility for wrongful acts. This is stressed in the commentary to Article 66 of the International Law Commission (ILC) Draft Articles on the Responsibility of International Organizations (DARIO), which underscores that if the conduct of an individual is attributed to an international organization or a State, this does not exempt that person from the individual criminal responsibility that he or she may incur for his or her conduct.[1] The commentary also notes that: 'individual responsibility could also relate to damage caused by an act of a person acting on behalf of an international organization. For instance, when the victims of an international crime suffer damage, the responsible individual may have an obligation to make reparation'.[2]

Usually, individual responsibility will be in addition to any responsibility the international organization incurs as a result of the unlawful acts, with some exceptions. Acts of individuals undertaken in a purely private capacity will not incur the responsibility of the organization.[3] Acts of individuals undertaken as part of official functions may implead the organization; and hence the language of section 29(b) of the Convention on the Privileges and Immunities of the United Nations (CPIUN) that: 'the United Nations shall make provisions for appropriate modes of settlement of ... (b) Disputes involving any official of the United Nations who by reason of his official position enjoys immunity, if immunity has not been waived by the Secretary-General'.

Individual employees, experts on mission, contractors, and troop contingents operating in connection with an international organization have been accused of a variety of unlawful acts including murder, disappearances, torture, sexual exploitation and abuse, trafficking in persons, assault, theft, corruption, fraud,

[1] ILC, Draft Articles on the Responsibility of International Organizations, 'Report of the International Law Commission on the Work of its 63rd Session' (26 April–3 June and 4 July–12 August 2011) UN Doc A/66/10 (DARIO) Commentary to art 66.
[2] ibid. [3] See Chapter III.2.1.

and misappropriation of funds.[4] Each of these acts, whether they are committed individually or jointly, and regardless of whether they stem from direct participation or from ordering, soliciting, or inducing the act, or aiding and abetting its commission may give rise to criminal, disciplinary, and/or civil liability. Often these unlawful acts occur in the context of peacekeeping operations and humanitarian crises and have involved some of the most vulnerable women and children.

The Independent Review on Sexual Exploitation and Abuse by International Peacekeeping Forces in the Central African Republic was established in response to allegations that a number of children in the M'Poko Camp for internally displaced persons had been forced to submit to sexual acts in exchange for military food rations or small amounts of cash by members of international peacekeeping forces, mainly from the French Sangaris forces. The review faulted the way in which UN agencies responded to the allegations, finding that: '[t]he welfare of the victims and the accountability of the perpetrators appeared to be an afterthought, if considered at all. Overall, the response of the UN was fragmented and bureaucratic, and failed to satisfy the UN's core mandate to address human rights violations'.[5] Human Rights Watch's investigation of sexual abuse allegations in the African Union's mission in Somalia found similar failings.[6]

Ultimately an international organization's failure to adequately respond to widespread criminality over which it has responsibility may engage its due diligence obligations and result in a separate internationally wrongful act giving rise to an obligation to afford reparation. The due diligence obligation is one of means, not of result. So, what matters is the reasonableness of the measures taken in light of the risks involved and the capacity to act. This chapter focuses on the narrower question of whether victims can pursue criminal investigations and civil claims for damages against the alleged direct offenders.

VIII.2 Individual Criminal Responsibility

An employee, expert on mission, contractor, or troop contingent may incur individual criminal responsibility for crimes that he or she perpetrates.

[4] For instance, in the Secretary-General's 2016 report on criminal accountability, it recorded 'United Nations officials and experts on mission for investigation and possible prosecution. Of those cases, eight concerned allegations of corruption and fraud; four concerned allegations of entitlement fraud; two concerned allegations of physical assault; two concerned allegations of sexual exploitation and/or abuse; one concerned allegations of sexual abuse and physical assault; one concerned allegations of corruption, fraud and sexual exploitation and abuse; and one concerned allegations of theft'. See UNSG, 'Criminal accountability of United Nations officials and experts on mission' Report of the Secretary-General (20 July 2016) UN Doc A/71/167 para 52.

[5] Marie Deschamps, Hassan Jallow, and Yasmin Sooka, 'Taking Action on Sexual Exploitation and Abuse by Peacekeepers: Report of an Independent Review on Sexual Exploitation and Abuse by International Peacekeeping Forces in the Central African Republic' (17 December 2015) http://www.un.org/News/dh/infocus/centafricrepub/Independent-Review-Report.pdf (last accessed 25 December 2016).

[6] HRW, '"The Power These Men Have Over Us": Sexual Exploitation and Abuse by African Union Forces in Somalia' (8 September 2014).

When such crimes occur, it is important that they are investigated and prosecuted. Prosecution serves a range of purposes including general and specific deterrence, satisfaction, reinforcing the rule of law, and avoiding impunity. Some of the crimes at issue are ones for which the competent authorities have a recognized obligation to investigate under human rights law. Also, the unequal power dynamics and the extreme breaches of trust that form the underlying context for the crimes make investigations and prosecutions crucial, also to preserve the dignity and reputation of the organization.

Victims do not necessarily have a right to see a particular offender prosecuted and punished. This was underscored in *Mustafić-Mujić v Netherlands*, where the applicants argued that the Netherlands breached its obligations under Article 2 of the European Convention on Human Rights (ECHR) when the Dutch authorities refused to order the prosecution of three members of the Dutch peacekeeping force who had been implicated in the deaths of Mr Rizo Mustafić, Mr Ibro Nuhanović, and Mr Muhamed Nuhanović in the context of the Srebrenica massacre. The European Court of Human Rights (ECtHR) affirmed that: 'there is no lingering uncertainty as regards the nature and degree of involvement of Lieutenant Colonel Karremans, Major Franken and Warrant Officer Oosterveen respectively'.[7]

It was therefore not possible for the ECtHR to find that the investigations were ineffective or inadequate, nor that there was insufficient evidence to proceed with a prosecution. However, according to the ECtHR this did not imply necessarily that the victims had an independent right to see those individuals prosecuted; the ECtHR rejected the applicants' complaints that that decision not to prosecute had been biased, inconsistent, excessive, or unjustified by the facts. The Court did not fault the prosecutorial decision which flowed from an investigation which was in all other respects Article 2 compliant, given the wide margin of appreciation afforded to States to determine whether to bring a prosecution.[8]

Nevertheless, human rights violations that constitute crimes give rise to an obligation on the competent authorities to carry out prompt, impartial, and thorough investigations capable of leading to the identification, and if appropriate, prosecution of the authors.[9] A State's failure to prosecute when there is clear evidence of criminal wrongdoing and jurisdiction over the offender is subject to clear limitations; victims may have a right to challenge the decision not to investigate or prosecute and any discretion exercised by the competent authorities to refrain from prosecuting must not be fettered. Victims should be entitled to a reasonable degree of certainty about the application of the criminal law. This would seem to require

[7] *Mustafić-Mujić v Netherlands* App no 49037/15 (ECtHR, 30 August 2016) para 106.

[8] The ECtHR refers to its rulings in *Branko Tomašić and Others v Croatia* App no 46598/06 (ECtHR, 15 January 2009) para 64 and *Armani Da Silva v United Kingdom* [GC] App no 5878/08 (ECtHR, 30 March 2016) para 259.

[9] *Barrios Altos v Peru* (Merits) Ser C no 75 (IACtHR, 14 March 2001) paras 42, 43; *Kaya v Turkey* App no 158/1996/777/978 (ECtHR, 19 February 1998); *Assenov v Bulgaria* App no 24760/94 (ECtHR, 28 October 1998); *Cantoral Benavides v Peru* (Merits) Ser C no 69 (IACtHR, 18 August 2000); *Güleç v Turkey* App no 21593/93 (ECtHR, 27 July 1998) [80]–[82].

that any exercise of discretion not to prosecute complies with established criteria on how such discretion is to be exercised, is appropriately reasoned and subject to review. These rights and their arguable impact on the case were not scrutinized fully by the ECtHR in *Mustafić-Mujić v Netherlands*.

Also, victims have recognized rights throughout the criminal justice process, such as the right to information,[10] the right to privacy and to be treated with humanity and respect for their dignity,[11] and the right to be protected from re-traumatization and reprisals.[12]

VIII.2.1 Immunities applicable to the alleged criminal acts of organization employees, contractors, and military contingents

One of the main impediments to the prosecution of persons connected with international organizations is immunity. Immunities will exempt certain individuals from being investigated or prosecuted by otherwise competent bodies and courts. The criminal law immunities applicable to different categories of personnel acting in some relationship with an international organization operate in much the same way and for many of the same reasons as the immunity of the organization itself, already discussed in Chapter VI. Criminal law immunity belongs to and is the absolute privilege of the international organization; it is not the prerogative of the individual who is accused of a crime. The main rationale for such immunity is the need to preserve the independence of the international organization.

Criminal law immunities provide a measure of insulation for such accused persons; however, they are not absolute. The extent of immunity from criminal investigation and/or prosecution will depend on the individual's status, function, and relationship to the international organization, the organization's constituent agreement, and applicable status of forces and status of mission agreements, headquarters agreements, and other relevant protocols.

[10] *Anguelova v Bulgaria* App no 38361/97 (ECtHR, 13 June 2002); see also Convention on Action against Trafficking in Human Beings (CATHB) (adopted on 16 May 2005, entered into force on 1 February 2008) CETS no 197 art 15; *Zontul v Greece* App no 12294/07 (ECtHR, 17 January 2012) [115]; OHCHR, 'Recommended Principles and Guidelines on Human Rights and Trafficking' (20 May 2002) UN Doc E/2002/68/Add.1, 9.2.

[11] *AT v Hungary* (CEDAW Committee, 26 January 2005) UN Doc CEDAW/C/32/D/2/2003 para 9.6(II)(vi); UN Human Rights Committee, 'General Comment 31' Nature of the General Legal Obligation Imposed on States Parties to the International Covenant on Civil and Political Rights (26 May 2004) UN Doc CCPR/C/21/Rev.1/Add.13 para 15; UN Committee on the Rights of the Child (CRC Committee), 'General Comment 5' General Measures of Implementation of the Convention on the Rights of the Child (3 October 2003) UN Doc CRC/GC/2003/5 para 24; Basic Principles and Guidelines on the Right to a Remedy and Reparation for Victims of Gross Violations of International Human Rights Law and Serious Violations of International Humanitarian Law, UNGA Res 60/147 (16 December 2005) (Basic Principles and Guidelines) 12(c); *Aksoy v Turkey* App no 21987/93 (ECtHR, 18 December 1996) [98].

[12] Basic Principles and Guidelines on the Right to a Remedy and Reparation for Victims of Gross Violations of International Human Rights Law and Serious Violations of International Humanitarian Law, UNGA Res 60/147 (16 December 2005) (Basic Principles and Guidelines) (n 11) 10, 12(b).

Unless the immunity is waived, personal immunity (which may be applicable to the head or deputy head of an international organization and is premised on the high-ranking status of the official) prevents an individual who holds this status from being subject to the criminal jurisdiction of a foreign State during the term of their office for acts carried out in both an official and private capacity. This principle stems from comparable personal immunities recognized for diplomats, heads of State, and foreign ministers, which arise from the recognition that such full immunity is necessary for the term of office to avoid interferences with the exercise of their official duties.[13]

Functional immunity (which may apply to other categories of employees and experts connected to an international organization) is restricted to those specific acts which are carried out as part of the official's functions or an expert's mission.

(1) The nature of immunities recognized for different categories of personnel (host state and troop contributing country jurisdiction)

(i) Military contingents

According to the UN Model SOFA which is the basis for the SOFA signed between the UN and the Host State[14] troop contributing countries have the exclusive responsibility to discipline and criminally sanction their military contingents. Troop contributing countries enter into a memorandum of understanding with the UN which also stipulates that only the troop contributing country can prosecute members of its military contingent for crimes committed on mission. The same framework is in place in African Union missions.[15]

The approach taken in the model SOFA differs from the NATO SOFA, which privileges the jurisdiction of troop contributing countries, but does not prevent the Host State from exercising jurisdiction in all circumstances. For instance, the troop contributing country is understood as having primary (as opposed to exclusive) jurisdiction in respect of acts carried out solely against the property or security of that State, or offences solely against the person or property of another member of the force or civilian component of that State or of a dependent or offences arising out of any act or omission done in the performance of official duty. In any other circumstance, the Host State has primary jurisdiction.[16]

The model EU SOFA has taken a similarly nuanced approach with respect to the potential jurisdiction of the Host State in respect of alleged crimes perpetrated by military contingents.[17] Similar to the NATO SOFA, it gives both

[13] *Arrest Warrant of 11 April 2000 (DRC v Belgium)* (Merits) [2002] ICJ Rep 3 para 53.

[14] UNGA, 'Model Status-of-forces Agreement for Peace-Keeping Operations' (9 October 1990) UN Doc A/45/594 (UN Model SOFA).

[15] 'Status of Mission Agreement between the Transitional Federal Government of the Somali Republic and the AU on the AU Mission in Somalia' (6 March 2007) art 55(b) AU para 9.

[16] See 'Agreement between the Parties to the North Atlantic Treaty regarding the Status of their Forces' (adopted 19 June 1951, entered into force 23 August 1953) art VII(3).

[17] See generally Aurel Sari, 'Status of Forces and Status of Mission Agreements under the ESDP: The EU's Evolving Practice' (2008) 19(1) EJIL 67.

the troop contributing country and the Host State jurisdiction over many criminal offences and establishes a framework for determining priorities when both States have concurrent jurisdiction.[18] Nevertheless, the model EU SOFA provisions on concurrent criminal jurisdiction do not feature in many of the SOFAs the EU has agreed with non-EU Member States. For instance, the agreement with the Central African Republic on the status of the European Union-led forces in the Central African Republic provides that: 'EUFOR personnel shall enjoy immunity from the criminal jurisdiction of the Host State under all circumstances'.[19]

Given the challenges associated with securing accountability for abuses taking place on mission, the Report on the CAR inquiry into sexual exploitation and abuse recommended the UN to 'consider building on the model status of forces agreement ("SOFA") adopted by the North Atlantic Treaty Organization ("NATO"). Where the NATO SOFA applies, primary or subsidiary jurisdiction is established over selected crimes committed in the host state, depending on the specific nature of the offense. If the country that has primary jurisdiction chooses not to exercise it, then the other country may choose to exercise its subsidiary jurisdiction. NATO SOFA also provides for mutual assistance between the TCC and the host State in carrying out the investigation and sharing information'.[20]

The immunity for military contingents which is set out in the model SOFA is only an immunity which concerns the Host State. It is not designed to provide the contingents with a blanket amnesty and serves the more restricted function of regulating the place where accountability should occur. In principle, the troop contributing country has absolute control over any investigation, any decision to prosecute (or not) and any decision regarding disciplinary sanctions.

In accordance with the model SOFA, if suspects are returned to the troop contributing country, contingents can and should be subject to that country's criminal and disciplinary jurisdiction. However, this does not always happen, owing to the limited capacity of some troop contributing countries and the limited willingness of countries to hold troop contingents accountable for acts which occurred abroad. There will also be practical difficulties to hold such trials including the difficulties to access evidence in the Host State; local laws will not always allow for extraterritorial

[18] ibid 91–92. See also EU, 'Agreement between the Member States of the European Union concerning the status of military and civilian staff seconded to the institutions of the European Union, of the headquarters and forces which may be made available to the European Union in the context of the preparation and execution of the tasks referred to in art. 17(2) of the Treaty on European Union, including exercises, and of the military and civilian staff of the Member States put at the disposal of the European Union to act in this context' (adopted 17 November 2003, not yet in force) art 17.

[19] EU, 'Council Decision 2008/389/CFSP of 7 April 2008 concerning the Conclusion of the Agreement between the European Union and the Central African Republic on the Status of the European Union-led Forces in the Central African Republic' (24 May 2008) OJ L 136/45, Council Decision 2008/389/CFSP art 6(3); See also 'Agreement between the European Union and the Gabonese Republic on the Status of the European Union-led Forces in the Gabonese Republic' (8 July 2006) OJ L 187/43.

[20] See Deschamps, Jallow, and Sooka (n 5) 87.

prosecutions, and there may be gaps or loopholes preventing certain categories of persons, or certain types of offences, from being prosecuted.

Largely as a result of these deficits and because of the significant pressures on the UN and its member States following numerous media reports of sexual exploitation and abuse taking place on mission that had not been investigated or prosecuted, the model memorandum of understanding between the UN and troop contributing countries was revised in 2007.[21] The impetus for the revision was the particular problem of sexual exploitation and abuse by peacekeepers; however, the revisions are not limited to those unlawful acts; the revisions apply to any alleged crimes. While the revised memorandum did not change the ultimate balance of power—troop contributing countries still retain exclusive jurisdiction to prosecute and discipline their troops, the troop contributing country provides a number of assurances in the memorandum which give greater impetus for, and transparency of, investigations and prosecutions. Under the memorandum, the troop contributing country provides an assurance that it shall 'exercise such jurisdiction'[22] and that: 'the case is forwarded to its appropriate authorities for due action' ... by authorities who 'shall take their decision in the same manner as they would in respect of any other offence or disciplinary infraction of a similar nature under its laws or relevant disciplinary code'.[23] While this assurance is not legally binding, it carries moral weight and provides a framework for dialogue between the troop contributing country and the UN on the implementation of the commitments.

The 2007 memorandum also requires the troop contributing country to 'notify the Secretary-General of progress on a regular basis, including the outcome of the case'.[24] In addition, it authorizes the UN to carry out its own preliminary fact-finding investigations in cases of serious misconduct if necessary to preserve evidence and where the troop contributing country does not conduct its own fact-finding proceeding.[25] The UN is also authorized to initiate an 'administrative investigation', if the troop contributing country is unwilling or unable to conduct such an investigation.[26] This may help safeguard evidence and establish at least on a preliminary basis, the relevant facts.[27]

The revision of the memorandum has improved the prospects for accountability but only marginally. A UN Office of Internal Oversight Services (UN OIOS) report from 2015 which considered the implementation of enforcement and remedial assistance efforts for sexual exploitation and abuse cases noted that:

> '[s]enior mission officials expressed doubts about the functioning of the MOU and called for its revision. A majority of conduct and discipline teams (CDTs), senior leadership interviewees, and senior military interviewees also perceived a lack of independence and an inherent and irreconcilable conflict of interest in requesting national

[21] UNGA, 'Report of the Special Committee on Peacekeeping Operations and its Working Group on the 2007 Resumed Session', Annex, Revised draft model memorandum of understanding (12 June 2007) UN Doc A/61/19 (Part III).

[22] ibid art 7 *quinquiens*. [23] ibid art 6 *sexiens* para 1. [24] ibid art 6 *sexiens* para 1.

[25] ibid art 7quater para 2. [26] ibid art 7quater para 3(a).

[27] See Carla Ferstman, 'Criminalizing Sexual Exploitation and Abuse by Peacekeepers' (USIP, September 2013) Special Report 335.

investigators to investigate their own troops. They viewed the TCCs as being strongly risk averse to the stigma of sexual exploitation and abuse (SEA) allegations and powerfully motivated to exonerate their personnel'.[28]

Another gap is that the revised MOU only applies to those troops that operate under UN command. Thus, foreign troops that work alongside but independent from UN mandated peacekeeping operations are not covered. This was a particular problem identified in respect of the French Sangaris forces operating in the Central African Republic. The Central African Republic (CAR) inquiry report recommended in this regard that: 'the UN should bridge the gap between the rules governing TCCs under UN command and those applying to troops not under UN command by negotiating provisions into its agreements with *all* TCCs that are consistent with the obligations under the existing SEA policies and human rights framework'.[29]

In 2016, as a result of further scandals implicating peacekeepers reported by the media, the UN Secretary-General adopted several further measures, such as 'naming and shaming' those troop contributing countries against whom there are allegations,[30] reporting more fully on follow up investigations and repatriating commanders and entire troop contingents as needed, in cases of widespread and systematic sexual exploitation and abuse and/or where there has been a failure of a troop contributing country to investigate and prosecute, as appropriate.[31] In addition, the Secretary-General encouraged military contingents to establish on-site court martial proceedings, which 'may be effective at demonstrating accountability, especially given that witnesses and physical evidence would be located in the host State and would respond to the interest in accountability by the international community and, most critically, victims'.[32] He also urged Member States to agree to obtain DNA samples of members of contingents who are alleged to have committed sexual

[28] UN OIOS, 'Evaluation of the Enforcement and Remedial Assistance Efforts for Sexual Exploitation and Abuse by the United Nations and Related Personnel in Peacekeeping Operations' (15 May 2015) IED-15-001, 15–16.

[29] See Deschamps, Jallow, and Sooka (n 5) 85.

[30] UNGA, 'Special Measures for Protection from Sexual Exploitation and Sexual Abuse: Report of the Secretary-General' (13 February 2015) UN Doc A/69/779 Figure II: Number of allegations for uniformed personnel per nationality; Annex IV (A): Allegations by mission, reported to the Office of Internal Oversight Services in 2015 involving military personnel of missions supported by the Department of Field Support (as of 31 December 2015).

[31] ibid; see also UN Security Council resolution 2272, which 'endorses the decision of the Secretary-General to repatriate a particular military unit or formed police unit of a contingent when there is credible evidence of widespread or systemic sexual exploitation and abuse by that unit' ... and '*Requests* the Secretary-General, when a particular troop-contributing country whose personnel are the subject of an allegation or allegations of sexual exploitation and abuse has not taken appropriate steps to investigate the allegation and/or when the particular troop- or police-contributing country has not held the perpetrators accountable or informed the Secretary-General of the progress of its investigations and/or actions taken, to replace all military units and/or formed police units of the troop- or police-contributing country in the United Nations peacekeeping operation where the allegation or allegations arose with uniformed personnel from a different troop- or police-contributing country as applicable ...' (11 March 2016) UN Doc S/RES/2272 (2016) paras 1, 2.

[32] UNGA, Special Measures for Protection from Sexual Exploitation and Sexual Abuse: Report of the Secretary-General' (n 30) para 68.

exploitation and abuse.[33] However, prosecutions remain the exception rather than the rule.

(ii) Employees and experts on mission

In accordance with the CPIUN and like treaties, heads of mission of international organizations cannot be arrested or detained, and they are immune from legal process of every kind during their term of office, aside from very limited exceptions.[34] This is similar to the personal immunity recognized for diplomatic envoys, heads of State, and foreign ministers.

Other employees of international organizations only enjoy functional immunity from host State jurisdiction. This comprises immunity from legal process in respect of 'words spoken or written and all acts performed by them in their official capacity'.[35] Similarly, 'experts on mission' have immunity from legal process in respect of words spoken or written and acts done by them in the course of the performance of their mission.[36] An expert on mission can be an independent Special Rapporteur acting in according with a UN mandate or in the context of a peacekeeping mission, military and civilian observers, formed police units, internationally recruited staff, and other persons so designated.

Thus, whether an employee or expert on mission or contractor will benefit from functional immunity will depend on whether the impugned act was done by them in an official capacity or in the course of the performance of their mission. The usual practice in peacekeeping operations in accordance with the UN Model SOFA is for the Host State to seek 'permission' from the UN prior to instituting proceedings; the UN certifies that the act in question is not related to the individual's official duties and would thus not fall within the scope of immunity, or if the UN determines that there is indeed immunity for the impugned conduct, it will decide whether immunity will be waived.[37] This practice diverges slightly from the approach taken in the jurisprudence of the ICJ, which has affirmed that an international organization's position as to whether an official has immunity serves as a 'presumption' which is to be given great weight and can only be set aside for the most compelling of reasons.[38]

There is a right and a duty to waive the immunity of any official in any case where the immunity would impede the course of justice and can be waived without prejudice to the interests of the United Nations.[39] Indeed, it has often been

[33] ibid para 69.

[34] Convention on the Privileges and Immunities of the UN (adopted 13 February 1946, entered into force 17 September 1946) 1 UNTS 15 (CPIUN) s 19; Convention on the Privileges and Immunities of the Specialized Agencies (adopted 21 November 1947, entered into force 2 December 1948) 33 UNTS 261 s 21.

[35] See eg CPIUN (n 34) art 18(a); Convention on the Privileges and Immunities of the Specialized Agencies (n 34) s 19(a).

[36] See CPIUN (n 34) s 22.

[37] UN Model SOFA (n 14) art 47(a).

[38] *Difference Relating to Immunity from Legal Process of a Special Rapporteur of the Commission on Human Rights* (Advisory Opinion) [1999] ICJ Rep 62 [88]–[89] (*Cumaraswamy Case*) [61].

[39] See CPIUN (n 34) s 20; Convention on the Privileges and Immunities of the Specialized Agencies (n 34) s 22.

recommended that the Host State should exercise jurisdiction with more frequency (with assistance from the UN or other States as appropriate).[40] While the exclusive jurisdiction of the troop contributing country to investigate and prosecute military contingents is unchallenged, in respect of other categories of persons over whom the Host State has jurisdiction, either because immunity has been waived or functional immunity does not apply to the alleged crimes, it has been recommended that the Host State does more. Yet, investigations and prosecutions by the Host State may be difficult. They are either unlikely because of the weaknesses of the justice system associated with the post-conflict context, or potentially flawed, due to the lack of independence of the justice system or the notoriety and high visibility of the cases.[41] The challenges for Host States to exercise jurisdiction has been emphasized by African States, who have argued that due to gaps in legislation and limited capacity for the Host State to exercise jurisdiction, the State of nationality of the alleged offender (the troop contributing country) is a preferable jurisdiction.[42]

In practice, there are instances when the determination of whether an employee, expert on mission, or contractor benefits from functional immunity is delayed or simply not decided, or in the case that immunity is recognized, it is not waived. Even for those types of personnel for whom the troop contributing country does not have exclusive jurisdiction,[43] the practice has been for the UN to refer the case to the troop contributing country anyway.

This problem was noted in a case concerning the MINUSTAH operation in Haiti. There, a Pakistani police officer had been accused of raping and abducting a 13-year-old Haitian male. As a police officer, the suspect would have only benefited from functional immunity which would not have been applicable to a rape and abduction case. Nevertheless, the Haitian government requested that the police officer's 'immunity' be lifted. The Pakistani government instead 'decided' to initiate a court martial proceeding, and 'United Nations Headquarters agreed'. The Pakistani government informed the UN that:

'it would not accept any decision by the Host State's courts, and would not allow any of its observers to the court-martial proceedings, as to do so would contravene [Pakistani] law on court martial. In the quickly convened and concluded court martial, no observers were allowed. Two members of the [Pakistani formed police unit] were found guilty and repatriated. However, none of the commanders was sanctioned ... It informed the United Nations that it considered the case closed. It remains unclear if verbal assurances

[40] See eg Prince Zeid report (n 615); UNSG, 'Ensuring the Accountability of United Nations Staff and Experts on Mission with Respect to Criminal Acts Committed in Peacekeeping Operations' UN Doc A/60/980 paras 27, 44.

[41] See Ferstman, 'Criminalizing Sexual Exploitation and Abuse by Peacekeepers' (n 27).

[42] UNGA, '"Small Number" of Officials, Experts on Mission Who Commit Crimes, Damage Organization's Reputation Must Be Held to Account, Sixth Committee Hears' (16 October 2015). Informal summary record of the Sixth Committee, session 70, 8th & 9th Meetings, UN Doc GA/L/3500.

[43] The different categories and status of persons on missions is described in UNCHR, 'Working Paper on the Accountability of International Personnel Taking Part in Peace Support Operations Submitted by Françoise Hampson' (7 July 2005) UN Doc E/CN.4/Sub.2/2005/42.

from the PCC to the United Nations of compensation to the Haitian victim were honoured'.[44]

Thus, there is a question about the ability of the Host State to exercise its sovereign jurisdiction, the conciliatory role played by the UN in shepherding the case to a Pakistani court martial process which arguably failed to meet fair trial standards and impeded the victim's access to justice. There is also a question of priority of jurisdiction. Arguably, Pakistan did have jurisdiction over the matter but so did Haiti. The absence of a clear rules framework and the relatively weaker negotiating position of the Host State made its exercise of jurisdiction less obvious, regardless of the position of the victims.

But separate from the Haiti case described above, in many other cases, the Host State is simply incapable, reluctant, or disinterested in exercising jurisdiction. The troop contributing country would normally have some jurisdiction to entertain an investigation and prosecution over a non-military suspect; however, the obligation to proceed is not clearly stipulated in the revised memorandum of understanding, and there are often gaps in the troop contributing country's domestic legislation pertaining to extraterritorial investigations and prosecutions of alleged offenders who are civilians as opposed to serving members of the military. Many countries restrict extraterritorial jurisdiction over civilians to specific treaty crimes such as torture, genocide, or war crimes. Sexual exploitation and abuse, fraud, and assault may not feature among the list of extraterritorial crimes. There are instances when this has prevented investigation and prosecution of experts on mission and civilian contractors.[45]

In addition to functional immunities, another challenge with the pursuit of criminal investigations against UN employees and experts on mission is the difficulties for troop contributing countries or Host States to take over investigations initiated by the organization. This problem was noted in the Central African Republic investigation report in respect of the administrative investigation initiated by UN staff in that country. The procedural bureaucracies associated with transferring the findings of the internal administrative investigation to the French authorities who had embarked upon their own investigation of the conduct of the Sangaris troops was time consuming and problematic. As part of its findings it recommended that: '[p]rivileges and immunities should not be a bar to UN officials and experts on mission to testify as witnesses to crimes of sexual violence, particularly where the UN has itself referred alleged incidents of sexual violence to the responsible national authorities for investigation or prosecution'.[46] Furthermore, it recommended that: '[t]he Office of Legal Affairs should adopt an approach to immunity that presumes cooperation and active participation of UN staff in accountability processes; immunity should stand only in circumstances where the

[44] UN OIOS, 'Evaluation of the Enforcement and Remedial Assistance Efforts for Sexual Exploitation and Abuse by the United Nations and Related Personnel in Peacekeeping Operations' (n 28) 17–18.

[45] See Ferstman, 'Criminalizing Sexual Exploitation and Abuse by Peacekeepers' (n 27).

[46] See Deschamps, Jallow, and Sooka (n 5) 91.

UN has determined that disclosure of information by staff members could result in a security threat to the victims or witnesses, or where the victim did not provide his or her informed consent to the disclosure of the information'.[47]

(2) *The role of other states and/or international tribunals to help address justice gaps*

Because of the ongoing challenges to progress investigations and prosecutions in the Host State and the concomitant failure of troop contributing countries to pursue investigations and prosecutions of their nationals in the majority of incidents (both for military contingents in which the troop contributing country has exclusive jurisdiction, and for other categories of persons where the Host State is incapable or unwilling to assert jurisdiction), it has been recommended that additional modalities for prosecution be put in place. In 2006, a Report of a Group of Legal Experts that had been commissioned to consider this issue, proposed a number of strategies to end impunity, including the possibility for States to agree a new convention on the subject.[48]

The proposed draft convention included an 'extradite or prosecute' regime,[49] the rationale being that when a crime is carried out in the peacekeeping context, the abuse of power implicit in the crime makes what would normally be an ordinary crime (not normally giving rise to extraterritorial jurisdiction) into an international crime which all members of the International Community have an interest in prosecuting.[50] However, which other States would exercise criminal jurisdiction? States other than the Host State and the troop contributing country might have an interest to prosecute if an alleged offender is found on their territory; however, it is less likely that they would request extradition of a suspect if that suspect is not their national and the offence had no impact on their citizens.[51] Under a classical extradite or prosecute framework, the obligation to act stems from an accused person's presence in the jurisdiction.

The Group of Experts report has also pointed to the possibility of establishing a hybrid tribunal[52] in the Host State which would contain international elements, as has been done in relation to the prosecution of mass crimes under international law in Sierra Leone, East Timor, and Cambodia, and the most recent example of the Extraordinary African Chambers which operates pursuant to Senegalese law. The Group of Experts report is persuaded by this type of model because, although costly, it would have the flexibility to deal with any type of crime; 'hybrid tribunals can be established to deal exclusively with domestic crimes including those committed by peacekeeping personnel which do not rise to the level of international

[47] ibid xii.

[48] UNSG, 'Ensuring the Accountability of United Nations Staff and Experts on Mission with Respect to Criminal Acts Committed in Peacekeeping Operations' (n 40).

[49] ibid para 44(a). [50] ibid paras 55–58.

[51] See Ferstman, 'Criminalizing Sexual Exploitation and Abuse by Peacekeepers' (n 27).

[52] UNSG, 'Ensuring the Accountability of United Nations Staff and Experts on Mission with Respect to Criminal Acts Committed in Peacekeeping Operations' (n 40) paras 33–37.

crimes'.[53] Yet, if these hybrid tribunals are established after the fact, in response to crimes which have already taken place, then this would not only be costly but also time-consuming. Further, it would be necessary for those crimes covered by the hybrid tribunal operating in accordance with the domestic law of the Host State to have already been clearly reflected in the statute books of the Host State to satisfy the principle of legality; this will often not be the case, particularly for acts amounting to sexual exploitation and abuse.

A more permanent solution might be a fixed structure untied to a particular Host State which would attach to the mandates of all current and future peacekeeping operations, and be incorporated into the SOFA and memorandum signed with troop contributing countries, the acceptance of which could be a precondition for a troop contributing country to engage in a particular peacekeeping operation. Or, it could form the basis of a new statute, which would need to be ratified by troop contributing countries prior to deployment. If accepted and supported by States, this type of structure could well have the greatest chance of tackling impunity. This model is somewhat similar to the 'new, independent system of special courts' that has been proposed by the 'Code Blue' campaign.[54] Crucial is for a scalable structure to exist independent of any particular peacekeeping operation which can be easily transported *in situ* to quickly address allegations as they arise, and for troop contributing countries to agree to be bound by the model as a condition for troop deployment. This might scare certain countries from contributing troops; however, the significant benefits for many countries derived from participation in peacekeeping should not be overlooked.[55]

Another suggestion that has been made is to vest jurisdiction in the International Criminal Court or another comparable tribunal. However, this may be a difficult option given that many troop contributing countries are not States Parties of the International Criminal Court statute. It may also cause a revisiting in the UN Security Council of an attempt to adopt a new version of Resolution 1422/02 which, using Chapter VII of the Charter, requested that the ICC suspend any investigation or prosecution of a matter concerning current or former officials or personnel from a troop contributing country not party to the Rome Statute.[56] The possibility for peacekeepers to perpetrate war crimes is recognized in respect of operations with enforcement mandates[57] and the prospect that human rights, international humanitarian law, and refugee law may be engaged is recognized by the UN's due diligence policy. In theory, the International Criminal Court may have jurisdiction to investigate and prosecute crimes perpetrated by peacekeepers when the Host State or troop contributing country is party to the Rome Statute and is unwilling or unable to investigate or prosecute domestically. Nevertheless,

[53] ibid para 34.

[54] Code Blue, 'A Practical Plan to End Impunity for Peacekeeper Sexual Abuse' (13 October 2016) http://www.codebluecampaign.com/press-releases/2016/10/13 (last accessed 4 January 2017).

[55] See Ferstman, 'Criminalizing Sexual Exploitation and Abuse by Peacekeepers' (n 27).

[56] UNSC, Res 1422/2002 (12 July 2002); renewed by Res 1487/2003 (12 June 2003).

[57] UN Secretariat, 'Observance by United Nations Forces of International Humanitarian Law' ST/SGB/1999/13 (6 August 1999) UN Doc ST/SGB/1999/13 Chapter I para 3.

the likelihood of the ICC Prosecutor pursuing such an investigation is limited, given that most peacekeeping crimes will not meet the required gravity threshold.[58]

These myriad suggestions were never pursued by Member States, who for the most part preferred to focus their attention on strengthening the capacity for troop contributing countries to assert jurisdiction directly. But because of the continued failings in this regard, the Secretary-General has revisited some of these decade old suggestions. In his 2016 report, he encouraged Member States 'to explore alternative means to achieve accountability, including extraterritorial jurisdiction for United Nations personnel who commit sex crimes', and encouraged Member States 'to catalyse progress on the questions raised more than ten years ago in the report of the Group of Legal Experts on ensuring the accountability of United Nations staff and experts on mission with respect to criminal acts committed in peacekeeping operations (A/60/980) and finalize their deliberations'.[59] These options have also been revisited favourably by certain other international inquiry processes.[60]

VIII.3 Civil Responsibility

Organization employees, experts on mission, contractors, and military contingents may incur individual responsibility when they cause harm or damage. This may give rise to an individual obligation to afford reparation.

Similar to criminal law immunities, the degree of civil law immunities for international organization personnel and affiliated persons will depend on the individual's status within the organization and their functions. Usually, the individual will benefit from functional immunity for claims which relate to acts carried out as part of the individual's official functions or an expert's mission. Depending on the treaty framework, the Secretary-General or person of similar rank within an international organization may also benefit from personal immunity for the time in which they hold that post.[61]

In accordance with Article 29(b) of the CPIUN, the UN is obliged to make provision for appropriate modes for settlement in respect of 'disputes involving any official of the United Nations who by reason of his official position enjoys

[58] Carla Ferstman, 'Prosecutorial Discretion and Victims' Rights at the International Criminal Court: Demarcating the Battle Lines' (2016) Acta Juridica 17, 24–34.

[59] UNGA, 'Special Measures for Protection from Sexual Exploitation and Sexual Abuse' (n 30) UN Doc A/70/729 paras 65, 66; this is also repeated in UNGA, 'Combating Sexual Exploitation and Sexual Abuse' Report of the Secretary-General (23 June 2016) UN Doc A/71/97 para 72.

[60] UN Women, 'Preventing Conflict, Transforming Justice, Securing Peace: The Global Study on the Implementation of United Nations Security Council Resolution 1325' (2015) 148–49.

[61] See CPIUN (n 34) s 19; Convention on the Privileges and Immunities of the Specialized Agencies (n 34) s 21. In the case of the former head of the IMF, Dominique Strauss-Kahn, a New York court determined that he was not entitled to personal immunity because the USA did not ratify the Convention on the Privileges and Immunities of the Specialized Agencies and Mr Strauss-Kahn did not raise his immunity in respect of his criminal case, and thus was prevented from raising it in the civil case. The Court determined that, the acts in question did not in any event fall within his official functions so he did not benefit from functional immunity. See *Nafissatou Diallo v Dominique Strauss-Kahn, Index* No 307065/11 (11 June 2012) Supreme Court New York, 9.

immunity, if immunity has not been waived by the Secretary-General'. Thus, a defendant in a civil claim will either: (i) not be immune because the acts the claim relates to were done in a purely private capacity; (ii) not immune because the international organization waived any immunity which would otherwise apply to the claim; or (iii) immune, in which case the civil claim would not be allowed to proceed. In the third scenario, the UN would be obliged to establish another mode for settlement of the claim.

In the peacekeeping context, the model SOFA specifies that when the claim relates to official duties, the UN and the host country shall settle the dispute by a standing claims commission established for that purpose. In practice, such commissions have never been established, and such claims are settled through internal claims review boards established by the UN.[62] The EU model SOFA provides for a somewhat different framework. In accordance with Article 18(6), claims against military or civilian staff 'arising out of tortious acts or omissions in the receiving State not done in the performance of official duty' are first considered and assessed by the authorities of the receiving [Host] State. The findings of this assessment are then delivered to the authorities of the troop contributing country, who will decide whether they will offer an ex gratia payment. The claimant would then be offered the ex gratia payment, failing which 'nothing in this paragraph shall affect the jurisdiction of the courts of the receiving State to entertain an action against military or civilian staff unless and until there has been payment in full satisfaction of the claim'.[63]

The full implementation of the above framework could ensure a modicum of justice for civil claimants. In practice, however, gaps have resulted. With respect to the UN framework, the majority of claims lodged before civil courts have referenced the organization as the defendant as opposed to a named official. Thus, the provision for appropriate modes of settlement have proceeded in accordance with Article 29(a) of the CPIUN, not 29(b) and as indicated in earlier chapters, no alternative settlement procedures have been established for claims concerning human rights and humanitarian law violations because these have been determined to be 'public' as opposed to 'private' claims.[64] Furthermore, in regards to the UN, local claims review boards have not always been made available to claimants in accordance with 29(b). As canvassed in Chapter VI, the failure to establish an alternative settlement procedure has not always impacted on the recognition of applicable immunities.

A part of the reason for the failure of the system is practical. If a victim raises a claim, it will be raised to the institution, it will not necessarily be taken by a victim to a local court (which would then set in motion a process for the UN to certify

[62] The limitations of these boards are discussed in Chapter V.

[63] Agreement between the Member States of the European Union concerning the status of military and civilian staff seconded to the institutions of the European Union, of the headquarters and forces which may be made available to the European Union in the context of the preparation and execution of the tasks referred to in Article 17(2) of the Treaty on European Union, including exercises, and of the military and civilian staff of the Member States put at the disposal of the European Union to act in this context (EU SOFA), Brussels, 17 November 2003, OJ [2003] C 321/6 art 28(6)(a)–(d).

[64] See Chapter V.4.3(6).

its immunity (or not) in respect of a named defendant and/or waive immunity for it to indicate what alternative remedy it will establish). Local courts are hard to access in many countries, expensive and many will not approach because of the lack of the means or because of the belief that immunities are more extensive than they actually are in law. The victim will simply bring an allegation to the attention of the organization with the expectation that this will lead to something. In a domestic setting, from a human rights perspective the lodging of a complaint (even an oral one) would require that complaint to be followed up, for the victim to be kept up to date about the complaints progress, and for the victim to be told about any other avenues of justice that may exist.

In the UN case, when a complaint is made, the victim may simply have no response at all. Using sexual exploitation and abuse as an example, the victim will report the offence to the UN office in country. The matter, if taken seriously will be taken up by OIOS and/or the Conduct and Discipline Unit who will carry out an administrative investigation; however, these bodies have no mandate to address criminal or civil claims. They cannot grant monetary compensation, restitution or other forms of reparation, nor do they necessarily point victims and claimants towards the limited victim assistance programmes set out in Chapter VI. If the UN unilaterally finds that the claims are not substantiated, the claim does not come before any court system or independent adjudicator.

Civil claims are also hindered by a lack of clear evidence. In the case of sexual exploitation and abuse the Secretary-General has urged troop contributing countries to provide DNA samples of deployed troops,[65] and the organization has developed a collection protocol to aid with sampling. However, this remains a voluntary process.[66] Access to a DNA bank is crucial for paternity claims; however, this is just the first step. In any other context such evidence would form the basis for a formal declaration of paternity following which a child support order and enforcement structure for negligent debtors would be put in place.

In the UN context, there has been an emphasis only on offering DNA sampling assistance to troop contributing countries, and a recognition of the need for children born from sexual exploitation and abuse to benefit from the planned assistance programmes described in Chapter VI. Occasionally there are *ex gratia* payments but these are not negotiated with the victim. In one reported case concerning a Uruguayan peacekeeper which DNA tests proved he fathered a Haitian child, the mother 'Rosa Mina Joseph, whose son was born in 2011, said she received an envelope with $300 in cash from the UN two years ago when it established paternity. She had to drop out of school to care for the son and her dreams of becoming a nurse have all but vanished. Posse [the father] sent her $100 once from Uruguay, she said, but has not sent anything more'.[67]

[65] UNGA, Special Measures for Protection from Sexual Exploitation and Sexual Abuse: Report of the Secretary-General' (n 30) para 69.

[66] ibid para 31; see also Associated Press, 'UN Silently Offers DNA Testing to Prove Paternity Claims for "Peacekeeper Babies"' (14 June 2015).

[67] David McFadden, 'United Nations Faces Civil Suit over "Peacekeeper Babies"' Associated Press (15 July 2016),

It is expected that victims should pursue paternity claims directly through the local courts. This is not a realistic expectation for the vast majority of victims who come from the most vulnerable sectors of society in States with poorly functioning legal systems. Local courts in the Host State will face a difficult job assessing victims' evidence in the absence of conclusive DNA evidence supplied through the troop contributing country. The contingent will invariably have been shipped out of the country and presence may be unknowable to the Court without the assistance of the troop contributing country. Extra-territorial child support orders have become increasingly frequent in regular (non-conflict) circumstances though they rely on enforcement protocols between the countries where the victim and defendant are living, respectively. One can imagine that these are unlikely to be in place in the majority of countries hosting peacekeeping missions.

VIII.4 Administrative or Disciplinary Sanctions

Wrongdoing can also result in administrative or disciplinary sanction.

Employees may be suspended, dismissed, or demoted for wrongful acts which violate the human rights and humanitarian law obligations of the organization. Importantly, when they are experts on mission on short-term or temporary assignments, such conduct will impact their ability to have their contract extended and to obtain a new contract. Equally, employee entitlements may be suspended or withheld. The internal employee dispute tribunals of international organizations have adjudicated numerous cases which concern sanctions imposed on employees as a result of their alleged wrongful conduct.

For instance, Mr Oh, an engineer working with the UN Operation in Côte d'Ivoire, was summarily dismissed for having procured sex from prostitutes who were victims of trafficking kept in debt-bondage in the capital Abidjan.[68] An employee with UNICEF was summarily dismissed for having sexually harassed four young men,[69] as was the officer-in-charge for security at MINURSO, for having taken nude pictures of local women in his apartment in Western Sahara.[70] An employee of the UN Mission in Sudan who physically assaulted a female civilian was determined to be unfit for further service. The UN Appeals Tribunal determined that:

> 'It is clear that the General Assembly will not tolerate the immunity of the United Nations being used as a shield permitting the criminal behaviour of staff members and experts on mission from being properly prosecuted. Indeed, the preamble of A/RES/64/110 continues to state that the General Assembly is "[d]eeply concerned by reports of criminal conduct, and conscious

[68] *Oh v Secretary-General of the UN* (UNAT, 17 October 2014) Judgment no 2014-UNAT-480, Case no 2014-554.

[69] *Applicant v Secretary-General of the UN* (UNAT, 28 March 2013) Judgment no 2013-UNAT-302, Case no 2012-334.

[70] *Massah v Secretary-General of the UN* (UNAT, 1 November 2012) Judgment no 2012-UNAT-274, Case no 2012-301.

that such conduct, if not investigated and, as appropriate, prosecuted, would create the negative impression that United Nations officials and experts on mission operate with impunity" '.[71]

Military contingents may be repatriated and barred from future service. With respect to sexual exploitation and abuse, additional sanctions have been put in place such as repatriating an entire troop contingent, and it has been proposed to suspend 'the portion of payments due to troop or police-contributing countries in connection with a specific individual suspected of sexual exploitation and abuse on the basis of credible evidence, from the time that the troop or police-contributing country is notified of an incident until the completion of its participation in an investigation, noting that the suspended payments will be returned to the Member State if, after an investigation, the allegations are not substantiated'.[72] In the General Assembly's July 2016 budget resolution, it approved the transfer to a trust fund for victims of withheld payments in substantiated cases of sexual exploitation abuse by civilian, military, and police personnel.[73] But, the prospects for implementation are extremely limited when so few cases have been substantiated.

VIII.5 Conclusions

The *status quo* is one of impunity and an absence of redress for victims of the myriad of unlawful acts that are perpetrated by individuals serving with international organizations in a variety of capacities. The UN has focused its attention on trying to encourage troop contributing countries to investigate and prosecute the alleged perpetrators of criminal acts and while important reforms have been put in place in recent years to tackle sexual exploitation and abuse, these reforms remain piece-meal, have not filtered to other areas of criminality and the track record of prosecutions remains extremely poor. The African Union has been even slower to respond.

Civil remedies have been all but illusory for victims. Even in those instances where immunity is not a bar, claims concerning criminal acts including human rights and humanitarian law abuses have not been received by local claims review boards or other internal administrative processes and access to domestic courts—whether

[71] *Toukolon v Secretary-General of the United Nations* (UNAT, 2 April 2014) Judgment no 2014-UNAT-407, Case no 2013-457 para 19. See for a similar ruling *Abu Ghali v Commissioner-General of the United Nations Relief and Works Agency for Palestine Refugees in the Near East* (UNAT, 17 October 2013) Judgment no 2013-UNAT-366, Case no 2012-414 para 43.

[72] UNGA/UNSC, 'Report of the High-level Independent Panel on Peace Operations' UN Doc A/70/95-S/2015/446 (n 203) para 283.

[73] UNGA, Res 70/286 (8 July 2016) UN Doc A/RES/70/286 para 75; see also UNGA, 'Special measures for protection from sexual exploitation and sexual abuse' (n 647) UN Doc A/70/729 para 76 (the Secretary-General's request to approve transfer of payments withheld for substantiated cases of sexual exploitation and abuse by any United Nations personnel to a trust fund set up to support victims); UNSG, 'The Future of United Nations Peace Operations: Implementation of the Recommendations of the High-level Independent Panel on Peace Operations' (2 September 2015) UN Doc A/70/357–S/2015/682 para 120.

in the host State or the sending State are not realistic venues for the majority of victims.

Administrative and disciplinary remedies—usually the separation from service, have been used to some effect and the risk of such sanction can serve as an important disincentive for would-be offenders. However, these remedies do little to meet comprehensively victims' needs and rights to justice.

IX

Some Concluding Thoughts—Where the Solutions Lie

The gaps identified in this book are multiple, often cross-cutting, and there is no easy or one-off solution capable of redressing the balance in favour of victims of human rights and international humanitarian law violations caused by the acts and omissions of international organizations.

That more *can* be done is a simple, rather uncontroversial conclusion. Why more *must* be done will depend on one's vantage point. As a matter of law, more must be done because international organizations have obligations under human rights and international humanitarian law which, when breached, give rise to secondary rules which require reparations. The failure to afford reparations cannot be justified by the absence of adequate procedures; to the contrary, the failure to afford reparations constitutes an additional internationally wrongful act.

But also, more must be done in order to preserve the integrity of the international organizations. This is not a simple moral imperative but a necessary consequence of international organizations' mandates and to fulfil their functions. The rules must necessarily reflect the different contexts in which international organizations now operate, and arguably the practice of international organizations will need to shift to meet growing responsibilities, including to refrain from prohibited conduct, to take adequate positive steps to prevent conduct where such an obligation exists and to afford remedies and reparation in the case of breach. International organizations must not only embrace the principle of human rights and international humanitarian law compliance, but also the consequences of such compliance. This will inevitably introduce challenges, as can be seen with the stalled process for the European Union (EU) to accede to the European Convention on Human Rights (ECHR). This requires a significant change in orientation, which is overdue.

What is required is a total reconfiguration of the placement and standing of victims to exercise rights on the international plane, and for mechanisms to be made available for them to do so, and for these mechanisms to have the power to adopt decisions which can be independently enforced against the organizations. While this is easier said than done, it is worth considering the key areas in which changes are required in order to move towards a model that achieves greater compliance. Indeed, should it be accepted that international organizations must afford remedies and reparation for breaches of human rights and international humanitarian law that correspond to the standards that exist in those specialized fields then there is a corresponding obligation for them to establish the framework for that to happen. Naturally, given the breadth of the gaps, a series of interlinked measures are required.

IX.1 Strengthening Human Rights and International Humanitarian Law Standards from the Inside

To date, the recognition by international organizations of their human rights and international humanitarian law obligations has been progressive (following media attention and/or claims lodged with domestic or regional courts regardless of their outcome—the sanctions de-listing process being one example). Voluntary or declaratory codes and other self-imposed ethical standards have been introduced slowly and have been helpful to clarify the limits of acceptable conduct and for training and discipline purposes. However, there has been less emphasis in such voluntary or declaratory codes to the secondary rules that become applicable upon a breach of a primary obligation and on the measures needed to enable those secondary rules to be enforced.

Artificial barriers that impede the enforcement of secondary rules remain firmly in place. These barriers would need to be removed by international organizations in order for them to comply fully with the obligation to afford reparation to injured individuals. For example, it is important for the UN to affirm that, in accordance with the progressive expansion of its mandate since the Convention on the Privileges and Immunities of the United Nations (CPIUN) was adopted in 1946, it is now obligated to make provision for appropriate modes of settlement for any and all disputes to which it is a party, regardless of whether those disputes stem from acts of a 'private' or 'public' character. Barring such voluntary recognition, it would be important for section 29 of the CPIUN to be subjected to independent judicial scrutiny. However, as detailed elsewhere, the lack of standing of injured individuals to seek such independent judicial scrutiny conspires to maintain the *status quo*. Another possibility (however lengthy and difficult) is for a new protocol to the CPIUN to be negotiated concerning the regulation of disputes of a 'public' character.

A further area in which international organizations should act on their own initiative to strengthen standards is with respect to the regulation of their own immunity. Domestic courts have rarely entertained claims against international organizations because of operable immunities. Yet, there has been insufficient emphasis in the jurisprudence on the functional character of international organizations and of the need for organizations' immunities to accord with wider institutional mandates, such as encouraging and promoting respect for human rights and rule of law. International organizations could do much more to recognize a need to relax immunities in certain circumstances. Furthermore, they are best placed to develop rigorous and transparent doctrine to guide decisions taken by them to waive (or not) immunity and to publicize those decisions. Without such doctrine and carefully and faithfully applied, the organizations simply perpetuate the sense of arbitrariness and seemingly inconsistent results.

IX.2 Independent Oversight

In addition to enabling individuals to access an international court to have their claims adjudicated, it would be important to develop an independent oversight structure with the capacity to receive and investigate complaints from injured individuals and others, and to carry out *proprio motu* investigations concerning human rights and humanitarian law abuses of international organizations. Such a free-standing structure, which would be internal to each international organization could help to encourage more regular reflection on the problem areas, receive any concerns and input from injured individuals and other sources and report on them to the appropriate international organization political organs. It could also help resolve disputes informally and contribute to reflection on the need to change organizational culture. Many international organizations have established ombudsperson structures to deal with employee disputes. An ombudsperson with a mandate relating to the listing and de-listing procedures of the Al-Qaida sanctions committee was established and has played a useful role in somewhat increasing access to procedural safeguards for persons on sanctions lists,[1] and one was put in place in Kosovo to address issues related to the UN administration,[2] before it was eventually overtaken by the Kosovo Human Rights Advisory Panel.[3]

This type of oversight function has occasionally been adopted by UN special rapporteurs even without a precise mandate for so doing, because of their concern by the lack of institutional accountability in respect of issues relevant to their mandates, such as the cholera epidemic in Haiti[4] and the proliferation of sexual exploitation and abuse in peacekeeping missions.[5] Given their limited available time, only few Special Rapporteurs have devoted attention to such matters, and even fewer have managed to do so over an extended period. A somewhat less *ad hoc* structure would be to create a new thematic mandate with a specific focus to

[1] UNSC Res 1904/2009 (17 December 2009) and extended by Res 1989 (17 June 2011) and Res 2083 (17 December 2012).

[2] See eg UN Secretariat, 'Office of the Ombudsman—Appointment and Terms of Reference of the Ombudsman' (15 October 2002) UN Doc ST/SGB/2002/12; UNMIK Regulations 2000/38 (30 June 2000), 2003/8 (15 April 2003), 2006/6 (16 February 2006), 2007/15 (19 March 2007); Law No.03/L–195 on the Ombudsperson (Kosovo).

[3] UNMIK, 'Regulation 2007/3 amending Regulation 2006/12 on the Establishment of the Human Rights Advisory Panel' (12 January 2007).

[4] UN Human Rights Council, 'Report of the Independent Expert on the Situation of Human Rights in Haiti, Gustavo Gallón' (7 February 2014) UN Doc A/HRC/25/71 para 77. See also UNGA, 'Report of the Special Rapporteur on Extreme Poverty and Human Rights' (26 August 2016) UN Doc A/71/367.

[5] UNGA, 'Report of the Special Rapporteur on Violence Against Women, Its Causes and Consequences, Rashida Manjoo, Mission to Somalia' (14 May 2012) UN Doc A/HRC/20/16/Add.3 para 27; UNGA, 'Report of the Independent Expert on the Situation of Human Rights in the Central African Republic' (22 July 2016) UN Doc A/HRC/33/63 paras 81–88.

assess international organization compliance with human rights and international humanitarian law and the implementation of reparations obligations.

Both the ombudsperson and thematic mandate approaches would give greater visibility to the concerns of injured individuals; however, they are not on their own likely to provide the impetus for the adjudicative framework to be strengthened. The example of the recommendations on reparations made by the independent Human Rights Advisory Panel (HRAP) being routinely ignored despite the findings of (often serious) violations of human rights does not inspire hope.

One step further would be to provide the ombudsperson or mandate holder with the licence to take up such matters with independent judicial or quasi-judicial authorities, as necessary. If, for instance, reference questions were referred to the International Court of Justice (ICJ) in order to provide Advisory Opinions to clarify aspects of law, this would provide a significant layer of independent review of international organization action. Clearly, an ombudsperson or thematic mandate holder would not at present have access to the ICJ to request such opinions; they would need to be requested through an organ of the UN. Thus, in order for such a model to work the rules would need to be revised so as to enable direct access to the ICJ (a difficult and unlikely prospect), or to limit the discretion of the relevant UN agencies to respond other than favourably, to the mandate holder/ombudsperson's request to forward requests for advisory opinions (perhaps equally difficult).

IX.3 Transforming Internal Adjudicative Mechanisms

As explained throughout this book, there are many fundamental flaws with the internal adjudicative mechanisms of international organizations. The simplest route to strengthen injured individuals' access to reparations is to reconfigure the adjudicative mechanisms so that they become fairer, more transparent, impartial, and accessible, and so that they have the potential to afford adequate and effective reparation.

As the book has reflected, both the procedural aspects of redress (in particular the degree of access to a redress mechanism, how it functions, its impartiality from the organization) and the reparation that might ultimately be afforded (the quantum and quality of reparation, for what types of harms, with which caveats) are extremely limited. Adjudicative decisions which consider international organizations' practice are mainly taken by bodies established and run by the organizations themselves. The few arms-length bodies that have been established invariably have only recommendatory powers, and thus the decision whether to comply with any recommendations rests with the international organization itself. The decision on whether to provide reparation, and if so the form that it should take is left to executive bodies, which have often failed to heed recommendations where these have been made and left victims without a substantial remedy. Very few mechanisms are able to afford compensation, and of those that do, often there are restrictions with respect to quantum, or the factual scenarios that may qualify.

There are several ways in which internal adjudicative mechanisms can be strengthened.

First, it would be appropriate to consider whether the types of tribunals established by many international organizations to adjudicate employment claims can be used with necessary modifications as a model to develop quasi-independent and quasi-judicial permanent structures to which injured individuals who are not employees and are otherwise unaffiliated with the organizations may address claims concerning human rights and international humanitarian law abuses.

Second, with respect to the particular context of wrongful conduct occurring in the context of peacekeeping operations, it should be possible to increase accountability and access to reparations for human rights and international humanitarian law breaches occurring in the context of a mission at the field level. This could be done by extending the mandates of local claims review boards to (i) include the possibility for claims of a public nature or involving policy questions; (ii) include claims which concern the conduct of a particular peacekeeper or official on mission for which the international organization is arguably jointly and severally liable; (iii) remove or significantly restrict the limitations on liability that are in place for claims of a private nature for these new categories of claims; and (iv) make the decisions of local claims review boards publicly accessible, or at least in summarized format.

Such modifications would remove the central lacunae; however, they would not address the procedural limitations of local claims review boards which are not designed for dealing with mass liability stemming from systemic organizational failings or incidents involving large numbers of victims, nor their lack of independence.

Consequently, a different option would be to establish a special panel for peacekeeping claims (other than claims concerning contracts and car accidents which could continue to be dealt with by the local claims review boards) which could operate differently to the standard review boards, with more independence and more accessible procedures for vulnerable victims. This should work as an independent structure to the peacekeeping mission and be attached to other independent quasi-judicial structures within the UN system, such as the UN Dispute Tribunal and the UN Appeals Tribunal.

Another option would be to develop a two tiered system whereby 'small' claims could be resolved by an on-site claims board which is mandated to resolve claims up to a maximum amount. Claims which go beyond this amount could be addressed to a central venue which would have greater latitude to determine with precision appropriate and effective reparations. For reasons already described, injured individuals would need direct access to this central venue; it would be inappropriate and insufficient for such claims to be absorbed by States of nationality.

There is also a need for independent oversight of such structures, even if the mechanisms themselves are strengthened. At present, what the international organization provides by way of redress mechanism is like a form of charity offered up to the injured individual: the individual is forced to take what is on offer because there is no venue to challenge it. This affords the organization a monopoly over the law and its procedures and is the antithesis to a rule of law based approach.

With respect to criminal law accountability, there has been a combined failure of troop contributing countries to prosecute their formed military contingents and for the peacekeeping missions to either waive immunity of other personnel in favour of the Host State or provide adequate technical assistance with respect to investigations to enable any competent State to exercise criminal jurisdiction. A more radical approach to the problem is now needed. It would be appropriate for the Group of Experts' recommendation for a new convention on the criminal accountability of peacekeepers to be pursued.[6] Also, it would be appropriate to consider a scalable structure to exist independent of any particular peacekeeping operation which can be easily transported in situ to quickly address allegations as they arise, and for troop contributing countries to agree to be bound by the model as a condition for troop deployment.

IX.4 Standing of Injured Individuals to Bring Claims before International Courts

A key area in which progress is needed is in regards to the recognition of injured individuals as right holders with the capacity to access justice independently. Standing is necessary not only to give injured individuals a venue to assert a claim but to account for the failure of their States of nationality to take up cases on their behalf and to address what are now unaccountable internal mechanisms.

International courts are a reasonable complement to organizations' internal adjudicative mechanisms. They would be more independent and impartial than internal processes. They would be fitting venues in light of international organizations' international character and having regard to the desirability of a model that has the potential to influence organization practice while safeguarding international organizations' independence from the possibility of State interference, arguably better than municipal courts could do. For similar reasons, international courts are arguably more appropriate forums to adjudicate claims concerning international organizations than regional ones. Not least, adjudication by international courts is better suited to claims which concern international organizations with universal mandates and could help avoid conflicting jurisprudence emanating from regional courts.

But it would be a complex route to make claims against international organizations justiciable before international courts and even more complicating—but still necessary—to allow individuals to lodge such claims. This would have the benefit of affording independent judicial oversight and would ensure that individuals are not overly reliant on their States of nationality. However, it would require significant reconfiguration of the current legal order and significant political will which is not evidently in place. And, there would be a need not only to afford notional

[6] UNSG, 'Ensuring the Accountability of United Nations Staff and Experts on Mission with Respect to Criminal Acts Committed in Peacekeeping Operations' UN Doc A/60/980.

access to existing international courts, but to ensure individuals in remote areas have practical access, even if rules of standing did not also present formal obstacles.

At present, injured individuals have no standing to assert claims against universal international organizations before international courts, aside from certain specialized regimes like the UN Convention on the Law of the Sea or in respect of international arbitration tribunals for staff employment claims. No regional or international court enables individuals to make a direct claim against a universal international organization pertaining to human rights or international humanitarian law. Individuals' standing to bring claims against universal international organizations before domestic or regional courts is curtailed by the application of immunities and the limited jurisdiction of those courts. Regional integration organization courts have no jurisdiction over universal organizations or other international organizations outside their regional system.

A State can put forward a claim against an international organization for the benefit of individuals or entities that it seeks to protect, under the principle of diplomatic protection. This can be done by using negotiation, conciliation, mediation, or arbitration procedures, which are incorporated into some agreements between States and international organizations.

An often cited example is the settlement of claims concerning Belgian, Swiss, Greek, Luxembourg, Italian, Zambian American, British, and French nationals arising from the United Nations operation in the Congo.[7] Disputes concerning the privileges and immunities of the UN or specialized agencies may be referred to the International Court of Justice for a request for an advisory opinion on any legal question; the opinion given by the Court shall be accepted as decisive by the parties.[8] But these are rare practices, particularly in respect of claims brought on behalf of nationals of a Host State. International organizations operate in some of the most fragile countries where security, the rule of law and democratic accountability to citizens is particularly weak. States have no recognized obligation to put forward a claim on behalf of their nationals, nor do they do so as of route. The State of Haiti never brought a claim against the UN on behalf of the thousands of cholera victims, nor did Kosovo bring forward a claim on behalf of victims of lead poisoning in Mitrovica.

It should be possible for injured individuals to use negotiation, conciliation, mediation, or arbitration procedures to secure reparations from international organizations, when their States of nationality do not take up these matters directly. However, individuals are not parties to the agreements made between States and international organizations where such arbitration or related clauses are listed and

[7] Discussed in ILC, Draft articles on the responsibility of international organizations, 'Report of the International Law Commission on the Work of its 63rd Session' (26 April–3 June and 4 July–12 August 2011) UN Doc A/66/10 (DARIO) Official Commentary art 36.

[8] Convention on the Privileges and Immunities of the UN (adopted 13 February 1946, entered into force 17 September 1946) 1 UNTS 15 (CPIUN) s 30; Convention on the Privileges and Immunities of the Specialized Agencies (adopted 21 November 1947, entered into force 2 December 1948) 33 UNTS 261 s 32.

thus there is not a defined and mutually agreed legal relationship between them and the organization.

The case for an international court with the mandate to adjudicate directly the acts of international organizations, especially the universal ones, is therefore clear. Difficult as this may already be, such a solution would only be worthwhile if injured individuals had direct access to such a court. The proposition of an international court with standing for injured individuals and competence over the human rights and humanitarian law violations of international organizations has already been made by scholars, so far without success.[9] It continues to be worth pursuing.

Applying a more restricted model, the International Court of Justice already has the power to receive and determine requests for 'binding' advisory opinions concerning any legal question which concerns the conduct of international organizations under certain treaties (such as the CPIUN). It would be appropriate to consider whether this power can be extended to other legal matters concerning the conduct of international organizations, and to develop a framework whereby injured individuals can address the Court on such matters, when their State of nationality has failed to take up the matter on their behalf.

The first proposition is relatively straight-forward (although not without difficulty) and may require new or amended language to be incorporated into agreements with international organizations. Reference to the International Court of Justice as the venue to resolve disputes is already featured in the Model SOFA.[10] However, under Article 96 of the UN Charter requests for advisory opinions may be made only by authorized organs of the UN and thus it is unlikely that the procedure is sufficiently robust to *require* the UN to make a request in contentious matters where doing so may be against the organization's own interests.

The second proposition of some form of subsidiary standing to be afforded to injured individuals when their State of nationality does not take up the matter on their behalf, is even more challenging. There is some practice which shows that certain individuals will not be able to avail themselves of the protection of their States of nationality—particularly stateless persons and refugees. The UN Claims Commission adopted a procedure whereby an 'appropriate person, authority, or body appointed by the Governing Council may submit claims on behalf of persons who are not in a position to have their claims submitted by a Government'.[11] However, as detailed throughout this book, it is not only refugees and stateless persons who will not be able to avail themselves of the protection of their States of nationality, when seeking to obtain reparations for human rights and humanitarian law breaches attributable to international organizations. Sometimes individuals' very competent and able States of nationality will simply decide not to take up the cases of their nationals because to do so is not in their perceived interest. Therefore,

[9] See Chapter VII.2.1.

[10] UNGA, 'Model Status-of-forces Agreement for Peace-Keeping Operations' (9 October 1990) UN Doc A/45/594 (UN Model SOFA) para 54.

[11] UNCC, Provisional Rules for Claims Procedure (26 June 1992) UN Doc S/AC.26/1992/10 art 5(2).

a more fundamental change in approach is required so that such injured individuals can access justice to assert their rights. This reconfiguration is likely to receive stiff opposition from most States.

While it is unlikely that individual standing to lodge claims against international organizations would result in a floodgate of cases, there are ways to ensure efficient processing. Some regional human rights courts have become adept at screening and weeding out those cases which are outside the jurisdiction of the court or are manifestly unfounded. A fall-back option would be to use an ombudsperson or commission structure to whom individuals can address such claims, which could provide some form of external screening of cases before they reach a court.

IX.5 Full and Effective Reparations

Once responsibility is established, it is but for reparation to be determined on the basis of the underlying violation and the harm caused. There is no further contingency introduced at the stage of reparations even if there is an apparent difficulty for the wrongdoer to make full reparations. While parties to a dispute may come to their own settlement arrangements for disputes between them, as I have argued, the international organization is incapable of agreeing with its Member States rules modifying its obligations on reparations, when injured individuals (as opposed to Member States) are the ultimate beneficiaries.

Despite this, the standards of fullness, adequacy, and effectiveness have not framed international organizations' approaches to reparations. One of the few bodies that has ordered reparations for human rights violations attributed to international organizations—the Human Rights Advisory Panel in Kosovo, has run into problems at the enforcement stage.[12] Part of the difficulty stems from UNMIK's position that it is bound by the UN General Assembly instruction which seeks to limit the UN's liability in peacekeeping operations, the terms of which have since been incorporated into agreements with States.[13]

But it is not only compensation which is lacking and/or inadequate to address the harm; other forms of reparation which have been recognized as necessary and appropriate to address violations of human rights and international humanitarian law[14] such as restitution, rehabilitation, satisfaction, and guarantees of non-repetition, hardly feature in the reparations practice of international organizations.

[12] Chatham House, 'The Kosovo Human Rights Advisory Panel' (International Law Meeting Summary, 26 January 2012) 10; European Commission for Democracy Through Law (Venice Commission), 'Opinion on the Existing Mechanisms to Review the Compatibility with Human Rights Standards of Acts by UNMIK and EULEX in Kosovo' (21 December 2010) 545/2009, CDL-AD(2010)051 para 46.

[13] UNGA, 'Resolution on Third-party Liability: Temporal and Financial Limitations' (17 July 1998) UN Doc A/RES/52/247.

[14] Basic Principles and Guidelines on the Right to a Remedy and Reparation for Victims of Gross Violations of International Human Rights Law and Serious Violations of International Humanitarian Law, UNGA Res 60/147 (16 December 2005) (Basic Principles and Guidelines).

Part of the reticence to afford measures of satisfaction such as unqualified apologies appears to stem from the fear that this would constitute an admission of liability and lead to a hefty compensation bill. The available financing for reparations can thus have implications beyond the sum which is ultimately afforded to injured individuals or groups.

The funding to implement reparations is a real challenge for international organizations, who struggle to have their annual budgets approved by States. Organizations' lack of real fiscal independence provides an interesting backdrop to the positions they take on liability for claims of a 'public' nature, reparations owed to individuals as well as immunities from suit. With respect to peacekeeping, individual missions tend to have a limited budget for claims and adjustments to cover third-party claims;[15] however, there has been a constant worry about the number and size of claims which eventually led the UN General Assembly to introduce temporal limitations and restrict the recoverable amounts,[16] including a usual cap of US$50,000; a bar on compensation in the event of 'operational necessity', a bar on compensation for non-economic loss, such as pain and suffering or moral anguish, as well as for punitive or moral damages. The introduction of caps to limit claimant recoverability does not align with the overall purpose of reparations (which is designed to address the harm) and seems ill-judged for human rights and international humanitarian law claimants, who had no choice about their engagement with the organization, unlike commercial contractors or employees.

For the few instances in which wide scale victimization has been alleged, the institutional response has been to refrain from accepting liability—as in the case of the Haiti cholera claims, or to argue that liability lies exclusively with others—as in the case of sexual exploitation and abuse by peacekeepers. In the latter example, status of forces agreements make clear that troop contributing countries have sole competence to address claims stemming from abuses perpetrated by formed military contingents; however, the UN, similar to the African Union and other regional organizations involved in peacekeeping, has refrained from developing a framework for reparations for abuses perpetrated by other types of personnel who would only benefit from functional immunity and for abuses over which the organization's joint and several liability is arguably engaged. In both these instances, humanitarian assistance programmes and trust funds have been established in lieu of reparations, and funding is made contingent on voluntary contributions. The use of assistance frameworks and trust funds can be important ways in which to deliver services to victims; however, the reliance on voluntary contributions is inconsistent with victims' rights to reparation flowing from the commission of an internationally wrongful act.

It is important that the regular budgets of international organizations account for the real possibility that the organizations will need to pay reparations to injured individuals for human rights and international humanitarian law violations.

[15] UN OLA, 'Memorandum to the Controller' (23 February 2001) UN Juridical Y pt 2 ch VI 381 para 15.

[16] UNGA, 'Resolution on Third-party Liability: Temporal and Financial Limitations' (n 13).

Advance planning and preparation for such eventualities is prudent and appropriate, given the limited unrestricted resources available to the organizations at any given time and the foreseeable liability risks. Internal funds can be built progressively to develop a sufficient pool of resources to insure against claims, the size of which can be determined by a careful and frequently updated risk analysis. In the alternative, organizations can contract with private insurance companies to underwrite those risks.

At present, the organizations are simply passing on the risks to the victims.

Index

Printed and bound by CPI Group (UK) Ltd, Croydon, CR0 4YY